THE LINER

THE LINER

Retrospective & Renaissance

Philip Dawson

W.W. Norton & Company

NEW YORK   LONDON

Previous pages: *At the height of the liner era, and themselves a generation apart, Cunard's* Queen Mary, *left, and* Aquitania, *right, are seen here together at Southampton Docks, probably during the late 1930s, when these two great ships would have been in peacetime commercial service together prior to the outbreak of World War II.* (CPL)

To the memory of my late father, Edward Stewart Dawson (1914-1996), from whom in my early childhood I first acquired my life-long fascination with, and love of, ships, shipping and sea travel.

First published in North America in 2006
by W. W. Norton & Company

W. W. Norton & Company
500 Fifth Avenue
New York, NY 10110
www.wwnorton.com

ISBN 0-393-06166-3

Design: Stephen Dent, Neil Stevens and Sholto Walker
Editorial: Nicki Marshall and Stuart Robertson

Printed by Times, Malaysia

1 2 3 4 5 6 7 8 9 0

▪ CONTENTS ▪

·ACKNOWLEDGEMENTS·

Awork such as this is inevitably a collaborative effort, completed with the support of loved ones, good friends, neighbours, and other acquaintances, as well as the valued help of various people in the shipping and shipbuilding industries, the design and architectural disciplines, academia, museums and libraries.

I am as ever eternally grateful to my dear friend and good neighbour Gordon Turner, who continues to make his own library and rich collection of liner-related material available to me, and who avidly shares in the delight of seeking out details of various liners, shipping companies, their lives and times and the personalities who made these memorable. With Toronto itself being a less ship conscious place than one such as myself could wish for, having a friend of some fifteen years standing such as Gordon, and indeed a veritable maritime library and archive in the apartment building where I live in most fortunate. The Lang family, who operate the Toronto-based travel agency, The Cruise People, are likewise friends of long standing, where John Lang is always willing to share his perspectives and thoughts on passenger shipping, both from his own love of its ships and social institutions and his appreciation of its business side and historical background. John and Diana's daughter, Fiona, and her good friend Thomas were most kind in sharing her own personal impressions of *Queen Mary 2* in the final chapter.

My thanks also to Ellis Stern, work colleague from my former career in data processing (as it was then known), fellow Montréal expatriate and friend of some twenty five years, for his general interest and moral support in projects such as this, and his timely thoughts and observations on transport and industrial development, particularly his own great interest in railways. During this book's preparation I also had the pleasure of meeting and working on another project with Bruce Peter, who is with the Department of Historical and Critical studies at the Glasgow School of art. This acquaintance was first made on the basis of our shared fascination with ships and their design, and has since provided me with the benefit of Bruce's unique insight into these things as we continue to keep in touch and exchange ideas.

It is a privilege also to count Stephen Payne and Robert Tillberg among my friends and those who have always been willing to help out with the great value of their own knowledge, insight and love of ships. Stephen, who is now Vice President and Senior Naval Architect of Carnival Corporate Shipbuilding, a fellow of the Royal Institution of Naval Architects and honoured with the Order of the British Empire (OBE) for his contribution to the shipping industry, co authored several ship design articles with me a decade or so ago, from whence we have continued to share our mutual fascination with passenger shipping as and when the opportunities permit. After writing the introduction for my earlier book, *Cruise Ships: An Evolution in Design*,

Stephen has virtually been my personal guide through the myriad complexities of *Queen Mary 2*'s planning, design and construction. Through various writing assignments and other projects, I have also enjoyed the great privileged of a close working relationship with Tillberg Design, and their affiliates, SMC Design in London and Fort Lauderdale-based Tillberg Design U.S., headed by Robert's eldest son Tomas. A very special thanks to Andy Collier of Tillberg/SMC in London and to Frederik Johansson of Tillberg's Viken office in Sweden for their assistance and guided tours of the *Queen Mary 2* at the yard during her final fitting out stages.

It has also been a great pleasure to speak with the late Doris Thompson of Blackpool Pleasure Beach about her crossing aboard *Normandie* in 1935 and to learn of her general impressions of sea travel over the years, and to speak at length on several occasions with Keith Gledhill of Blackpool about his experiences working in the purser's department aboard the old Cunard *Queens* and to share his more recent impressions of *QE2* and *QM2* as a discerning passenger. I am eternally grateful to Pat Collier, Personal Assistant to the late Geoffrey Thompson of Blackpool Pleasure Beach, for her role in brokering both of these most valuable contacts for me during a short visit to the UK in 2002.

My sincere thanks too to John Maxtone-Graham, author of Cunard's official *Queen Mary 2* inaugural book, for sharing his own first-hand thoughts and impressions of the ship's maiden voyage in January 2004, as well as to M. Philippe Kasse, Communication Manager, for Alstom Chantiers de l'Atlantique for his ongoing support of my writing endeavours from the standpoint of his position. I am indeed indebted to him and his colleagues Natalie Hjan and Gwénola Jutel for facilitating my visit to the yard during the final weeks of *QM2*'s construction, as well as to Jean-Jacques Gatepaille and Eric Chapuis for the time they spent with me on the naval architecture and technical aspects of shipbuilding at Saint-Nazaire. My gratitude also to Thérèse Dumont of Ecomusée de Saint-Nazaire for her help in securing photographs from the shipyard archives now vested with the museum, and to Andrea Klose from Saint-Nazaire's remarkable Escal'Atlantique for her hospitality in introducing me to this remarkably interactive museum and the compelling impressions of shipboard life in the liner era that it evokes.

Among the many others who have touched this project on one way or another, whose names may be victim of time and space here or of lapse in recollection on my part at this late stage of working, again my sincere and heartfelt gratitude. Last, and by no means least, it is a great pleasure to work again with Nicki Marshall, Stephen Dent, John Lee and Stuart Robertson on this, the third book I have been privileged to produce with this singular dream team. ●

FOREWORD

BY

STEPHEN M. PAYNE, OBE BScEng(Hons) FRINA CEng
VICE PRESIDENT & CHIEF NAVAL ARCHITECT,
CARNIVAL CORPORATE SHIPBUILDING, SOUTHAMPTON
DESIGNER, CUNARD LINE *QUEEN MARY 2*

For many generations past, nothing in the world could rival the sight of a majestic ocean liner in her natural element at sea. With their long sleek hulls, towering superstructures and smoking funnels, they were the epitome of man's engineering genius. National steamship lines vied with each other on routes around the world with bigger and faster ships, many sponsored by their respective governments. In the 1930s a profusion of spectacular ocean liners, dubbed the 'Ships of State', were built, and which, seen in retrospect, clearly represented the golden age of travel.

The liners were always viewed as technological marvels. Steam turbines, reciprocating engines, diesels and, latterly, diesel/gas turbine electric plants of colossal proportions, propelled them at ever-increasing speeds, fuelled initially by scores of stokers performing Herculean feats of stamina in shovelling tons of coal into the boilers. Technology moved on and oil-firing improved efficiency, reduced manning and negated the filthy process of 'coaling ship'. Steam gave way to diesel propulsion, firstly with direct drive, then mechanically manipulated with a gearbox and more recently with electric drive.

Passenger comforts and amenities also moved forward with the times. Gas lamps gave way to electric lighting, lifts appeared providing ease of access between decks where previously there had been only stairs, and squash and tennis courts for active recreation became commonplace. Public rooms increased in size, grandeur and number, and grandiloquent restaurants provided epicurean experiences.

Philip Dawson, author of several previous acclaimed passenger ship works, has carefully researched and studied the liner form, mystique and contribution to the movement of mankind across the oceans of the world. Step aboard this voyage of discovery and celebration, intermixed with calamity and reflection. It is all here.

Liners have worked hard in both peace and wartime doing what they do best – carrying passengers across the globe. During conflicts some were transformed into auxiliary cruisers and even aircraft carriers. Liners survived until cheap air travel became available with the introduction of large jet airliners such as the Boeing 747. One by one their routes succumbed until there was but one left – the original North Atlantic route. Happily this crossing is still alive and well into the 21st century with the latest and most spectacular liner of them all, Cunard Line's RMS *Queen Mary 2*. ●

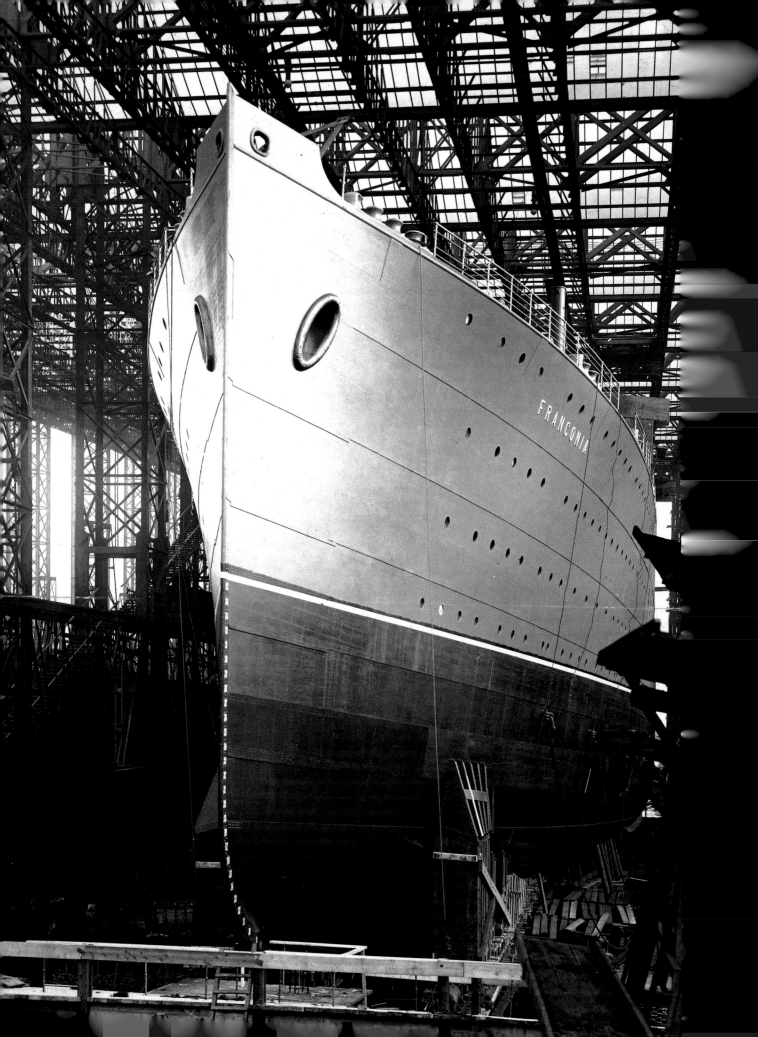

·INTRODUCTION·

A few years ago someone participating in an ocean liners internet chatroom worked out the cost of producing a functional cruise-ship replica of the 1930s liner *Normandie*, with the challenge, 'Why doesn't someone build it?' No doubt anyone who is aware of this legendary French Line flagship has secretly mused about the same thing at one time or another.

Countless design changes would be needed for such a ship to meet current safety regulations and to suit the way we now live, travel and use our leisure time. Stringent modern fire-safety codes would have to be met, with significant changes being made to *Normandie*'s original axial plan and the arrangement of its legendary flow of spectacular open spaces. The ship would require a lower lifeboat location at the base of the superstructure, rather than atop it in the traditional ocean-liner arrangement. *Normandie*'s naval architect, Vladimir Yourkevitch, had himself already planned such an arrangement for *Bretagne*, an avant-garde fleet mate he proposed for the French Line flagship. Unfortunately this was one among a number of highly progressive shipbuilding projects never realized thanks to the outbreak of World War II.

Perhaps even more onerous in their impact on such a ship would be the considerations of modern cruise ship design to provide the type of ocean-going living the experienced traveller now expected. There would no doubt have to be far more accommodation with hotel-style balconies than *Normandie*'s original 24 Promenade Deck Verandah Staterooms and two Grande Luxe Suites on Sun Deck, each with its own part of the Sun Deck. The main Upper and Lower Embarkation Halls in First Class, with their elaborate sequences of processional stairways extending through five decks, would probably have to be reworked into a fully fledged modern atrium, and a full-production theatre for cabaret shows provided. *Normandie* had no casino, no interactive TV or mini-bar in the cabins, little of today's cruise ship health and beauty and other specialist lifestyle amenities and only limited shopping facilities. Even the most avid liner enthusiast today would probably become bored after but a few hours of enraptured exploration of such a ship if it were built.

Normandie belonged to an era where the standards of First-Class luxury were set largely by the attentive personal service offered by the ship's company in an essentially passive environment where people provided much of their own entertainment and amusement. By contrast, the ultra-luxe sectors of

today's cruise industry is built on similarly high standards of service that tend to be focused more on the unique and diverse stimulation the shipboard experience can offer, both by virtue of the amenities offered and voyage itinerary. Apart from fine gastronomy, attentive valet service and professional entertainment, this may include specific facilities for personal stimulation and enrichment.

The 21st-century cruise passenger likes to mix his or her own cocktail from the stateroom minibar and takes for granted the convenience of a self-service launderette, but is also likely to want the service of a personal trainer in the ship's spa, and seeks the adventure of making out-of-the-way excursions in a Zodiac, viewing glaciers from a helicopter or exploring the Great Barrier Reef by submersible. Where the art of conversation and the shipboard rituals of promenading and celebrity watching once flourished on the high seas, today's shipboard experience is more geared to involving the passenger directly in a diversity of activity, day and night. This has come about largely as the cruise industry began to realize that passengers are prepared to pay for many of the additional services and facilities offered onboard.

While the exclusive preserves of First Class often occupied as much as two thirds of the passenger space aboard an express liner, more than twice as many passengers might well be carried in the less glamorous milieu of the Cabin, Second, Third, Tourist, Tourist Third or Steerage classes. A hundred years ago, ladies and gentlemen lived largely segregated social lives aboard ship. Gentlemen in First Class had exclusive use of the smoking room, while the main lounge, or on some ships a separate Ladies' Salon, was the non-exclusive daytime female preserve. Ladies and gentlemen were free to mix on the promenade and open decks, in the dining room and for a few hours of evening dancing or entertainment in the main lounge or ballroom.

Life in the nether regions of the lower decks tended to become less formal the farther down the ocean-going social companionway one descended. Yet, often these lesser echelons of the ship's passenger hierarchy offered a more relaxed and informal shipboard experience, perhaps in its own right more akin to today's main-market cruise sector. There were probably more interlopers who descended the social ladder than there were those aspiring to climb it. Thankfully, the abolition of multiple classes in cruise service, with its inherent duplicity of facilities and services, greatly simplifies the design of the 21st-

Opposite:
Bow of the Cunard line's first Franconia, *of 1911, pictured just prior to launch at Swan, Hunter & Wigham Richardson's yard at Wallsend-on-Tyne.* (CPL)

century passenger ship, allowing more usable space per passenger and far greater flexibility of the overall layout.

The age of the ocean liner began as steam propulsion created the possibility for ships to be operated on a regularly scheduled basis, no longer at the mercy of the winds. With mechanical propulsion came also the iron and steel hulls that in turn made possible larger ships and higher standards of accommodation and onboard creature comfort. Towards the end of the 19th century, there emerged an ocean-going architecture, born out of the belle époque's Grand Hotel formality. Indeed César Ritz's own house architects were to turn their creative hands to some of that era's most notable and memorable ocean-going interiors. With the ships of this era, there emerged for the first time an ocean going lifestyle in its own right.

Many of the features of today's cruise tonnage can rightfully trace their origins back to the liner era. The modern shipboard atrium, largely seen as a cruise-ship adaptation of architect John Portmann's 1970s Hyatt Regency Hotel designs, traces its ocean-going origins back to various liners of the early 20th century. Compagnie Générale Sudatlantique's l'Atlantique of 1931 can be seen as the contemporary origin of the linear atria featured in the early-1990s-built Baltic super-ferries Silja Serenade and Silja Symphony, as well as in the 1998 cruise-ship example, Voyager of the Seas. l'Atlantique's trend-setting axial plan was most recently adopted as a key design reference for Cunard's Queen Mary 2, the first true express ocean liner to be built in more than three decades. Arguably the vestigial origins of this type of space can be traced as far back as the mid-19th century and the outstanding deep-sea example of Great Eastern, and to some of the larger fresh water ferries and river

boats built for service on North America's great waterways.

The cabins with private verandas that now make up the vast majority of modern hotel-style cruise accommodation were in fact first introduced on the Great Lakes in the early days of the 20th century. More contemporary conceptions of the idea later appeared in a few notable liner examples, including the 1927-built Italian Cosulich liner Saturnia, where virtually all outside cabins on the aptly-named Veranda Deck featured their own private deck spaces. Other liner-era examples included a unique arrangement aboard the French Line flagship France of 1962, where a number of what would otherwise have been inside cabins were grouped around an inner court open to the sky. Generally the modern ocean liner's development was characterized by a progressive de-formalization of luxury ocean-going living from the 1920s onwards, with ever greater consideration being given to a duality of service between line voyages and cruising. Indeed Swedish American Line was a proponent of progressive dual-purpose ship design from the design of their first Kungsholm of 1927 to their final liner of the same name commissioned in 1966.

The express Norddeutscher Lloyd liners Bremen and Europa introduced a uniformly high standard of American-style hotel accommodation in the 1930s, along with other trendsetting ideas aimed at increasing their versatility and overall public appeal of modern ocean travel. Meanwhile, l'Atlantique made her debut as one of the first modern passenger ships built without the traditional curvilinear forms of deck sheer and camber. This remarkable ship also introduced much of the structural daring that would characterize Normandie's design a few years later. The outstanding contemporary architecture of Orient Line's Orion, Holland America's Nieuw Amsterdam, and of the many outstanding Italian ships brought a gracious informality of living to ships of otherwise more traditional technical planning.

With the widespread introduction of air-conditioning throughout liner interiors in the 1950s and 1960s, the once divergent characteristics of the North Atlantic and tropical liners dissolved into a universal single ship type, virtually interchangeable between one type of service and another. Built of modern and durable materials in the contemporary styles of the jet age, these asserted a sleek image that greatly helped to set the tone for the metamorphosis of the ocean liner into the cruise ship. Holland America's Rotterdam, P&O's Canberra, French Line's France and Cunard's Queen Elizabeth 2 were among the pivotal elements of that era that made the successful transition from line service to cruising alongside their new counterparts from Scandinavia. Rather than being the reincarnation of a bygone era in ocean travel, Cunard's new Queen Mary 2 commenced her service career in early 2004 as an entirely state-of-

Below: *Ship's bellboys being inspected by Mr. Joe Rigby, chief second steward, on board the* Queen Mary *in April 1947 as she prepared to resume passenger service after World War II.* (CPL)

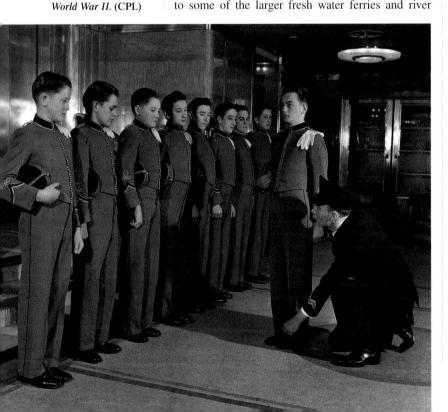

the-art express ocean liner, developed with a service approach rooted in the modern hospitality and cruise industries, and combined with all the facilities of an ocean-going resort to meet the needs of both her Atlantic and worldwide cruising role.

What has changed most perhaps is the extent and scale of the ocean-liner features now offered, the way they fit into today's cruise experience and how they are used and enjoyed by the passenger. For instance, a large multiple-deck space that would have enhanced the social experience of dining aboard a '30s-era liner is now more apt to be created as a circulating and gathering space such as an atrium, or as a fully fledged theatre for cabaret entertainment. Shipboard gastronomy has become more diverse and specialized, with the main dining room being supplemented by various specialty restaurants. The smoking room, card rooms, library and writing room have diversified into various alternative facilities, such as casinos, internet cafés and business centres more appropriate to the lifestyles in the 21st century. Perhaps one of the most significant developments has been a progression from the Turkish baths, indoor pool and gymnasium introduced aboard ship a century ago to the elaborate and extensive health and beauty centres of today's cruise ships.

The concept and function of these features was devised to suit the vogue and lifestyles of the times, but then as now was intended to create a distinctive and memorable experience for the paying passenger. The development of the traditional ocean liner will be rediscovered through the following chapters, but rediscovered from the vantage point of the dawning 21st century, and from the knowledge and understanding of passenger shipping as it is viewed today. The enquirer in the internet chat room who challenged the industry to replicate *Normandie* can now see much of this realized aboard *Queen Mary 2*, for which the legendary French flagship is indeed a significant design prototype.

Rather than endeavouring to chronicle a complete history of ocean-going passenger transport per se, this work aspires to explore the subject through the examples of those factors that have been most influential in the industry's development. This seeks to go beyond the tonnage itself and the business of transporting passengers across the world's oceans to explore also the human factors of service and life on board, and to view these in the historical and social context of an eternally changing world beyond the decks and saloons of the ocean liner. The public's perception of ships has evolved through the machine age and the background of great worldwide engineering works, into which steam navigation was born and grew through its adolescence, through its high social standing during the late Victorian and Edwardian era of La Belle Époque. Onwards into the 20th century, the demographics of travel were significantly altered by two world wars that relied heavily on liners for mass trooping operations, and later by the airborne challenge of the jet age. Yet through all of this the classic image of the great ocean liner, with black hull, white superstructure and traditional funnels has flourished as one of the most powerful and enduring icons of human civilization and accomplishment. ●

Above: *Crowds welcome the* United States *as she arrives at Southampton in July 1952, at the end of her record-breaking maiden voyage.* (CPL)

1

OUT OF THAT 'PREPOSTEROUS BOX'

The commercial development of the modern ocean liner traces its origins to the mid-19th century. This was the time of Samuel Cunard's idea of establishing a scheduled shipping service, operated on a business basis similar to the railways then spreading out across the continents. Likewise Isambard Kingdom Brunel envisioned his steamers *Great Western* and *Great Britain* as as but an extension of the Great Western Railway he had built from London Paddington to Bristol, bringing its services clear across the North Atlantic to New York. By the time Cunard's *Britannia* and Brunel's *Great Western* first sailed to the New World, there were rail networks of some 2,925km (1,755 miles) already serving the British Isles and Europe, and more than 4,534km (2,720 miles) in North America, capable of assembling and distributing large numbers of steamship passengers to and from the major sea ports.

While the railway networks might have been viewed as less influential themselves in the development of longer routes to India, Australia and South America, men of vision such as P&O's Arthur Anderson and Brodie McGhie Wilcox were well aware of the far greater mobility and hastened pace of life and commerce they were bringing to the world as a whole. Like the railway locomotive, the steamship was viewed as a product of the dawning machine age with an essential role to play in providing the means of transport and communication that global industrialization would itself ultimately create and thrive upon.

The great advantage of machine-propulsion over sail was that ships needed no longer to be entirely at the mercy of the prevailing winds, and voyage durations and arrival times could be precisely scheduled. The sailing packet lines that had established the standards of deep-sea travel up to that time were at best able to schedule the departures of their ships, usually on the basis of two or three sailings per calendar month on the North Atlantic routes between Europe and the New World. Sailing dates tended to be less frequent on the longer routes to India, Australia and South America, where voyage durations were considerably longer. Yet within the time frame of a generation or so, steam brought regularly scheduled steamship services to all of the world's great oceans and numerous other waterways. The comprehension of distance was changed and the numbers of people who travelled progressed from being measured in but a few thousand to tens of millions. Where overland and sea travel had been a privilege of the few for thousands of years, the railways and steamships had suddenly put the whole world within comparatively quick and easy reach of its many nations and their peoples. While the North Atlantic has always attracted the greatest numbers of passengers, and usually offered the largest and fastest ships to carry them, the development of other routes to India, Australia and South America was no less illustrious in meeting the special needs of these longer passages through hot tropical latitudes and the severity of seasonal mistrals and monsoons.

On the North Atlantic, a typical passage from

Opposite top:
Cunard Britannia *arriving in Boston, 1840.* (Gordon Turner collection)

Opposite bottom:
Liverpool docks in the mid-19th century; today the site of the Three Graces – the Royal Liver Building, the Cunard Building and the Mersey Docks and Harbour Board headquarters. (CPL)

Liverpool to Halifax, Boston or New York under sail could take anything from 16 days to three weeks or more, depending on prevailing sea and wind conditions. A number of days would be spent in port at the voyage's destination for cargo and mail handling, victualling and general servicing of the vessel. The Philadelphia packets, for instance, sailed from Liverpool in rotation on the eighth and twentieth days of the month, with cargo closing the day before. The London packets set out for New York from St. Katherine's Dock on the first, tenth and twentieth of each month. Among the best-known of these privateer enterprises was the Black Ball Line of New York, which had started a transatlantic service to Liverpool in 1816. The solidly built and stocky 500-ton vessels of their fleet set the pace for much of the sailing-packet Atlantic shipping of the early-to-mid 18th century.

Passengers were offered Saloon Class passage between Liverpool and New York, berthed in cabins, with mattresses, bedding, and with all food, wine and other stores necessary for the voyage being provided at a price of around 35 guineas per adult. The Philadelphia packet *Dorothea* was reputed to offer some of the finest accommodation in any American ship of her time, having been originally built for the East India trade. Ships then serving India under the charter of the East India Company offered a standard of accommodation and service second to none and generally well beyond the realm of those private enterprises vying for their shares of the Atlantic and other deep-sea trades.

In those early days of the North American emigrant trade, some packets advertised that, 'a few respectable passengers can be accommodated in the steerage'. Fares for Steerage passage were between £3 and £6 per adult, with the passenger having to reckon on spending at least an additional £2 each to buy the food and provisions they needed for the voyage. Space in Steerage was allocated on the lower deck for each family and their belongings, including furniture, which would be made fast by the ship's carpenters before sailing. They were provided only with a moderate quantity of potable fresh water and with 'firing' or access to a communal stove where they did their own cooking.

In 1837 the New York-bound packet *Diamond* was 100 days at sea on her way from Liverpool. Although this in itself set no record, the incident attracted attention as there were 17 deaths among the Steerage passengers aboard who had simply run out of the food they had brought with them for the journey. With the ship's crew themselves having been put on short ration, and many of their fellow passengers themselves close to starvation, there was little that could be done for these poor souls. One of the slowest Atlantic crossings known was attempted in 1741, by a Captain Higgins, who abandoned his ship after running out of provisions 144 days out from Dublin on his way to Philadelphia. There were no doubt oth-

ers who simply foundered without ever being known.

The newer and more prestigious sailing ships of this era were significantly larger and more comfortable to travel aboard than the vessels that had brought the Pilgrim Fathers to Plymouth Rock in 1620. They were also much improved on the 'coffin brigs' that had long traded to the Americas, the Far East and the Antipodes, and taken British convicts and their families to the penal colonies in New South Wales and Van Diemen's Land during the late 18th century. The big packets of the 1830s set a standard of passenger accommodation and service that prevailed well into the formative period of steamship design and development.

Saloon passengers were for the most part berthed aft, in the quietest and most stable part of the ship, on the uppermost enclosed deck. Small cabins were arranged along either side of the ship and the centre space between these formed an open communal space used for dining and other indoor social activity – such as it was in those days. Known as the saloon, this was usually fitted out with long trestle tables and fixed benches along either side. The crew were usually berthed forward, and the lower decks were either used exclusively for cargo, mail and provisions, or were partially adapted to carry Steerage passengers. Layouts of this type prevailed in the design of early paddle steamers, where the intrusion of boilers and machinery amidships across the hull's full beam resulted in accommodation deftly segregated into two separate enclaves forward and aft below the open main deck. Only later, with larger hulls built of iron and steel, could ships be designed with passenger accommodation above their propelling machinery rather than around it.

By the late 1830s, Samuel Cunard (1787–1865) was already thinking outside the proverbial box, as he immediately realized the need for a fleet of ships with similar capacities and performance that could maintain his timetable of regular sailings. His business model also stressed a preference for the tried and proven over the avant garde. This recognized the key importance of speed without compromising safe, secure and comfortable passage; others for whom record performance was the primary concern would experiment with breaking the limits. Cunard's approach emphasized the 'ferry-boat' model. Sufficient tonnage was already available to offer frequent departures and arrivals of the line's ships to keep pace with the steady demand for mail, passengers and a limited quantity of special or 'fine' cargoes to move back and forth across the Atlantic.

SAMUEL CUNARD'S MAIL STEAMSHIP SERVICE

In 1838 the British Admiralty called for tenders to operate a regular transatlantic postal service steamship service to the United States. A seven-year contract was awarded to Samuel Cunard, originally on the basis of the service being provided by three 800 GT steamships, with the additional provision that any improvements in steam navigation considered essential by the Lords of the Admiralty during the life of the agreement would have to be implemented at the shipowner's expense. The agreed annual fee to be paid to Cunard was set at £50,000 per year. Wood and Napier, the Glasgow firm of shipbuilders and marine engineers, was commissioned to design, build and engine the ships, based on their preeminent experience in producing many of the more significant steamers then in both coastal and deep-sea service. A number of these had been built for the East India Company, of which Cunard himself had been the Canadian agent.

Cunard wanted his Atlantic steamships to be as identical as possible, so as to establish a uniform standard of design, performance and operation. For his passengers, a consistency of shipboard design, service and comfort would be identifiable more with the line itself than with any particular ship in its fleet. In this regard Cunard's mail steamers were to have a degree of uniformity in outward appearance and onboard experience, much like the consistency of the railways and their coaches.

As planning proceeded, the original contract tonnage rose to 1,139 and the propulsion power was increased from 300 to a total indicated horsepower of 420 as the first ship, *Britannia*, was delivered. Cunard was in the meantime convinced by his friend and business associate, J. N. Stayner, deputy Postmaster General of Québec, that a fourth vessel should be added to counteract the inevitable delays caused by fog and bad weather and meet the advertised schedules. Cunard had to apply to the Admiralty for an additional £5,000 to cover the increase in price of the larger ships from £30,000 to £32,000, as well as the cost of the fourth vessel. He was forced also to seek additional outside backing for his steamship venture. In May 1839 he formed a partnership with shipowners George Burns, owner of the Burns Line, and David McIver, who was agent for the City of Glasgow Steam Packet Company. After careful deliberation they jointly subscribed to a 50 per cent interest in the £270,000 enterprise. Accordingly, this was officially registered as The Glasgow Proprietary in the British and North American Royal Mail Steam Packets, the line itself having been chartered in Liverpool as The British and North American Royal Mail Steam Packet Navigation Company. This cumbersome name was soon popularly reduced to The Cunard. The fashion of prefacing an owner or proprietor's name with the definite article indicated reference to his business rather than himself.

As part of the overall business arrangement, the Burns Line steamer *Unicorn* was sold to Cunard for the feeder service between Pictou and Québec City,

with the mails being carried between Halifax and Pictou overland by stage coach. Also designed and engined by Napier and built in 1836 for the coastal service between Glasgow and Liverpool, the 648-ton *Unicorn* can be seen as being a prototype of the new Cunard ships by way of similarity of her overall layout and machinery arrangement. Her positioning voyage with 27 passengers aboard in May 1840 was in reality Cunard's first transatlantic sailing, although it was made outside the Admiralty contract, carrying no mail.

Britannia sailed on her maiden voyage from Liverpool at 2:00 pm on Friday, 4 July, 1840, completing the crossing to Halifax two days ahead of schedule in the pre-dawn hours of 17 July and arriving in Boston on Saturday evening, 18 July. She was followed by *Acadia* and *Caledonia*, entering service in August and September the same year, and by *Columbia* in January 1841. Once all four ships were in service, The Cunard was able to offer a regular fortnightly liner service to the New World, from March to October and once a month between November and February. With this began a remarkable progression, first to a weekly high-season service in 1848, with the help of four additional ships, then to the two-ship express service of the first *Queens* in the 1950s, continuing to the dual-function *Queen Elizabeth 2* commissioned in 1969, and onwards into the 21st century with the addition of *Queen Mary 2* in 2004. Although the transatlantic service is now a seasonal operation, this indeed represents the longest running passenger-ship service in maritime history.

With the four new Cunard steamers in service by early 1941, earlier steam packets were for the most part relegated to their place in history as the one-off experiments that had proven the new technology to be fundamentally viable. Popularly credited as being the first steamship to cross the Atlantic, the American-built *Savannah* made a 28-day crossing in 1819 from Savannah, Georgia, to Liverpool, with no passengers and little cargo aboard. Unable to carry the quantities of fuel to sustain continuous operation

Above: *A rendering showing 'Clyde of 1841' as representative of the wooden hulled steamers used in deep-sea and coastal services on both sides of the Atlantic.* (CPL)

of her machinery for the entire crossing, the ship's paddle wheels were fitted so that they could be hoisted on deck, allowing her to proceed unencumbered by them under sail for much of the voyage. Although in reality a 'power-assisted' passage, this nonetheless showed the possibility of things to come, as did the first powered flight carrying a human made by Wilbur and Orville Wright at Kitty Hawk, North Carolina in December 1903.

Later steamships made the crossing with a far greater reliance on permanently installed paddle wheels and greater fuel capacities, though still with the need to conserve coal under favourable sailing conditions and to stop the machinery frequently while their seawater boilers were cleaned and descaled. A successful steam crossing was made in 1826 from Antwerp to Paramaribo in Dutch Guiana (now Surinam) aboard a Clyde-built paddle steamer of 320 tons with a 100-horsepower engine, bought by Dutch merchants and named *Curaçao*. The Canadian paddle steamer *Royal William*, built with accommodation for 50 Cabin passengers and an additional 80 in Steerage, made a successful crossing from Québec to London in 1833, with coaling stops made en route at Pictou and Cowes. This was in reality a positioning voyage, with only seven passengers and a small amount of revenue cargo, made while trying to find a buyer for the ship after her original service on the St Lawrence river had become a financial failure. *Royal William* was engaged for several successful charters in European waters before being sold to the Spanish government for use as a warship.

Sirius and *Great Western* were best known among a number of other ships making moderately successful revenue-earning Atlantic crossings in the late 1830s, carrying passengers and mail. A second *Royal William*, built in 1836 for the City of Dublin Steam Packet Company's London to Dublin service, was

later put into transatlantic service by an entity calling itself the Transatlantic Steamship Company. Her passengers were even offered the cruise-style contingency of a 10-day stay in New York allowing time for them to tour the scenery of the Hudson river and to visit Niagara Falls. By 1838 this line was eager to establish a modern fleet service, returning *Royal William* to her original owners upon purchasing the large new two-funnelled steamer *Liverpool* as the first of several planed acquisitions. *Liverpool* alone remained in Atlantic service until the Transatlantic Steamship Company closed and sold her to the new Peninsular and Orient Steam Navigation Company in 1840 for their service to the Orient. Without her planned fleet mates, *Liverpool*, like *Sirius*, *Great Western* and other contemporaries, was unable to deliver the reliability of machine propulsion on a sufficiently frequent scheduled basis.

Great Western was significant for her conception as an integral part of the Great Western Railway's development, envisaged as an extension of its rail services between London and Bristol, all the way across the North Atlantic to New York. In terms of today's intermodal transport strategies, this can be seen as an early conceptualization of integrated rail and sea travel in the visionary mind of Isambard Kingdom Brunel, the indefatigable Victorian engineer who built both the railway and the ship. Although *Great Western* was ultimately unsuccessful commercially, her safe passages of the North Atlantic under steam power have long been viewed by many historians as having set a precedent for establishing the Admiralty mail services first contracted to Cunard and P&O. As discussed in the next chapter, *Great Western* was followed by two further ships of significant design and technical influence built by Brunel.

As the lead unit in a four-ship class-building,

Below: *Working plan of the* Royal William, *drawn by James Gaudis in 1831.* (CPL)

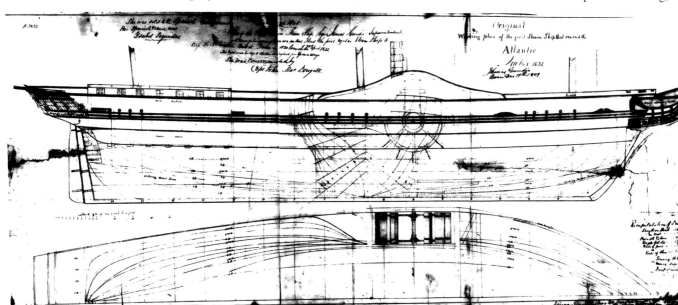

Britannia offered little that was revolutionary or in itself trendsetting. Structurally, she was a three-masted wooden barque, built as a steamship with paddle wheels driven at 16 revolutions per minute by a single side-lever steam engine. Steam was generated by four return-flue-type boilers at a modest nine pounds per square inch, consuming about 37 tons of coal per day. With a bunker capacity of 640 tons, *Britannia* had the capacity to steam at 8.5 knots for 17 days, enough to make the 2,534-mile (4054km) crossing from Liverpool to Halifax with a comfortable reserve for delay due to storms and heavy seas. The stop at Halifax was included largely to provide an opportunity for topping up the ship's bunkers to ensure that the contracted schedule to Boston could be met. As the ship carried a full sailing rig, Cunard instructed its captains to conserve coal by proceeding under canvas whenever the winds were favourable.[1]

In addition to her hold capacity for 225 tons of mail and special or 'fine' cargoes, *Britannia* was fitted out with accommodation for 115 Cabin passengers, with no provision made for Steerage trade. As part of the Admiralty mail contract, the ship was readily convertible as a troop transport in case of war. Passenger accommodation was located on the main deck, where it was arranged forward and aft of the machinery spaces amidships. In line with the latest trends for larger steamers of her day, *Britannia*'s state rooms were for the most part arranged alongside two parallel passages between the outer rows of cabins at the ship's sides, and two files of inside rooms arranged back-to-back along the centreline space. The saloon was given new pride of place on the deck above, where it retained the original centre-line location and proportions of its sailing-packet forebears, with the added attraction of windows overlooking the open decks to either side. Officer accommodation, the galley, cow houses, sheep and pig pens, chicken coops and hen roosts, along with a few water closets, machinery and crew accesses, and the entrance vestibules to the passenger accommodation below, were all contained within a group of small deckhouses forward of the saloon, arranged around the base of the funnel and engine room uptakes, between the paddle-wheel boxes.

Britannia's passenger accommodation was comfortable and pleasant for its time, though less luxurious than that of the era's more opulent sailing packets and some of the steam tonnage to follow quickly on Cunard's success. The saloon was dining room, lounge, bar, card- and writing-room all in one. Cabins were, for the most part, each fitted with two berths, one above the other, a sofa (which in reality was little more than an upholstered bench), a washstand and several clothes pegs on the walls. When Charles Dickens (1812–70) and his wife occupied one of these meagre wooden cubicles on their sailing to America in early 1842, he described it in his later-published *American Notes* as: 'this utterly impracticable, thoroughly hopeless and profoundly preposterous box'. The matter of ensconcing himself and his lady, along with their luggage in that space was no easier, 'than a giraffe could be persuaded or forced into a flower pot'. It is a thought that many economy-class airline passengers today can no doubt readily identify with. His reference to the saloon as being like a 'gigantic hearse with windows in the sides' was scarcely any kinder.[2]

By modern-day standards *Britannia*'s state rooms would have been little more spacious than the basic couchette-style sleeping accommodation offered on Channel and North Sea ferries built during the 1960s and 1970s, but then rendered without the conveniences of electric light and mechanical ventilation. A North Sea crossing on a stormy winter night in such accommodation aboard one of the smaller ferries still in service, with the lights switched off while listening to Wagner's *Ride of the Valkyries* on your Walkman, especially if you are wearing damp clothing and in need of a shower, might give a reasonable impression of an Atlantic voyage aboard *Britannia* or one of her contemporaries.

All in all the sheer hardship of being at sea on the rolling and heaving decks of those frail ships left the average passenger with little energy to enjoy much of the normal pleasures of life. They would spend much of their time between meals in the saloon, whiling away the long days in conversation, reading or dozing. Some of the ladies might sew or do needlework, and during the evenings the gentlemen would engage in a few hands of whist, playing from their pockets if the sea was too rough for the cards to stay put on the saloon tables. Those wishing to smoke were only permitted to do so on deck, where they would congregate in the lee of the funnel around the engine room vent uptake. Weather permitting, ladies and gentlemen would play an early form of shuffleboard on the open expanse of the quarter deck above their accommodation or would dance to the music of a fiddle, tin flute or concertina played by a shipmate or a crewman.

Although passengers were not permitted on the navigating bridge, which then literally was a bridge formed by a platform extending across the space between the paddle-wheel boxes, they were allowed in good weather to venture onto the small railed-in platform at either side of it. As *Britannia* and other steamships of that age were still structurally built as sailing packets with high solid bulwarks, the outlook beyond the ship's sides from the open deck was largely blocked. Even from the top of the saloon or other deck houses, the view would have been obstructed by the lifeboats, along with the ratlines, chain plates and other items of the ship's sailing rig. Thus, the occasional opportunity of ascending the iron ladders to the tops of the paddle boxes offered the best outlook to the sea and horizon and gave a sense of contact with the outside world's vastness during the long voyage. Yet passengers were accorded a much closer look at their ship and its workings than those who would travel in the more hotel-like accommodation of steamers built a decade or so later. *Britannia*'s fascinating side-lever steam engine could be viewed through the deck openings above the engine room and the stokers could be glimpsed at their brutal toil in the boiler room. As passengers promenaded forward, around the main and fore-masts, they could look into the galley, bakery and cow house. It all helped to pass the long days under way and to stave off the mental stagnation, then still a concern of ocean travel.

Meals were served in the saloons, to which the food had to be hurriedly carried on covered tureens, from a small pantry in the galley by way of the open deck.. The fare was plentiful and wholesome, consisting mainly of pork, beef and lamb roasts, preserved meats and salt fish, served with split peas, baked potatoes and roast apples, along with breads and biscuits baked on board and steamed rice or suet puddings of one kind or another. With the only form of limited shipboard refrigeration then being dry ice packed in sawdust, suckling pigs, cows and poultry were carried for slaughter. A few fresh eggs could be had as long as the hens lived, though milk was available only to women, children and invalids. Breakfast was taken at 6:00 am, lunch at noon, dinner at 4:00 pm, and tea at 7:30 in the evening. Supper, for those wanting it, could be ordered before 10:00 pm. The saloon pantry provided bar service, dispensing ales, wines, port and spirits from 6.00 am to 11.00 pm.

In those days, before the introduction of electric light aboard ship, oil lanterns were used in the saloon and candles in the cabins. Stewards and other ship's crew on duty after dusk carried lanterns as they went about their watches and attended to other tasks. Sanitation, such that it was, consisted of chamber pots, water jugs and wash bowls provided for passengers in the cabins. There was no running water for showers or baths, and only four communal water-closets located on the upper deck for daytime use, along with a few additional WCs adjacent to the main deck cabins, no doubt primarily intended for the use of lady passengers. There were generally no laundry facilities, and saloon tableware was hand washed in buckets on the same open deck where livestock would have been slaughtered and butchered for the meals eaten with these utensils. Animal carcasses, bones and other waste were simply thrown overboard

There was only natural ventilation inside the accommodation, admitting salt spray, cooking odours, soot and engine smuts, along with the chilly damp air of the North Atlantic to the crowded interiors. Considering the level of personal hygiene then possible at sea, the inevitable amount of sea sickness on board much of the time, and the fact that salt water

was used for washing and bathing, the accommodation would no doubt have been quite unpleasant smelling by today's standards, even at the best of times. The livestock carried on deck, along with the grains and fodders needed to keep them alive, contributed a strong agricultural odour to the heavy coal fumes from the boiler furnaces below. In those days, however, before modern hygiene, prepared foods and refrigeration, when there were horses in the streets everywhere and the air was heavy with coal fumes and soot, the population in general, regardless of their station in society, were oblivious to many odours and fumes that today would be considered unacceptable.

While Charles Dickens creates a perhaps rather dark impression of sea travel in his writings, there has nonetheless always been a unique character of informality and comradeship, of being drawn together on the high seas, that has long attracted people to sail aboard ships for reasons other than abject necessity. In a letter written home to his mother, Alexis de Tocqueville, a passenger aboard one of *Liverpool*'s voyages to New York, gives a rare insight into the human side of shipboard life:

> You cannot imagine, dear Mother, what a droll life one lives in this great stagecoach called a ship. The necessity of living on top of each other and of looking each other in the eye all the time establishes an informality and a freedom of which one has no conception on terra firma. Here each one carries on in the middle of the crowd as if he were alone: some read aloud, others play, others sing; there are those who write as I do at this moment, while close by a neighbour is supping. Each one drinks, laughs eats or cries as his fancy suggests. Our cabins are so narrow that one goes outside them to dress; and but for publically putting on one's pants, I know not what part of one's toilet doesn't take place in the face of Israel...[3]

Indeed there was a lighter side to sea travel, which Dickens himself admitted to in describing his own experience aboard *Britannia* as 'one-fourth serious and three-fourths comical'.[4] While the passenger trade of those days was made up mainly of those booking saloon passage in the line of business or other duties, and others emigrating to the New Worlds of North America and Australia in Steerage, there were nonetheless the adventurous few who merely sought the pleasures of an ocean voyage and the adventures of discovery in foreign lands. It was for these people that the Transatlantic Steamship Company had in 1836 offered its passengers the opportunity for excursions during *Royal William*'s turnaround in New York. A number of steamship voyages to the Mediterranean were advertised in the 1830s as round-trip excursions or cruises. Starting in 1840, P&O offered round-trip escorted excursions on the ships engaged in its regular liner services to the Mediterranean and the Middle East. Cunard, however, remained entirely committed to his Admiralty mail contract and the business of his Atlantic line service before venturing later into cruising.

The standards of conduct expected from passenger and crew, the order of the day, and indeed much of life aboard ships of the Cunard line, were precisely laid out in code of company Rules and Regulations, similar to those enforced ashore by the railway companies. In the beautifully articulate prose of its day, the preamble to this as it applied to passengers explained its raison d'être:

> It being obvious that on a passage of some days' duration, the comfort of a numerous body of passengers must very much depend upon the manner in which they themselves assist in promoting it, a cheerful acquiescence is expected in the following Regulations and Suggestions which, if in any instance at variance with the opinions, habits or inclinations of the few, are framed with regard to the comfort of the whole.[5]

Slops from cabin water jugs, washbowls and chamber pots were to be emptied overboard to the leeward side of the ship while passengers were at breakfast. Bed linen was to be changed every eight days, and ladies' cabins swept each morning before breakfast. Passengers were responsible for keeping their own cabin ports closed and for extinguishing their candles at the 'lights out' hour of midnight. The third officer's duties included issuing all stores on board, including wines and spirits, effectively designating him as the ship's purser. The officers' mess was made up of the first, second and third mates, chief engineer, the Admiralty officer responsible for the mail, the chaplain and surgeon. The captain and surgeon were the only officers to dine in the passenger saloon, while passengers considered to be of 'respectable' character could be invited to the officers' mess.

There was a separate mess for the engineers, while the deck crew, firemen and coal trimmers housed forward in the forecastle were to have breakfast at 8:00 am, dinner at noon and supper at 6:00 pm in their own quarters. Officers and engineers were entitled to reasonable quantities of sherry, ale, port and spirits, while ratings were to receive a glass of grog for each four-hour watch served, with extra ration for deck crew being at the discretion of the first officer and at the chief engineer's option for engine ratings. As mentioned earlier, frugality was paramount, and captains were instructed to economize on fuel and proceed under sail wherever possible. They were to attain a 'Character for speed and safety', with vigilant look-outs, careful steering, and precaution against the hazards of fire and principal elements.

The British and North American Royal Mail Steam Packet Navigation Company's contracted transatlantic mail service immediately satisfied the line's obligations to the Admiralty and the Post Office. After sailing with their saloons half empty for the first few voyages, Samuel Cunard and his business partners soon found themselves hard-pressed to keep up with the demand for passage in their ships. Most significantly, a viable prototype had been created and standards set for the coming era of passenger ship travel.

AMERICA'S FIRST NORTH ATLANTIC CHALLENGES

Cunard's position on the North Atlantic was countered for the first time when the United States started its own government-subsidized postal steamer service to Britain and Europe. Despite the pioneering role of *Savannah*, in 1819, American transatlantic shipping had continued to focus its progress on the nation's supremacy in building and operating fast sailing packets. Among those who could foresee the ultimate need for a modern steamship line registered under the Stars and Stripes, was Boston shipowner and industrialist R. B. Forbes, who ordered the 770-ton wooden screw steamer *Massachusetts* as the first of a proposed fleet of ships for a liner service between New York and Liverpool. The ship's steam machinery was in reality an auxiliary feature, provided with an unusual arrangement for uncoupling the propeller and hoisting it out of the water while navigating under canvas. After two round-trip voyages made in the autumn of 1845, the ship was found to be too small for her intended North Atlantic service and was finally sold to the United States government.

While the American public maintained its love affair with the age of sail, *Massachusetts* nonetheless stimulated enough interest in steam shipping to give the United States a chance to regain lost time and catch up with British and European commercial developments. It also showed that the prohibitive cost of building steam tonnage in the New World would have to be borne in part by the government in the form of subsidies of one kind or another. This cause was enthusiastically championed by Georgia senator Thomas Butler Kink, who suggested that Washington should put up a million dollars a year for carriage of the mails by the fastest and most regular American-built and owned ships.

In 1845, the United States Postmaster General was mandated by an Act of Congress to contract for carriage of the nation's mails to foreign countries by merchant shipping lines, 'wherever he thinks it necessary for the public interest'. Tenders were invited from American-owned shipping interests for a transatlantic service, preferably operated under steam, connecting New York with Liverpool, Bristol,

Cowes or Southampton, and the European ports of Lisbon, Antwerp, Brest, Le Havre, Bremen or Hamburg, as well as for other routes to Cuba, the West Indies, Central and South America. Bids were also sought from America's railway companies for gathering and distribution of the mails throughout the continental United States.

From among the four tenders submitted for the transatlantic service, Edward Mills was awarded a five-year contract at US$400,000 per year for twice-monthly year-round service between New York City, Le Havre and Bremen, with a call at Southampton. This was controversial as Mills owned no ships and there was a general consensus in New York's shipping circles that the subsidy should have gone to bidders with an established shipping background. The most likely choices would have been Junius Smith's American Atlantic Steam Navigation Company, Edward Knight Collins, founder of Dramatic Line in the sailing packet era, who had submitted a late bid for the Post Office service, or for that matter R. B. Forbes, whose *Massachusetts* had at least aroused an interest in Atlantic steam shipping.

Mills and his backers established the Ocean Steam Navigation Company in 1846, to which he assigned the mail contract, himself becoming General Agent. Orders were placed in the United States with the Westervelt and McKay yard for the large 1,825-ton wooden-hulled paddle steamers *Washington* and *Hermann*. These were the largest ships of their time, each with four decks, and accommodation for 112 Cabin passengers, following the high standards set by the best American sailing packets. They were also notable as being among the first steamships to introduce Second Class, with an additional 70 berths provided in this category.

Washington sailed on her maiden voyage from New York on 1 June 1847, the same day Cunard's *Britannia* started a regular scheduled sailing from Boston to Liverpool. The parallel coincidence of these crossings is seen as the first race for the Blue

Riband of the Atlantic. Despite *Washington*'s greater size and power, *Britannia* reached Liverpool two days before the newer ship made her European landfall. Yet to the credit of the new American venture, this established a preference for New York as a key transatlantic mail and passenger terminal, along with the convenience of also serving London from the much closer proximity of Southampton.

Cunard introduced their own service to New York under a new Admiralty mail contract with four additional ships. At 1,825 tons each, the new *America*, *Niagara*, *Canada* and *Europa* were of comparable performance, style and comfort to their American rivals. In 1848 Cunard inaugurated the world's first weekly transatlantic service, with a sailing every Saturday from Liverpool alternately between the direct New York service and the existing route to Halifax and Boston. As the original rolling schedules related to the calendar month and the old fortnightly schedule became related to a regular week-day time interval, the life beat of the North Atlantic became synchronized with the working week as a standard measure of time in the developing industrialized worlds of commerce and labour.

The Ocean Steam Navigation Company's fortunes were short lived, as the United States postal subsidy was changed from a fixed amount to a percentage of the postage on those mails actually carried. Under this arrangement the line would have lacked the capital needed to expand and modernize its fleet against new competition from both sides of the Atlantic. In 1857 the postal contract for mails to Bremen was awarded to the Vanderbilt Line, and the Ocean Steam Navigation Company was liquidated with their ships sold for further trading in Pacific waters.

Although the late bid from E. K. Collins received no consideration from Congress for the European services awarded to Mills, Collins ultimately secured a contract to carry the US mail to Liverpool, on the basis of a very ambitious weekly service to be inaugurated in 1849. Using five ships it promised to be far in advance of anything else in service on the Atlantic. Collins vowed to 'out steam' the Cunarders from the Atlantic and to 'build steamers that would make the passage from New York to Europe in ten days or less'.[6] The venture was incorporated as The New York & Liverpool United States' Mail Steamship Company, better known simply as the Collins Line. As the cost of building five ships ultimately proved to be prohibitive, the operation was scaled down to a four-ship bi-weekly operation, and Collins managed to secure a substantial advance on his fees. The service was inaugurated in 1850 with the four 3,000-ton paddle steamers, *Arctic*, *Baltic*, *Atlantic* and *Pacific*. Designed by George Steers, architect of the famous yacht *America*, for which the America's Cup race was named, these were created to accord the Blue Riband of Atlantic supremacy to America.

Below: Baltic, *one of the four near-identical steamers built in 1850 for Collins Line service between Liverpool and New York in competition with Cunard's already established services.* (CPL)

Among the innovations of these luxurious American-built and engined ships were steam heating in the accommodation and the introduction of an electric bell-call system for the cabin stewards. While these ships achieved what was expected of them, large sums of money had to be continually spent to repair structural damage caused by their overpowered machinery. After *Arctic*'s 1864 loss in a fatal collision while fog-bound off Cape Race, Newfoundland, *Pacific* mysteriously disappearing without a trace at sea two years later, and finally a reduction of its postal subsidy, this company too was eventually wound up in 1858.

The progress of world shipping development was slowed in the 1850s as ships from all services were requisitioned and chartered by the governments of Britain and its allies for transport duty during the Crimean War. This boosted the fortunes of the American lines for a few years while their rivals were engaged in other services. At the beginning of the following decade, however, the tables were turned as the financial and commercial impact of the American Civil War took its toll on the nation's shipping services, with many river and deep-sea vessels being used for inland and coastal transport. Later, other lines, including those of America and several European nations, were to take up the challenge in the coming era of metal hulls and screw propulsion.

THE PENINSULAR AND ORIENT TO INDIA AND THE FAR EAST

At the time of Samuel Cunard's conquest of the North Atlantic trade, the routes to the Far East were of the greatest administrative and commercial importance to the British Empire and its vast network of trading interests around the globe. Before the Suez Canal was opened in 1869, the only direct sea passage to India was by way of the route around Africa and the Cape of Good Hope, discovered by Vasco da Gama in 1497. Alternatively the journey could be made by way of the Mediterranean, overland between Cairo and Suez and onwards through the Red Sea and Arabian Sea to Bombay, or by the longer entirely overland route through the Ottoman Empire and Persia. Compared with the Atlantic, either of the two sea routes to India generally required larger ships of greater capacity capable of much longer voyages. Here too, there was a primary need for swift and secure passage of the mail, which in this case included the official correspondence of the English East India Company, its trading partners, and those British settlers the company's affairs had brought to India.

The East India trade was less diverse than its North Atlantic counterpart, largely without need to cater for the growing emigrant phenomena of North America, and later Australia. While there was also less of the New York route's keen competition for the cabin trade, the levels of service and comfort on the longer passages east was prescribed by the standards accorded by the East India Company for those privileged to travel on its affairs. With an abundance of cheap labour already available in India there was no call for those below management status, professional or technical standing such as doctors or engineers to travel outbound, and admission of people from the East to Britain was restricted only to the few so privileged in the line of business enterprise or those qualifying for higher education.

Although Samuel Morse's electric telegraph, invented in 1832, was already being extensively used ashore by the railways, with overhead cable strung along their right of way, the first successful long-range undersea cables needed to carry its dot-and-dash Morse Code from one continent to another were yet to be laid. The Atlantic cable between Ireland and Newfoundland went into service in 1866, followed by the Aden–Bombay cable completed in 1869. As telegraphy began to set the pace of instantaneous communication over the world's land masses, the need for postal services to close the remaining deep-sea links as quickly and reliably as possible became ever the more critical.

While the transatlantic routes from Britain to the Americas were direct, the overland routes to India inevitably involved passage through other countries, with even the sea route via the Mediterranean then relying on the mails having to be taken overland between Cairo and Suez. In those years following the end of the Napoleonic wars and restoration of Europe's national boundaries, governments and monarchies in 1815, the security of sending the royal mail by sea aboard British naval vessels or merchantmen was to be preferred, lest there be conflicts of this nature again or it should fall prey to robbers and highwaymen in foreign lands. Yet safe passage was not at the expense of significantly longer travelling times by sea, particularly as would be incurred by sailing all the way around Africa.

After the experimental steamer *Enterprise* had made an agonizingly slow steam-assisted passage of 113 days from Southampton to Calcutta in 1825, the East India Company began to focus their attention more on developing the alternative Red Sea route. Thomas Fletcher Weghorn (1800–49) of the Bengal pilot service, who had piloted *Enterprise* at Calcutta, was later appointed as a courier to the East India Company to help develop a steamer service by the alternative Red Sea route connecting overland with the Mediterranean. While the attempt to use *Enterprise* for this was ultimately unsuccessful, Weghorn made significant progress towards developing the all-important overland link between Alexandria and Suez. During his research he found, for instance, that coal could be bought far more cheaply at Cairo, and brought to Suez economically by camel train.

Above: *P&O's* Tagus *at sea, 1839.* (Author's collection)

During the time he spent in Egypt, Weghorn had established a friendly relationship with Mohemet Ali, Pasha of Egypt, and his officials as well as gaining the support of the land's nomadic peoples, in whose tents he had himself been welcomed, convincing them to work for pay rather than live by plunder and bakshis. The steamer *Hugh Lindsay* sailed between Suez and Bombay once a year until 1836, following the seasonal flow of the monsoon winds, southwest from May to September and northeast October to April. More frequent sailings became possible when the two larger ships *Atlanta* and *Berenice* were added that year. Meanwhile, through his travel agency in Cairo, Weghorn managed to significantly improve the transit between the Mediterranean and Red Sea. The experience involved travel by barge to Atfeh, where passengers transferred to the Nile steamers connecting to Cairo. The stretch of desert between Cairo and Suez had to be crossed overland. He secured improvements to the canal and Nile services and established a regular overland caravan service to safely convey travellers between Cairo and Suez, with eight rest stations, and eventually English carriages, vans and horses. Passage between Alexandria and Suez was scheduled at 88 hours for the transfer of passengers, and through relays of donkeys and camels the mail was carried directly from one ship to the other in about 64 hours. The highway trip between Alexandria and Suez can now be made by car in but a few hours.

An arrangement had been made in 1839 for the royal mail to be carried across France to Marseilles, where it was taken by Admiralty or British merchant steamers to Egypt by way of Malta, often involving a transfer from one ship to another at Valletta. Two years earlier two business partners had secured an Admiralty contract to carry mail around the Iberian peninsula to Gibraltar. The partners were Arthur Anderson (1792–1868), a Shetlander with some Merchant Navy experience, who had ended up in London at the end of the Napoleonic Wars, and

Brodie McGhie Wilcox (1786–1862), a London businessman and shipbroker who had given Anderson his first job in the City. Their company, The Peninsular Steam Navigation Company, was incorporated in 1837, and on winning the contract the 1828-built paddle steamer *William Fawcett* was chartered from the Dublin and London Steam Packet Company. Although the Peninsular mail service was actually opened using the steamers *Don Juan* and *Tagus*, *William Fawcett* has always been honoured as the line's first ship, with a model of the little 206-ton steamer being displayed in the William Fawcett lounge aboard P&O's ultra-modern turbo-electric *Canberra* of 1961.

Despite the grave misfortune of *Don Juan* being wrecked on the homeward leg of her maiden voyage, the venture was ultimately successful, particularly in regard to the establishment of the company's own eventual 'passage to India'. The Admiralty sought the advice of Anderson and Wilcox on a consulting basis to determine the feasibility of extending the direct sea route to Egypt and onwards to India and the Far East, before inviting tenders for the contract to provide the service. The wining bid came from Anderson and Wilcox, who not only offered the lowest price at £34,200, but were the only contenders with experience in the trade from their own earlier peninsular service.

Thus the Peninsular and Oriental Steam Navigation Company was incorporated under Royal Charter in December 1840, with the requirement to place two large steamers in service to Alexandria, and to commence operation between Suez and Bombay within a further two years. The voyage time between Southampton and Bombay was to be no longer than 30 days, including the 150 miles of travel overland in Egypt connecting the Mediterranean and Red Sea. Initially, however, the service had to be operated between Suez and Calcutta, as the East India Company maintained a strict monopoly of the Bombay route, despite P&O having been granted a mail contract with time constraints based on passage to Bombay. Passengers bound to or from Bombay had to travel aboard an East India Company vessel, connecting with P&O's services at Aden, often involving a wait of some days. Alternative overland travel in India only became a viable alternative when the rail link between Bombay and Calcutta was opened in 1870.

The line was, however, able to use an alternative port at Barygaza in much the same way that non-scheduled or neophyte airlines today have to, for instance, use Stansted or Luton airports when they are unable to have access to Heathrow. Today part of the modern Indian city of Bharüch, Barygaza was one of several ports that flourished on trade with Greek and Roman merchantmen who had developed routes to India from Arabia and East Africa in the 1st and 2nd centuries AD. This port's location north of

Bombay, at the mouth of the Narmada River, was unfavourable for P&O as its use would have increased the voyage times to the larger cities of Madras and Calcutta.

Its name soon shortened to The Oriental and later P&O in everyday parlance, and now diversified under the corporate structure of the P&O Group, the company today is a multi-faceted modern corporation with interests in various aspects of transport and communication, including ferry services and cruising – but, alas, no longer in the deep-sea passenger liner service.

The first two Peninsular and Oriental ships to operate on the 'thin red line' of the Admiralty's mail service to Alexandria, calling only at the British ports of Gibraltar and Valletta, were *Great Liverpool* and *Oriental*. The Transatlantic Steamship Company's by then redundant *Liverpool* was purchased and enlarged with the addition of a second accommodation deck. To avoid confusion with the line's 500-ton steamer *Liverpool*, already serving on the old Peninsular route, the new ship was appropriately renamed *Great Liverpool*.

This ship had a remarkably compact machinery installation, occupying less fore-and-aft space in her hull than other installations of similar performance. This was no doubt appreciated by the new owners, on the subtle distinction between ships of the East and West, in that Atlantic tonnage was then considered to be sail-assisted steam, where vessels trading over the longer routes to the Orient and Far East continued to be seen as primarily sail-powered with auxiliary steam. This in itself was probably a moot point, as captains in all services were instructed to proceed under canvas wherever possible. The longer routes to Egypt and onwards to India required greater quantities of coal to be carried and no doubt a more judicious economy in its use, mainly to make it last longer. The availability of greater revenue-earning space to carry mail, passengers or cargo, particularly with *Great Liverpool*'s enlargement for her new service to Alexandria, would have been a welcome benefit.

Great Liverpool also had the distinction of being one of the first passenger steamers equipped with a water distilling plant, which apart from the obvious progress over using seawater in the boilers, was promoted by the original owners as a welcome domestic amenity, producing water, 'equal in purity and coolness to that of the crystal well of the hermit'. The outstanding grade of passenger accommodation this ship offered to her Atlantic passengers was already up to the altogether-higher standards of the East India trade. There were a number of different cabin types available, including a variety of three-berth rooms and eight 'dormitories' for larger groups of people travelling together.

Oriental, another ship originally destined for Atlantic service was bought on the stocks from her

builders and completed for the Orient trade. This ship featured a distinctive accommodation plan, spread over two decks, and with two special cabins located above on the open quarter deck. The main deck cabins were arranged aft around a traditional sailing-ship style saloon, while the lower deck accommodation was divided between two groupings forward and aft of the machinery spaces. The lower deck rooms were, for the most part, arranged back to back along the centreline, with access from two lounging areas extending along either side of the ship. Part of the starboard-side lounging space was separated by a partition as a ladies' saloon, with several cabins reserved for women passengers travelling alone.

Of the two ships, *Oriental* was first to sail to Alexandria, making her maiden voyage in September 1840. She and *Great Liverpool* were followed in 1843 by the slightly larger *Hindostan* and *Bentinck*, delivered as the company's first new ships, designed and built specifically for the Egypt–India service between Suez and Calcutta with stops at Aden and Point de Galle, then the main port city of Ceylon, and a later addition Madras. The second ship was named for Lord William Bentinck, the Governor of India who had strongly advocated for the development of steam navigation east of Suez.

Getting the new P&O ships to Calcutta involved a lengthy positioning voyage around the Cape of Good Hope. Sailing from England on 24 September 1842, *Hindostan* reached Calcutta in 91 days, of which 63 were spent under way at sea and 28 in various ports along the route. The planning of these once-only passages for both ships was a major undertaking, with sufficient quantities of coal having to be shipped ahead of time by sailing packet to Gibraltar, the Cape Verde Islands, Ascension, Cape Town, Mauritius and Ceylon for bunkering of the new P&O vessels. Fresh water and provisions were also replenished at these stops.

The ships had to be large and stable enough to withstand the monsoon winds and rains, and needed to be robustly engined and outfitted so that they could be maintained easily far away from the facilities of their builders and machinery makers. They would also be expected to uphold the famed standards of passenger comfort and service long established aboard the East India Company's own ships. P&O took the opportunity to introduce a number of design innovations of their own, as one of the first lines to make significant concessions to the creature comforts of their passengers on long, hot equatorial voyages.

Departing from the original centreline-saloon plan of the sailing packet era and the various steamship adaptations of it, *Hindostan*'s layout featured a large full-beam saloon located aft on the upper deck, with windows astern and on both sides. Instead of the usual accommodation plan, with as many rooms as possible at the ship's sides enjoying their own port-holes, sidelights or windows, the cabins were arranged centrally between corridors at either side of the deck. The idea was to use the passage as a heat barrier between the sleeping accommodation and the ship's sides. Whatever breezes could be drawn into the ship in the heat of the Red Sea would pass through the open cabin doorway or through a jalousie in the door itself, without the heat from the ship's side also being felt inside the room. There were also the advantages that passenger berths would be closer to the centre of the ship, where the effects of rolling would be less pronounced and the rush of water against the hull less audible.

The passages themselves, which at the starboard side of *Hindostan* ran 170ft (52m) of the ship's 240ft (73m) full length, with windows on one side and the accommodation on the other, were similar to those later introduced in long-distance railway sleeping coaches in North America, Russia and Europe. The dimensions of the cabins and these outer passages would in fact have been close to those of their later Pullman counterparts ashore.

The cabins themselves included a number of rooms on the upper deck with skylights, as well as others with the luxury of their own private WC. A small group of cabins on the upper deck, as well as some of those on the lower deck, were laid out on a more conventional plan of inner and outer rooms on either side of a central passage. Other comforts included warm and cold baths and showers, a ladies' drawing room and, like *Oriental*, separate cabins for female passengers travelling alone.

Life aboard P&O's ships in the Mediterranean and Indian Ocean would have been similar in many ways to that of the line's Cunard counterparts serving the New York route. While those crossing between Europe and America had to endure North Atlantic storms, fog and rain, passengers on the way to and from India were inescapably subjected to the inferno of the Red Sea passage, along with the Mediterranean mistrals, high winds and torrential rains of the seasonal monsoons, not to mention the ordeal of making the overland connection between Alexandria and Suez. A narrow body of water bound by desert along either side, the Red Sea is notorious for the discomfort of its searing air temperatures. Without the benefit of mechanical ventilation and air-chilling systems, the saloons and cabin accommodation could become almost as hot as the boiler room as ships steamed with the prevailing winds, the smoke from their funnels rising straight up and the still air on and below decks becoming stifling. The traditional Indian punkah, a cloth sail hung from a rod above the saloon table, and steadily swung to and fro by a native punkah wallah to stir about the already hot and heavy air inside the saloon, offered one of the very few forms of relief.

From the earliest days of the Peninsular and Orient services to India, passengers were treated to the Indian cuisine that has remained a distinctive feature of P&O liner services around the world. Curried chicken, beef, lamb, fish and vegetables, traditionally served with plain and Pillau rice and all of the proper accompanying chutneys, poppadums, chapaties, sweet fruits, nuts, raisins and various other condiments, have been offered since the first Indian sea cooks were hired in the 1840s. The last curries were finally served in the air-conditioned dining rooms of the 1960s-built *Oriana* and *Canberra* as they ended their careers in 1981 and 1997 respectively. Generally lighter than English and North European fare, the piquant cuisines of India, the Middle East and Latin America are easier to eat and digest in hot climates, as their spices have the effect of drawing heat from the body. Whether one preferred the Eastern or English alternatives on the table, dehydration was a key concern of shipboard well-being for passengers and crew alike east of Suez. At first fresh water had to be brought to Suez by donkey and camel caravan until condenser plants were built there.

Then, before the advent of modern casual clothing, without the durable and easily-cared-for synthetic fabrics of today, and with virtually no facility for laundry to be done aboard ship, passengers travelled with incredibly large quantities of baggage. The First-Class allowance was four hundredweight, 448lbs (203.2 kilos), per adult passenger. All personal belongings were to be packed in trunks that would be stowed in the ship's baggage room, where they could be accessed as scheduled times, weather permitting, during the voyage. The trunks themselves could weigh no more than 80lbs each, with dimensions no greater than 2ft 3in x 2ft 1in x 2ft (68.5cm x 63.4cm x 60.9cm) so that these could be slung over the back of a camel for the overland trek between Cairo and Suez.

While steamship travelling conditions of the 1840s appear to be difficult and uncomfortable by the standards of present-day jet travel, these nonetheless represented the progress of their age and a new dimension of mobility and convenience for those wanting to travel. Travel then no doubt held a greater sense of adventure and exploration in a world less homogenized by the forces of globalization and by the instantaneous communication of late 20th-century electronic media. Doctor David Livingstone was yet to make his journey across Africa in 1856. Roald Amundsen was still to find a way through the North West Passage in 1903–06 and successfully complete the first ever expedition to the South Pole in 1911, three months ahead of Robert Scott. The lost Inca city of Machu Picchu was still to be found by Hiram Bingham in 1911 and the tomb of Tutankhamun found as late as 1922. For those among the wealthy who had no commission to carry out explorations for the Royal Geographical Society, sea travel offered the opportunity to explore and discover the known world in the company of a small group of like-minded individuals.

THE ORIGINS OF P&O CRUISING

As the Peninsular and Orient company built up its network of Iberian peninsula, Mediterranean and Black Sea routes, along with various auxiliary and feeder services, the company started to offer guided and escorted tours of the Mediterranean. At first this was probably done in part to sell excess capacity on the mail ships operating between Malta and the Ionian Islands. When the line finally obtained a release from their contractual obligation to continue this money-losing service in 1842, the by-then popular excursions were continued, using their alternative service to Greece and the eastern Mediterranean.

The voyage segment from Southampton to Malta was made aboard the company's Iberian-service steamers, with calls at Vigo, Lisbon, Cadiz and Gibraltar. After transferring to the eastern-Mediterranean-service ships at Valletta, the tour continued on to Athens, Smyrna (Izmir), Constantinople (Istanbul), Beirut and Jaffa (Tel Aviv). From here the journey was made on horseback or by carriage to Jerusalem, and again overland to Cairo, with excursions to Luxor and the pyramids of Cheops. The party would then sail down the Nile to Atfeh, by canal vessel to Alexandria, and back to England aboard a P&O steamer, again by way of Malta and the Iberian ports. The whole excursion, covering some 25,000 miles (40,233km), took about three months to complete.

Unlike modern-day cruises, where the ship makes a round-trip pleasure voyage without carrying regular passengers, mail and cargo, these were escorted parties of passengers travelling aboard regular line services engaged in their ordinary trades. Thus excursion passengers were brought in to much closer contact with the places and peoples served by the ship, with longer stays ashore and some parts of the tour being made overland, using local transport and lodgings. In 1844 P&O offered one of these voyages to William Makepeace Thackeray (1811–63) in an effort to help

publicize the pleasures of leisure ocean travel, and which he chronicled in his *Diary of a Voyage from Cornhill to Grand Cairo*, published three years later.

Thackeray recounts that these local encounters were not always as pleasant as might have been expected during such a prestigious travel experience by a young and fashionable Londoner such as himself. He describes the swarm of local passengers who sailed to Jaffa on the same ship with his party as a mix of 'Christians, Jews and Heathens'. 'In the cabin were Poles, Russians, French, Germans, Spaniards and Greeks; on the deck squatted several little colonies of peoples of different race and persuasion', he continues, describing 'a profusion of stinks they raised... the horrible messes cooked in filthy pots and devoured with nasty fingers'.

He describes also the 17 days he and his party had to spend in a quarantine lazaretto at Malta before returning to England as being 'pleasant and quiet....almost agreeable after the incessant sightseeing of the last two months'. As an overall impression of the tour he writes:

> I didn't see the dancing dervishes, it was Ramazan [Ramadan]; nor the howling dervishes at Scutari, it was Ramazan; nor the interiors of Saint Sophia, nor the women's apartments of the seraglio, nor the fashionable promenade of the Sweet Waters, always because it was Ramazan. On account of the same holy season the royal palaces and mosques are shut, the people remaining asleep all day, and passing the night in feasting and carousing.[7]

While there were the inevitable disappointments of so extensive a journey, Thackeray nonetheless had the highest genuine praise for his hosts, their ships, captains and crews. His writings achieved what the line had hoped for, and its directors were no doubt as pleased as Thackeray himself with the experience.

Indeed from the preposterous shipboard boxes occupied by Charles Dickens and William Thackeray there came a literary account of ocean travel and shipboard living that was to reach the wider public and fire its imagination, as well as its thirst for ocean travel. ●

THE WONDERMENT OF THE VICTORIAN ERA

Queen Victoria was crowned in 1837, at about the time Samuel Cunard began to envisage his dream of a regular transatlantic steamship line and when Arthur Anderson and Wilcox incorporated their Peninsular Steam Navigation Company. This was an age of wonderment, when in 1851 the Great Exhibition in Hyde Park had served as the greatest congress of engineering and technological talent the world had yet witnessed. From the scientific discussion and business proposals inspired by the Exhibition, housed in the magnificent iron-and-glass Crystal Palace designed by Joseph Paxton, there emerged a number of significant initiatives: the conceptualizations for building the Suez Canal; new ideas for a tunnel under the English Channel; and plans to build the world's greatest steamship. This was indeed an age of great development and accomplishment.

The unbridled optimism of the era was expressed in projects such as these, whose unprecedented vastness often fell far short of what was expected of them commercially, as was the case with *Great Eastern*. Yet this was also a time of remarkable evolutionary progress. The daring and the bold also seemed to wield an enormous influence in stimulating a relentless pace of innovation going on in the background out of the limelight. As sail gradually yielded to steam, shipbuilding itself progressed from wood construction to iron and then to steel. The paddle wheel eventually gave way to the screw propeller, as each innovation brought with it a steady progression to larger ships, higher speeds, and inevitably to greater stability, safety and onboard comfort.

The large paddle steamer *Persia* was built by Robert Napier & Son of Glasgow in 1856 as Cunard's first iron-hulled Atlantic liner. She was a remarkably beautiful ship, with a perfect visual balance to the massing of her two funnels, paddle enclosures and long clipper bow. Her accommodation was the best available on the North Atlantic. Apart from her First-Class cabins for 200 passengers and an additional 50 in Second Class, *Persia*'s public facilities included spacious saloons occupying much of the upper deck's full length, forward and aft of the machinery and other working spaces amidships. The accommodation plan provided a full-length promenade deck along the centre of the ship for passenger use above these. *Persia*'s 3,214-ton size permitted a through plan of the main deck, with internal passages at the ship's sides, bypassing the machinery spaces amidships between the forward and aft cabin blocks. Achieving a top speed of 14 knots, *Persia* regained the Blue Riband record passage honours for Cunard from the Collins liner *Arctic* in July 1856, with a passage time from Liverpool to New York of 9 days, 4 hours, 45 minutes. The prestige of this, however, came at the cost of a horrendous 150-tons-per-day fuel consumption, amounting to six tons of fuel being burned for every ton of cargo carried. She was, nonetheless, a very popular ship, remaining in the line's Atlantic service until 1868.

The shipyard drawings for *Persia* were made by

Opposite:
Detail from an original painting by Mark Myers depicting the paddle steamer **Great Western** *running before a storm.* (CPL)

Napier's draftsman, David Kirkaldy, whose personal interest in design and shipbuilding was to lead him to discover methods for oil hardening steel for ship-building. Foreseeing the need for ship yards to adopt standard ways of estimating requirements of draft, speed and economy of operation in larger new ships, he also developed a structured system of mechanical testing. Kirkaldy obviously took great pride in his work, and appears to have made *Persia*'s drawings as much for his own pleasure as for paid work. These were so exquisite that they were the first drawings of their type ever to be exhibited at the Royal Academy in London. They were later shown at the Paris Exhibition of 1855, along with drawings of *America*, *Niagara*, *Canada* and *Europa*, earning Napier a gold medal and League of Honour recognition as the exhibitor and a medal for Kirkaldy himself as drafts-man. His drawings were later put in the Louvre museum after being presented to Emperor Napoleon III (1808–73).

Persia was joined in 1862 by *Scotia*. The new ves-sel had the further refinements of additional water-tight bulkheads and buoyancy chambers in the for-ward compartments formed by a double-hull shell. While *Persia*, built only six years earlier, was Cunard's first iron-hulled ship, *Scotia* would be their last paddle steamer. At about the same time as *Scotia*'s completion, the line also took delivery of their first screw-propelled Atlantic liner, *China*, which sported compact geared oscillating engines. Although two knots slower than *Persia* and *Scotia* and about two thirds their size (with only half their fuel consumption), the new *China* carried 150 Cabin passengers, 770 Steerage and 1,400 tons of mail and cargo against the *Scotia*'s exclusively Cabin capacity of 275 and hold space of 1,050 tons. In 1867, *Persia* and *Scotia*'s size and speed were matched by the new screw steamers, *Cuba*, *Java* and *Russia*, and later that year *Persia* and the line's last wooden-hulled paddler, *Africa*, were withdrawn from service. *Scotia* remained in Cunard service until 1876, when she was finally withdrawn from the Liverpool–New York service.

Through this era, the style of cabin accommoda-tion and onboard passenger service evolved only through an increase in the size of the ships them-selves, with the added stability affording greater comfort. While ships such as *Persia* offered larger saloons and greater areas of open deck space for pas-senger enjoyment, the cabin accommodation itself changed only in regard to the quality of its outfitting. The greatest advance was in the way that emigrant travellers in Steerage were treated due to the devel-oping emigrant trades during the emerging steamship era.

Cunard and his partners resisted any temptation to go head-to-head with their rivals on excessive ship-board luxuries and pampering of their passengers. The line maintained its solid contractual commitment to the swift, regular and safe passage of Her Majesty's mail, with passengers being carried as but a secondary priority. The point is abundantly illus-trated by a commentary from Samuel Cunard's part-ner David McIver on the question of providing table napkins for saloon passengers, whose view was: 'Going to sea is a hardship. The Cunard Company does not undertake to make anything less out of it, and that if people want to wipe their mouths at a ship's table, they could use their pocket handker-chiefs'.[1] This represented the bluff and honest senti-ment that characterized the line's whole approach to its business. In that era, when going to sea was indeed realistically viewed by many as a hardship, this in itself was a valued source of solace and reas-surance to the timid.

THE STEERAGE EXODUS

Originally, the emigrant trades to America and Australia were handled almost exclusively by the sailing packet companies, while the early steamers fulfilled their mail contracts and catered to the exclu-sive Saloon-Class trades. Steerage passengers were effectively carried as cargo, more or less as livestock that brought along its own possessions and had the capacity to feed itself. Their numbers were not reck-oned in the specification of ships' passenger capaci-ties, as they occupied the same holds on outward pas-sages that were used to carry cargo on the home-bound leg of the voyage. Steerage passengers were embarked, along with their meagre belongings, by way of makeshift ships' accommodation ladders, or companionways as these were called, erected in the cargo hatchways.

As described in the previous chapter, Steerage passengers were only given small quantities of fresh water and had access to the open deck, weather per-mitting, for airing, exercise and 'firing' to cook their own food. Through periods of storm and heavy weather, Steerage passengers could be confined below decks for days, without fresh air, cooking facilities, or even adequate light, ventilation and toi-let facilities. There was only space enough to stand between the rows of triple-tier berths, and nowhere to sit even to eat one's food. The best one could do was to squat atop a coil of rope or some other piece of ship's paraphernalia on deck or upon one's own pile of possessions. These people found that they could be mercilessly flogged for any infraction of ship-board regulation and protocol, and were often abused and bullied by the crew.

Apart from the misery of seasickness, there were periodic epidemics of cholera or typhus, and the fatigue brought on by mental stagnation or 'ship fever', as it was called. There was no doctor or med-ication available, and those who died simply had their mortal remains unceremoniously committed to the deep, probably without so much as the event being acknowledged in the ship's log. Yet these conditions were scarcely worse than in the workhouses and slums of the British and European industrial cities from which many of these poor souls were trying to escape.

While the exodus began during the years of economic depression following the Napoleonic Wars and as a consequence of the Irish potato famine of the 1840s, ultimately it grew as a byproduct of industrialization and urban development. The modern urban metropolis had grown as a phenomenon of industrialization. The railways aided this transformation by moving great volumes of raw materials, components, fuel and other consumables to centres where manufacturing could be concentrated enough to make it economically viable. The railways would also bring the required labour to these centres and distribute the finished goods to their markets. As vast numbers of people moved in from the countryside to find employment in the factories and the promise of learning and social development, inevitably there were those who were unable to find places for themselves in the new urban economies. Far from their homes and family backgrounds, these growing masses of jobless, disenchanted and utterly impoverished people found that they were trapped in a wholly impersonal milieu, with no state welfare resources, without the traditional lines of support from family, neighbours or their church.

Many sought to move on rather than try to go back. Between 1846 and 1932 more than 60 million people migrated from the British Isles, Europe, Scandinavia and Russia. Among these were some two million Irish citizens, estimated as a quarter of the nation's population at the time. Many of the emigrants poured out of the heavily industrialized British Midlands and the German Ruhr Valley, with the greatest numbers going to the United States. British emigrants settled also in Canada, Australia and the other dominions of the Empire, while the Italian exodus was divided between the United States and Latin America, and those from Spain preferred the Spanish-speaking countries of Central and South America. Argentina and Brazil were particularly popular destinations for emigrants from continental Europe, as these countries themselves were aggressively industrializing and in need of workers.[2] This great migration of humanity fluctuated with the ebb and flow of commercial progress, attenuated during its boom cycles and boosted by its periodic bust. It finally subsided to a mere trickle when immigration to the United States was curtailed in the early 1930s during the Great Depression.

Many of these unfortunate people irrevocably took leave of their homelands, families and friends, with scarcely more than the clothes on their backs. With photography then in its infancy and any form of art likewise a luxury of the wealthy, they took with them no images of their loved ones and homes other than in their memories. As many could neither read nor write, correspondence with those left behind, no matter how long letters took to reach their destinations then, offered no possibilities for maintaining family ties and keeping in touch. The best they could do was to keep their recollections alive through the arts of storytelling, ballads, song and dance. Even as late as the 1920s many of those who left their homes as part of this great emigrant exodus were never again to see their old homelands, families and friends.

Industrialization and development of the United States in the late 19th and early 20th centuries provided a steady demand for both skilled and unskilled labour. Unlike Australia and New Zealand, the USA and Canada imposed no restriction on immigration of English-speaking settlers. This created opportunities for many people throughout the British Isles, Europe and Scandinavia to emigrate by choice rather than by abject necessity, bringing with them valuable skills and trades, to seek new opportunities and a better life in the Americas. By 1869 transcontinental rail service had been inaugurated across the United States, allowing comfortable, relatively quick and secure access to the interior and west coast within the timeframe of only a few days.

Aboard ship, men, women and families would be berthed together in the same holds; there was no privacy, nowhere even to sit and little respect for even the most basic levels of human dignity. Conditions were on average probably worst aboard the privateer sailing packets then still carrying the bulk of the North Atlantic trade. Those making the much longer voyage to Australia and New Zealand tended to fare best, as each passenger was provided with a bunk and a storage box for his or her personal belongings, food and utensils. Trunks and other items of baggage were secured at the centre of each passenger compartment, where these served as places to sit and as makeshift saloon tables. Steerage passengers on these routes were strictly segregated into separate compartments, with single men forward, married couples and their families amidships and women travelling alone aft.

Government legislation introduced on both sides of the Atlantic as late as the 1840s and 1850s finally imposed standards to limit overcrowding and to provide such basic necessities of life as water closets within the accommodation for use by women and children. Although passengers still had to prepare their own food, prescribed rations of water, ship's biscuits, wheaten flour, oatmeal, rice and molasses had to be provided to each passenger as part of the ticket price. In 1861 this was revised to include beef, pork, preserved meats and salt fish in lieu of the earlier diet's less wholesome items.

The first significant improvements in emigrant-class accommodation were introduced in the 'iron age' of steam shipping by the Inman Line. Their pioneering screw-propelled iron ship *City of Glasgow* was purchased from Tod and McGregor of Glasgow, who had built her for their own transatlantic passenger and cargo service. William Inman was one of the first shipping people to view the business from the passenger's perspective, and to foresee that its future development would depend more on the travelling public's perceptions of sea travel itself, rather than merely on the technical and engineering progress of the ships. He was also aware that the continuing industrialization of the United States was going to demand a vast influx of labour, emigrating from overseas as Steerage. No doubt he realized that ultimately there would even be competition at this level. Inman and his wife made a number of voyages themselves in emigrant accommodation to experience the hardship first-hand and determine what could reasonably be achieved to make this class of travel more comfortable.

City of Glasgow was built as a ship of modest size and performance, with cabin accommodation for 52 First-Class passengers and 85 in Second Class along the full length of her upper deck. This was arranged on a traditional plan with cabins at the ship's sides flanking central saloon and public areas 16ft (4.87m) wide. With the exception of two four-berth rooms, First-Class passengers enjoyed the luxury of being berthed only two to a cabin, while Second Class was comfortably berthed four or eight to a cabin. The ship's most notable passenger amenity appears to have been the inclusion of a single bath with a device for pumping seawater in and out of it for bathing. The pleasures of using this were described in promotional literature of the time as, 'an enervating experience to be countered by an alcoholic stimulant.'[3] The lower deck had space for 1,200 tons of cargo, itself no doubt sufficient to assure the ship's profitable operation without carrying passengers at all.

After the ship went into the service of her new owners in 1850, and had completed a couple of successful voyages between Liverpool and Philadelphia, Inman convinced his business partners to engage in the emigrant trade. Basic accommodation and service were provided for 400 Steerage passengers on the lower deck. They were still accommodated sailing-packet style in triple-tier berths. These were arranged in blocks four-or-five deep from the ship's side and two fore-and-aft, which one climbed into from their outward ends. The lower deck where these were located was well ventilated, with its height of 7ft (2.13m) offering good air circulation and with spaces along the centre of the ship for passengers to eat their meals and congregate socially. There was freer access to the open decks above, as well as the unprecedented Steerage-Class luxuries of a ladies' lounge and a medical dispensary tended by the ship's surgeon.

Although Inman put the needs of his passengers first, *City of Glasgow* was, nonetheless, of technical interest in her own right. As one of the first successful screw-powered iron steamers she had an unusual machinery arrangement. Her two engines were positioned on one side of the ship with their working beams crossing the centreline, and the three-to-one reduction gearing was arranged on the opposite side. Her iron hull enclosed three full-length decks and was partitioned by five iron bulkheads into six watertight compartments. Yet she was also of the classic exterior appearance typical of Clyde-built ships of her time, with a long clipper bow and a particularly voluminous barque sailing rig.

Despite her loss at sea without trace in 1854, *City of Glasgow* was the prototype for what became known at the time as 'Inman's Iron Screws'. She was followed by the slightly larger *City of Philadelphia* and *City of Baltimore*, also built by Tod and McGregor, as well as the American-built City of Pittsburgh. More significantly, these ships also set the pace for development of the North Atlantic emigrant trade, both through the 42 years of the Inman Line's own existence, and in the model it set for others to follow. A number of forward-looking steamship owners also realized the value of humane treatment of their poorest passengers. They also noted the commercial potential of economy made possible by screw-propelled steamships able to transport large numbers of these people on minimum fare. Those interests of the Ismay, Imrie & Company and the Oceanic Steam Navigation Company, which eventually suffused into the White Star Line, were later to offer similar service aboard their distinctive ships constructed in the 1860s by the Belfast shipbuilders Harland & Wolff.

By 1871 White Star guaranteed to provide a separate berth for each adult, along with a ten-cubic-foot baggage allowance for the Steerage fare of about 6 guineas. Children sharing berths with adults were carried at half price, while passage was denied outright to those the line considered to be in unfit mental or physical health. The ticket price also included meals, with breakfast served at 8:00 am, dinner at 1:00 pm, supper at 6:00 pm, and an optional serving of oatmeal gruel available at 8:00 pm. The fare itself consisted mainly of porridges, stews and gruels that could be prepared in quantity and ladled out from cauldrons into the pannikins, or messing tins, from which it was eaten. Steerage passengers still had to bring their own bedding and eating utensils, against the odds that, if included in the passage fare, most of these items would have found their way ashore as these people disembarked.

Many of those emigrating in the latter decades of the 19th century would have found that even the most basic accommodation aboard an Inman or White Star ship was more comfortable or humane than they would likely have experienced ashore in working-class city neighbourhoods and company enclaves. The sense of security from merely having the privilege to travel aboard one of the great steamers, although no doubt frightening for many, would have been awe inspiring. There was also the promise of better things to come in a new land, free from the social barriers and class-oriented restrictions of British and Continental society. Even as the seas became rough, the steady turn of those great reciprocating engines below deck would have been steadying and reassuring.

BEYOND CALCUTTA

In the meantime, P&O began extending its Indian Ocean services onwards to Penang, Singapore, Hong Kong, Australia and New Zealand. The line had already built its own extensive network of facilities to service the overland link between Alexandria and Suez, with coaling stations, workshops and other amenities to service its fleets east of Suez, and had already overcome the most difficult part of reaching the Far East.

P&O's Far Eastern route to Singapore and Hong Kong was inaugurated in 1845, using the 533-ton Peninsular-service steamer *Lady Mary Wood*, aboard which William Thackeray had made part of his Mediterranean cruise the previous year. This was at first run as a connecting service based in Point de Galle, Ceylon, where the Far Eastern mails would be transferred to and from the mainline ships serving Calcutta. *Lady Mary Wood* made her positioning voyage to Singapore in a remarkably short time of only 41 days, less than half the time taken for *Hindostan* to reach Calcutta from Southampton four years earlier. This would appear to have been largely a result of improved shore support along the way, with less time being spent in ports during the voyage. The steaming time from Point de Galle to Penang was six days, another two days to Singapore, and an additional week to reach Hong Kong. With the additional port time required for mail and cargo handling, bunkering, victualling and other ship's services, a second ship, *Braganza*, was also transferred from the Company's original Peninsular route to maintain a year-round monthly sailing schedule to the Far East.

In that era prior to radio broadcasting, semaphore of one sort or another was a widely used form of communicating important messages to the general public. The authorities in Singapore decided to announce the closing times at the post office for mails to Britain and Europe by flying a Red Ensign from the flagstaff on Government Hill, with a yellow signal flag indicating the closing of the China and Far Eastern post. The first time the yellow flag was run up there was near panic throughout the colony, as this was widely recognized as the Quarantine signal, raising concern that there had been an outbreak of cholera, bubonic plague or yellow fever. Many feared that a hapless Arab pilgrim ship may have brought some epidemic or plague, and that the whole colony might be quarantined, other ships diverted from its

port, as well as passengers and ships' crews from Singapore being quarantined elsewhere. The incident was soon cleared up, although with considerable embarrassment to the Singapore Post Office and to P&O, who, as so often happens, had clearly underestimated the public's general knowledge and understanding of such things. It also supports the common knowledge as to how few people take the time to read public notices.

From its ancient origins in the trade of silk and other precious commodities, the Silk Road had also become the Opium Road, as silk and tea moved west and opium went east. Apart from the privately-owned China tea clippers that thrived as much on the drugs trade as on other legitimate cargoes, P&O, the Dutch East India Company and others were also quite responsive to the 'hidden hand' of the opium trade. These prestigious companies would not themselves engage in buying and selling narcotics, although they saw no reason why they should not transport opium from the Middle East and India to China as they would any other commodity. While this suited the prevailing moral standards of the time, P&O found itself in conflict with the clipper owners who had built their businesses on the opium trade, without the benefit of government mail contracts to fall back on. Charges were made that P&O and other lines were compromising their postal service obligations, and that ships were being overloaded, with opium chests carried in the bunkers and coal heaped on deck. These charges were disproved by an Admiralty investigation of the line's activities, although an onwards service from Hong Kong established beyond the postal contract was subsequently curtailed.

Other routes were tried with varying degrees of success, including services to Shanghai and Japan. These were outside the constraints of the company's Admiralty mail contracts, and could run on a somewhat ad hoc basis, as dictated by the availability of cargoes and passengers.

P&O was, however, as anxious to extend its services to Australia, as were the Australian people to have the benefit of regular mail and steamship connections with the rest of the world. The most direct and commercially advantageous routing for this would be as a service from Bombay, where the East India Company continued to maintain its monopoly of traffic between India and Britain. In 1849 the line made a bid to carry the royal mail by steamship to Bombay and onwards to Australia for the same rate of £50,000 per year as was being paid to the East India Company for the service it operated by sailing packet to Bombay alone. The financial difference, including the additional £50,000 the service was costing the East India Company, was to be made up by the additional cargo and passenger revenues these routes could generate.

The East India Company was finally forced to relinquish its Bombay shipping monopoly, as it faced

Above: Chusan, *the modest screw steamer of 1854 that opened up P&O's world to Australia, and to services that were retained until* Oriana *and* Canberra *were finally switched to full-time cruising in the 1970s.* (CPL)

increasing difficulties in meeting its postal service obligations. The end came after an entire shipment of mail bound for Aden was lost without trace after being consigned to a native sailing dhow when there was no company vessel available to carry it. In 1862 P&O successfully tendered as the low bidder against the Eastern Steam Navigation Company to operate a bundle of five separate mail services for an annual fee of £199,600 for eight years. These included:

- Twice-monthly service between Southampton and Calcutta
- Twice-monthly connections of Marseilles and Malta with the England–Egypt service
- Monthly service to Bombay, Ceylon, Singapore and China
- Monthly service to Calcutta, Singapore and China, combining with the Bombay service to reach India and China twice a month
- Service every two months between Singapore and Australia, calling at King George's Sound, Adelaide, Melbourne and Sydney

The first P&O ship to reach Australia was the new 699-ton screw-propelled iron steamer *Chusan*, arriving in August 1852 at the end of her positioning voyage from England via the Cape of Good Hope. The regular scheduled passage between Britain and Australia could then be made in about 70 days, depending on the amount of time taken for the Alexandria–Suez overland connection and for transferring between ships in Ceylon and Singapore. Passenger fares 'including bedding and provisions' were advertised at £10 10s First Class and £6 6s Second.

The impact of these new steamship services in such far-away corners of the British Empire and other parts of the world was enormous. Passages no longer had to be made to coincide with the seasonal monsoons, and ships were freed from the whim and mercy of nature. Although telegraph was yet to come, business and social correspondence could be

answered more quickly, in a matter of only weeks or months, and the response could be anticipated with the predictability of a scheduled service. With passage between Britain and Australia under sail taking anything from 94 to 159 days, communication had been incredibly slow, even by the standards of those times.

Perhaps most significantly, those travelling to such distant destinations as Singapore, China, Japan and Australia no longer had the feeling that they were embarking upon epic once-in-a-lifetime voyages from which returning home was a daunting prospect. Business travel became more feasible, with the possibilities of making a round-trip to just about anywhere in the world in only a matter of months. Although the voyage times were longer, steamship travel was beginning to make Australia, China and Japan as accessible as the Americas and West Indies. A steamship network of world communication hubs had been brought into existence by the private enterprise of two remarkable English companies, Cunard and P&O. In a sense the idea of the railways, with their timetables and clockwork regularity of service, had bridged the high seas. The world was starting to become a smaller and more familiar place to an increasingly wide variety and number of passengers.

INFLUENCES OF BRUNEL AND HIS *GREAT EASTERN*

The Admiralty's research of possible trading routes to Australia showed that there were in fact three alternatives, each of which could be covered by steamship in about 70 days. Apart from the route via Egypt, these included the sea route around the Cape of Good Hope and a westward route across the Atlantic and Pacific Oceans with an overland crossing of the 49 mile- (82km-)wide Isthmus of Panama. The Cape of Good Hope offered the only direct sea route without an overland crossing and the inherent need for mail, passengers and cargo to be transferred from one vessel to another. The greatest difficulty with both alternatives lay with their very long open-sea passages and the need to carry huge amounts of fuel. While provisioning ships with fresh water and food on long voyages at various port calls along the way was easy enough, sufficient quantities of coal were generally unavailable in these same places. As P&O had already learned, this usually had to be shipped out from Britain ahead of time to various bunkering stages such as Aden or the African ports.

There had been only a gradual progression to larger ships. Shipowners and builders remained cautious, as the longterm service implications of building and sailing metal-hulled ships were still unknown, and there was still the need for most ships to also be able to proceed under canvas, both as an economy and a fail-safe measure. Cunard, P&O and other steamship companies were keen to keep up with the pace of engineering and technological progress, but remained reluctant themselves to be the pioneers. Any ship represented, then as now, a substantial longterm investment for its owners and builders. Before committing themselves to something new, most shipowners need to be reassured by the existence of a working prototype, to substantiate any significant new direction, either in design or scale. As recently as 1997, when the order was placed to build the 140,000-ton *Voyager of the Seas*, Royal Caribbean International CEO Richard Fein needed to see for himself that, at just over 100,000 tons, the new *Carnival Destiny* had avoided creating any impression onboard of being too large.[4]

Sometimes the impetus to do something different must originate from other fields of endeavour or the vision of enlightened outsiders to stimulate change and foster progress. In 1851 the eminent British engineer, Isambard Kingdom Brunel (1806–59) brought to the Great Exhibition his ideas of building ships on a far greater scale than the world had yet seen. Already the architect and builder of the Great Western Railway and many of its structures, including London's Paddington Station and the Clifton Suspension Bridge over the River Avon at Bristol, Brunel was a man whose accomplishments always seemed brilliant, radical and larger than life itself. His work on other projects included the Thames Rotherhithe Tunnel, the Royal Albert Bridge over the River Tamar at Saltash, as well as countless railways, piers, dry-docks and bridges in England, Ireland, Italy and India.

In the year 2001, the BBC asked the populace to choose the person they thought to be the Greatest Briton, as those born or who lived in Great Britain and whose life played a significant part on the history or life of the British Isles. Sir Winston Churchill was voted the Greatest, followed by Isambard Kingdom Brunel, Princess Diana, Charles Darwin and William Shakespeare. In the television documentaries made of the top ten Britons, which also included Queen Elizabeth I, John Lennon, Sir Isaac Newton, Oliver Cromwell and Horatio Nelson, narrator Jeremy Clarkson said of Brunel:

> Brunel built modern Britain, and Britain built the world, which means that Brunel built the modern world, and that makes him a pretty damned great Briton in my book.

Standing only 5ft 4in (1.6m) tall, the usually top-hatted Brunel was affectionately known in his own time as The Little Giant. He moved about London through the seemingly endless whirlwind of his day-to-day activities in what he called his 'Flying Hearse', a fast horse-drawn Britzka outfitted with a bed so that at

Below: *A painting by Mark Myers showing Brunel's* Great Western *arriving in New York in April 1838 to begin the first successful steam ship service between Britain and America.* (CPL)

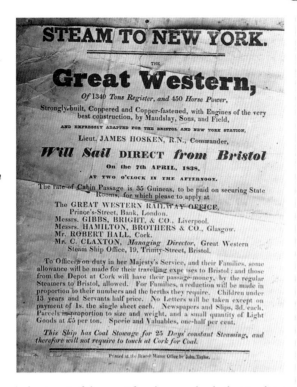

Below: Photographic pioneer W. H. Fox Talbot's famous picture of Great Britain *afloat in Bristol harbour in 1843.* (CPL)

for building a shield that could be advanced using jack-screws as the brick shaft is completed behind it for tunnelling under the Thames. This was indeed the first prototype of the modern tunnelling machines used for projects such as the Euro Tunnel.

Brunel's shipbuilding exploits were among his greatest achievements. Even if these were ultimately less successful commercially than his railways they proved to be enormously influential in the development of modern merchant shipping. They included the Atlantic steamers *Great Western* and *Great Britain*, built in 1838 and 1843 respectively. Of these, *Great Britain*, built for Great Western Steamship Company, was the first transatlantic ship both to be built with an iron hull and to have screw propulsion. It also introduced a hydrostatically researched steamship hull-form with a flat double bottom and no outside projection of the keel. The ship was divided into six watertight compartments by bulkheads extended all the way up to the main deck, rather than to the first deck above the waterline, as later became standard practice for merchant ships. After a brief career on her original transatlantic service, *Great Britain* was later used for many years in an emigrant service to Australia via Cape Horn, eventually being converted into a sailing ship after her machinery had worn out. After being dismasted during a gale in 1886, she was beached near Port Stanley in the Falkland Islands, where she remained until 1970, before finally being rescued and restored to her original home port of Bristol.

Great Britain's epic 7,600-mile homecoming voyage was made by way of Montevideo, where her weather-beaten and scared iron hull was mended for the journey. She was floated on to a submersible pontoon upon which she was towed at an average speed of five knots, arriving at Avonmouth 49 days later. She made the final eight miles upstream to Bristol under tow afloat on her own bottom. Her great sea-hardy iron hulk was showered with confetti and flower petals by enthusiastic well-wishers as she passed beneath Brunel's Clifton Suspension Bridge, while ships' whistles and sirens sounded, bugles and horns were blown, church bells pealed and crowds cheered throughout her regal passage up the Avon to her birthplace. On 19 July 1970 the tide was just right to lift her keel clear of the gate sill as she was gently nudged into the drydock from which she was launched on the same day in 1843.

As the essential work of her preservation was immediately taken in hand, the key decision was made to restore *Great Britain* as closely as possible to Brunel's original plans. This entailed the controversial removal of the wood cladding fitted around her hull in 1882 and other remaining vestiges of her later career as a cargo ship. A crack in the hull that had developed while she was beached in the Falklands – and would have eventually caused the ship to break apart if left unattended – and the steel

least part of the scant four hours a day he lost to sleep could be taken while travelling. Apart from his great engineering and building conquests, he also ran a hotel, was an active lobbyist for railway development, an accomplished parlour magician and a skilled watercolour painter. Even through his art, he devised the interior colour schemes for his railway carriages, stations and ships. While making a casual examination of a common shipworm under the powerful magnifying glass he was accustomed to carrying, Brunel observed how its destructive work was accomplished so effectively thanks largely to two hard plates that protected its siphons while tunnelling into wood. This gave The Little Giant the inspiration

plate used to temporarily repair it were, however, retained as a symbol of the call for *Great Britain*'s salvation and new lease of life.

During the more than three decades since her return to Bristol, *Great Britain* has continued to attract immense public enthusiasm as the world's only surviving deep-sea passenger ship of the Victorian era. Over the years, part of her promenade deck, with its various deck houses, captain's quarters, navigating bridge, funnel and masts has been reconstructed. Below, the dining saloon, ladies' drawing room and some of the passenger cabins were constructed after meticulous research into the ship's original design and the times of her early Atlantic crossings. The forward main deck is still in its stripped-out condition as a cargo hold, revealing the ship's robust structure. A replica engine is being fabricated for installation on board, along with the boiler fronts that are already in place.

While *Great Britain* is herself minuscule compared with Cunard's vast new *Queen Mary 2*, which dwarfs even her great forebears of the 1930s, a great sense of massiveness is conveyed to a visitor to Bristol by this great clinker-built riveted iron hull, seen up close as it would have been in 1843 against a backdrop of the same surviving buildings. To venture

in to the meticulously reconstructed interiors is again a rare perception of the ship's greatness from the viewpoint of her passengers. It suggests the sense of awe, and at times no doubt of fright, that they would have experienced at a time when *Great Britain* was one of the largest moveable objects of human fabrication.

Brunel's third ocean-going ship project started life under the name the *Great Ship* before it became known as *Leviathan* and ultimately *Great Eastern*

Above: **Great Britain** *at sea; lithograph by H Papprill, after an 1845 painting by J Walter.* (CPL)

Left: *The forlorn state of the* **Great Britain** *lying in Sparrow Cove in the Falkland Islands, before her return to Britain in 1970.* (CPL)

when finally launched in 1859. This vessel brought Brunel in to contact, through the Great Exhibition, with John Scott Russell, a noted shipbuilder and marine enginemaker who had the expertise and facilities to construct the vessel, as well as to provide consulting services and technical drawing support. Financial backing was secured from a group of investors headed by Henry Thomas Hope, who had led the Great Eastern Steam Navigation Company bid for the mail contract lost to P&O. Although it had been customary for an individual shipbuilder to construct the ship, its machinery and to do all of the fitting out, the magnitude of this project demanded the same kind of collaboration of equipment suppliers and sub-contractors familiar today in the shipbuilding industry. Many of these were, however, also members of the consortium whose capital was needed to build and operate her.

Building of the hull and paddle engines was contracted to the John Scott Russell yard on the Isle of Dogs in the Thames, while James Watt and Company would build the boilers and screw-propulsion engine. The huge crankshafts for the paddle engines were forged by Fulton & Neilson of Lancefield Forge, Glasgow, one of the few foundries able to fabricate so large a piece as this, while the ship's revolutionary steam steering engine was made by the noted inventor, J. MacFarlane Gray. Professor Piazzi Smyth, Astronomer Royal of Scotland, was to devise a gyroscopic navigation system for this greatest-ever metal ship. The support of numerous other suppliers was engaged to provide everything from sailing gear and interior furnishings to the two steam launches the ship would carry under a special set of davits.

So vast a project as this, with its involvement of various builders, machinists and suppliers working at different locations, called for an unprecedented level of organization and coordination among all involved. Draughting became critically important, so that detailed and thoroughly reliable working drawings would be available as a universal and authoritative source of information. The highly detailed line drawings made by Scott Russell's draughtsmen were lithographically reproduced for distribution to other parties involved in the ship's construction and fitting out. Colour was added to a number of these, creating a very fine set of presentation illustrations, including an elevation view, detailed plans of each deck, longitudinal- and cross-sections diagrams. These were remarkably artistic, with their use of subtle shadow and shading making them almost photorealistic.

John Scott Russell himself was also an avid proponent of industrial photography, realizing its potential as a means of controlling and recording large technical processes such as construction and shipbuilding. As joint secretary to the Great Exhibition of 1851, he arranged to have the entire process of the Crystal Palace reconstruction at Sydenham photographed in great detail. As construction of *Great*

Eastern began, he commissioned Joseph Cundall, a member of the Photographic Institution in London, to photograph two views of the ship at the beginning of each month illustrating progress of her building. Another photographer, Robert Howlett, was separately engaged to photograph the attempts made to launch *Great Eastern*. These rare images, along with the drawings and lithographs in the archives of the National Maritime Museum in Greenwich, London, still provide a valuable documentation of this great project as well as an insight in to that era of British industrial history.

The whole concept of *Great Eastern* was developed from the old shipbuilding premise that two larger ships could do the work of at least three smaller ones at a lower cost. Thus by doubling the length and beam of a reference ship such as *Persia* or *Scotia*, the internal volume is increased eight-fold for a hull of similar form, by virtue of volume being the cubic measure of the linear dimensions enclosing it. Taking in to account the limiting factors of more machinery and greater quantities of fuel being needed to propel the larger vessel, Brunel calculated that he could build a ship effectively five to six times larger than anything then in service. This could be operated economically against the higher volume of cargo and greater numbers of passengers on the basis of what the industry today calls 'economy of scale'. Greater speed could also be achieved as a function of the more powerful machinery and maintained economically on the basis that once such a mass was brought in to motion, its progress could be better maintained against the resistance both of the water and the atmosphere.

Great Eastern's backers were assured that their investment of £600,000 to build the ship would net them a return of 40 per cent per year with the ship in service between Portsmouth and Trincomalee, Ceylon. A key operational aspect of this bold venture was that the ship's great size allowed enough coal to be carried to negate the need for bunkering en route during the 22,000-mile round trip. The voyage time to Ceylon or India was foreseen to be 30 days, or direct service to Australia in 33 days. As Ceylon was the distribution point for all services east of India, it was claimed that *Great Eastern* could in effect monopolize British trade to the Far East and Australia. No doubt the thought of this would have been sweet revenge to Hope and his partners at the Eastern Steam Navigation Company for their loss of the Admiralty mail contracts to P&O.

At a measure of 18,915 tons, 689ft (210m) in overall length, with a beam of 82ft 10in (25.3m), five funnels and six masts carrying a total sail area of 54,900 sq.ft (5,100 sq.m), this great ship outclassed anything else either already in existence or even dreamed of. The largest ships of the 1850s were Cunard's *Scotia* and *Great Britain*, each of which measured around 3,200 tons. The closest precedent

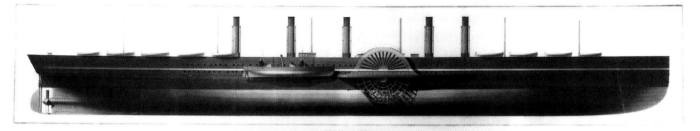

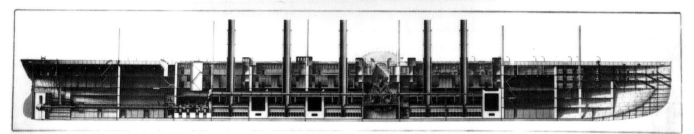

Above: *A set of presentation illustrations from the naval architect's drawings of the* Great Eastern, *showing the side elevation and longitudinal section.* (CPL)

for anything of *Great Eastern*'s size, albeit of a perhaps somewhat ethereal nature rooted in general interest rather than technical precedent, was at the time said to be Noah's Ark. Based on calculations made some time earlier by Sir Isaac Newton (1642–1727), who had reckoned the Biblical cubit to be 20½ inches (51.5cm), the Ark would have been built at a length of 515ft (154.5m), 86ft (26.8m) wide, and with a displacement of around 18,231 tons, against *Great Eastern*'s displacement of 22,500.

Great Eastern's size record stood through four decades from the time of her launch, before being eclipsed by the White Star liner *Oceanic*, completed in 1899. The midship cross-section of *Great Eastern*'s hull was of remarkably similar overall dimensions, with approximately the same depths to the lower and upper passenger decks, as the 1907 Cunard ships *Lusitania* and *Mauretania*, although the later ships bore no direct design influence from Brunel's *Great Ship*. It is difficult to visualize *Great Eastern* in terms of today's cruise tonnage, as the design and shape of ships has changed so radically, as have the rules for measuring tonnage. *Great Eastern*'s 689ft (210m) length compares with the present-day cruise ships *Patriot* (built in 1983 as *Nieuw Amsterdam*) and *Horizon* at 698ft 4in (214.7m) and 675ft (207.6m) respectively, although today's ships tend to be beamier. The 1977-built gas-turbine ferry *Finnjet* comes closer to the length-to-beam ratio of *Great Eastern* with a 699ft (214.9m) length and beam of 81¼ft (25.4m).

The visual impression of *Great Eastern* would have been far more overpowering. The ship's whole 18,915-ton capacity was contained within a vast hull, with no superstructure but rather six great masts and wide yardarms towering above her five tall stovepipe funnels, arranged two forward and three aft of the enormous paddlewheel enclosures at her sides. Yet although her appearance was unlike today's passenger ships, this behemoth of the Victorian age nonetheless introduced innovations of design that

were ultimately to shape the building of larger ships with far greater amounts of passenger accommodation. For the first time ever, her designers found themselves confronted with the difficulties of planning accommodation for decks whose greater width would require light and ventilation to be brought to a far greater proportion of inner cabins and living spaces. With three accommodation decks, there was also the need for light and fresh air to be brought down from above, as well as in from the ship's sides.

Great Eastern was still designed essentially as a vast sailing ship with all accommodation in the hull below her open Spar Deck. These were arranged around two sets of five vast saloons, one above the other, along the ship's centreline, and with double files of cabins along either side of these. The uppermost of these, on the 2nd Deck, housed First Class in high-ceilinged spaciousness and comfort throughout. The double height of the saloons was achieved by their extension up inside a combing through the Spar Deck. The Second Class domain below on 1st Deck had its own double-height saloons by virtue of the mezzanine-like Middle Side Decks housing a second tier of cabins along either side of the ship. The saloons were arranged two forward of the machinery spaces and three aft, with the cabins grouped into small enclaves at either side.

The larger First Class rooms were for the most part in blocks of four to six, and the Second Class rooms in groups of seven to nine. The larger cabins were arranged in inner-and-outer pairs at either side of alleyways extending to the ship's side from the saloons, while the smaller rooms were grouped around a cruciform arrangement of a sideways alleyway and short fore-and-aft passage. The whole plan respected the full watertight subdivision of *Great Eastern*'s hull, with transverse bulkheads segregating the passenger accommodation at regular intervals of 63ft (18.9m). The lengthwise boundaries between the saloons and sleeping accommodation were likewise determined by the longitudinal bulkheads running parallel 36ft (11m) apart for a distance of 262¼ft (106.7m) through the hull's mid-body. This was perhaps one of the first examples of the type of grid-planning that would be adopted in passenger ship design in the mid-to-late 19th century.

Brunel himself solved the problem of bringing daylight into the accommodation by arranging a continuous riband of skylights along either side of the saloons, with linear light wells in the 2nd deck to bring light farther down into the decks below. He also had the cabins arranged in blocks, laid out so that cabin locations corresponded from one deck to the next, allowing ventilation shafts to be brought down to the inner rooms. Without too great a stretch of the imagination the vestigial origins of the modern liner's double-height saloons and lounges, and perhaps even the linear atria of several cruise ships and Baltic ferries of our own age, can be seen in *Great Eastern*'s exceptional structural design.

Yet despite all of this great ship's structural and engineering marvels, she was also the product of technologies that were beginning to fall short of the demands being made of them. Her machinery was for the most part merely a proportional enlargement of the engines used in the smaller tonnage her size had eclipsed. Her great range was achieved simply as a function of sheer volume: 15,000 tons of coal were carried, to a depth of around 30ft (9.1m), in bunkers occupying the compartments outboard of the transverse bulkheads alongside her boiler rooms and machinery spaces, as well as in the centre compartments above the boilers. Against this, *Great Eastern*'s cargo capacity was just 600 tons. The ship was derided by some as being 'a floating coal mine', while others moaned that monsters of her type would reduce traditional seafaring to the drudgery of 'foundry work'.

The success of bigger ships would ultimately be achieved through developments such as more powerful reciprocating and turbine engines, high-compression watertube boilers that would greatly improve propulsion efficiency, and smaller machinery installations that would reduce the amount of fuel consumed. This would again bring development back to an evolutionary process.

Unfortunately, *Great Eastern* never served the route for which she was designed and built. Delays and cost overruns in her building forced her owners into liquidation. After offering the ship to prospective buyers, including P&O and the Admiralty, to whom it was suggested that her size and speed would allow the great iron ship to simply ram-sink anything on the seas, *Great Eastern* was finally acquired by a venture called The Great Ship Company for a transatlantic service to New York.

Meanwhile Brunel himself fell ill from a stoke while visiting the ship just before she finally sailed. He was gently carried ashore through a lower-deck hatch and slowly driven home in his Britzka. He died in his bed a few days later after learning of an explosion onboard that had killed one of the crew. Although *Great Eastern* herself survived the minor blast, sadly it was believed by many that through the strain of realizing this vast undertaking, the great iron ship taken the Little Giant as one of its own casualties. As the nation grieved his passing, his obituary in the *Morning Chronicle* commented:

> Brunel was the right man for the nation, but unfortunately he was not the right man for the Shareholders....They must stoop who gather gold, and Brunel could never stoop. The history of innovation records no instance of grand novelties so boldly imagined and so successfully carried out by the same individual.[5]

As the ultimate test of any ship's worth, the North Atlantic Ocean showed that in fact the great iron ship was under-engined for her size. *Great Eastern* ultimately achieved success as the world's greatest cable

Right: *Great Eastern ended her days as a floating advertisement on the Mersey.* (CPL)

ship, where she was used for laying the first Atlantic undersea cable between Ireland and Newfoundland in 1866 and the Aden–Bombay cable three years later. She ignominiously ended her days in the Mersey as a floating *bon marché* for David Lewis's well-known Liverpool firm of tailors and clothiers, before finally being sold for scrap and broken up at Birkenhead between 1889 and 1891.

Despite being one of the greatest white elephants of shipping history, *Great Eastern* was in many regards a great and wondrous accomplishment. Apart from the structural sophistication of her double-skinned cellular hull and the many ideas introduced in the design of her passenger accommodation, she was also a pioneer in the automation that would become necessary in the larger ships that followed. She was first to use McFarlane Gray's steam steering engine, by necessity of her rudder being far too large to be hand turned. Following sailing ship practice, earlier steamers were hand steered from a position fully aft above the rudder stock. Orders would be communicated aft from the bridge amidships using an officer's whistle or bullhorn, where the wheel would be turned by hand. In larger ships it was customary for several wheels to be ganged together so that in heavy seas six-or-more men could put their shoulders to turning the rudder. This innovation allowed the ship to be steered directly from the navigating bridge. *Great Eastern* was also among the first ships to use mechanical telegraphs and semaphores of one sort or another so that instantaneous communication could be made between the bridge, engine rooms and other working parts of the vessel, where the distances would have been too great for speaking trumpets or pipes to be used. Although inside electric lighting was yet to be tried at sea, there were plans at the early stages of development for a powerful electric arc lamp to be installed on one of the masts that would floodlight the ship during the night hours.

Perhaps most significantly, *Great Eastern* stood for the triumph of Victorian-era engineering, when seemingly nothing was too bold or too audacious to be tried. The Great Exhibition of 1851 helped to bring together the artistic, scientific and intellectual worlds with the emerging industrial realm, to foster business relationships, create greater mobility for the masses and produce manufactured goods that would influence the public's desire for consumer products and services. It was a time when just about everyone believed that the engineering mind could conquer all.

THE SUEZ CANAL

The opening of the Suez Canal on 17 November 1869 was a momentous occasion for its French creator, Ferdinand de Lesseps, the Suez Canal company and its backers. The event celebrated one of humanity's greatest engineering works, in the conquest of a natural geographical obstruction to the progress of our ever-more mobile civilization. Although the long-awaited waterway joining the Mediterranean with the Red Sea was wondrous, scientifically and technically, for those who had long invested in the overland route and the ships that served its Mediterranean and Red Sea ends, the Canal introduced the realities of industrial obsolescence.

The P&O overland connection had brought with it the development of a self-contained economy, with vast investment in the harbours, shipping line offices, warehouses, coaling facilities, workshops and ship repair yards at Alexandria, Suez and Aden. The company had developed its own farms near Cairo to produce the poultry, eggs, vegetables and fruit for consumption aboard its steamers, as well as financially backing the building and operation of the Egyptian railway system and a series of lighthouses on the Red Sea. A large new hotel built in Cairo to meet P&O's accommodation needs during the peak winter tourist season, along with various other commercial facilities in several Egyptian cities, were in grave peril of being rendered redundant by the new Canal.

Worst of all from P&O's standpoint was the reality that none of its ships was suitable to transit the Suez Canal, or indeed to make the through passages between England, India and points beyond. Much of the line's existing tonnage was designed either for service in temperate European waters or for the hot Equatorial passages beyond Aden, but was unsuitable for both. New propeller-driven steamships with flat-bottoms and with no projection of the keel beneath the shell plating were needed to navigate the original Cut's 182ft (55.5m) width and 26ft (7.9m) depth.

Apart from all the other concerns about the Canal's viability at the time, including fears that the prevailing winds would simply fill it with sand and silt, there were two other factors of the shipping business that either no one had foreseen or were underestimated. The first of these was that the Suez Canal simply eliminated the need for all of the ground support facilities in Egypt that P&O had developed over the years on the strength of their mail contracts, and that they alone could use exclusively for their own gains. Thus the routes were opened up to competition from other shipowners who would simply have no additional overhead other than payment of the fees for using the Canal.

Although perhaps less a direct influence of the Canal itself, the second of these came as a coincidence of other developments in cargo shipping. Completion of the North Atlantic and Aden–Bombay undersea cables at about the same time of the Suez Canal's opening brought instantaneous communications to much of the world, as perhaps the first sign of today's Information Highway. Among the many other services electric telegraphy made possible, it enabled shippers and shipowners to maintain absolutely up-to-the-minute data on the availability and movements of cargoes and ships virtually around the globe. Out of the commercial possibilities offered by this intelligence there emerged the shipping phenomenon of tramping. Rather than running a line service on a fixed route and regular sailing schedule, tramp operators follow the movements of cargoes on a more ad hoc basis. Thus there was no obligation for tramp freighters to maintain scheduled service to ports where there was insufficient trade to make the call pay, and the owner, or even the ship's master, had the freedom to divert and change the schedule as immediate circumstances dictate.

As steam tramping developed in the late 19th century, its overall effect on the shipping industry was a drastic reduction in cargo shipping rates. While world industrialization created the need for ever more shipping capacity, both for raw materials and manufactured products, cargo became an increasingly significant part of the industry. Liner services were forced to compete with tramp operators for their share of the cargoes and the revenues to be earned from carrying them. Generally the liner companies were able to offer cargo shippers the benefit of regular sailings, and often the advantage of larger and faster ships. These lines, many of which were comparative newcomers to the trade, also found themselves in a strong competitive position to bid for the government mail contracts that had long been the lifeblood of such prestigious lines as Cunard and P&O. As the competition grew, so the value of the government post office contracts declined.

To this point P&O's business had been developed out of the mail contracts and a fairly exclusive passenger business, carrying only small amounts of valuable cargoes in its ships. The company seemed confident enough in its view of the future to add 23 new ships to its fleet for the same type of trade, even as the Suez Canal was being built and their competitors were planning and building for a greater emphasis on cargo.

British competition was also to come from Orient Line, formed as an offshoot of Anderson, Anderson and Company, whose original founders had started operating periodic services to the West Indies and Australia under sail since the early 19th century. In 1876, Anderson, Anderson and Frederick Greene & Company jointly chartered three surplus steamships from the Pacific Steam Navigation Company and a fourth vessel from Dutch owners to inaugurate a new passenger and emigrant service to Australia. This began in June 1877, with bi-monthly sailings from London to Melbourne and Sydney by way of the Cape of Good Hope and returning home through the Suez Canal. By the time of the fourth ship's departure, the venture was organized under the name Orient Line. The longer outbound route enabled Orient's captains to pick up favourable prevailing winds under canvas and to take advantage of the Westerly Drift across the southern reaches of the Indian Ocean between South Africa and Australia,

with the result that London to Melbourne could be covered in as little as 40 days.

The venture was an immediate success, with the new line ordering their first purpose-built ship *Orient*, delivered by John Elder & Co, in 1879. At a measure of 5,386 tons, she was considerably larger than anything then in the P&O fleet. *Orient* was one of the world's first ships to be fitted with electric light in the passenger accommodation, as well as first in service to Australia with refrigerated holds. The ship's deckhouses were extended to the full beam of the hull, where they were enclosed by an upwards extension of the hull plating, painted white. Passengers were provided with the novelty of their own promenade deck and the ocean-going architectural marvel of an oval-shaped drawing room with a central light well opening to the dining saloon below. The saloon had a tiled ceiling, which was shaken loose during some rough weather on the maiden voyage, with passengers dining for the remainder of the journey under a canopy of netting into which more of the ceramic tiles periodically dropped like ripe apples.

Orient set the pace for the very progressive development of the Orient Line and its fleet. By 1883 the line negotiated its own mail contract with the government of New South Wales, as well as an agreement to carry emigrants to Australia for which the government paid them £14 per person for the first 400 carried per voyage and £14 10s a head for those above that number. The contracted postal schedules, however, forced Orient to abandon the romance of its tranquil longer Cape route in favour of Suez in both directions.

Competition between these two British lines continued until 1918, when a controlling interest in the Orient Line was purchased by P&O. The services of both companies were combined and rationalized, with the Orient name remaining as a division of the P&O group of companies until 1960.

With the modern steam-shipping industry then still very much in its infancy, there was little in the way of precedent to guide owners and steamship line management, especially in the area of managing changes to their trading circumstances. The stability of long-established trades and businesses was inescapably upset by the relentless march of industrialization that had to be absorbed and adapted to constantly. The sheer magnanimity of projects such as *Great Eastern* and the Suez Canal was unprecedented, and the scope of their impact was well beyond the full technical and business comprehension of many. The Post Office, for example, even insisted that the mails still be carried overland between Alexandria and Suez for several years after the Canal had opened, because they lacked trust in so great and unprecedented an undertaking of human endeavour.

Yet despite steadily falling revenues against its newfound competition, P&O chose to rebuild its entire fleet with versatile new tonnage capable of making the longest voyages between Britain and Australia, by way of the Suez Canal, and with the added cargo capacity to meet the challenge of its competitors. Yet the line also planned to retain the highest possible standards of service for its passengers and to retain the solid reliability of its service to the Post Office and its established valuable-cargo clientele. This was believed to be the best longterm approach, aimed at ultimately reasserting the line's preeminence, rather than merely going head-to-head against its competitors in a spiral of undercutting one another. P&O's British home port was changed from Southampton to London, so as to directly serve its passengers and cargo shippers in the nation's railway hub.

The first new ships, including *Australia*, *Peshawur* and *Cathay* went into service in 1870 to 1873, as a series of around a dozen essentially class-built iron-hulled steamers of about 3,800 tons each, built by Caird & Co in Greenock, Scotland. These modest vessels set the standard of combined cargo-passenger operation and began to establish the long equatorial routes via the Suez Canal, to India, Australia, New Zealand, the Far East, and onwards across the Pacific Ocean to North America, that would serve the company through to the times of its final two ocean liners, *Oriana* and *Canberra* of the 1960s.

LATE VICTORIAN DEVELOPMENTS

Although the 19th century and the Victorian era closed without other developments in shipping as spectacular as *Great Eastern* and the Suez Canal, there was nonetheless continued technical development, a steady progress to larger ships and the introduction of many new technical developments and onboard auxiliary services.

White Star Line's first *Oceanic* appeared in 1871 with the innovation of having the usual cluster of wooden deckhouses suffused into a single enclosure extending along much of the ship's length. Gone too were the old-fashioned solid sailing-ship bulwarks, replaced by an open metal deck railing and a neat row of white stanchions. The stanchions supported a full-beam deck above with its own accommodation block inboard of the lifeboats in their modern quadrant davits. This replacment of the bulwarks represented probably the most significant outwardly visual change in ship design since the old paddle boxes had given way to the screw propeller's unseen presence below the waterline. Although the classification authorities at first only allowed very few passenger cabins on these upper decks, this represented the first manifestation of the modern ship's superstructure and boat deck.

Below decks, the ship's machinery plant became ever more complex and sophisticated, particularly as various auxiliary services were added. Evaporators and distillation plants were added to produce desalinated boiler and domestic water supplies.

McFarlane Gray's steam steering machinery of the type introduced aboard *Great Eastern* was used in the 1869-built Inman liner *City of Brussels* as one of several alternatives vying for supremacy in the late 19th century. Ultimately, the quadrant-type steering gear made by Brown Brothers of Edinburgh, and fitted in the Cunard liners *Campania* and *Lucania* of the 1890s, was adopted as an industry standard until well into the 20th century. The Brown Brothers system used a small steam engine attached to a tiller arm fitted to the head of the rudder stock. This was engaged to a geared quadrant attached to the deck so that the engine could move the rudder to either side under control of the wheel on the ship's bridge. It was more compact and intrinsically simpler than many other systems where a pair of stationary

Below: The mail and passenger steamer Cathay *of 1872, photographed at Gravesend. She was built by William Denny & Brothers Ltd of Dumbarton for P&O, with whom she served until 1890 before being sold.* (CPL)

engines were used to turn the rudder stock one way or the other.

Electric dynamos were added to provide lighting and a variety of other onboard services. Following the mid-19th century introduction of small dynamos to power lighthouse lanterns ashore, machinery of similar design was adapted for shipboard use, first by the Royal Navy, and later the merchant marine. Compagnie Générale Transatlantique's steamer *Amerique* of 1874 is believed to be the first passenger liner to have electric navigating lights, including a 'lighthouse' beacon at the top of her foremast. *Orient* and the 1879-built Inman liner *City of Berlin* were among the first passenger liners to introduce electric light at sea, with the Inman ship having six incandescent filament lamps in her saloon. As changeable light bulbs came into wider use ashore, ships' accommodation and deck lighting quickly became more extensive and advanced. By 1881, *City of Rome*'s interior illuminations extended to 100 electric lights in the saloons, 150 additional lamps in the cabins and other passenger areas and a further 10 incandescent fixtures in the Steerage communal areas.

Illumination was seen as the most important first use of electrical power at sea, with arc-lighting also being used in search lamps, running lights and lighting of engine rooms and other continuously manned working spaces. As larger generators were produced and power distribution systems were developed for shipboard use, numerous auxiliary systems could be added aboard passenger ships. These included fans and mechanical ventilation systems for the accommodation, domestic water heaters, as well as laundry and galley equipment. Electric motors were used for a variety of other applications, including hoists for cargoes and mails, various items of deck machinery, as well as pumps and other auxiliary engine-room functions.

Refrigeration was undoubtedly one of the most significant applications of electrical power at sea. Following the French steamer *Paraguay*'s 1878 success in transporting a refrigerated cargo of 5,500 frozen beef carcasses from Argentina to Le Havre, one of the first passenger ships to be equipped with a refrigeration plant was Cunard's *Servia* of 1881. This, of course, had the great advantage that live stock no longer needed to be carried, and that the old ice rooms, with their limited-time cooling capacities, could be replaced by cold rooms that could be maintained at various temperatures for the longterm storage of fruit and vegetables, meat, fish and poultry, as well as wines and other consumables. A number of express liners of this era, including most notably White Star's *Majestic* and *Teutonic*, were also fitted with refrigerated holds for carrying meats and other perishable revenue cargoes.

As steel-hulled ships became larger and faster, and their machinery more reliable and efficient, the auxiliary sailing rigs once needed to conserve coal under favourable winds, and as a failsafe measure, gradually became redundant. The first large P&O

Below: *P&O's Garonne of 1871.* (Author's collection)

Left: *The* Teutonic, *with HRH Prince Albert Victor on board, opening the Alexandra Graving Dock, Belfast, on 21 May 1889.* (CPL)

Below: *Stern view of the* Teutonic, *now in dock, showing her propellers dismantled.* (CPL)

The P&O steamer China. *On 27 March 1898 she ran aground off Perim Island at the mouth of the Red Sea. The lower photograph shows her passengers being disembarked, efforts to refloat her having proved unsuccessful. (CPL)*

ships to appear without auxiliary sails were *Himalaya*, *Australia*, *Caledonia*, *India* and *China* of the 1890s. Meanwhile *Umbria* and *Etruria* were the last Atlantic liners to carry auxiliary canvas in Cunard service before *Campania* made her debut in 1893 as the line's first steam purebred.

Towards the close of the long and illustrious Victorian era, the first Marconi wireless sets were installed aboard *Kaiser Wilhelm der Grosse* and *Lucania* in 1900, finally ending the total isolation of ships as they crossed the deep waters. These early sets had only a comparatively short-range capability to transmit Morse code, allowing ships to signal one another at sea over distances of perhaps as little as 50 miles. Ship-to-shore communication had to be relayed from one vessel to another to cover the greater distances. Although Guglielmo Marconi himself demonstrated the possibilities of long-range wireless when he received the first transatlantic message in Newfoundland at the end of 1901, commercially available equipment capable of this performance would take a while to develop. Even as late as 1912, radio messages from the Cunard liner *Carpathia* regarding the rescue of *Titanic*'s survivors had to be relayed to New York by way of the wireless operators aboard *Olympic*.

Wireless aboard ship was originally envisaged purely as a navigational and safety device for the exchange of information about sea conditions, fog and ice. Yet as soon as the first Marconi sets and their operators appeared at sea, passengers who had once been content to distance themselves from the worries of the world during a sea crossing, were immediately eager to keep in touch with friends, family and business associates on both sides of the ocean. At first, captains would occasionally oblige with the courtesy of allowing a message to be sent on behalf of a well-known or regular passenger. Although official communication remained the highest priority, private messages very soon became the main part of the Marconi operator's routine day-to-day work, as well as a valued source of additional revenue. As wireless attained something of the public appeal that mobile cellular phones now hold,

shipping lines quickly found themselves obliged to provide the most up-to-date radio facilities as much for the use of passengers as for their own purposes. In addition to the fastest passage times, the greatest luxuries of accommodation and service, passengers then also started to seek the communications facilities to keep them in touch with the world beyond the horizon.

Various rival systems were developed by others, including the German Telefunken company, bringing technical incompatibilities and proprietary operating practices with the operators of one system refusing to handle messages from another. This, one of the first deadlocks of 20th-century technical incompatibility, was eventually resolved by agreement at the 1906 Radio-Telegraphic Conference, deciding that wireless communication should be a free enterprise, with all messages being handled on a mutually-compatible basis in the interest of the safety of ships at sea and those aboard them.

By the time of Queen Victoria's death in early 1901, White Star Line's *Oceanic* was completed as the world's first liner to exceed *Great Eastern*'s overall length, although the earlier ship's tonnage was not to be eclipsed until later. Forty years after his death, Isambard Kingdom Brunel's dreams of great ocean liners were being realized, albeit perhaps in forms other than he himself might have envisaged. ●

Above: **Built for service to Adelaide, Melbourne and Sydney,** Carthage *was the first P&O ship to surpass the gross registered tonnage mark of five thousand, with a measure of 5,013.* **(CPL)**

3

THE SPLENDOURS OF LA BELLE ÉPOQUE

By the late 19th century, the express passenger liner was emerging to be one of modern industrial civilization's greatest achievements. Ships of this type had become the largest moving objects ever to be created by human endeavour. These magnificent accomplishments were widely publicized the world over, often with extensive features in magazines such as *The Illustrated London News* and *Illustration*. The liners were in their own times what the Boeing 747 jumbo jet, Concorde supersonic airliner, Japanese Shinkansen Bullet Trains and high-speed TGV of the French railways are to theirs; the commercial impact and public wonderment of the Victorian liner was in fact far greater, as nothing of its size and might had ever been accomplished before. Apart from the natural wonders of the world and the marvels of its great castles, palaces and cathedrals, there had been nothing to so stir and intrigue the minds of ordinary people, whose own lives could accord them the opportunity at least once in their lifetime to travel by rail, cross the ocean in a steamer or ride to the top of a skyscraper in a lift.

Ships still offered the only means of crossing the oceans from one continent to another, and were still relied on almost exclusively for travel in parts of the world with extensive coastal and inland waterways such as the Americas, Europe and Russia. Yet with the increased demand for passenger and cargo traffic, and the quickened pace of business life set by the relentless metronomes, first of the dot-and-dash electric telegraph and later wireless telegraphy, there was increasing demand for ever more, greater and faster ships.

As various nations industrialized and engaged in world trade, they sought to build up merchant fleets of their own. Fast modern liners were becoming important symbols of progress and prosperity to be asserted as much in the interest of national identity and pride as of individual company supremacy.

A DIVERSITY OF NATIONALITY

Belgium was among the first European nations to enter the North Atlantic trade in 1855. At this time the iron-hulled screw steamer *Belgique* was commissioned as the first of two Dutch-built ships for the Société Belge Des Bateaux á Vapeur Transatlantiques, also known as the Compagnie Transatlantique Belge (Belgian Atlantic Line). Although the ship was claimed by her owners to have a Lloyd's A1 classification, she developed serious technical and performance difficulties on her way from Antwerp to Southampton at the start of her maiden crossing to New York, and was forced to undergo extensive repairs in the British port before re-starting her voyage again from Antwerp some months later. The second ship, named *Princess Charlotte*, was given a precautionary overhaul at Hartlepool to ensure that the shortcomings of her sister had indeed been overcome. The following year, *Leopold 1*, built by Cockerel in Antwerp, appears to have avoided any startup difficulties, although the

Opposite: *The long-serving* Aquitania, *completed in 1914, is pictured here in 1950 at the end of her final voyage to be broken up just along the coast from where she had been built.* (CPL)

careers of all three ships under the Belgian flag were remarkably short. The service folded by the end of 1857, and the ships sold to British owners, with service from Antwerp being continued by the Red Star Line. (The Compagnie Maritime Belge, which operated cargo and passenger services to the Belgian colonies in Africa, was founded much later with no relationship to this venture.)

In France a programme of government subsidy proposed by Emperor Napoleon III to revitalize the nation's merchant marine brought in to being the progressive modern steamship line Compagnie Générale Transatlantique, later generally known as French Line in the English-speaking world. France had suffered severe losses of merchant tonnage during the Crimean War, as well as a number of commercial failures, including that of the short-lived Compagnie Franco-Américaine, which had tried to establish regular steamship services to the United States and Brazil in the early 1850s.

In 1858 the company L'Union Maritime was founded in Le Havre by Michel Victor Marziou, with financial backing from members of the Rothschild family, to operate a regular mail steamship service to the Americas under the French flag. As this vast venture revealed itself to be beyond the scope of the new company, its already-negotiated concession to operate the services was transferred to the Compagnie Générale Maritime, which had been founded in 1855 by the Parisian industrialists Emile and Isaac Péreire. This company had already built up a diversity of European short-sea steamer services, along with various trades under sail on longer routes to Central and South America, as well as to California by way of Cape Horn.

Under this arrangement the Compagnie Générale Maritime was re-constituted in 1861 as the new Compagnie Générale Transatlantique (CGT). It received an annual subsidy of 9.3 million francs to carry French mail to the United States, the West Indies, Central America and Brazil. For its flagship New York service, the company was required to provide a fleet of five steamships, each with a minimum of 759 horsepower and speed of 11.5 knots, and guarantee to run 26 round-trip voyages each year.

All services were initially operated under the CGT houseflag. The Compagnie de Navigation Sud-Atlantique, which was absorbed under CGT management in 1913, was founded in 1910 by the owners of the Société Générale des Transports Maritimes and a consortium of French banks. The Compagnie de Navigation Sud-Atlantique was retained as a part of CGT until 1972, when both lines were merged with Messageries Maritimes, and the name reverted once again to Compagnie Générale Maritime. The Compagnie Générale Transatlantique and Messageries Maritimes identities were, however, retained within the new corporate structure.

The service between Le Havre and New York was inaugurated in 1864 with four 3,400-ton iron paddle steamers: *Washington* and *Lafayette*, both built by Scott's Shipbuilding & Engineering in Greenock, Scotland; *Napoleon III*, built in London by Thomas Ironworks of London; and the Robert Napier & Sons-built *Péreire*. These were followed in 1866 by the screw-propelled *St. Laurent* and *Ville de Paris*, of which *St. Laurent* was the company's first French-built liner for North Atlantic service.

At the time of its incorporation, CGT also established their own shipyard on a strip of land known as Penhoët, along the north bank of the Loire estuary at Saint-Nazaire in Brittany. There was at the time no other yard in France with the capacity to build the larger vessels that would be required for the New York mail service. Incorporated in Saint-Nazaire as Chantiers de l'Atlantique, the yard was initially run by Scott's Shipbuilders & Engineering, who provided a core of management and technical expertise to build up and train a workforce in France, recruited from the vicinity of Saint-Nazaire. The new French yard continued to work exclusively for CGT until it was constituted in the year 1900 as a separate company named Société Anonyme des Chantiers et Ateliers de Saint-Nazaire Penhoët. While the yard would continue to build most of CGT's significant ships of the 20th century, it was also better positioned to obtain other commissions from outside the line. The company reverted to its original name, Chantiers de l'Atlantique again in 1955 when it was merged with the Chantiers de la Loire yard.

The first ship to be built at Penhoët was the iron-hulled paddle steamer *Impératrice Eugénie*, completed on 23 April 1864 and put into Central American service between Saint-Nazaire and Vera Cruz. Her sister ships *France* (the first of three Penhoët ships to bear the name) and *Nouveau Monde* went into West Indies service the following year. There appears, however, to have been considerable use made of these vessels also on CGT's North Atlantic service to maintain the contracted level of service to New York.

The French naval architects Clapeyron and Eugène Flachat adopted Cunard's much admired paddle steamers *Persia* and *Scotia* as design references for their first ships built at Chantiers de l'Atlantique. The design of *Persia* had, as noted in the previous chapter, been shown at the Paris Exhibition of 1855, and David Kirkaldy's outstanding presentation drawings of the ship subsequently deposited with the Louvre museum. Following the example of Cunard's 1862-built steamer *China*, originally planned as an identical sister ship to *Persia* and reworked for screw propulsion in the course of her building, *St. Laurent* was likewise adapted during her building to become CGT's first propeller-driven liner. As soon as *St. Laurent*'s superior performance in service could be ascertained over that of her paddle-driven fleet mates, the line decided to quickly modernize much of its North Atlantic fleet in the late

1860s by likewise rebuilding and re-engining *Washington*, *Lafayette* and *Péreire* as screw steamers.

CGT's on-going North Atlantic fleet development kept pace with Cunard's continuing growth and modernization. Following the inevitable interruption of commercial progress caused by the Franco-Prussian war in 1870, the line continued for a while to redevelop and redeploy its existing tonnage to meet increased requirements of the new 1873 mail contracts. The weekly North Atlantic sailings between the months of April and October amounted to 40 voyages to New York each year.

The considerably larger North Atlantic liners *La Champagne* and *La Bretagne* were delivered from Penhoët in 1886 at 7,087 tons each, along with the 7,395-ton *La Bourgogne* and *La Gascogne*, whose building was contracted to Forges et Chantiers de la Méditerranée at Le Seyne. These, to all intents and purposes, rivalled the latest Cunard ships *Servia*, *Umbria* and *Etruria* in their standards of accommodation, service and technical performance. Ships of this type were beginning to emerge as large express liners of an international standard, with Germany also emerging with a formidable presence of its own on the North Atlantic.

With French, German and other lines usually calling at Southampton or London en route, there was the opportunity to attract a portion of the First- and Cabin-Class trades interested in enjoying something of the culture, cuisine and social ambience of another nation during the crossing. France has always been especially keen to offer passengers aboard her ships a 'French atmosphere' throughout the voyage, extended from its premiere grades of accommodation through all passenger classes aboard.

The first German challenge in North Atlantic shipping came about in 1871, when Reichskanzler Otto

von Bismarck unified Prussia with its surrounding German states and principalities into a modern German nation that can be recognized today. This in itself had the potential of creating a confident and buoyant atmosphere for trade and commercial development. The rapid industrialization that followed was accorded the full support, not only of the government, but also of the intellectual and scientific elite. Shipbuilding and commercial sea trade were given a very high priority in the overall scheme of asserting a strong and unified German industrial presence. This went beyond the postal contracts and subsidies granted in Britain, the United States and France, to set policies for the structure and operation of the nation's merchant shipping activities in much the same way that other German industries were being developed.

Starting in 1874, all orders for German naval tonnage were placed at home in a bid to stimulate the nation's shipbuilding industry. This provided the opportunity for the nation's existing privately owned

Above: Cunard Line's Umbria *of 1884, which despite her steam propulsion, and advances in hotel-style passenger accommodation and service, still retained the operational backup of a full sailing rig. (Gordon Turner collection)*

Below: Passenger accommodation plan for Cunard's Umbria/Etruria *of 1884/5. (Author's collection)*

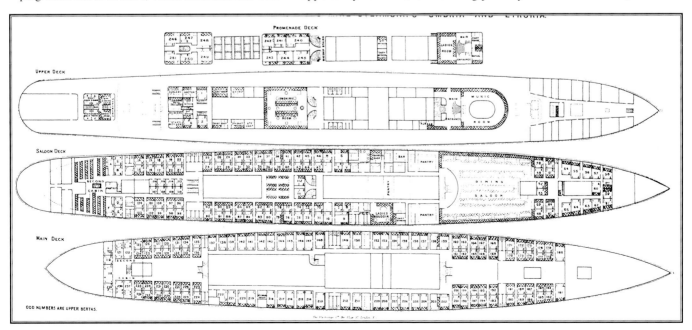

yards to expand and modernize their facilities and to hire and train younger workforces. Lest German yards should merely become fabricators, the ships had to be built of German materials, and as far as possible in those formative years of the nation's industrialization, were required to use domestically built machinery, auxiliary equipment and fittings.

Other important developments were taking place that would ultimately help to shape German shipbuilding. In 1883 Emil Rathenau founded the Allgemeine Elektrizitäts Gesellschaft in Berlin to produce electric light bulbs and other components. Its name shortened to the now more familiar AEG, this company quickly grew into a vast industrial concern with worldwide business interests and a wide diversity of domestic and industrial products by 1890. Siemens is another example of a well-known German corporation which traces its origins to this period. Indeed electrical equipment and machinery from these firms were soon to find their way aboard not only German ships, but also those of Britain and other nations. While the government naval contracts alone were insufficient to sustain the longterm growth of shipbuilding in the new German federation, the plan was that these would place the shipbuilders and their suppliers of machinery, equipment and fittings in a more competitive position to secure other work on their own merit.

Meanwhile, the Hamburg-Amerikanische Packetfahrt Actien-Gessellschaft (HAPAG), or Hamburg-Amerika Line as it is better known in both languages, and Norddeutscher Lloyd (NDL) or North German Lloyd, had both started their own transatlantic steamship services in the mid 1850s. HAPAG had in fact operated services to New York under canvas since 1848. Each had built up a fleet of modest-sized steamers constructed at various British yards, and the two companies had even gone so far as to negotiate pooling of their services during the winter seasons. As these were both publically held companies, operating without government subsidies, there was no requirement for them to follow the government policies covering naval shipbuilding.

HAPAG was among the first to commission tonnage built domestically, with orders for the 3,500-ton intermediate class *Rugia* placed with the AG Vulcan yard at Stettin in 1882 and *Rhaetia* with Reicherstieg at Hamburg in 1883. In turn the awarding of a postal contract to Norddeutscher Lloyd in a bid to develop German-flag mail steamer services to the Orient resulted in orders for five more ships to be built in Germany.[1]

At that time German merchant shipping already had the basic ingredients for success, with its established steamship companies, various ship yards and supporting industries capable of supplying the machinery and other components. Although the nation's yards then had little experience in building large ocean liners, they were capable of doing so. The only real problem was that companies such as HAPAG and Norddeutscher Lloyd were still reticent to entrust orders for their larger and more prestigious liners to fledgling domestic builders.

At first only less-important contracts, for ships usually of no more than around 3,500 tons, were entrusted to German builders. This trend was eventually broken towards the end of the 1880s when Norddeutscher Lloyd placed orders for their 6,963-ton North Atlantic sister ships, *Spree* and *Havel*, with Vulkan's Stettin yard. These commercially successful ships, with their three-class passenger capacity of 826, speed of 20 knots and powerful triple-expansion machinery, served as an excellent example of the nation's industrial expertise. From then on the line turned wholeheartedly to their countrymen for all future tonnage, with the vast majority of the work being done by Vulkan.

At the end of the decade, HAPAG followed with their first large German-built steamers, *Augusta Victoria* of 7,661 tons and *Fürst Bismarck* at 8,430 tons, both built at Vulkan's Stettin yard. *Fürst Bismarck* exceeded her contract speed of 19 knots by a knot and a half on trials, and continued to serve her owners reliably for many years. However, the Hamburg firm continued for some time to maintain strong ties with their British shipbuilders, as *Columbia* and *Normania* were built in Scotland by Laird Brothers and Fairfield respectively.

The challenge of these modern 20-knot ships was quickly taken up by Norddeutscher Lloyd, which sought also to increase their share of the trade between Britain and America. Orders were placed for their own large express liners *Kaiser Wilhelm der Grosse* with Vulkan at Stettin, and *Kaiser Friedrich* from the Schichau yard in Danzig. The building contracts for both ships made the unusual provision that they could be refused by their owners and returned to

Below: *By the time Cunard's* Lucania *was completed in 1893, the shipbuilding art had progressed to elimination of the secondary sailing rig and a visual assertion of the prominence of steam with much larger funnels.* (Gordon Turner collection)

the yard unaccepted if they failed to maintain their contracted speeds. When delivered in 1898, the twin quadruple-expansion engines of the three-funnelled *Kaiser Friedrich* barely managed to achieve a sustained speed of 20 knots on her maiden voyage. After persevering with the new liner's sluggish performance for nearly a year, the owners finally rejected her. After making a few charter voyages for HAPAG, she was eventually sold in 1912 to the Compagnie Sud-Atlantique for service to South America and renamed *Burdigala*.

Kaiser Wilhelm der Grosse became an immediate success, with her triple-expansion machinery achieving outstanding performance throughout her maiden voyage in September 1897, made at an average speed of 21.39 knots, according her the honours of then being both the world's largest and fastest ship. She thus became the first European-flag liner to hold the Blue Riband of the North Atlantic, taking the honour from Cunard's *Lucania*, and conceding it to HAPAG's *Deutschland* three years later. Interest was also attracted by her clean-lined modern profile with twin masts and the unusual arrangement of her four funnels in pairs fore and aft of a large accommodation light shaft amidships. The ship had large capacities for 332 passengers in First Class, 343 Second and 1,074 Third or Steerage. As the prestige and speed of a new ship were of great attraction to the travelling public, *Kaiser Wilhelm der Grosse* was heavily booked for the ten voyages she made in 1898, carrying a total of 71,118 passengers, reckoned by some accounts to be 24 per cent of all transatlantic passenger movements through New York for that year.

In little more than two-and-a-half decades Germany had secured a high standing in North Atlantic and world shipping, largely through the development of the nation's own shipyards and their associated industries. While the prestigious liners of HAPAG and Norddeutscher Lloyd offered their passengers the cultural experience of their homeland and the best of its hospitality and cuisine, perhaps most significantly the ships themselves were a veritable showcase of German industrial development and technological advancement. In essence they had become the statement of the official administrative policies that had stimulated their development.

Among the many other steamship lines that were born of this era, Holland America is one of the most notable, which like Cunard, P&O and Germany's current entity Hapag-Lloyd, has remained in continuous service to the present day. Founded during 1873 in Rotterdam as the Nederlandsche Amerikaansche Stoomvaart Maatschappij (NASM), the line started its primary North Atlantic trade as a reorganization of the business established by the Plate Reuchlin company two years earlier. This venture had been inaugurated with the 1,694-ton steamer *Rotterdam*, built by Henderson Coulborn & Company of Glasgow.

Construction of the sister ship *Maas* the following year had led to financial difficulties for Plate Reuchlin, which were resolved through NASM's creation. The business was completed under the new ownership in 1877 with the addition of the Robert Napier-built steamers *W. A. Scholten* and *P. Caland* in 1874, and with *Schiedam*.

Unlike its French and German counterparts, NASM was a privately owned venture without mail contracts or government subsidies, built up from the emigrant trade. The line's early steamers each carried about 400 steerage passengers from Flushing to New York at a fare of about US$10 for the ten-day passage. On their return voyages to Europe these ships could carry about 800 tons of cargo in the accommodation spaces.

From a mere eight Cabin-Class berths on the *Maas*, Holland America gradually introduced more First- and Second-Class accommodation. When the larger 10,000-ton-class *Statendam* and *Rotterdam* were built by Harland and Wolff in 1897–98, the line had progressed to a three-class service, accommodating 200 passengers in First Class, 150 in Second and

Above: *No doubt commissioned for publicity purposes, this fine painting of* Lucania *conveys a compelling impression of the ship's size and power – note the high open navigating bridge above the forward deckhouses, typical of many late Victorian-era liners.* (Gordon Turner collection)

2,000 Steerage. While *Zaandam* had been ordered in 1882 from Nederlandsche Stoomboot Maatschappij in Rotterdam as Holland America's first Dutch-built ship, the line continued to maintain a longstanding relationship with Harland & Wolff, particularly for the building of their larger liners.

Statendam and *Rotterdam* were significant ships in asserting the NASM image and reputation for comfort and reliability. At the same time the less formal title, Holland America Line and Holland Amerika Lijn, became the official alternate English and Dutch name of the company. Throughout its illustrious history, Holland America Line has never aspired to set records for speed or for the size of their ships, but rather to succeed in maintaining a world-standard of hotelier service to their passengers across all classes. As other new deep-sea steamship lines were born in the late 19th and early 20th centuries, some, such as the Italian lines that would ultimately become Italian Line, would contend for the North Atlantic Blue Riband prestige and honour. Others, including perhaps most notably Norwegian America Line and Swedish American Line, would opt for the more human scale and personal service of the Holland America example.

THE OCEAN-GOING HOTEL

Throughout much of the early steamship era, cabin passengers were carried in what was essentially an extension of ships' officer accommodation, and Steerage was at best berthed in open dormitories below decks. Even *Great Eastern*'s lofty saloons were in essence little more than great messing halls for the vast numbers of passengers she was designed to carry. Apart from separate ladies' lounges and a few private toilets being provided for the convenience and comfort of women and children passengers, there had been little concession made to creating any sort of innkeeper hospitality at sea.

Travellers aboard ship lived virtually as supernumeraries, with no ship's duties to perform but entirely at their own devices between mealtimes. There were few ships with smoking rooms or other such specific-function public amenities, and deck space was limited and expendable as required for the vessel's operation. It was only during the mid-1880s that the first vestiges of what was then called 'hotelism' started to appear at sea. The whole idea of the luxury Grand Hotel living was itself comparatively new, having grown largely from the ability of the railways to move large numbers of people around with the need for places to stay as they travelled.

In fact many of the first large urban hotels were constructed and run by the railway companies as accessories to their mainline terminals. Among the finest examples of these were the Paddington and St. Pancras hotels of 1854 and 1865 respectively, designed to reflect the architectural magnificence of the head-of-line stations to which they were attached.

The French château-style Paddington Hotel, for instance, was planned so that its restaurant, lounges and other public rooms were at the same level as the station's concourse and platforms, on the notion of making a seamless transition between the luxuries of First-Class rail carriage and grand hotel. During its early years, the hotel was for a while managed by Isambard Kingdom Brunel, who found his role in the emerging hospitality field, 'a very agreeable relaxation from the more important duties'.[2] Now, nearly 150 years later the hotel's original connection with the station, the Great Western Railway and the sea connections from Bristol to the rest of the world were realized anew as Paddington Station became the London terminus for the new Heathrow Express.

Following a major modernization, the establishment was reopened in March 2002 as the four-star Hilton London Paddington Hotel, providing its guests with direct access to station airline check-in facilities and the 15-minute express rail connection to Heathrow Airport's passenger terminals. The vast gothic-style Midland Grand Hotel at St. Pancras Station, which has long been unoccupied, is about to undergo a similar renaissance as St. Pancras becomes the main London terminus of the cross-Channel Eurostar express rail service to Paris and Brussels in 2007. No doubt Brunel himself would have been thrilled, and one wonders how The Little Giant had he been alive now would have been involved in the development of today's world of air and fast rail transport.

These and their counterparts in other cities no doubt played a significant role in creating the demand for a hospitality industry whose pace would be set by John Jacob Astor, César Ritz, Louis Adlon and others. The 1897 opening of the skyscraper Waldorf Astoria Hotel in central Manhattan was a landmark achievement, creating the world's largest hotel. The opening of the Paris Ritz the following year at Place Vendôme and that of the Berlin Adlon at Pariser Platz in 1907 set the standard by which the world has since judged classic grand-hotel luxury and service ever since.

Coincidentally, the Beaux Arts-style buildings of the Ellis Island Immigration Center opened in 1900, replacing the facility's earlier wooden structures which had been destroyed by fire in 1897. The main building with its Great Hall where arriving Third Class passengers were processed for entry at least gave these humble masses an impressive, though for many no doubt intimidating, impression of their new homeland and its official institutions.

Meanwhile, as hotels were being built ashore, and steamships were becoming progressively larger, the hotelier hospitality available on land as an accessory to rail travel started to be introduced as an integral part of the passenger's life at sea. Cunard's *Umbria* and *Etruria*, built in 1884–85, are believed to be among the first ships promoted to the travelling public as floating hotels. These were somewhat urgently needed to modernize the Cunard fleet against stiff competition on the North Atlantic, where the Blue Riband speed honours had passed back and forth among Inman, Guion and White Star Line.

The *Servia* and *Aurania*, completed but a few years earlier, were notable for their steel hull construction and introduction of numerous technical refinements, including electric lighting in their passenger accommodation, but neither of these ever achieved an Atlantic speed record. Yet despite these advances, gentlemen still had to smoke their pipes and cigars on the open deck, much as their fathers had done 40 years earlier aboard *Britannia*, while the saloon continued to live its dual lives as dining room and social hall. These were, nonetheless, the first of what came to be known as express service liners, where the space needed for their powerful machinery left only limited room for cargo. The functions of express passenger and mail service began to separate from that of the intermediate-class ships carrying both passengers and cargo.

The 7,718-ton *Umbria* and *Etruria* were ordered from John Elder & Company of Glasgow, which later became Fairfield Shipbuilding & Engineering Company. They were conservatively designed with giant single-screw propulsion plants using three-cylinder compound engines of proven performance to give them the best chances of sustained record speed in service, based on a contract speed of 19.5 knots. With a waterline length of 501ft (153m) and moulded beam of 57¼ft (17.4m) their 8.75:1 length-to-beam ratio was close to *Aurania*'s figure of 8.2:1. *Aurania*'s ratio was itself a return from the longer and narrower hull proportions of nearly 10:1 that had been widely used in shipbuilding of the 1870s, and seems to have been greatly favoured by Harland & Wolff in that period. This slightly stockier build of the *Aurania*, *Umbria* and *Etruria* type were proven to offer better stability, and thus greater passenger comfort, without loss of performance.

The passenger accommodation aboard *Umbria* and *Etruria* were notable for their well-articulated overall plan and layout, as well as for the added facilities and services they offered, along with the genuine sense of Grand Hotel bon vivant these brought to the North Atlantic. Cunard and their builders realized that the hotel-conscious carriage trade of the late Victorian era needed a greater variety of public spaces in which to pass the days at sea between Liverpool and New York. In addition to the full-width dining room, similar to that of the line's earlier *Servia* and *Aurania*, and some of the special features of the latest Inman, Guion and White Star ships, *Umbria* and *Etruria* each also had a gentlemen's smoking room, a music room, barber's shop and ladies' salon. As remarkable as these were in themselves, there was also a great deal of care taken in

their planning, so that each had direct inside access from the passages and deck vestibules. This added greatly to the comfort of life on board over most earlier ships, where inevitably one had to pass from one part of the accommodation to another by way of the open decks.

These ships offered a remarkably high standard of sanitary facilities, including 13 marble baths and an abundance of lavatories throughout their First Class accommodation. Lady passengers were provided with an elaborate boudoir, including its own private lounge and an array of scented baths and mirrored toilette facilities. A number of cabins were arranged so that they could be combined for wealthy families or VIPs travelling with their own entourages. Hands of whist were dealt in the smoking room rather than on the saloon tables, as the dining room could then became a fixed-purpose venue opened exclusively for meal times.

The interiors were lavishly and, by today's standards, excessively decorated in the hotelier styles of the Victorian era. During the daytime hours diffused light passed to the public interiors through their ornate stained glass windows and a cupola above the music room with its central opening to the dining room below; through the evening hours the rich veneer panelling of these plush interiors shimmered in the glow of incandescent electric light. 'Hotelism' brought to these early adaptations of its shoreside grand luxe a reassuring sense of luxury and security, which combined with the strength, stability, speed and reliability of the ship's technical design and engineering.

Remarkably, *Umbria* and *Etruria* were also the last of their kind. The again larger, faster and more powerful *Campania* and *Lucania* that would join them in service during 1893 would be the line's first twin-screw ships, and would also dispense entirely and irrevocably with the auxiliary sailing rig. Late in her career, *Etruria* lost her propeller during an eastbound crossing in February 1902, and diverted under sail towards the Azores, until she was taken in tow by the Leyland Line steamer *William Cliff*. Yet the some-

Below: Lucania's sister ship Campania *is seen here in profile, clearly showing the well articulated relationship of her funnels and masts to the accommodation and navigating bridge. (Author's collection)*

what elitist *Umbria* and *Etruria* were significant as being among the first to attract a social standing of their own among the wealthy of their time and to have asserted the origins of a distinct ocean-going lifestyle.

SOCIETY AT SEA

By the end of the 19th century steamship travel had come of age. It had attained a class consciousness of its own, reflecting the stratification of society ashore. Sea travel was no longer the hardship it had once been, and was beginning to be enjoyed for its own pleasures, with the cognoscenti savouring the merits of particular ships and lines over others. For the upper classes it had attained the snob appeal of 'one-upmanship'.

This belonged to an era of social history known loosely as La Belle Époque. It was a time of relative peace and great prosperity. The prospects of continuing commercial and industrial conquest seemed boundless, sustaining the wealth of the upper classes and ensuring an abundance of employment for the masses, albeit often at the lowest possible wages and in unspeakably poor working conditions. There was unshakable confidence in the learning, scientific progress and engineering achievements of the age. This was a time when it was said that, 'the sun never sets on the British Empire', and when France, the Netherlands, Belgium and Germany likewise tended their own colonial possessions around the world. Human conquest seemed invincible to many of wealth and authority, who cast their eyes upwards and forwards, without daring to ledge the simmering cauldrons of social injustice and unrest and the growing following of Marxist and Leninist teaching in the lower classes.

For those who chose to emigrate from Europe, this same era also offered the opportunity to travel in relative comfort and security to other parts of the globe in search of new lives and homes, gainful employment and betterment. At the same time, there was also a close-knit circle of Western European and American high society who were devotees of the 'Grand Tour' and avid followers of all the latest developments in luxury travel and accommodation. Many of them were members of the same exclusive clubs, showing up often by coincidence at the newest and most fashionable hotels in London, New York, Paris or Madrid; the same resorts on the French Riviera or in the Alps; and inevitably very often aboard the newest and fastest ocean liners. This elite and well-heeled clientele popularized ocean travel and made it fashionable, as much through the social and gossip columns of the newspapers as by the publicity the steamship companies themselves sought as endorsement of their ships and the services they provided.

With the hotel luxury, or at least home comforts, of liners built in the late 19th century there came also an altogether greater sense of safety, comfort and general wellbeing, at least for those passengers in the First and Second or Cabin Classes. Ships with a greater measure than 10,000 tons and of more than 600ft (180m) in length could better ride the high seas, and were at least a little less prone to the pitching and rolling of their smaller predecessors in rough weather. Accommodation was designed for direct inside access to all public areas and other ship's facilities, without passengers having to cross stretches of open deck. Apart from providing protection from the cold, damp and salt spray on deck and minimizing the risk of tripping over the high hatch sills of the deck entrances, this also offered refuge from the smoke and soot from the funnels and the ashes blown up from their ejector ports in the hull's side. The cowl ventilator came into being, with its circular metal right-angle hood which could be turned to face leeward away from the wind, mist, steam and fumes, admitting cleaner, drier air to the cabins and public rooms below.

Inside, First-Class passengers started dressing in their finery for dinner. The old clothes that Cabin passengers kept aside for wear aboard ship, and consigned to steamer trunks for storage at the pier between the outbound and homeward voyages, became relegated to daytime deck wear. Gentlemen unpacked their dinner jackets, tuxedos and cummerbunds to escort their ladies to the dining room in long evening dresses, silk stockings and dress pumps. The long saloon benches secured to the deck were replaced with individual swivel chairs, each with ornately carved wooden backs and metal bases likewise attached to the deck. These made getting to and from the table far easier, especially for the ladies. Eventually the long tables gave way to circular replacements, seating six to ten passengers. Here, in the glow of newfangled Edison incandescent lamps, the wealthy could enjoy a leisurely dinner with all of the service and comfort of the latest London or New York hotels.

After dinner, gentlemen would retire to the smoking room for their cognac and cigars, some talk of business or sport and a hand or two of whist, while the ladies would gather in the music saloon for conversation of their own and perhaps an impromptu piano recital. Late Victorian and Edwardian societies in Great Britain and Europe were stringently stratified vertically between the wealthy and aristocracy, the middle or merchant classes and the proletariat, as the working masses were referred to in Marxist and Leninist terms. The upper classes also tended to be partitioned laterally between gentlemen and ladies, who for much of the waking hours circulated in separate social spheres. Ladies were barred from ships' smoking rooms, as they were ashore from taverns, private gentlemen's clubs and most hotel-lobby cocktail bars. Where couples would stroll in London's Hyde Park, the Jardin des Tuileries in Paris or

Berlin's Tiergarten, the ship's promenade deck started to become a significant focal point of conjugal daytime social life at sea.

As Cunard dispensed with auxiliary sailing rigs on *Campania* and *Lucania*, and P&O likewise from their 1892-built *Himalaya* onward, the clutter of deck paraphernalia required for handling canvas overhead also disappeared. This allowed for a more modern steamship arrangement of deckhouses as a superstructure surrounded by sheltered outer decks. *Umbria* and *Etruria* each featured promenades surrounding the upper deck music room, smoking room, cabins and other enclosed spaces. These were sheltered overhead by the open promenade deck above, encircling the ladies lounge, luxury cabins and officers' accommodation, inboard of the lifeboats.

Campania and *Lucania* each had an additional superstructure deck, effectively separating the passenger promenade from the crew thoroughfares connecting various working parts of the ship forward and aft on upper deck. Above, on the Promenade Deck, as the added layer of deckhouse was called, a broad veranda for the virtually exclusive use of First-Class passengers completely surrounded its internal spaces. The lifeboats were on the deck above this, which was accessible to passengers by way of outside stairways.

For the first time in Cunard history, deck chairs were offered for rent at the price of four shillings (about one American dollar) each for the voyage. With these simple collapsible wooden chaise longue chairs there arrived also a daytime shipboard lifestyle that continued well into the mid-20th century. The morning and afternoon hours would be passed cosseted beneath a steamer rug, and eventually with the ministering of hot bouillon by deck stewards. The promenade decks became the boulevards on the high seas, where one could watch shipboard society, spot celebrities and other important passengers, renew friendships and acquaintances, and be seen and rec-

Below: *Teezimmer interior of HAPAG's* **Victoria Luise** *of 1911 (ex-*Deutschland, *1899).*
(Author's collection)

Above and below: *Smoking room interior of HAPAG's* **Victoria Luise.**
(Author's collection)

Above, left: *Cunard postcard of* Carmania/ Caronia *of 1905; lounge interior with passengers.* (Gordon Turner collection)

Above, right: *Smoking room interior with passengers.* (Gordon Turner collection)

ognized by others. Whether one watched from the vantage point of a deckchair or took the more active role of strolling around the deck, there was a cordial informality about promenade deck life, where passengers at least shared the social bond of travelling together aboard the same ship.

Promenading was a daytime activity, passing the times between breakfast and lunch, and again from early afternoon until teatime. By dinner time, the decks would be virtually deserted of passengers; the steamer rugs would have been stowed in deck lockers, and perhaps the deckchairs themselves folded flat and stacked to facilitate the teak decks to be hosed down before breakfast the following morning.

Inboard of their promenades, the ornate Victorian-style public rooms aboard *Campania* and *Lucania* included both a spacious lounge and a music room amidships and forward of the smoking room, as well as a library fully forward, corresponding to the music room's location in the earlier *Umbria* and *Etruria*. These rooms were essentially laid out and furnished as parlours, where the art of conversation flourished and people were generally content to amuse themselves. There were no dance floors, stages or bandstands. The lounge and music room in fact combined to form a doughnut-shaped space surrounding a windowed light shaft above the dining room on the deck below. Although there was a piano and an American organ these tended to be used only when there were passengers aboard who could play them. In those times, before radio broadcasting and sound recording, many educated people, particularly ladies, could play the piano or other musical instruments.

Beyond the occasional concert given by passengers themselves or perhaps by musically talented crew members, and apart from meal times and promenade deck life, male and female social activity remained fairly segregated. The music room and library tended to be predominantly female preserves, although their use was never restricted as was access to the smoking room. In that era, when letterwriting flourished, the library tended to be a quiet place for reading or penning one's thoughts.

As seen from on deck and from within the accommodation, the liner of this period presented two rather different impressions. Venturing up from the promenade to the boat deck, one was still in the engineer milieu of the ship's inner workings that had fascinated earlier generations of travellers aboard *Britannia*, *Great Britain* or *Hindostan*. Fifty years of progress was indicated by the great funnels towering overhead, each held steady with a rake of some five degrees by guy wires and cables, and surrounded at its foot by a cluster of hooded ventilators. An open skylight would reveal a glimpse down the wide engine-room casing, with its steep crew-access ladders to the great compound steam engines in the care of their boiler-suited engineers and oilers. The acrid smell of coal fire, smoke and steam from the funnels in the damp chill air bore quiet testament to the unseen brutally hard labour of the stokers, firemen and trimmers who tended the boilers. All the while, there was a steady and reassuring throb from the turn of the machinery below and the hum of numerous auxiliary items, perhaps only subliminal in deep, still waters, reflected a silent and unspoken confidence in such great engineering accomplishments as these.

The exterior design of the ship was then purely as functional as the engineering of its inner workings. There was no need to make anything less of it through styling or adornment of any kind. Yet *Campania* and *Lucania* seem to have been designed with remarkably large funnels, seemingly in compensation for the lack of yard arms, rigging, ratlines and sails.

The interior impression was, however, allowed to introduce an element of fantasy or illusion, at least in First and Second Classes. This was done partly to follow the trend of an atmosphere of bon vivant, where the experience of being away from one's home and family could be enjoyed to the fullest, as well as to provide the steamship passenger with a reassuring sense of solid shore-side hominess while at sea. A century ago travel was far less likely to be taken for granted the way it is today. People were unaccustomed to the universal mobility of the private auto-mobile, while many still approached rail travel with great trepidation, let alone contemplating crossing the ocean aboard a steamship. To accommodate passengers within a reasonable semblance of the surroundings they were familiar with ashore and at home was to offer them the most effective bromide against fear, anguish and sea-sickness. While the architecture and styles used varied from one line or nation's ships to another, the overall effect was that the First-Class passenger could in fact cross the Atlantic or make any other sea voyage securely cosseted within surroundings bearing absolutely no resemblance to a ship and having little or no contact with the sea.

Second Class, or Cabin as it was often called, generally tended to be a scaled-down rendition of First Class, catering to fewer passengers in less opulent surroundings. Against their First-Class capacities of 600, *Campania* and *Lucania* each carried 400 Cabin passengers in accommodation farther aft on the upper, saloon and main decks. Here they were provided with their own dining saloon, lounge and smoking room, covered and open deck spaces and an array of two- and four-berth cabins. The general axiom was that the Second- or Cabin-Class accommodation of any given ship were generally as good as the First-Class facilities had been on its predecessor of a generation earlier.

Steerage, or Third Class as the fashion of late Victorian and Edwardian nomenclature would have it, was generally located forward on the lower decks or divided between the two ends of the ship, making use of a working alleyway for access between the two sections. Passengers were for the most part still accommodated in open berths, segregated among single men, single women and married couples, although cabins were beginning to be introduced by some lines. They had their meals at long tables in the sleeping compartments, with most lines by this time providing each person with a pannikin, tin cup, knife, fork and spoon which he or she was responsible for keeping clean and returning at the end of the voyage. Airing space was provided in the well deck forward of the superstructure or in the upper hold decks where openings in the hull shell plating provided light and fresh air. There were no deck chairs, seldom any benches, leaving passengers to perch themselves on the hatch covers, deck lockers and bollards. These areas would be taken over by the crew when required for such things as baggage and mail handling at the beginning and end of the voyage.

DEBUT OF THE MODERN LINER

The large ocean liner of the 20th century, which endures to this day as an icon of human endeavour, was to emerge largely out of a conglomeration of architectural and engineering creativity. There was at first little collaboration between the two professions,

as architectural firms were engaged merely to decorate the First-Class public interiors, and the technical disciplines of naval architecture and marine engineering continued separately in their own quest for speed, reliability and stability.

As the standards of luxury accommodation and service ashore were being established by the emerging hotel industry, so the shipping lines sought to compete for their First-Class trade on the same terms of reference. Inevitably, they started to look to accomplished hotel architects to assist in designing their ships. Some of the most outstanding work in this field was then being done for César Ritz by the French architect Charles Mewès. The work Mewès did in the Paris hotel during the late 1890s was quickly followed by an extensive refurbishment of the old Carlton Hotel in London for the Ritz chain with his British colleague Arthur Davis, and then the Madrid Ritz, designed with the Spanish designer Luis de Landecho. These were followed in 1906 by the London Ritz, again a collaborative work of Mewès and Davis.

Mewès based his work on an interpretation of Louis XVI and other classic 18th-century architectural styles, rendered with a sense of understated elegance, human scale and great attention to detail. These were never intended to be period revival schemes per se, but emerged rather as a characteristic grand-luxe hotelier style. It was hoped that this would create its own sense of comfort and luxury without being overwhelming, intimidating or at odds with anyone's individual preferences of style and taste. Mewès and his associates realized that the purpose of hotel architecture was to create a mood of wellbeing for the guest by way of a classic elegance to be enjoyed and interpreted in his or her own way.

This also recognizes that the design of hotels, and for that matter ships, must appeal to a far broader cross-section of society than would comprehend the more highbrow styles used in palaces, private residences or institutions of higher learning. Even in modern times, the architect Philippe Starck cautioned against overdoing good taste lest there be too few 'beautiful people' around to fully appreciate it.

Albert Ballin (1857–1918), the indefatigable head of HAPAG's passenger department, was immediately struck by the appropriateness of the Mewès approach. He had dined at the Ritz-Carlton Grill on his way home from a visit to the Harland & Wolff shipyard in Belfast, and decided that the restaurant's elegant French interior, outstanding cuisine and attentive personal service should set the standard for his First-Class trade. Mewès was commissioned to design the First-Class public rooms on the line's *Amerika* which were to include, for the first time aboard any liner, an exclusive added-charge restaurant located high up in the accommodation. Ballin also made arrangements for the alternative restaurant to be managed and staffed by Ritz-Carlton.

Amerika's exclusive Ritz-Carlton restaurant and Mewès-designed First-Class public spaces, based on a seamless melding of classic Louis XV and John Adam styles, both won immediate favour with the travelling public when the ship went in to service in 1905. Having found the cost of running their 1899-built blue-Riband contender *Deutschland* to be prohibitive, HAPAG had also by this time decided to follow the White Star Line example of building for comfort rather than record-breaking speed. Ballin lost no time in engaging the articulate Frenchman as the line's house architect, with the work being handled through the architect's Cologne-based partnership of Mewès & Bischoff. This enabled Mewès to continue his hotel and other shoreside work separately, and when he was approached later by Cunard to design interiors for their ships, to handle the work through his Mewès & Davis office in London. Although the architect had to agree that work for the two competing lines was never to be discussed between the two offices, his own creativity continued to set the pace for the remaining few years of his life, and continued to be carried on by the work of his protégé Arthur Davis well into the 1930s.

From the work of these designers there emerged a specific ocean-going counterpart of the era's grand-luxe hotel architecture. This combined the Mewès impressionism of classic style rendered in muted luxury with a special sense of the ship's structural and technical milieu that appears to have been a particular speciality of Arthur Davis. One of the key differences between shoreside and ocean-going architecture, then as now, is that the scale of ships made from metal, no matter how large these may be in themselves, is altogether smaller and lighter than that of masonry and concrete construction on land. Economies of structural weight are a far greater concern at sea than on land, even in the case of modern glass-and-steel construction. Thus the supporting columns and ceiling beam are less massive, the walls thinner, window and door openings shallower than in a space of identical size in a building ashore. Deck heights tend to be lower, with the result that, even in a double-height space, barrel vaults or Romanesque arches may need to be *flattened* into shallower arced lines or ovoid forms.

As ships were then built with their decks sheered upwards towards the bow and stern, and cambered downwards to the sides of the hull, the architect had to find ways of rendering essentially rectilinear designs into these uniquely curvilinear spaces. The cornices of a large room would have to follow the curved forms of the deck above, while avoiding the visual discord of being at odds with horizontal door and window-frame tops.

Daylight was found to be a special concern of ocean-going architecture. Large full-beam spaces such as dining rooms were lit only by rows of portholes, considerably smaller than the windows normally used in buildings. On the superstructure decks, where large rectangular windows were possible, these usually opened in to a sheltered promenade deck, with considerable loss of light. Also to be taken in to consideration were the special characteristics of daylight at sea, where the ship's orientation to natural light sources is constantly changing, and the far greater tendencies of sunlight to be reflected upwards on to the ceilings. Arthur Davis also noted that the cold green light of overcast days made lighting ship interiors from above by way of clear-glass skylights or domes far less satisfactory than lateral illumination from windows or clerestories.

Similar approaches were adopted by various other architects in Britain and Europe. The interiors of *Empress of Asia* and *Empress of Russia*, designed by George A. Crawley for Canadian Pacific, along with James Miller's *Lusitania* interiors, came perhaps closest to the Mewès & Davis classic. However, the public rooms on Orient Line's *Orvieto*, designed by Andrew Prentice, were of a more eclectic nature.

Norddeutscher Lloyd's *George Washington* was completed by the Vulkan yard at Stettin in 1909 with First-Class public interiors designed by the contemporary German architects Bruno Paul and Rudolf Schröder in a comparatively simple and clean-lined Art Nouveau style. Schröder's restrained treatment of the ship's single-deck-height main lounge and modernistic three-deck-high dining room, decorated in bright solid colours, were in marked contrast to the overly ornate Rococo interiors of the line's ships from a decade earlier. The inspired combination of the practical and the chic aboard *George Washington*, with its elements of the Charles Rennie Mackintosh and Frank Lloyd Wright schools remained unique to this ship alone until other manifestations of modernity were to appear in the 1920s.

Meanwhile, below decks, marine propulsion was being revolutionized by the introduction of the steam turbine. The turbine is a power generator of intrinsically lower mechanical complexity than earlier compound engine types, where the sequenced compression and decompression of steam cylinders is used to turn a shaft by way of pistons or levers. The turbine principle uses alternating sets of stationary guide blades attached to the cylinder casing and moving blades connected to a drive shaft which does the work. Each ring of blades is arranged to act as a wheel of nozzles so that, as the steam pressure decreases, its velocity is maximized against the next turbine ring, be it rotating or fixed. At each successive stage of the turbine its diameter is increased to extract the greatest amount of power from the steam as it becomes spent.

This is essentially the same approach as that used in aircraft jet engines, which are gas turbines rather than steam and an outer turbofan cylinder is used to generate the thrust to fly the plane. Marine steam turbines, as used in ocean liners and other large, fast vessels, usually use an aggregate of separate high-, medium- and low-pressure cylinders to generate the necessary amount of mechanical power. Since turbines, by their nature, turn at higher speeds than piston engines, the required thrust can be achieved with smaller-diameter propellers. By virtue of its potential strength and compactness this type of machinery was capable of far greater performance than its predecessors.

Development of the marine steam turbine is generally attributed to the work done by Charles Parsons and Gustaf de Laval during the late 20th century. Of these, it is Parsons who is the more popularly acclaimed, primarily for the audacious promotional stunt of sailing his turbine launch *Turbinia* through the line-up of the 1897 Spithead Naval Review. After being successfully tried in various excursion vessels and short-sea ferries, the first ocean-going applications of steam turbine propulsion in Britain were for Allan Line. The line changed their plans in order to use them in their new Atlantic liners *Victorian* and *Virginian*, both completed in 1904 by Workman Clark & Company of Belfast.

Cunard's *Caronia* and *Carmania* were delivered for North Atlantic service in 1904 and 1905 respectively, with steam turbines fitted aboard *Carmania* while her sister ship was completed with quadruple-expansion reciprocating engines. This was done primarily as a means of gaining experience in building and operating larger marine steam turbine machinery, towards its introduction aboard their planned new express liners *Lusitania* and *Mauretania*. Although the decision had already been made to adopt turbine propulsion for the larger ships, comparison of the otherwise nearly identical *Caronia* and *Carmania* showed a considerable operating economy in favour of the turbine-powered ship.

Caronia and *Carmania* were significant as the prototypes of the modern 20,000-ton, 20-knot liner that was to become the backbone of 20th-century liner trades around the world. Nicknamed 'the pretty sisters', these ships had an attractive modern exterior, with their hull plating extended upwards to the height of the first superstructure deck. Their First-Class accommodation was positioned on the two decks above surrounded by open promenades contained within solid balustrades. They had very straightforward and well-articulated accommodation plans, with the added sophistication of a passenger lift for First Class, as well as modern pedestal flush lavatories and running water piped to the communal bathrooms.

Sanitary facilities for personal cleanliness and grooming in cabins was still provided by way of a quaint ocean-going device known as the compactum. Originally a product of Pullman railway ingenuity, this was a cabinet containing a flat water container concealed behind an eye-level mirror, a drop-leaf washstand with attached basin at about waist height and a second waste water reservoir below. The washstand flap would be lowered and the basin filled from the upper tank by means of a spigot, and once ablutions were complete, the bowl emptied into the lower reservoir by simply tipping the flap up again. The railway counterpart, today still in use throughout much of the world, is filled from an overhead water

Below: *While still sporting tall 'stovepipe' steamer funnels,* Caronia *was among a number of ships to debut in the early years of the 20th century with a high modern super-structure, having its lower deck plated in and promenades surrounding those above.* (CPL)

Above: *Port view of Lusitania's original paint scheme.* (Author's collection)

tank serving an entire coach, and unceremoniously emptied on to the tracks below; the ship's compactum, on the other hand, was at the mercy of the cabin steward who had to keep its upper supply tank filled, and most importantly, drain the slops from the lower container. Until well into the 1930s many lesser ships continued to provide cabin chamber pots, which were encased in a wooden box secured beneath one of the lower beds to ensure the contents would stay put against the ship's roll.

Third-Class passengers were given a large full-beam dining room amidships on the bulkhead deck, a social hall forward on the shelter deck and their own promenade space as an extension on the aft mooring deck. They were accommodated in four- and eight-berth cabins. There were no compactums in these rooms, so occupants had to use lavatories and washing facilities at the opposite ends of the deck above their accommodation. On average, the cabins here would have each been about the size of the 'preposterous box' Charles Dickens had occupied aboard

Britannia in 1842, although with electric light, mechanical ventilation and the stability of a large 20,000-ton ship no doubt considerably more comfortable.

At slightly over 30,000 tons each, and contracted for service speeds of 24.5 knots, Cunard's elite express liners *Lusitania* and *Mauretania* were two-and-a-half times the size of *Lucania* and *Campania*, the line's last record holders in 1893. *Lusitania* was built on the Clyde by John Brown & Co. Ltd, while *Mauretania* was booked at Wallsend-on-Tyne with Swan Hunter & Wigham Richardson. With both ships achieving maximum trial speeds of more than 26 knots, *Lusitania* regained the Blue Riband honours from Norddeutscher Lloyd's *Kaiser Wilhelm II* on her maiden voyage. These two express Cunard liners steadily worked up to higher speeds during their service lives, improving on their own (and one another's) records until *Lusitania* was lost in May 1915. After this, *Mauretania* alone continued to serve as the fastest liner on the North Atlantic until con-

Below: *Lusitania's later paint scheme.* (Gordon Turner collection)

ceding the honour to Norddeutscher Lloyd's new *Bremen* in 1929.

Apart from their superlatives of size and speed, there was a sense of perfection about these two great ships that has accorded them a special place in seafaring history as two of the most famous and best-loved liners of all time. Their exterior appearance showed absolutely classic lines of form and balance between the massing of hull, superstructure and funnels. Rather than there being an open well deck between the fo'c'sle and the superstructure, the forward part of C deck (previously named the upper deck) was fully enclosed, with the shell strakes continued up to B deck above, whose open foredeck extended in a single sheered sweep to the bridge front. This diminished the visual impact of the superstructure height, creating the leaner and lower overall impression of speed and strength. The solid bowed bridge front continued along the ships' sides as a sheer upwards extension of the hull plating to a point aft of the second funnel and ending at the curved forward entrance to their promenade-deck openings. This made a classic statement of beautifully functional clean-lined form representing the timelessly elegant greyhound of the seas. *Lusitania* was originally painted white from the level of her solid C-deck bulwark upwards, creating a band of white shell plating surrounding the uppermost row of fo'c'sle portholes. When it was seen that *Mauretania* presented a sleek, longer and lower appearance with her hull painted black up to B deck, *Lusitania* was soon after touched up to follow suit.

The possibilities of engine noise and propeller vibration is a great concern in designing and building any new ship of high performance. While turbines themselves are intrinsically smooth running and quiet, propellers can be the cause of great difficulties, as much a factor of hull form and hydrostatics, the location and shape of their shaft bossings and supporting brackets as by their own design. Without wishing to introduce any difficulties through the differences in her design from that of *Lusitania*, *Mauretania*'s builders carried out five days of highly secretive trials in the North Sea before the ship's delivery.

While *Mauretania*'s engineers were enjoying a full-speed run during these tests, a peremptory order was unexpectedly rung down from the bridge, requesting an immediate reduction of speed. When later discreetly asked off the record about his action, the captain apparently answered, 'because I was being shaken off my bridge'.[3] Corrective measures were taken before *Mauretania* ran her official sea trials for Cunard from Liverpool.

The First-Class accommodation of both ships made an especially elegant statement of Edwardian-era hotel luxury. *Lusitania*'s First-Class lounge and smoking room design reflected classic 18th-century English themes, with dark polished wood walls and

Above: *Upper part of the* **Lusitania**'s *first-class dining room with a dome above to create an airy piazza-style circular expression of plan within an otherwise rectangular shipboard space.* (**Author's collection**)

Below: Lusitania's *main lounge interior. The glazed dome at the room's centre serves instead as a principal source of natural daylight while dark panelled wall coverings lend a sense of richness, similar to hotel interiors.* (**Author's collection**)

Above: Mauretania. (CPL)

Below: Mauretania, *early in her career before boats were added on the open midships part of her boat deck*. (CPL)

ornately detailed cream plaster work in coves of their stained-glass ceiling vaults. The mahogany-panelled main lounge featured an elegant ersatz fireplace with a marble mantle and chimney piece. The smoking room was panelled in walnut, with light pear wood friezes. The Louis XV and XVI main lounge and library/writing room aboard *Mauretania* were especially successful, with an Italianate style being adopt-

ed for the smoking room. *Lusitania*'s double-height domed dining room on D deck, designed in French Louis XVI motif with carved cream coloured wood-work and gold-lead detailing, was especially delight-ful.

The most remarkable characteristic of both interi-ors was the incredibly human scale they offered 560 First-Class passengers aboard each ship. Although they were considered to be very large and powerful by all standards of their time, the impression these created for the passengers on board was never over-whelming or overpowering. The A-deck lounges aboard *Mauretania* in particular were laid out with seating alcoves enclosed in window bays at either side, while the arrangement of the smoking room, surrounding a pair of vent shafts near its forward end, likewise offered a degree of seclusion for those seek-ing it. The mezzanine-plan dining rooms also avoid-ed creating any impression of large messing halls.

Lusitania and *Mauretania* also introduced a num-ber of significant improvements in their cabin accommodation. Each ship offered two regal suites, with private parlours and bathrooms, which could also be allocated their own private segment of the promenade deck. There were also ten groupings of cabins that could be combined en suite with their own private bath rooms, as well as four additional combinations of rooms to form two deluxe parlour suites.

Accommodation for the two lower classes was also of a high standard, with an attractive range of

public rooms and cabins available in Second Class, including lounge, music salon, smoking room and a range of two- and four-berth cabins. For the first time, the Third-Class accommodation even offered the comparative luxury of a few two-berth cabins, in addition to the large full-beam dining room forward on D deck and their own smoking room and general room above on C deck. Remarkably, C deck divided the First-Class accommodation at its vertical mid-point, with only the upper level of the dining room and entrance foyer at this level. The forward part of this, which was in essence the ship's lower promenade as well as a working deck, was occupied also by the Third-Class entrances and communal toilets, flanked at either side by their covered promenades. Aft there was a block of engineer's accommodation and Second-Class cabins further astern. Operationally, these provided a four-ship weekly transatlantic service, with Saturday sailings from Liverpool and Tuesday departures from New York, running with *Caronia* and *Carmania*.

White Star Line, CGT and HAPAG each challenged Cunard's dominance of the North Atlantic ferry route on the basis of even higher levels of luxury and comfort rather than greater speed. White Star progressed to the unprecedented mark of 45,000 tons in their orders placed with Harland & Wolff for *Olympic*, *Titanic* and *Britannic*. These were hybrid triple-screw ships, where the outer shafts were driven by reciprocating steam machinery and the centre shaft was turbine propelled.

Inside, the accommodation and public areas were of an unprecedented standard, yet without the excesses of creating double-height spaces even for First-Class lounges and dining room. Rather, space was lavished on the cabins, with a large number of hotel-style rooms being offered, each with full-size bedsteads, occasional chairs and its own porcelain wash basin with hot and cold running water and en-suite

bathroom and lavatory. Other passenger amenities were introduced, including squash courts, Turkish baths, a gymnasium, an exclusive alternative restaurant and one of the first indoor ship's swimming pools.

After *Olympic* had completed her first few voyages and the service was assessed, various improvements were made to *Titanic*'s passenger accommodation during her completion and fitting out. The most outwardly noticeable of these was the enclosing of the forward half of her promenade deck with sliding glass windows. A precedent for this had been set by Harland & Wolff in 1909 in Holland America's second *Rotterdam*, amid unfounded ridicule at the time that the glass would all be smashed to pieces by the first Atlantic gale the ship would encounter. *Titanic*'s lower promenade was for the most part eliminated in

Above: *Port view of* **Mauretania** *with white hull, as she appeared when used in cruise service during her later career.* (Author's collection)

Below: *Cross section comparing* Lusitania *with* Great Eastern. (Author's collection)

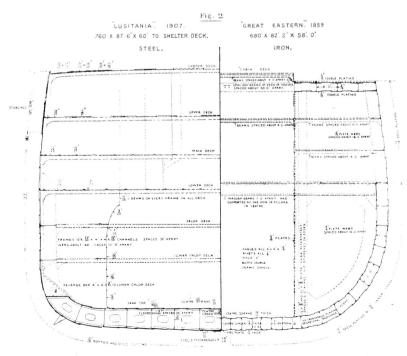

favour of adding more hotel-style cabins, including two elaborate suites, each with its own private, enclosed veranda. The restaurant on this deck was itself extended out to the port side, with an informal Parisian Café being created as an enclosed deck space to starboard. This feature seems to have acknowledged a growing need of the early 20th-century society for places where ladies and gentlemen could gather informally.

Of the three ships ordered, only *Olympic* was ever to reach New York. *Titanic* was lost on her maiden voyage in April 1912, as discussed in the next chapter. The third ship, *Britannic*, was only completed after the outbreak of World War I, and after being engaged in government service as a hospital ship was sunk in November 1916 after striking a mine in the Aegean Sea, without ever having entered commercial service.

Meanwhile the steam-turbine *Aquitania* was completed in 1914 as the long-awaited consort of *Lusitania* and *Mauretania* that would finally establish Cunard's three-ship New York service. With a service speed of 23.5 knots, she was designed to keep pace with the two earlier ships without being a record breaker herself, and at a measure of 45,647 tons, offer at least the same level of passenger comfort as *Olympic*. *Aquitania*'s overall plan was generally similar to the White Star ship, although as indicated by her significantly higher passenger capacity of 3,230 against *Olympic*'s of 2,435, less space was lavished on the First-Class sleeping accommodation. *Aquitania* had more than double the Third-Class capacity, with accommodation for nearly 2,000 guests. Although the First- and Second-Class figures were actually slightly lower than those of *Olympic*, there were fewer large hotel-style rooms with en-suite bathrooms, and a generally greater proportion of inside cabins in First Class.

Otherwise the First-Class public spaces were the epitome of the Mewès and Davis oeuvre. Following on the basis of their hotel work ashore, designs of these and the deluxe cabins were for the most part based on French Louis XVI themes. The architecturally-designed main suite of public rooms on A deck also encompassed two attractive garden lounges at either side of the main foyer, which were in fact the enclosed mid sections of the promenade. The interior decoration was further enriched with the addition of genuine antique furniture pieces as well as classic art reproductions suitable to the styles of the rooms themselves. The general arrangement of *Aquitania*'s First-Class public rooms, with the drawing room as a quiet area forward, main lounge amidships and smoking room aft, along with a long gallery extending aft from the main lounge, was adopted as something of a standard layout. It was replicated with variations of scale and detailed plan through several later generations of Cunard liners up to the time of *QE2*'s planning in the mid 1960s.

Opposite top: *The ill-fated* Titanic. (John Bowen)

Opposite bottom: *A Cunard Line publicity poster featuring a rather whimsical cross section through* Aquitania, *showing all that the ship had to offer those travelling in her divergent classes.* (Corbis)

Left: *White Star* Olympic, *1911 starboard view.* (Author's collection)

Below: *Cunard* Aquitania *1914 port bow quarter at Southampton.* (Author's collection)

The final ocean liner splendours of La Belle Époque were to emerge in the form of *Imperator* and *Vaterland*, HAPAG's last two North Atlantic liners to be completed before the outbreak of World War I. Both ships were built in Hamburg, with the 51,969-ton *Imperator* ordered from Vulcan Werke and *Vaterland* at 54,282 tons from Blohm & Voss. These went into service in the spring of 1913 and 1914 respectively, while a still larger third ship to have been named *Bismarck* was only completed after the war. In their outward appearance these liners presented an especially good impression of their great size. Their hull lines were conventional for the most part, and the massive superstructures were of the same rectilinear type as their British counterparts, *Olympic* and *Aquitania*. The geometric proportions of *Imperator*'s superstructure, funnels, masts and other deck fixtures were painstakingly planned to present a balanced exterior profile. In comparison with Cunard's *Aquitania*, *Imperator* created a far stronger impression of size, although she was only 6,321 tons larger. The shorter funnels and improvements in the arrangement of deck equipment atop *Vaterland*'s superstructure conveyed a far more clean-lined appearance than that of the first ship.

Like *Aquitania*, *Imperator* and *Vaterland* were among the first ships to be completed since new requirements to provide 'lifeboats for all' were put in place following the loss of *Titanic*. In the case of *Imperator* this amounted to 40 conventional davit-launched lifeboats as well as 43 decked craft carried mainly on the fore- and after-decks where they could be launched using the cargo booms. To minimize the topside weight and compromise of vertical instability that might occur by carrying 40 boats and their launching gear in conventional fashion atop the

Left: *HAPAG's*
Imperator *of 1913,*
starboard view.
(Author's collection)

already high superstructures of both ships, 28 boats were carried two decks lower down along the aft part of C deck, where 12 of these were nested beneath the B-deck promenade. Although this feature created no immediate trend for nested lifeboats in any of the large ships that followed in the 1920s and 1930s, it was to return much later in the Dutch liner *Willem Ruys* of 1947, as well as P&O's *Oriana* and *Canberra* of the 1960s, and is now virtually a standard feature of modern cruise-ship design.

The Cologne office of Mewès and Bischoff were consulting and coordinating architects for the vast suites of First-Class public rooms in both ships, with a number of the individual interiors being contracted to prominent specialist architects in Germany, Britain and France. Yet the diversity of their work appears to have been discreetly moulded into a clear overall cohesion at the skilled hand of Mewès himself. *Imperator* and *Vaterland* were among the first large liners to offer a diversity of public spaces, themselves virtually occupying the full length of the promenade deck. In addition to the usual main lounge, smoking room and ladies salon or library, *Imperator* also featured a large winter garden amidships, adjacent to the Ritz Restaurant.

The winter garden was an ocean-going rendition of similar spaces in the leading hotels ashore, where it provided an informal daytime gathering place for ladies and gentlemen to meet and socialize together. Its main focus, though, was as a forecourt of the restaurant, which was raised above its floor by several steps as something of a showpiece in itself, as well as to provide its diners with an overhead vantage point of their surroundings. Forward of the centre funnel casing and main vestibule, the main lounge (or Social Hall as it translated from its German

moniker *Gesellschafts Zimmer*) was also noteworthy for the large raised bandstand at its forward end and parquet dance floor at the centre, from which the daytime carpeting and occasional furniture would be removed during the evening hours.

With the aft end of the promenade deck taken over by the Ritz restaurant, and its catering facilities and a separate veranda café overlooking the stern, the English Tudor-style smoking room was relegated to the forward part of A deck, above the ladies' lounge. *Imperator*'s greatest architectural marvel, however, was the elaborate mosaic-tiled indoor swimming pool, modelled on the Pompeiian Baths of the Royal Automobile Club in London designed by Mewès and Davis a few years earlier. Appropriately scaled to the

Below: *HAPAG's*
Admiral von Tirpitz
Wintergarten interior.
(Author's collection)

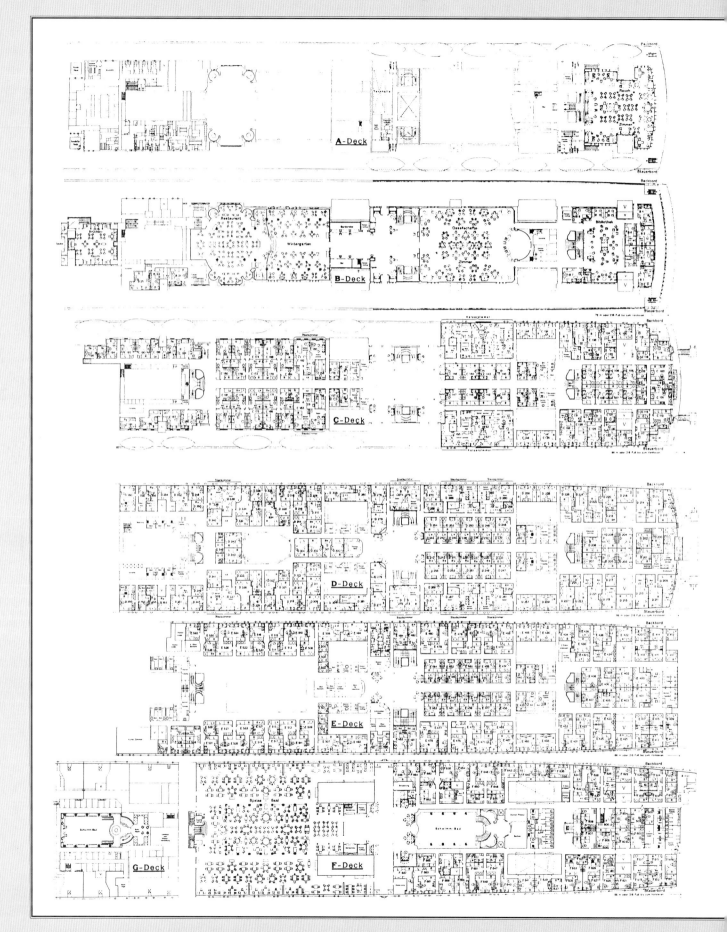

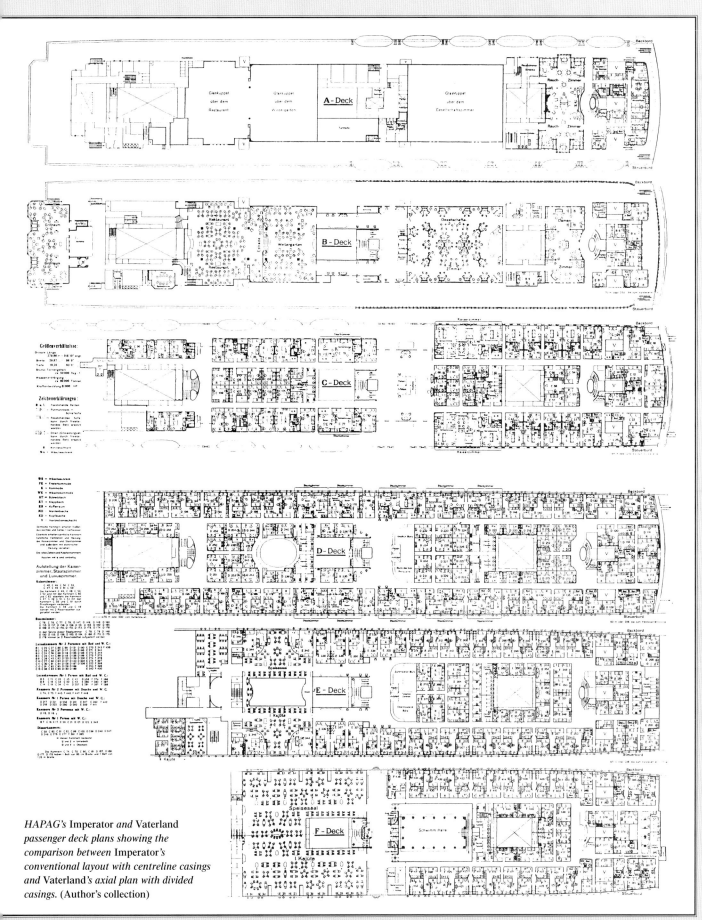

HAPAG's Imperator *and* Vaterland
*passenger deck plans showing the
comparison between* Imperator's
*conventional layout with centreline casings
and* Vaterland's *axial plan with divided
casings. (Author's collection)*

Above: *The Grand Salon aboard French Line's* France *of 1912, showing the impeccably good taste and gracious elegance of La Belle Époque's classically-inspired grand hotel hospitality.* (Author's collection)

ship's dimensions, this retained the double-height hall above the pool tank, and was given the added shipboard feature of a spa with steam and speciality baths.

Vaterland followed the same overall plan, but with the significant innovation of the funnel casings and central stairway and lifts being divided, or 'split', towards the sides of the ship, rather than being arranged along the centreline. This was done to create a grand central thoroughfare through the main public rooms with a clear vista from the social hall's stage forward through to the raised floor of the Ritz Restaurant aft, a distance of some 262ft (80m) along the ship's centreline. The second ship also reflected a number of other refinements of plan: the main staircases and lifts were located at either side of the centreline, between the divided centre funnel uptakes; the bandstand likewise was placed between the forward uptakes, with the result that more fore-and-aft space was made available for the social hall, effectively balancing its internal volume against the combined extent of the winter garden and Ritz Restaurant aft.

As magnificent as this axial plan was for the lounge deck, it was far less satisfactory on the cabin decks below. Whereas *Imperator* featured a classic cabin plan, with two parallel corridors flanking a file of funnel and engine casings, stairways, lifts and other services arranged along the centreline, *Vaterland*'s single, wide central hallways on each deck were too far in from the sides to allow for a

straightforward hotel-style layout. Smaller secondary passages were needed to access the majority of higher-priced outer cabins, and numerous variations of individual cabin layouts were required to fill the areas between the casings and the ship's side and other irregular spaces created by this approach. The plan was further compromised by the dining room dome and the swimming pool hall, inevitably located along the centreline on the lower decks. Despite the comparative natures of their cabin-deck layouts, both ships offered the largest and most elaborate suites that had ever been available at sea. The two Kaiser suites each featured two bedrooms with en-suite bathrooms, sitting room, breakfast room, a private enclosed veranda, a service pantry and storage room for trunks.

As head of HAPAG's passenger department, Albert Ballin was concerned with the well-being of those aboard his ship in all classes. He was particularly concerned with serving the emigrant trade, then in its heyday. The business rationale of his approach was simply that the revenue earned from the masses on lower decks was significant against the fares paid by First-Class passengers for the spacious luxury of the upper decks. The humanity of this lay in his firm belief that the well-treated passenger in HAPAG's emigrant classes was the future good-will ambassador who was more likely to write to those who would follow later, recommending that they too travel with the same line. A further technical advance that benefited all classes of passengers and crew alike was the Frahm anti-rolling tanks. The cost, both in terms of space taken up and the price paid for Doctor Frahm's invention, no doubt greatly outweighed its limited success. Nevertheless it was considered worthwhile enough to be installed on many liners, including Norddeutscher Lloyd's later *Bremen* and *Europa*, before the advent of modern compact and efficient fin stabilizers.

Although little was seen of them in their original service careers before the outbreak of World War I, *Imperator* and *Vaterland* emerged nonetheless as the veritable prototypes of the sophisticated modern North Atlantic liner of the coming decades. Yet these were the final expressions of a genteel yet elitist section of society that had flourished in Europe and North America, and on the high seas between the two continents, out of the prosperity, confidence, and above all, the newfound mobility of late-19th-century urban life. It was largely luxury travel, and the enjoyment of experiencing it, that had brought together the close-knit elite of the age. ●

Left: *Postcard of Mauretania, port view as a hospital ship in World War I.* (Gordon Turner collection)

Below: Mauretania *in 1918, in 'dazzle camouflage' designed to break up the ship's outline and so hinder identification.* (CPL)

4

THE INFORMAL MODERNITY OF PARIS

The assured well-being enjoyed by the genteel high society of La Belle Époque, and indeed the confidence and pride of virtually the whole western world, was profoundly shaken by the loss of *Titanic* on her maiden voyage to New York during the night of 14 April 1912. Through the new medium of instantaneous wireless communications and the widespread distribution of daily newspapers this was one of the first calamitous events of world history whose shock and pain were immediately felt on both sides of the Atlantic. The immediacy of its publicity captured the human emotion of the event as the rescue effort was completed, the search for additional survivors continued, and above all, the quest for information and answers continued. It created the sort of media-led awareness the world has endured since, including President Kennedy's 1963 assassination, the 11 September 2001 terrorist attacks and the devastating Indian Ocean tsunamis of late 2004.

There had been little special publicity about the debut of the new White Star Line ship, as she was but the follow-on ship to *Olympic*, and there was no question of her being a contender for the Blue Riband. Quite by coincidence, though, a cadre of high-society personalities, including John Jacob Astor and Benjamin Guggenheim, had booked First-Class steamship passage to New York at the same time. They all turned up aboard *Titanic* probably for no other reason than that her Wednesday, 10 April sailing date from Southampton best fitted in with their own travel plans.

Titanic was only very slightly larger than her earlier sister *Olympic*, which had gone into service in 1911. Like most large new liners of the era, her steel hull was compartmentalized, with the connecting watertight doors equipped for simultaneous operation from the bridge, allowing the compartments to be sealed off one from the other in an emergency. Yet the economies of building ever larger ships had brought compromise. Watertight bulkheads were no longer built to the hull's full height, but rather only to the first deck fully above the waterline, known accordingly as the bulkhead deck. Calculations had shown that this was sufficient to maintain stability with any two adjacent compartments flooded. Where the double-skinned hulls of *Lusitania* and *Mauretania* had in effect been turned upwards into longitudinal cofferdams forming the coal bunkers along the full length of the boiler and engine rooms, the double bottoms of *Olympic* and *Titanic* stopped at the turn of their bilge keels, with the bunkers being arranged laterally between the boiler rooms. One of the most onerous compromises was the unquestioned adherence to outdated Board of Trade regulations where lifeboat capacity for passenger ships was determined by tonnage and watertight subdivision of the hull rather than the actual numbers of passengers and crew carried.

The judicial investigations carried out in Britain and the United States following the tragedy generally concluded that the ship was proceeding at excessive speed despite warnings of icebergs. While

Opposite: Canadian Pacific poster from around 1929. (Corbis)

Titanic herself was found to be of sound design and construction generally, apart from the inadequacy of her lifeboat complement, the report from the Merchant Shipping Advisory Committee recognized the difficulty of embarking the large numbers of passengers into lifeboats within the likely time-frame of an emergency at sea. As inadequate as *Titanic*'s lifeboats were, for one reason or another, only about two thirds of their total capacity of 1,178 persons was actually filled. The new Board of Trade rules brought into effect on 1 January 1913 required lifeboat capacity for all persons on board. They also specified the number of boat davit sets to be provided according to the length of the hull to ensure that a reasonable number of the boats could be simultaneously launched in an emergency.

There has long been debate as to whether the actions of simultaneously reversing the propellers and turning the ship hard to port might have counteracted one another, causing the iceberg to graze *Titanic*'s steel hull below the waterline for a third of its length and opening up six compartments to the sea. This suggests that reversing the propellers alone would have resulted in a non-fatal head-on collision with only the forward compartments being breeched, or that turning *Titanic*'s bows to port alone would have avoided the collision altogether. While much has been learned from various expeditions made to the wreck of *Titanic* in the late 20th century, many of these questions remain unanswered, and are still a source of controversy, more than 90 years after the event.

There was, however, a great deal more to the *Titanic* disaster than the questions of lifeboat capacity, procedures for abandoning ship and excessive speed while navigating in ice conditions. There was suspicion that the captain was under pressure from the line's managing director, who was travelling aboard the ship and wanted the prestige of an early arrival of his new ship in New York to capture newspaper headlines. There was also the mysterious existence of the small Leyland Line cargo/passenger vessel *Californian*, which was within sight of *Titanic* as she was sinking yet without a 24-hour radio watch and agonisingly unresponsive to the stricken liner's visual distress signals. The confidence of progress had been compromised by expedience, rationale, economy and perhaps most of all, by the characteristic human shortcomings of misjudgement, error and incompetence. All of this serves to fuel a culture of conspiracy and conjecture that tragic events of this sort seem to engender.

The *Titanic* disaster continues to live on. Heirs of the families who lost loved ones are still trying to identify remains of the bodies retrieved from the sea by the cable ship *MacKay Bennett* during the weeks following the sinking and buried in numbered graves at a cemetery in Halifax, Nova Scotia. In a number of cases, modern DNA matching is now being used to

establish links between the remains from these graves and samples either from living direct descendants or taken from the buried remains of other blood relatives who have died in the meantime. There is still controversy over recovery of more artifacts from the wreck or whether the entire site should be declared as a grave site and left in peace.

The enduring fascination of this tragedy is itself legendary in its power to continue capturing the minds and imaginations of people around the world. Apart from *Titanic* enthusiast organizations, memorials, special events and exhibitions, vast quantities of literature have been produced on the subject, including numerous books and several motion pictures.

The 1958 British film *A Night to Remember*, directed by Roy Baker and based on Walter Lord's bestselling book of the same title published three years earlier, stood alone through four decades as the best and most historically accurate account of the disaster. The film's almost austere documentary nature and unbiased impartiality reflected the integrity of Walter Lord's book as more of a historical work than a dramatization. It succeeded also in portraying a very real human sense of the night's events, largely as seen through the eyes of *Titanic*'s second officer, Herbert Lightoller, played by Kenneth More and of others among the ship's crew and passengers, including a very much in love Mr. and Mrs. Lucas, portrayed by John Merivale and Honor Blackman. Some of the most real deck scenes of the lifeboats being prepared, loaded and lowered down the ship's sides were filmed aboard the 1927-built Royal Mail Line ship *Asturias*, whose classic style and outfitting of 15 years later still portrayed much the same Edwardian character as the ill-fated White Star Line steamer.

While being perhaps less complete as a historical drama, James Cameron's epic 1997 film *Titanic*, starring Leonardo DiCaprio and Kate Winslet, uses modern film-making techniques to create a riveting impression of what the experience of being aboard *Titanic* might have actually been like. A virtually full-scale model of the ship was used for many of the deck and onboard scenes, as well as for a simulation of the actual sinking. Advanced computer imaging was used to create a number of the more stunning visual effects as the ship breaks her back and goes down. The scenes of water pouring into the lower deck and inundating the accommodation as it tore furniture and fittings loose, and of the bridge front being breached as it slipped below the surface, were startlingly convincing. These effects, along with the modern wide-screen format and surround Dolby sound, more than compensated for the picture's few inevitable anachronisms and a trite Hollywood love plot between two fictitious passengers that pales in contrast to the real-life drama experienced by those actually aboard *Titanic*.

The great commercial success of the James Cameron film, and its remarkable appeal to younger cinema audiences, quickly translated itself into a surge in bookings for Cunard's *Queen Elizabeth 2*, as movie-goers sought to experience the only remaining vestige of the liner era for themselves. This came about at a time when Cunard was studying the economic feasibility of building a new liner to ultimately replace *QE2*. Although the enthusiasm for sea travel created by the film was encouraging, the decision to build was based on longer-term business projections over a service-life expectancy of 40 years for the new ship.

Almost three years after *Titanic*'s loss, in the early afternoon of 8 May 1915, *Lusitania* was sunk by a single torpedo fired from a German U-boat as she approached the Irish coast on a regular commercial voyage, inbound from New York. The ship sank in as little as 20 minutes, with a death toll of nearly 1,200. The extensive lateral and horizontal watertight subdivision of *Lusitania*'s hull was quickly rendered ineffective, as she rapidly listed heavily to starboard, since many of her portholes which had been opened in the warmth of that spring day slipped below the surface.

As tragic as this incident was, its horror was more immediately and readily comprehended as an act of aggression against a defenceless civilian target, without ever attaining as much popular intrigue as *Titanic*'s loss. Yet *Lusitania*'s demise was a harsh early introduction to the ugly reality of 20th-century acts of violence, where military conflict was no longer confined to battlefields and combat at sea among naval vessels. A largely unheeded warning from the Imperial German embassy in Washington DC, published in many New York newspapers the morning of *Lusitania*'s sailing, reminding would-be passengers that British merchant ships were subject to attack, seems almost to have been prophetic. However, large and fast ships continued to sail with impunity, seemingly confident that traditional values of gentlemanly conduct with which World War I had started would continue to prevail and that they would be spared. The shock and outrage at *Lusitania*'s sinking and the loss of American lives among her passengers were instrumental in creating the public support needed to bring the United Stated in to the conflict with Germany in April 1917.

As ships of various nations were requisitioned, chartered or seized as prizes of war, the Atlantic ferry was for a time reinstated as a trooping run. The grand ballrooms, elegant dining saloons and luxurious staterooms that had once catered to the wealthy and important, were filled to several times their original capacities in a military-style adaptation of Steerage mass transit, as thousands of American troops were transported to fight in the trenches of France and Belgium. On yet other ships the upper deck lounges became ocean-going hospital wards where the injured from the various theatres of war were received and treated, while their deluxe suites were hastily converted to operating rooms and medical laboratories. German ships impounded in American ports, including the prestigious new *Vaterland*, were seized and pressed into trooping service, while their caretaker crews were processed through the Ellis Island Immigration for internment in the United States. What could hardly have been foreseen or envizaged at the time was that passenger shipping, and indeed the world that would continue to rely on it as the only viable means of intercontinental travel for at least two decades yet to come, had changed irrevocably and that things would never be quite the same again.

REBUILDING AND MODERNIZING

Once the troops and the injured had been brought home, and prisoners, internees and detainees repatriated, the world was faced with recovering from the loss of some 11 million tons of merchant shipping sunk during four years of hostilities. The big liners had fared best, with *Mauretania*, *Olympic* and *Aquitania* being duly returned to the service of their original owners after extensive refurbishment following their war service. Likewise, HAPAG's *Imperator* and *Vaterland* withstood the conflict intact, along with the third ship in the series, *Bismarck*, which was left undisturbed at her fitting out basin in Hamburg since work on her had halted during the war. Of these, *Imperator* was allocated to Cunard, becoming *Berengaria*. *Vaterland*, renamed *Leviathan* when seized and put into trooping service in 1917, remained with the United States Shipping Board who

Left: *Probably the last ever photograph taken of the* Lusitania, *heading out on her final voyage in 1915. The loss of 123 American lives in her sinking was an early factor in turning the then neutral United States against Germany.* (CPL)

from 1921 operated her and several other former German vessels under a commercial subsidiary called United States Line. This was a forerunner of the later United States Lines formed through its acquisition by International Mercantile Marine Company in 1931. *Bismarck* was completed by Blohm & Voss and delivered to White Star Line as *Majestic*.

With the high cost of building resulting from shortages of materials and labour, as well as a lack of available building capacity while yards catered to the demand for refit work, many lines looked to acquiring surplus German tonnage to meet their immediate post-war needs. White Star Line abandoned plans for their new *Homeric* to be built by Harland & Wolff in favour of purchasing the unfinished Norddeutscher Lloyd liner *Columbus*, and having the ship completed for them as *Homeric*. Likewise, HAPAG's *Tirpitz*, one of three ships built as half-size versions of *Vaterland* planned for the line's South Atlantic service, was purchased by Canadian Pacific and renamed *Empress of Australia* for their own service. The two later ships in this series were completed for United American Lines as *Resolute* and *Reliance*. Red Star Line's *Belgenland*, which had been under construction at Harland & Wolff when war broke out in 1914, was first hurriedly completed (with only two funnels and minus her upper promenade deck) as a troop ship, before being later completed in her original

form. Holland America's *Statendam* was pressed into wartime service as *Justicia*, also in a half completed condition, with the misfortune of being sunk by German submarines in July 1918. She was ultimately replaced by a second ship similar to the original design ordered from Harland & Wolff and completed only in 1923.

The work done to prepare most of these ships for commercial service in the 1920s involved conversion of their boiler plants from coal to oil firing. The greatest advantage of this was that it eliminated the back-breaking manual labour of stoking the boilers as well as the filthy and time-consuming ordeal of coaling during the turnaround time between voyages. Surprisingly, the great march of engineering progress that had taken steam shipping from the age of the lever engine and paddle wheel to the sophisticated high-performance 25-knot turbine propulsion, had made no progress in mechanizing either of these tasks. The workers tipped coal by the bucket load into the bunkers of a liner boomed out from her dock for the operation, and then manually ladled it by shovel into the furnaces to raise steam. No matter how cheap coal might have been and inexpensive the labour, this practice seems to be utterly incongruous from the viewpoint of our own era of automation.

While the meticulously renovated Mewès-style First-Class interiors of these ships might have created

Below: *Norwegian America Line* Stavangerfjord, *passing Ellis Island., New York.* (Gordon Turner collection)

an impression of luxury travel having returned to its former glory, the reality was that the clientele itself had changed significantly. Americans from all walks of life who had done military service overseas during the war were anxious to return to Europe in the lines of business and leisure activity. Commercial enterprises, friendships and marriages had created new ties across the Atlantic, with the result that a much higher percentage of the trade was American. With this came the demands for additional space, privacy and sanitary facilities already setting the standards of hotel service in the United States. Living standards in America had continued to improve during World War I, where the nation's military involvement had been over a considerably shorter time-span and there had been no loss of civilian properties and domestic infrastructure at home. With the start of Prohibition in 1920, thirsty Americans who enjoyed the pleasures of the bottle were anxious to travel aboard the ships of any nation but their own, where they could at least enjoy some social alcoholic libation.

Below decks, the passenger accommodation on

many British and European ships were extensively rebuilt to meet the higher hotel standards of the times. Aboard Cunard's *Aquitania*, for instance, large numbers of First-Class cabins on C deck were rebuilt in 1922 to provide attached lavatories and showers. Originally these rooms were arranged in blocks of six, three either side of a short transverse passages leading off the main fore-and-aft corridors. The single centre cabin between the inner and outer twin-bedded rooms each side of the secondary passage was replaced with a shower and toilet shared between the remaining two rooms, with individual washbasins being retained in each room. While this reduced the number of cabins in each group from six to four, and the passenger capacity from ten to eight, the new rooms with their attached toilet facilities could be sold at higher prices to cover the loss of revenue from the reduced number of berths.

These same cabins were rebuilt a second time in 1933, when the inner cabins were replaced altogether with large bathrooms attached to each of the significantly enlarged outer staterooms, which could

Above, left: *Canadian Pacific* Empress of Australia, *steaming up Southampton Water.* (CPL)

Top, right: *Ladies participating in horse racing, Canadian Pacific style.* (Author's collection)

Lower, right: *'Crossing the Line' celebrations at sea, aboard the* Empress of Australia. (Author's collection)

then be sold as deluxe accommodation. Other changes included increasing the number of cabins offered for single occupancy, often accomplished by merely removing the upper berths from smaller rooms and by increasing the numbers of interchangeable accommodation that could be sold as either First or Second Class depending on the demand for space.

Meanwhile, the world emigration boom was coming to an end. Shipping lines that had depended on the high volume of this minimum-fare trade to help subsidize the luxuries of their premiere classes had to find new ways of filling their high-density accommodation on the lower decks. In 1921 legislation was introduced in Washington to end the era of virtually free immigration to the United States, with the implementation of a quota system based on the ethnic make-up of the American population as it stood in 1910. Other countries, including Canada and Australia, also became concerned about protecting their own labour resources and emerging cultural mixes.

Fortunately the amenities of Third Class had by this time risen far enough above the level of abject squalor for there to be a ready market with young and mobile people who were anxious to travel overseas at affordable fares as tourists. Ships such as *Mauretania*, *Olympic*, *Aquitania*, as well as the newly acquired *Berengaria*, *Leviathan* and *Majestic*, had been built with an acceptable standard of Third-Class accommodation, having individual cabins of two to six or eight berths, large and airy dining rooms, public spaces and deck areas already suited to this type of trade. With but a few added touches in the cabins, some refinements of cuisine and service and the catchy advertising pitch of 'Tourist Third' the concept gained instant popularity.

The minimalist railway-compartment-sized cabins usually had upper and lower bunks either side of a standing space, the washbasin at its inner end and enough space only for a pair of storage lockers between the foot-ends of the berths and the corridor wall. But they proved satisfactory for the thousands of adventurous students, teachers and seasonally or periodically employed persons who had the time for the voyage. In those days, most wage-earners in America only received two weeks' paid holiday a year, which was barely sufficient for the round-trip Atlantic crossing, let alone to spend time ashore at the other end. Tourist Third also served what the shipping lines called an 'old home' trade, of former emigrants and their families who had saved enough to visit their former homes in Europe or to bring their parents, friends or relatives to visit them in the New World.

The demographic of sea travel was becoming more diverse and democratic. The exclusive Ritz restaurants and their galleys had been removed from *Berengaria* and *Leviathan* as part of an effort to reduce weight on the upper decks and overcome the original vertical stability problems of these ships.

Their elitist pre-war extras appear to have gone without being too seriously missed, as their space became ballrooms and Palm Court lounges. By the late 1920s, passengers were beginning to watch motion pictures aboard ship as a new diversion to help pass the time at sea. Early shipboard film screenings were makeshift events, with a portable projector, loudspeaker and screen being set up in a lounge, where the furniture would be rearranged and the room darkened for the show.

Other amusements included bingo (known in the military as housey-housey, which was also its name on British ships), tombolas and the shipboard game of horse racing organized as afternoon or early evening activities. Horse racing was essentially a board game using a canvas 'track' with numbered lines painted on it which could be unrolled on the lounge floor and numbered wooden horse-shaped profiles moved along it to the roll of a dice. Canadian Pacific later came up with the charming idea of asking lady passengers to don number placards on their backs and stand as the horses.

A small orchestra would be carried aboard larger and more prestigious ships as the only source of professional entertainment. They would provide dance music and perhaps perform in the dining room through the dinner-hour. Yet, with the performance facilities that were by this time available, passengers became far more creative and imaginative in organizing concerts and performances of their own. Fancy dress parties also became a popular pastime, with ship's crews being quite helpful in securing all manner of items for creating everything from knights in shining armour and damsels in distress to witches, pirates and dragons.

Many shipowners foresaw that times were changing, and that the new Tourist Third experience was leading the way to a future inexpensive mass mobility (which would finally be scooped by the jumbo-jet age some 40 years on). Others foresaw that the diversity of increased mobility would also continue to demand an elite class of accommodation and service, perhaps in a modernized form, for those prepared to pay for it. While some looked to the agility of the modern diesel motor ship, which could be sent cruising in the off season, others foresaw the coming of even greater steamships as flagships of the nations that would build them.

Dawn of the Motor Ship

While the big-league players were vying for Blue Riband supremacy on the North Atlantic, the cream of the First-Class trade and Europe's mass emigrant exodus, the small Danish vessel *Selandia* was making history as the world's first commercially viable motor-propelled 'steamless ship'. She was built by the Refshaleoen shipyards in Copenhagen for the East Asiatic Company's cargo and passenger service between the Danish Capital and Bangkok. Apart from being without sails, *Selandia* distinguished herself visually by also lacking a funnel. Below decks, she was powered by a pair of eight-cylinder marine diesel engines built by the Danish engine makers, Burmeister & Wein, with a slender exhaust pipe being carried high inside the centre mast.

The oil-burning engine, which is largely credited to the German engineer Dr Rudolf Diesel (1857–1913), from whom it takes its name, produces mechanical power directly by sequenced combustion inside its cylinders. Unlike automotive gasoline, internal-combustion engines, which use an electrical sparking device to produce combustion by igniting vaporized fuel from a carburetor, the diesel works on the principle of compression. Air is admitted to the cylinder, then compressed by the up stroke of the piston causing its temperature to rise to the flash point of the fuel oil. Fuel is admitted into the cylinder under pressure where it ignites, causing the expansion of gases from the burn to push the piston back down to the point where the cylinder is cleared of exhaust gases, and then the cycle is repeated. The diesel engine has the advantage of more even fuel ignition and expansion of the gases it produces over the head of the entire piston, without the mechanical shock from the more localized firing of the spark-ignited gasoline automotive engine. Thus the diesel engine can more readily be produced in the greater

sizes and with the lower operating speeds required for the propulsion of ocean-going ships.

Although the diesel motor itself is a complex piece of machinery, requiring considerable care and upkeep over its lifespan, its use aboard ship was seen to offer a remarkably compact and efficient alternative to steam plants with their need for boilers and the inherent energy losses in the transfer from heat to steam and again to mechanical power. Diesel engines were being used in various installations ashore for quite some time, and had already been tried aboard various coastal and river vessels in Great Britain, Europe, Scandinavia and Russia by the time the first marine steam turbines were introduced aboard the Atlantic liners *Victorian* and *Carmania*. *Selandia*'s twin-engine, two-screw machinery arrangement established the prototype of motor-ship technical design for many years to follow. After 980 hours of running during the ship's maiden voyage to Bangkok, her engines were thoroughly overhauled and found to have stood up well in service. *Selandia* herself remained in service for the East Asiatic Company until 1936, when she was sold for further trading. She met her final demise as *Tornator* while under charter to Japanese operators by her third owners, when she grounded near Omaisaki and became a total loss.

Managing director of Harland & Wolff, Lord Pirrie, who had been involved in the planning of *Selandia*, was himself an avid proponent of diesel

Below: Union Castle Line's Carnarvon Castle of 1926 is a fine example of the Harland & Wolff-built motorships of her time, with twin squat funnels, angular superstructure lines and the forward promenade deck glass enclosed even for tropical routes such as the run to south Africa. (CPL)

Opposite, left:
*Swedish American
Line* Gripsholm, *starboard view later in
her career.* (Gordon
Turner collection)

Opposite, bottom:
Kungsholm, *after
being purchased by
the United States
Maritime Commission
in 1942 and renamed*
John Ericsson *for
trooping and other
government services
during and
immediately after
World War II, later
becoming* Italia *for
Home Lines.* (Gordon
Turner collection)

Below: *The motorship*
Asturias *of 1927,
showing Royal Mail
Line's preference for a
black hull on their
trans-equatorial ships
serving South
America.* (Gordon
Turner collection)

propulsion, and he and his successor Lord Kylsant were eager to build and engine motor ships at Belfast. Confident of the motor ship's longterm prospects, Lord Pirrie prophesied in 1925 that, provided the relative prices of coal and oil remain constant and there was no substantial undue disparity between the building costs of either type of ship, the steamship would ultimately be unable to compete with its diesel counterpart of the basis of operating economy. Accordingly, Harland & Wolff was soon to build a number of significant passenger motor liners during the 1920s.

Among the most notable of these were the Union Castle liners *Carnarvon Castle*, *Winchester Castle* and *Warwick Castle*, along with *Asturias* and *Alcantara* of Royal Mail Lines and White Star's *Britannic* and *Georgic*. From the standpoint of their overall appearance and general layout these represented a further development of the Harland & Wolff liner approach, with the forward half of the main promenade enclosed, a rectilinear superstructure front and covered forward well deck, as seen in the earlier examples of *Belgenland* and *Statendam*. The design of their passenger accommodation was also fairly traditional, generally still reflecting a pre-World War I style of First-Class luxury and liveable domesticity for the lower echelons. These were, however, given a distinctive motor-ship style with squat raked, ovoid funnels and modern cruiser sterns. Funnels were still an important part of the ocean liner's public image, which no owner was prepared to compromize in favour of *Selandia*'s exhaust-pipe masts. Yet the motor ship look made a statement of their modernity that was still acceptable by the standards of the romantic and traditionalist.

Asturias and *Alcantara* were unfortunately re-engined in 1935, with their original double-acting four-stroke diesels being replaced by steam turbines, seemingly as a belated result of early difficulties with the original machinery. Widely known as the Pirrie Kylsant motor ships, these were otherwise highly successful, with White Star's *Britannic*, delivered a few

years later in 1930, proving to be one of the most commercially successful ships in the line's history.

Meanwhile, Swedish American Line, founded in 1918 as part of the Brostrom family's interests, had already put their highly successful motor ships *Gripsholm* and *Kungsholm* into North Atlantic service in 1925–28. At about 20,000 tons each, and with a modest service speed of 17 knots, *Gripsholm* was built by Armstrong, Whitworth & Co at Newcastle-on Tyne, and *Kungsholm* three years later by the Hamburg yard of Blohm & Voss. While the Pirrie Kylsant motor ships built for Union Castle and Royal Mail were designed as tropical liners, with deep shade decks and high-ceilinged public rooms for coolness in equatorial latitudes, the new Swedish liners, and *Kungsholm* in particular, were among the first to make specific provision for cruising as a winter alternative to their high-season trades between Gothenburg and New York.

The accommodation was arranged so that the Second-Class public rooms on B deck aft were sufficiently elegant and comfortable that they could augment the principal First-Class lounges above on the promenade deck to offer a greater diversity of communal spaces. Likewise the dining rooms of these classes, below on E deck, were of similar standard so that they could also be served on an equal basis from the main galley located amidships between them. The First- and Second-Class cabins, which included a number of interchangeable rooms, could be combined into a single class, offering a wider variety of cruise accommodation. The change from two-class line service to cruising was a simple matter of removing the promenade-deck barriers aft and opening the doors in the accommodation passages on B and C decks. The accommocation for Third Class, at the extreme ends of the lower decks and along F deck beneath the dining rooms, would be closed off entirely at these times, reducing the three-class Atlantic passenger capacity of 1,344 to a mere 600 or so for cruising.

These ships brought a unique sense of luxury, rooted in the sedate elegance and customs of Swedish high society, and interpreted in a remarkably human scale for cruising. Service and hospitality were seldom lacking in comfort and congeniality, nor were they carried to the extremes of excess. This in itself reflected the uncrowded and unhurried pace of life in Sweden and its neighbouring Nordic kingdoms, where the comparatively small populations seemed to uphold a family-like affinity among their peoples.

In the overall patterns of human circulation about the world, by sea or by air, then as now, the geographical location of these countries places them far enough out of the way that they are less frequently travelled as thoroughfares, which helps retain a stronger sense of their own identities. Yet this in itself has set a standard of quiet comfort and impeccably good taste which has since drawn the rest of the world to Scandinavian hospitality. *Gripsholm* and

Kungsholm gained great popularity with British, Western European and American passengers, and laid the groundwork in their day for the American-based Scandinavian luxury-cruise business of future generations.

Of the two ships, *Kungsholm* was by far the more outstanding for the elegant modernity of her interiors. These were a veritable showcase of contemporary Swedish architecture and decorative arts. Here the designers and decorators dared to go beyond the hotel idiom itself and introduce elements of fantasy aimed at enriching the shipboard experience itself as well as depicting the cultural relationship that had grown between Sweden and America through the emigration era. The First-Class smoking room was, for instance, decorated with murals by Kurt Jungstedt

Above, right: *Swedish American Line's* Kungsholm, *port view with unidentified tall ships to left.* (Gordon Turner collection)

depicting stylized images of the Stockholm and New York skylines opposite one another on its forward and aft walls. Paintings by Jerk Werkmäster and Rolf Engströmer in the First-Class lounge and music room, with its African-pear wood ceiling and rich oriental carpeting, made an impressionist depiction of Gothenburg at the height of its trading exploits in the East India Company. In lieu of these fine art-works, the Second-Class lounge and smoking room were decoratively panelled in top-quality wall coverings and furnished to a high standard, delineating them from their counterparts on the deck above without creating any impression of their being inferior. The Javanese teak and ebony panelling in the Second-Class smoking room, along with the dark polished woods used in the adjacent lounge, set the tone of these as elegant club rooms in their own right.

The schemes were fanciful and whimsical, without reference to history and classicism that might be over-powering or perceived as pretentious or bourgeois.

Beyond the maritime themes depicted by some of the murals, and a healthy respect shown for the forms and shapes of the ship herself, *Kungsholm*'s architects and interior designers avoided the pitfalls of trying to embellish on the shipboard milieu by making any sort of surrealistic impression of it in their work. These liners were among the first to create a sense of ocean-going luxury based on the experience of the ship her-self and her ports of call in preference to restating the traditional hotelier notion of palatial grand luxe. *Kungsholm*'s distinctive architecture was radically different from the more traditional ocean-going hote-lier themes of her slightly older sister, *Gripsholm*, which was also a successful ship in her own right.

THE PARIS EXPOSITION DES ARTS DÉCORATIFS

During the interval between the deliveries of *Gripsholm* and *Kungsholm*, the 1925 Exposition Internationale des Arts Décoratifs in Paris had already asserted a significant influence over architec-tural design and the decorative arts. Le Corbusier's bright and crisply modern Pavilion de l'Espirit Nouveau illustrated a good use of space in modern dwellings of reduced area. Furnished with light-weight mass-produced 'type object' furnishings, space was maximized to create an attractive, contem-porary and more informal way of living. The func-tional attractiveness of the designs shown aroused great public appeal throughout France, Europe and the United States, as stunning contemporary archi-tecture, open planning of interior spaces, bold fluid lines of form and new manufactured consumer goods began to set the pace of an altogether more liberal-ized approach to living. Only in retrospect much later did 'Arts Décoratifs' became abbreviated as the now more familiar term 'art deco'.

The spirit of modernity ilustrated at the Paris exposition went to sea two years later through the decoration of CGT's *Ile de France*, completed as a companion ship to the line's *Paris*. The interiors of the two French ships were as radically different from one another as were those of *Gripsholm* and *Kungsholm*. *Paris*, whose keel had been laid in 1913, and which had remained uncompleted until after the war, was still very much a product of belle époque classic design styling and genteel living. The only advance of modernity suggested by the exterior of *Ile de France*, however, was that she was one of the first large liners to use overhead gravity davits, carrying her lifeboats high enough above the deck that the space beneath them could be used as an open prom-enade. Only on entering the First-Class interiors was one first struck by what cruise ship designers today call 'the wow factor'. The First-Class grand salon presented a modern coffered ceiling and indirect lighting scheme, blood-red columns and highly pol-ished veneer walls; the triple-deck-high dining room

Below: *A stylish 'Deco' French-language poster by Willy Fischer, from the 1920s or 1930s, promoting Cunard Line's services from the ports of Cherbourg and Le Havre to Canada and the United States.* (Corbis)

displayed vast expanses of marble cladding and stark overhead rows of rectangular lighting fixtures, boldly geometric carpeting and impressionist paintings. All these asserted a new expression of ocean-going luxury, expressed in the scale and geometry of the ship itself rather than the classical references of the traditional liner leitmotif.

Ile de France seemed almost to be more an extension of the exhibition itself than an expression of the modernity it represented. She effectively brought the Exposition Internationale des Arts Décoratifs to sea and onwards to New York, and the Americans loved her for it. This new French ship's interiors were bold, brash, and despite those who derided them as an expression of expensive vulgarity, they made her an immense commercial success: for the first few years of her career she carried more First-Class passengers than any other North Atlantic liner.

Both *Kungsholm* and *Ile de France* succeeded in conveying impressions of great modernity merely through the design of their public rooms, while otherwise retaining very traditional overall layouts, and relatively little other change in the way they were equipped and operated. While *Kungsholm* had been designed for amalgamation of her First- and Second-Class facilities in cruise service, anything below *Ile de France*'s First Class accommodation was as mundane as its equivalent spaces aboard *Paris*. In the case of either ship, the decision to adopt any new direction in design involved the considerable risk of failing to find favour with the travelling public, or of the decorative scheme going out of fashion. This had already happened when the impressive Art Nouveau architecture of Norddeutscher Lloyd's 1909-built *George Washington* proved to be a short-lived trend ashore, leaving the ship to look outmoded against the timeless classicism of HAPAG's Mewès and Bischoff interiors. While individual public rooms could be redecorated during a ship's periodic overhauls in drydock, any significant change in social structure and domestic living ashore would have to show some signs of greater permanence before being eagerly adopted full-scale aboard expensive new ocean liners.

Thus, for a while at least, the shipping industry continued to live with the limitations of an approach to accommodation design that had merely grown along with the steady increase in the size of the ships themselves, without necessarily being rethought or rationalized. While life ashore was becoming more democratized and far less stratified, most of the world's passenger-ship lines still believed they needed to maintain three, and some times four, classes of passenger service, with all the implicit duplication of public rooms, deck spaces, access facilities and ship's services. In the early days of steam, when Steerage was effectively carried as human cargo without proper sanitary facilities, there was a practical need for complete class segregation. Yet during the 1920s and 1930s, when Third Class had achieved

a cachet of social acceptability among artists, teachers and students as Tourist Third, there was hardly the need any longer for its total isolation, though the standard prevailed on some lines until the 1960s.

There was also the perception that passengers expected a vast range of cabin types in various price ranges to the point that on some ships virtually no two rooms were the same. Modern hotels were by then being built with standardized room plans, arranged so that the layout of each floor was identical, with the plumbing being efficiently run through vertical conduits. The shipping lines nonetheless continued to believe that the same people who stayed in these hotels ashore would be unlikely to accept a similar degree of standardization at sea. This was probably rooted in the belief that a ship must herself provide a greater sense of diversity and individuality to those aboard for a crossing of five or more days than is expected of a hotel, where one is free to come and go at will and to experience its surrounding vicinity as a natural extension of its own facilities.

The diversity of cabin planning was, however, sel-

Above, top: *French Line's* Paris, *1921, port bow quarter view, under way with steam blasting from her whistles.* (Gordon Turner collection)

Above, bottom: *French Line's* Ile de France, *1927, starboard view against New York skyline.* (Gordon Turner collection)

Above: *The* Ile de France*'s Grand Salon Premiere Classe,* bringing to the American travelling public an irresistible taste of European chic and modernity.
(Archive Chantiers de l'Atlantique/Cliché Ecomusée de Saint-Nazaire)

Right: Ile de France*'s Salon de Thé Premiere Classe, view forward port side towards the head of the triple-deck-high open grand stairway and main foyer before the large mirror on the forward wall.*
(Archive Chantiers de l'Atlantique/Cliché Ecomusée de Saint-Nazaire)

dom reflected in the range of public rooms and other communal facilities. The traditional sequence of main lounge or social hall, drawing room (or 'Salon de Thé' as this was called aboard *Ile de France*) and, alas, the still predominantly male preserve of the smoking room, were still essentially parlours with no specific function. While passengers aboard today's cruise ships seldom spend more than a day or two at sea between ports, the range of mainly fixed-function public amenities available to them is vast by comparison. The various entertainment lounges, casinos, elaborate health and fitness spas, conference facilities, alternate restaurants, patisseries and speciality cafés leave few places for conversation and relaxation without something else going on and the continual opportunity to spend one's money from dawn until the early hours of the following morning.

Canadian Pacific's 42,350-ton *Empress of Britain* made her debut in 1931, virtually on a point of transition between the traditional approach to ocean-going Grand Hotel and the sort of modernity introduced in the arts decoratifs designs of *Ile de France* and *Kungsholm*. By that time Norddeutscher Lloyd's new *Bremen* and *Europa* had also asserted a rationalist leitmotif of their own, as discussed in the next

chapter. Since the Canadian Pacific Railway Company intended both to compete with the latest New York liners and to use their prestigious new flagship for long around-the-world cruises in the winter months they believed that *Empress of Britain* needed to retain a strong element of what the travelling public would be most likely to expect of her. They also no doubt took into consideration possibilities of switching tonnage between their Atlantic and trans-Pacific routes. The smaller *Empress of Japan* at 26,300 tons had been completed the previous year for Pacific service between Vancouver, Honolulu and Yokohama, and was to all intents and purposes interchangeable with *Empress of Britain*.

Empress of Britain was in fact a bold move on Canadian Pacific's part to capture the patronage of passengers travelling to or from the American mid and far west. This was based on the ability of the Canadian Pacific railway to provide direct connections between the ship's berth at Wolff's Cove near Québec City, and Chicago's Union Station, from where connections could be readily made with all points west. The shorter crossing distance between the St. Lawrence River and Europe could be covered in little more than four-and-a-half days, effectively

Above, left: Ile de France's *grand stairway seen from the centre level of the main first-class foyer, with the Salon de Thé ceiling reflected in the mirror forward of the staircases.*
(Archive Chantiers de l'Atlantique/Cliché Ecomusée de Saint-Nazaire)

Above, right: *A group of ladies in the Salon de Thé, October 1932.*
(Collection Ecomusée de Saint-Nazaire fonds Cdt. G. Burosse /Cliché Ecomusée de Saint-Nazaire)

Left: *Port view of Canadian Pacific's* Empress of Britain, *at Southampton.* (CP Rail Corporate Archive/Gordon Turner collection)

cutting many hours off the overall travelling time between, for instance, Southampton or Cherbourg and Chicago. While thus going head-to-head against the latest New York-bound liners such as *Bremen* and *Europa*, the line reckoned also that their cruise clientele would want a high standard of accommodation and service, with a harmonious variety of decorative styles and themes, all in the very best of good taste, that would be comfortable to live with for periods of up to four months at a stretch. Thus, within the clean-lined contemporary of the ship's classic white exterior, the essence of Canadian Pacific's railway hotel elegance from ashore was retained on a fairly traditional layout with enough of a modern touch to add diversity, yet without going to the point of being overly avant garde or trendy.

The almost-square main Mayfair lounge on *Empress of Britain* was an outstanding example of classic ocean liner elegance set in an exquisitely pro-

portioned room with a glazed vault above its central nave. The room was decorated in a Romanesque motif with polished walnut panelling, amber-glass skylights and richly upholstered furniture in subdued colours. Aft of this was a spacious card room in Spanish style and the Cathay Lounge, a democratized rendition of the shipboard smoking room where lady passengers were also welcome. The sincerity of this gesture was unfortunately betrayed by the inclusion only of a gents' lavatory in the room's immediate vicinity.

The Cathay Lounge was designed with a Chinese fretwork theme encompassing the room's four structural ceiling-support columns, which were sheathed in black vitrolite glass and joined at their tops by shallow arches of silvered metallic fretwork to create the impression of a canopy in the centre of the room. The lacquered vermilion-ebony furniture, bright red Chinese vases, green-and-gold glass fireplace, along with the inlaid Macassar ebony and Oak floor, creat-

Below: *Canadian Pacific's* Empress of Britain: *impressive construction photo at John Brown's yard, 1931.* (Gordon Turner collection)

Left: *Ballroom with band and dancers, aboard the* Empress of Britain. (Gordon Turner collection)

Below: Empress of Britain *pictured being towed out of Southampton.* (CPL)

Right: *The* Empress of Britain's *Mayfair Lounge reflected an entirely traditional ambience aboard an otherwise predominantly contemporary ship.* (Gordon Turner collection)

Opposite, top: *W. Heath Robinson applies the finishing touches to one of the ceiling panels for the Knickerbocker Bar aboard the* Empress of Britain. (Gordon Turner collection)

Right: *The Knickerbocker Bar interior, with barman and passengers.* (Gordon Turner collection)

Opposite, bottom: *Some of* Empress of Britain's *passengers taking refreshment on the promenade deck.* (CP Rail Corporate Archive/Gordon Turner collection)

ed a bold impact that was, to say the least, stimulating and undoubtedly quite modern. This can now be seen as an early forerunner of the type of themed interiors now to be experienced throughout the Carnival Cruises fleet and to varying degrees aboard other modern cruise vessels, especially those serving the American-based market.

Forward of the Mayfair Lounge the spacious main deck lobby and the wide galleries at either side of the two foremost funnel casings were decorated in an essentially modern art style using various blonde woods and light colours. This was created as an open-plan multi-functional space where people could gather, read, write letters or simply relax. The Empress Room forward, which served both as the ballroom and cinema, was a place of timeless hotelier elegance, decorated in soft hues of coral pink, blue pink and silver, with a deep blue dome resembling a starlit night sky above its polished Australian-oak parquet dance floor.

Among *Empress of Britain*'s most charming and whimsical interiors was the W. Heath Robinson-decorated Knickerbocker Bar. Well known at the time throughout the English-speaking world for his cartoons depicting outlandish scientific inventions rigged up with pulleys, plumbing fixtures, plungers, levers and bellows all held together with string (and usually worked by creatures running on treadmills or riding bicycles with the help of the odd bird or egg-laying chicken), the work inspired the expression 'Heath Robinson contraption' for just about anything newfangled, complicated or over engineered. He was commissioned to paint a series of decorative sycamore wall and ceiling panels for the room illustrating his impression of the history of the cocktail. Heath Robinson also designed the novel clock above the bar, which rather than using conventional hands displayed the time from a small opening in the circular casing revealing the edges of two concentric disks turning behind its solid front – indeed a real Heath Robinson contraption with a purpose. Essentially an American-style sit-up or stand-up bar, the Knickerbocker Bar was a popular spot, especially among the ship's male passengers.

As became of so many remarkable and popular ships of this era, *Empress of Britain* had a tragically short career. She ended up a casualty of World War II when bombed and set ablaze 75 miles from the Aran Islands on 26 October 1940 while serving as a troop ship. After the war, *Empress of Japan*, by then renamed *Empress of Scotland*, was extensively refitted and modernized for North Atlantic service. She remained in the Canadian Pacific fleet until 1958, when she was sold to Hamburg Atlantic Line, the forerunner of Deutsche Atlantik Line, when she was once again substantially modernized for the Cuxhaven–New York route, becoming *Hanseatic*. After a serious engine-room fire broke out at her New York pier on 7 September 1966, the 36-year-old was

P&O Strathmore. Left: *detail arrangement of C-deck single-berth cabins with bathrooms attached.* **Right:** *detail arrangement of vice-regal suite and alternative arrangements when converted to cabins de luxe.* (Author's collection)

found to be damaged beyond the point of repair, and after being towed to Hamburg was finally sold for scrap.

P&O's *Strathnaver* and Orient Line's *Orion* emerged as two highly successful trend-setting modern British ships of the 1930s. Both were designed for tropical service, and for the much longer voyages operated by these lines to India, the Far East, Australia and New Zealand. These differed from their North Atlantic counterparts in that their accommodation provided for a more relaxed and informal passenger lifestyle than was customary on the North Atlantic. They served what were then still considered to be 'colonial trades', with greater numbers of their First-Class passengers being government officials, military officers, functionaries of the civil services and business people. Those of British nationality were usually employed on long-term contracts with a period of leave, providing them and their families with round-trip fares to spend four to six months on holiday at home in Britain every three or four years. This in itself made up a substantial part of the premium-fare passenger trade, bringing as well an especially congenial atmosphere to these long tropical passages.

Strathnaver immediately presented a crisp, modern appearance when delivered by Vickers Armstrong of Barrow-in-Furness in 1931, in P&O's new colour scheme of light buff funnels and masts and a white hull. Prior to this, P&O's livery was black hull and light pebble-grey superstructure, with the notable exceptions only of the *Caledonia* delivered in 1894 with her hull painted white, as was the Aden–Bombay ship *Salsette* between 1908 and 1917. The Union Steam Ship Company's *Briton* of 1897 was one of the

few other large liners built with a white hull, apart from several smaller state, private and cruise yachts, including HAPAG's *Prinzessin Victoria Luise* of 1899. When Norddeutscher Lloyd's *Deutschland* was converted for cruise service in 1910–11, she re-emerged in cruising white as *Victoria Luise*. So long as ships were coal-fired and there was the messy ordeal of manual bunkering, black was the only hull colour that would maintain a clean appearance without constant cleaning and painting. Without the problems of upkeep, however, there was the advantage of white's light-reflective qualities to potentially lower a ship's inside temperature by as much as five degrees Fahrenheit (about 2.8 degrees Celsius).

Despite the rather angular lines of her superstructure and her three large traditional steamer funnels, *Strathnaver*'s light and cool appearance set a new and lasting trend in the appearance of tropical liners and cruise ships. She was joined in service the following year by her identical sister *Strathaird*, and in 1936–37 by the slightly larger and decidedly more streamlined *Strathmore*, *Stratheden* and *Strathallan*. The latter three *Straths* set the exterior style that became a veritable hallmark of P&O's liner fleet until the time of *Oriana* and *Canberra* in the early 1960s.

At slightly more than 22,000 tons each, the 20-knot *Strathnaver* and *Strathaird* were a further development of P&O's first turbo-electric ship *Viceroy of India* delivered by Vickers Armstrong in 1929. The first two *Straths* were similarly engined, following on *Viceroy of India*'s success as a remarkably quiet-running ship, although the later three liners reverted to geared turbine propulsion. While the public rooms aboard all five ships generally followed the traditional English colonial styling of *Viceroy of India*, considerable advances were made in standardized cabin planning, particularly in the later *Strathmore, Stratheden* and *Strathallan*.

The First-Class cabins were laid out on a simple and straight-forward plan, with large rectangular rooms directly accessed from the two fore-and-aft passages on C and D decks. As these ships catered to a large number of passengers travelling alone, the shallower deckhouse width inboard of the sheltered lower promenade on C deck was occupied by luxury single-berth cabins of a standard plan, each with its own private bathroom and with connecting doors in order to be combined in pairs for double occupancy. The larger twin-bedded cabins below these were likewise arranged on a fairly standard hotel-style plan, with the individual bathrooms forming a sound barrier between the room proper and the corridor at its inner side. The two vice regal suites on each ship were arranged as a reception room inboard of the suite's own private veranda, with provision for it to be joined with an adjacent pair of standard double cabins as required. The reception room could be furnished on request as a sitting room, dining room or, if need be, as an additional cabin. Since this also had its own bathroom, it could be booked along with its own veranda as an individual deluxe cabin.

From the standpoint of her general physical characteristics and overall layout, Orient Line's *Orion* was essentially an adaptation of the *Strathmore* concept. Orient likewise changed their livery, adopting the distinctive corn-coloured hull tried experimentally a year earlier with *Orama* and retained until *Oriana* was delivered as the line's last liner in 1960. However, it was the ship's stunningly modern open-plan interiors that created the greatest sensation when she made her maiden voyage to Australia in 1935.

Much of the credit for this is due to Colin Anderson, himself at the time a young and energetic director in the family-owned Anderson Greene and Company, managers of the Orient Line. This family's connection with P&O was made in 1934 when Donald Anderson (1906–73) transferred to P&O, later becoming its chairman and accepting a knighthood.

Colin Anderson meanwhile was sympathetic to the causes of new thinking in the shipping industry. He was given the opportunity to develop some of his ideas in *Orion*'s planning and to appoint a like-minded professional architect to design the passenger accommodation. His choice of Brian O'Rorke, a young New Zealander working in London with a diverse portfolio of architectural achievements already to his credit, proved to be ideal in that both men approached the project with the same values and similar dedication to the detail. O'Rorke also had the good fortune to be involved in the planning at an early enough stage to also influence the structural design of the spaces he would design and decorate, and to also be given the latitude to have some influence over the ship's exterior appearance.

The First-Class public areas on the promenade deck were arranged as a series of open-plan spaces that flowed seamlessly together without interruption. The main stairway rose directly into the aft end of the lounge, from where a wide U-shaped gallery extended aft around the funnel casing into an open-plan library and writing room to the ballroom, astern of which there was a café overlooking the long expanse of after-decks, with the swimming pool and its own adjoining tavern on the deck below. The ballroom, or 'dancing space' as originally named, was designed to also open outwards directly onto the promenade deck at either side by way of glass panels that could be swung up on to the deckhead above,

Left: *Orient Line's* Orion *of 1935; port view under way.* (Author's collection)

Right: Orion's *main lounge, clearly showing the elegant functionality of its spaciousness, clean-lined structural forms and extensive open planning.* (Author's collection)

Below: Orion, *docked at Tilbury in May 1963 at the end of her final crossing from Australia.* (CPL)

effectively blending the inside and outer domains.

While air-conditioning was installed in *Orion*'s First-Class dining room four decks lower down, as well as a select few of her First-Class suites, people in the 1930s were still more accustomed to acclimatizing themselves to their surroundings. Dancing has always been a particularly favoured pastime among British passengers, with its enjoyment on deck during a tropical voyage or cruise being especially romanticized. *Orion*'s ballroom could be either outdoors or indoors, depending on the climate, and was also suitable for a great variety of other daytime activities, either as deck space or a well-lit and airy enclosed room. Wherever possible, other rooms were given direct access to the decks, whose function was retained as a traditional shade veranda surrounding the public rooms. The entire plan in effect offered far more flexibility and functionality than its open planning might have at first suggested. Despite the lack of walls and other barriers, there was enough space between its various areas that passengers enjoying activities in one would not disturb those in another. The smoking room's designation as a café, augmented by the pool tavern directly beneath it, retained the essence of the traditional smoking room, but without being an exclusive male preserve.

The decoration of the public spaces and accommodation was elegant in its practical simplicity. O'Rorke avoided the temptation to get caught up in notions of streamlining or excesses of artiness or fancy. He realized that while streamlining is important to the design of aircraft and trains, at sea its only appropriate place is in the hull form below the waterline. Likewise, he avoided the pitfalls of trying to do any sort of nautical theme by using horizontal railings, circular ports and other marine forms inside the interiors. The idea was to retain the real feeling of the ship rather than trying to make an imitation of what was already there. He used durable, high-quality plywoods rather than exotic veneers and even allowed the white-painted metal of the superstructure itself to come into spaces such as the indoor/outdoor ballroom. Wall and ceiling finishes were matte wherever possible to diffuse and soften the glare from those omnipresent tropical seas beyond the deck rails. Yet his schemes also provided an abundance of colour and charm through the carpeting, soft furnishings and some of the purely decorative elements.

Great care was also taken with the design of *Orion*'s cabins, which was also an area of particular interest to Colin Anderson. Detailed surveys were made of the accommodation aboard existing Orient Line ships, and passengers and crew were asked for their opinions on the cabins and were encouraged to make suggestions of things they would like to be included in the new ship's facilities. It was found that what passengers really wanted was a sense of privacy and spaciousness in comfortable rooms with attentive though unobtrusive service. The crew want-

ed serviceable rooms that would be easy to clean and maintain, while the owners were keen to make the best possible use of space to accommodate as many passengers as possible without compromise to their standard of service.

O'Rorke succeeded in satisfying virtually all of these requirements with a compact, standardized plan featuring interlocking L-shape rooms designed to offer the maximum number of outer cabins with their own portholes or windows. These were furnished with standardized built-in fitments, scaled to the proportions of the rooms themselves and specifically dimensioned to accommodate the items of clothing and other personal belongings passengers were most likely to bring with them. The vanity mirrors above the dressing/writing tables were designed to conceal built-in shelves behind them for cosmetic bottles and other toiletry items. The rooms themselves were finished in light colours with modern decorative carpets and soft furnishings to increase their sense of spaciousness and coolness in the tropics.

While these were less artistically expressive than the lounges and dining rooms aboard *Ile de France* and *Kungsholm*, their character came much closer to realizing the ideas of rationalism and functionality

Below: Orion's *starboard-side gallery, looking forward towards the main lounge, showing here how the clarity of its architecture is compromised by a bewildering array of carpet and upholstery patterns.* (Author's collection)

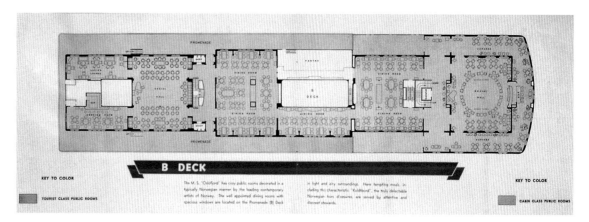

promoted by many participants of the 1925 Exposition Internationale des Arts Décoratifs. What Colin Anderson and Brian O'Rorke had achieved was genuine contemporary shipboard architecture in its own right rather than an ocean-going adaptation of hotel design, created also without recourse to the changing modes of style and fashion. A similarly contemporary approach, albeit rendered on a prodigious scale and the rather more luxurious interpretation of the characteristic French 'grande gesture', was at the same time being created for North Atlantic service aboard CGT's *Normandie* as discussed in the next chapter. *Orion* herself remained in Orient Line service, as a troopship through World War II, and again in passenger service until 1963, when after being sold and serving as a hotel ship in Hamburg for three months, she was finally broken up in Belgium.

Orion set the standard for all further Orient Line passenger ships, with O'Rorke himself being retained as the line's veritable house architect, and with many other lines adopting similarly modern and functional design. Tropical liners offered special design opportunities in that many served on longer routes demanding a greater variety of passenger amenities. These included the emerging trend towards on-deck swimming pools, Lidos and adjoining café, as well as other possibilities to vary the plan with dining rooms located on the upper decks and a greater degree of open planning than was then normally appropriate on the North Atlantic.

The Genoese designer Gustavo Pulitzer (1887–1967) created a stunning contemporary Italian style of architecture through both his work ashore and his extensive oeuvre in the shipping field. One of his first significant works was the Lloyd Triestino express motor liner *Victoria* of 1931, where his treatment of her interiors blended the divergent worlds of naval architecture and interior design without concealing the passenger's impression of the ship behind the image of a hotel. The materials, forms, colours and textures of the interior were brought together to set an aesthetic awareness of the unique beauties of the hull form and of the superstructure, funnels, ventilator cowls and other technical fittings the passengers would see around the ship. This was done with-

out necessarily copying these things inside, and creating a ship inside a ship, but rather adapting their characteristics to the functional realities to create an interior milieu of comfortable and livable elegance in its own right.

Pulitzer's greatest triumph of the 1930s was the extensive scheme of First- and Cabin-Class public interiors for Italia's prestigious and much-admired *Conte di Savoia*. As one of the period's most outstanding expressions of modernity, she was designed with a similar integration of technique and art. This was devised to give the enchantment of a luxury sailing journey aboard a great ship, rather than merely quick passage inside an ocean-going grand hotel. Yet Pulitzer resisted any temptation to fashion this along the lines of Le Corbusier's ideals of 'machines for living', or to restrict himself to the idea of modern interiors for modern people. The variety of architecture and art on *Conte di Savoia* recognized the great diversity of her passengers themselves, their individual tastes and preferences. Within the 'ship conscious' overall context of his work, individual public spaces ranged from the quiet modernity of the First-Class dining room, the sophisticated Genoese club atmosphere of the smoking room bar or the classic Italianate main lounge.

Among the most outstanding ships of this period was Holland America's 36,287-ton *Nieuw Amsterdam* completed by Rotterdamsche Droogdok Mij. NV in 1938. At the time the greatest ship to be built in the Netherlands, and also the world's largest twin-screw liner, *Nieuw Amsterdam* is still regarded by many to be one of the most beautiful examples ever of timelessly classic modern shipbuilding, both inside and out. Externally, she presented a perfect visual balance of hull, superstructure and funnels, classic lines of hull form and deck sheer and a radial superstructure front that appeared appropriately shipshape, without being too expressive of the trend towards exaggerated streamlining.

The interiors were designed by a number of leading modernist Dutch architects, including Hendrik T. Wijdenweld, whose greatest triumph aboard *Nieuw Amsterdam* was the First-Class Grand Hall, and J. J. P. Oud, responsible for most of the Tourist-Class public rooms. The general theme adopted by these lead architects, and the many designers and artisans who worked with them, was based on developing a straightforward and functional contemporary atmosphere of liveable comfort and elegance within the relatively compact confines of an ocean-going vessel. The role of decorative art was integral to the architecture so that one would support the other, without either trying to impress or dazzle the passenger with its own creative flights of fancy. Rather than being an end unto itself or exhibition pieces merely to be observed for a few moments and then forgotten about, or worse still disliked and avoided, the art elements were part of the whole, contributing to asserting and sustaining the passenger's overall impression of the ship and his or her experience of it throughout the voyage.

Nieuw Amsterdam's architectural and artistic themes were carried throughout the First- and Cabin-Class public areas and cabins, as well as being extended into Third Class, with but minimal compromise of their richness and quality. Like *Gripsholm* and *Kungsholm*, *Nieuw Amsterdam* was planned for alternative cruise service with her accommodation classes largely combined. Apart from serving as an Allied-forces troop ship during World War II, she remained in Holland America service, modernized and updated as needed, until the end of 1973, when she was finally withdrawn from service and broken up. Throughout the 1950s and 1960s *Nieuw Amsterdam* had developed a loyal clientele, both for her voyages and cruises. Her double-height Grand Hall, elite Ritz-Carlton Café and the elegant adjoining First- and Cabin-Class dining rooms with their high-vaulted ceilings retained their original lustre and great favour with the ship's passengers until the end of their love affair with 'the darling of the Dutch' as she was known colloquially.

Norwegian America Line's *Oslofjord* featured a similar contemporary style of architecture and decoration. This ship also had the distinctive feature of both her First- and Cabin-Class dining rooms being located on the promenade deck, separating the remaining lounges and other public facilities forward and aft. Catering was by way of a large pantry on the port side of the ship, itself served from a galley on the deck beneath. Rather than merely being lined with deckchairs, the enclosed deck surrounding the First-Class main lounge forward was fitted out as an attractive veranda lounge, serving more as an indoor space than merely an enclosed outer deck. This became a standard feature of all later Norwegian America ships as the Garden Lounge, until enclosed promenades eventually gave way to full-width public rooms aboard Scandinavian liners of the 1960s.

Unfortunately, *Oslofjord* was little-known as she, like a number of other significant ships completed in the late 1930s, was ultimately to fall victim to the carnage of World War II. Among the most tragic of

these losses was that of Swedish American Line's second *Stockholm*. After first falling victim to fire at the late stages of her fitting-out in 1938, this hapless ship was rebuilt for neutral Sweden in 1942, only to be entrapped by wartime activity in the Mediterranean, sold to Italian owners for conversion as a troopship and finally bombed at her fitting out berth. Had she seen commercial service, *Stockholm* would no doubt have been a great success, with her modern décor, axial public-rooms layout and remarkably straightforward centre-passage cabin plan. Attractive as they were, none of the post-war Swedish American Line liners ever repeated these most outstanding features nor the decorative artistry of the beautiful *Stockholm*.

While the gathering storms of World War II were setting the scene for much of Europe to be laid to waste and for the world's great passenger liner fleets to be culled yet a second time, there was a highly publicized event in 1927 that nonetheless went largely unnoticed in shipping circles, but would ultimately have an even greater influence on the future of world-wide passenger travel. On 20–21 May 1927 a shy young American pilot named Charles F. Lindbergh flew his single-engined plane *Spirit of St Louis* from New York to le Bourget airport in Paris. Although there had been several earlier solo and non-stop flights, this was the one that caught the newspaper headlines, and has continued to fire the public imagination ever since. Who would have believed that small and frail flying machines such as these could change the world, any more than anyone in *Sirius*'s day would have thought that ships propelled by machinery would carry 60 million people from Europe and Russia to new homes and lives around the globe. In 1927 the world's largest, fastest and most prestigious ships of the liner era were yet to be put into service. ●

Below: *NYK Line's* **Yawata Maru***: promenade deck view.* (Author's collection)

HAMBURG-AMERIKA LINIE

DEUTSCHLAND

NEW YORK

HAMBURG

ALBERT BALLIN

KOEKE

NACH NEW YORK

CA. **8 TAGE** „
AB HAMBURG

CA. **7 TAGE** „
AB KANALHÄFEN

5

LINERS OF SPEED AND NATIONHOOD

As the size, power and enormous prestige of the world's liners continued to grow, they began increasingly to assume the character of ocean-going city states, covering a complete cross-section of modern human civilization, in all walks of life and taking in virtually every human need from birth to death. As such, they began to take on something of an ambassadorial and diplomatic status representing the countries that built and operated them. In those days, when the ship was built in the nation of its registry and home port, and operated and crewed by nationals of the same country, passenger shipping tended to portray a far greater national identity than it does today, with ships constructed half way around the world, owned by an offshore holding company and staffed by people of 50 different nationalities.

National governments had long backed the growth of ocean shipping through postal contracts and subsidies granted to the steamship companies, as well as policies and incentives aimed at patronizing the shipbuilding and related industries of the homeland, and were generally keen on the phenomenon of national flagships. These could showcase the engineering achievements, architectural and industrial design, fashion, cuisine and hospitality, art and culture of their nationalities overseas with the potential of stimulating trade, tourism and cultural exchange. They could also make other significant statements of national progress, development and even government policy or ideology to the world at large.

Yet government influence of the industry has usually remained somewhat removed, providing subsidies and loan guarantees towards only the greatest shipbuildings developments of national significance. In Great Britain, Germany and Italy the mergers of rival shipping lines were required as a condition of financial assistance granted for the building of major liners during the Great Depression in the early 1930s. The governments of France and Italy did in fact assume partial ownership of lines that in effect became national flag carriers. Only the Soviet Union had a nationalized overseas passenger-shipping service marine, organized somewhat later under a group of regionalized state-run companies.

While Great Britain had long been shipbuilder to the entire world, the governments of France and Germany had taken various steps in the mid-19th-century to stimulate the growth of shipbuilding as part of their own programmes of industrialization. As an industrial leader in the New World, the United States had already built up a substantial shipbuilding industry to meet the needs of the nation's own domestic and coastal shipping services, as well as its deep-sea services to Europe, the Pacific and Far East, the West Indies and South America. The momentum of merchant shipping progress was lost with the outbreak of World War I, as the immediate needs of naval construction were met with any means available. The urgent need to replace lost tonnage afterwards was a burden the industry had to meet against shortages of materials and labour.

Opposite: *Poster from 1930 by Henning Koeke for the Hamburg-Amerika Line.* (Corbis)

BREMEN AND EUROPA SET THE PACE

Bremen and *Europa* were built during the difficult period of post-war recovery, under the burden of crushing war reparations imposed by the Treaty of Versailles. They were symbols of national pride and determination to catapult Germany once again to the forefront of the shipping world. To compensate the Allied Powers for their wartime shipping losses, Germany was forced to hand over all merchant vessels of greater than 1,500 tons, along with half of those between 1,000 and 1,500 tons, and a quarter of the smaller fishing craft.

Only *Hindenburg* remained in German hands, since the ship was at such an early stage of construction that she could be excluded through a technicality. With little more than her double bottom assembled and none of the hull frames erected at the outbreak of hostilities in 1914, she was effectively disqualified as being a vessel at all. She and her sister ship, which had become White Star's *Homeric*, were planned as very much larger follow-ups to Norddeutscher Lloyd's very successful *George Washington*.

Hindenburg was given her forfeited sister's original name *Columbus*, and was in due course completed to her original overall specifications. With the inevitable delays and shortages of materials in the immediate post-war period, it was only in November 1923 that she began her maiden voyage. During the five-year period of the ship's completion, the owners had time to modify her outfitting in response to the changing needs and expectations of a new post-war clientele. The emergence of a more affluent North American lifestyle and of Tourist-Class holiday travel were carefully assessed for future ship designs beyond *Columbus*.

As explained by Norddeutscher Lloyd's technical director, Paul Biedermann (1876–1955), the Americans had established the standards for First-Class travel and hence for the new liners that they would travel aboard. Priority also had to be given to the standard of comfort in the Second and Tourist Classes, with the possibility of combining these for off-season cruising. He also stressed that the entire arrangement of cabins in these classes be assembled together into a suitable accommodation block above the bulkhead deck in a similar manner to that of the First Class on the decks above. Through appropriate planning of the ships it would be possible to provide

1929
BREMEN
EUROPA
Die kommenden
GROSSBAUTEN
des
Norddeutschen Lloyd Bremen

Above: *A starboard bow quarter view of Norddeutscher Lloyd's Bremen.* (Author's collection)

these classes with the run of much of the bulkhead deck's length and with a greater number of well-planned and attractively outfitted cabins in the more comfortable centre part of the vessel. A larger number of these could be at the ship's side, with natural light and ventilation, and a greater emphasis placed on two- rather than four-or-more berth cabins. Indeed much of this accommodation could be of sufficiently high quality as to be interchangeable with First Class.[1]

Plans were at first made in 1926 for a single larger and faster sistership to run with *Columbus*. However, Norddeutscher Lloyd's then general director Ernst Glässel, who was an avid expansionist, wanted instead a pair of new express liners capable of making 27 knots, which would reinstate the pre-war Tuesday sailings from both Bremerhaven and New York. Accordingly, the proposed design was reshaped. The final dimensions of the new ships only emerged after further calculations and model tank-testing were carried out by the line's technical department. Plans also called for *Columbus* to be re-engined and modernized to keep up with her new sisters.

The new German superliners aroused great interest worldwide, as clearly these were being planned as record breakers that would ultimately capture the Atlantic Blue Riband honours from Cunard's venerable 1907-built *Mauretania*. Norddeutscher Lloyd had already made a remarkable comeback, re-establishing itself through a partnership formed in 1920 with the United States Mail Steamship Company using second-hand and chartered tonnage. When their American partner was absorbed in the formation of United States Lines in September 1921, Norddeutscher Lloyd was by then in a position to carry on by itself. By 1926 the line was carrying

about 87 per cent of the number of passengers between New York and Bremen as either White Star or Cunard were on their routes to and from Southampton.[2] Under the regime of the Weimar Republic, which governed the country from 1919 until the Nazis came to power in the early 1930s, the German nation was once again becoming prosperous. There was extensive rebuilding and industrial development, construction of housing, roads, railways, the opening of airline services and airports as well as a revitalization of the nation's merchant marine.

Finally, on 13 December 1926, simultaneous orders were placed with two German yards for a pair of 46,000-ton superliners at a cost of approximately 65 million Reichmarks each. These would materialize to virtually eclipse *Columbus* and flash past her in a new bid for the Blue Riband. To be named *Bremen* and *Europa*, they were not planned merely as record breakers, to also be the most modern and rationally designed ships the world had yet seen. Perhaps Norddeutscher Lloyd's design department had learned, from the excessive grandeur of *Imperator* and a number of her contemporaries, that modern-day standards of luxury and comfort could be built on functionality. There was an element of irony in the fact that these new ships would compete in trade with the then rather dated floating Grand Hotels which their British and American rivals had seized out of German hands as war reparations. No major shipbuilding was then going on in either nation, since both remained rather over-tonnaged thanks to these acquisitions.

The ships were launched in August 1928 on consecutive days, in what would now be described as a major media event. This was a carefully orchestrated piece of publicity aimed at focusing worldwide attention on the remarkable recovery of the German industrial economy.

On Wednesday, 15 August, *Europa*'s huge hull took to the water shortly after 5:00 pm, at the Blohm & Voss yard in Hamburg, following an address by the American Ambassador to Berlin, Dr Schurmann. The ship was launched by Miss Ines Glässel, daughter of the line's managing director. Among the more than 100,000 people who had assembled for the event were 200 invited reporters representing the world's press. After the launch itself and a round of congratulatory speeches at a reception held in the builder's offices, these special guests were escorted to a hall where all the necessary telephone and telegraph facilities were ready and waiting. Transcripts of the proceedings were expertly prepared on the spot in various languages to help them get their coverage of the great event out to the world as quickly and efficiently as possible.

The next day special trains made their way to Bremen. At the nearby Deutsche Schiffe-und Machinenbau AG's Weser yard, Reichspresident Paul von Hindenburg (1847–1934) bestowed that city's name upon the second ship. In contrast to the mild diplomatic rhetoric of the previous day's launch address, von Hindenburg plainly told his people that the Treaty of Versailles could not crush their faith in Germany's future on the high seas as exemplified by the building of the two great new ships. He asserted that so remarkable a revival was only possible by the concentrated and unified effort of all Germans to win back their land's former position in the world.[3] Following his words *Bremen* slid quietly into the waters of the Weser as if to immediately take up his challenge.

Norddeutscher Lloyd and the builders of both ships were anxious to show off what promised to be the world's fastest and most sophisticated ships. However, they were careful not to share any trade secrets on technical matters. Those among the visitors who were in the know could guess for themselves what the trial speeds and propulsion power might be, given only the overall dimensions, approximate tonnage and the fact that these liners would make the voyage between New York and the English channel in five days, and Bremen in six.

Launchings do however afford a unique view of a ship's hull, her underbody fully exposed to view high overhead on the inclined launchways. Following her ceremonial immersion in seawater she is only ever to be so exposed to technicians and yard workers during periodic drydockings. What visitors could see of *Bremen* and *Europa* were some startling new ideas in hull form and hydrodynamics that would be key to their performance. The smooth curvilinear underwater hull form devoid of bilge keels and with a bulbous shape of the bow forefoot gave credence to claims that these were lines not seen on other ships which had gone before.

Conflicting with the traditional idea that great speeds were to be achieved by an acutely knife-like bow form, the bulb was described as being shaped like the head of a salmon or cod, both of which are notably fast-swimming fish. What had been gleaned from nature here was that the bulb's blunt 'fish head' would push a hole through the water for the hull to follow in, rather than slicing its way forward like the knife-edge entry of earlier ships' bows. The bulb was found to create smoother flow lines along the sides of the hull, as well as improving the ship's overall stability. Now a familiar feature of most modern ship types, the original brainchild was credited to an American, Admiral David Taylor, who had advocated its use by the United States Navy. The American-flag *Malolo*, built by William Kramp & Sons of Philadelphia for Matson Line and appearing on the Pacific in 1927, was one of the first liners to adopt it.

Above, the long sweeping lines of futuristic-looking streamlined superstructures on both ships bore the promise that these were indeed ships of the future. Even in this unfinished state it was clear that they were to present, virtually for the first time, a modern, streamlined profile on the high seas. But why streamline styling?

Formal scientific recognition of streamlining as

Below: *The Matson Line's* Malolo *on her maiden arrival in Honolulu. Albeit notable for the arrangement of her public rooms high above the lifeboats, the full significance of her design by William Francis Gibbs would only become fully manifest in his later role as naval architect for the ultimate Blue Riband liner* United States. (Author's collection)

physical and mathematical phenomena probably originated with the 18th-century work of Daniel Bernoulli (1700–1782) and Leonhard Euler (1707–1783) in hydrostatics and hydraulics. This knowledge subsequently began to be applied in the design of fast sailing clippers during the 19th century. The term 'streamlining' itself did not come in to use until around 1909, when it was borne in to the obscure engineering jargon of aircraft research and development. The 1925 Exposition Internationale des Arts Décoratifs in Paris had promoted the stark cleanliness of streamlined form as a core styling element in the emerging field of domestic industrial design. American consumer goods in particular were being designed with rounded edges and corners, flush surfaces and recessed details such as control knobs, dials, handles and latches. Likewise, the wheels of automobiles and locomotives were recessed and covered within wells contained inside the streamlined body casing.

Streamlining was the 'in thing' of American design influence the world over. If Norddeutscher Lloyd were to follow through with Paul Biedermann's ideas of courting the lucrative American market, then homage at least must be paid to their taste in styling. Whether streamlining of the superstructure and funnels would contribute significantly to performance was not the real issue; this was a matter of image so that *Bremen* and *Europa* presented the right appearance to their prospective clientele.

The traditional rectilinear open-decked steamship superstructure was usurped by the sweeping curves of *Bremen* and *Europa*'s semi-circular fore-structure form and clean-cut, long horizontal lines of the fully glass-enclosed promenades. Where this line of large windows had to be interrupted because of structural elements behind the shell plating or around the expansion joints, the gap was kept as narrow as possible. This minimized the visual impact of all such interruptions, which in turn strengthened the horizontal expression of each ship's lines. The sleek impression of a long and low profile was enhanced by extending the black hull paint up one deck higher than usual. This helped to also diminish the impression of superstructure height and also made the ships appear longer, with a modernistic cut-away look to their foredecks.

Perhaps the strongest impression of modernity was imparted by the funnels, which were to be stepped at a later stage of construction. Instead of tall *Aquitania*-like stacks, each ship could carry a pair of broad low-profile motorship-style funnels, slightly raked in profile and virtually flat-topped. Those of *Bremen* would be streamlined while *Europa*'s builders favoured an elliptical shape. The absence of traditional-style ventilator cowls in favour of fan houses built into the superstructure itself further heightened the strategically important impression of speed and contemporary chic.

Structurally, *Bremen* and *Europa* were near-identical sisterships, both of Paul Biedermann's overall design. However, in many details of construction they differed considerably, each one representing her respective builder's particular design approach. In this regard shipbuilding is a fairly subjective matter in which there are recognized to be several workable solutions to any given issue. The builder is usually free to develop those alternatives best suited to their own way of doing things, so long as it falls within the owner's expectations of the completed ship.

Bremen and *Europa* both represented a significant advancement to geared turbine propulsion from the direct-drive machinery of the *Mauretania*, *Aquitania* and *Imperator* generation. Since the times of their earliest development, turbines were recognized to be inherently most effective at high speeds. To obtain satisfactory results from direct drive marine installations, either the propellers had to be of small diameter, or the turbine diameters had to be increased to reduce their running speeds. Both cases were compromises which were costly both in fuel consumption and the bulkiness of the larger machinery needed. One of the first ocean-going ships to overcome these problems through the use of reduction gearing was

Below: *The* Bremen *alongside in New York, showing the streamlined shape of her bridge and superstructure.* (CPL)

the 5,791-ton cargo ship *Urundi*. Built and engined by Blohm & Voss, she was delivered to the Deutsche Ost-Afrika Linie in 1920. Cunard's *Franconia* and *Ascania* had been constructed with geared-turbine machinery by British yards in 1923 and 1924, while *Malolo* was a notable American example.

The internal plan of both ships adopted a rational further development of the axial layouts first introduced in the HAPAG *Imperator* and *Vaterland*. It also stressed virtually absolute horizontal divisions between communal spaces and sleeping accommodation. This arrangement was thought to be the most effective means to satisfy Paul Biedermann's vision of hotel-standard accommodation aboard ship. The areas allocated to each passenger class were arranged so that its own public rooms were on the uppermost

deck, dining room well below, where greater ceiling heights would be needed. On the four cabin decks between these, a uniformly lower height was acceptable, even preferable, in view of the comparatively small dimensions of the private passenger and crew accommodations. Nearly 40 years later similar thinking was adopted in designing Cunard's *Queen Elizabeth 2*.

The promenade-deck suite of spacious and well-proportioned First-Class public spaces was exceptional. The rauchzimmer or smoking room was forward, an enormous halle, or social hall as the Germans liked to translate it, amidships, followed by the library and writing room opposite one another, and finally, the ballroom aft-most. These were joined by a 22½ft- (6.75m-) wide central thoroughfare

Above: *Norddeutscher Lloyd's* Europa, *later in her career after her funnels were extended. This gave her a more traditional stance (with less soot falling to the decks too), though to some degree this was at the expense of her original sleek image.* (CPL)

Europa.
Top, left: The Winter Garden in the promenade deck's semi-circular forward end.
Top, right: The library, lying across the central axial passage, passing through the wide entrance portal to the right.
Bottom, left: The social hall, remarkable as being a large rectangular space without skylights or glazed domes.
Bottom, right: The ballroom, decorated in contemporary style.
(Author's collection)

measuring some 446ft (135m) in length from the smoking room bar forward to the ballroom bandstand aft. The halle was designed to be the *treffpunkt*, or meeting place, at the hub of shipboard social activity. Furnished with movable easy chairs, settees, tables and standard lamps it could be readily rearranged to suit a variety of occasions, daytime bridge, the afternoon *kaffestunde* (coffee hour) service, evening musical shows and concerts or even special banquets. In that era prior to the professional shipboard entertainment of today, a portable stage had to be assembled for concerts, while the ballroom aft had its own bandstand and permanent parquet dance floor. Directly above the halle on the sun deck, there was spacious high-ceilinged restaurant with its own kitchen, operated as an alternative dining option on an extra-charge basis. Situated well above the lifeboats, with high windows along either side, this provided the exceptional experience of being atop the ship.

Following the original concept of giving priority to the standard of comfort in Second and Tourist Classes, the public areas of these were similarly arranged farther aft on the promenade and A decks with those of Second Class in particular also being given the high-ceilinged luxury of their First-Class counterparts forward. The Second-Class dining room was also notable for its double-height plan, similar in concept to that used in First Class although rendered in a less opulent fashion. These rooms were successful in giving their own clientele a good sensation of the same modern features both ships offered their First-Class passengers. In cruise service these could serve as an extension of the main First-Class rooms, with occupants of the combined Second- and Tourist-Class cabins using the Second-Class dining room.

The axial layout was also extended below to the First-Class accommodation on A and B Decks. Here, the normal two parallel cabin alleyways were augmented by a third corridor following the centreline. This avoided *Imperator*'s complexity of lower-deck layout by providing a central link among the principal stairways with access to the inner cabins. The two outer corridors passed outboard of the divided

uptakes, likewise giving direct passage access to the outer rooms along the full length of the accommodations. The Second- and Tourist-Class accommodation layouts on the two decks below was similar, although slightly less well articulated owing to the greater numbers of cabins and the arrangement of crew quarters along the port side of D deck.

In line with Norddeutscher Lloyd's design policy of providing hotel-standard accommodation aboard their ships, the majority of rooms in First Class were rectangular in shape and all were provided with their own bathrooms. Instead of the wardrobes then usually fitted in ships' cabins, each had a built-in closet in the style of the most up-to-date American hotels. This arrangement of the bathroom, closets and entrance vestibule along the inside wall of each room formed a virtual sound barrier against noise from the corridor. The whole plan followed as nearly an identical layout of staterooms one directly above the other throughout three decks as the ship's overall design would permit. As in a hotel building, this offered the advantage of allowing for vertical rather than horizontal runs for plumbing, ventilation and other services.

The First-Class cabins were standardized to a much greater extent than was usual at that time in ship accommodation of any kind. Most were of nearly identical dimensions and similar layout within a limited number of categories. They were, however, decorated in a variety of modern styles and colour schemes to diminish any impression of mass institutionalism. This rationale, however, seems to have stopped short of the Second- and Third-Class accommodation, where it might have been applied to making the most efficient use of space. Instead, the usual shipboard mix of individual cabin layouts and dead-end alleyways prevailed.

In their choice of architects, Norddeutscher Lloyd stopped short of embracing anything quite so radical as the Bauhaus movement. They opted instead for established contemporary designers with a sense of the hotelier-type approach. The approach recognized the lifestyles of the times, with their dependancy on modern convenience and functionality, while retaining a sense of understated traditional luxury and comfort within a timelessly modern theme. Professor Fritz August Breuhaus (1883–1960) of Dusseldorf was appointed as coordinating architect for *Bremen*, while the majority of passenger accommodation aboard *Europa* was handled by Munich architect Professor Paul Trost (1878–1934).

Both *Bremen* and *Europa* brought forward a refreshing and long overdue break from an international standard of shipboard architecture still dominated by an over-dressed and outmoded Grand Hotel style. Even Trost's successful earlier interiors for *Columbus*, and her smaller 1920s-built fleet mates, *München*, *Stuttgart* and *Berlin*, already seemed dated by comparison. Yet the modern functionality of the

Top: *The* Europa's *Social hall, where a rather more light and bright interior decor served to take full advantage of daylight from the large windows to either side.* (Author's collection)

Middle: *The* Bremen's *sun deck restaurant, designed as a high-ceilinged room well above the lifeboats with an unobstructed view out to sea.*

Bottom: *Interior of the main dining room aboard the* Bremen. (Author's collection)

new German record-breakers was neither cold and austere, nor even mildly expressive of the machine-age eclectic. The forms and materials chosen conveyed an honest, traditional sense of richness and comfort. The inside spaces created an ambience of unostentatious luxury and harmony, which was both impressive and elegant.

Professor Trost's treatment of *Europa*'s interiors showed a slightly more classical touch than that of his counterparts working on her sister ship. For instance, the First-Class halle had a wood-panelled ceiling supported by its two rows of slender cylindrical columns, themselves mounted on pediments and topped with decorative capitals. The room was furnished with high-backed settees and wing-backed club chairs arranged in groups of varying numbers around low tables. Aboard *Bremen*, Breuhaus stressed simpler lines of form, with completely straight, unadorned columns and a modern ceiling treatment with both direct and cornice lighting. Here the furnishings, themselves more substantial, were given a more substantial presence in the room by the addition of tall standard lamps, usually arranged on four rows along its length. Windows here and throughout the majority of public rooms were generally flush with the walls, lacking the decorative frames used in *Europa*. Elsewhere, surprising touches of modernity could be found, such as the display gallery joining the halle with the rooms farther aft which held at least a subtle impression of Bauhaus styling. Professor Karl Wach's design of the indoor swimming pool on G deck showed the greatest impression onboard of the international style, which would later emerge as the Bauhaus legacy, with its uninterrupted flat surfaces, square-section columns and translucent illuminated ceiling.

Bremen had the unusual distinction of being fitted with a swivel-based aircraft-launching catapult, positioned high up above the sun deck restaurant. Its function was to launch a light Heinkel He-12 seaplane to speed 440lbs (200k) of first-class post across the last 600 miles (1000km) of the crossing to its destination, arriving a few hours ahead of the ship's own arrival. This had been tried earlier aboard *Ile de France*, and in reality can have been little more than a fascinating gimmick. A perhaps far more worthwhile, though less spectacular, innovation was that all of *Bremen*'s 26 lifeboats were powered as motorized launches.

Both ships were to have entered service together in a simultaneous bid for the Blue Riband, but *Europa*'s delivery was delayed eight months after she was all but lost to fire while fitting out. Meanwhile, *Bremen* ran her sea trials in the summer of 1929, achieving a top speed of 28.5 knots. Starting her maiden voyage from Bremerhaven to New York on Tuesday, 16 July 1929, the new German ship proved her staying power with a record crossing made at an average speed of 27.83 knots. In New York,

Mauretania's master, Captain S.G.S. McNeil, made the trip by taxi from his ship's berth in the Hudson to the Norddeutscher Lloyd piers in Brooklyn to congratulate Captain Leopold Ziegenbaum for *Bremen*'s victory. The new German liner clinched her lead with a record voyage home at an average of 27.92 knots between New York's Ambrose Channel Light Vessel (ACLV) and Queenstown Eddystone Lighthouse off the coast of Ireland.

Mauretania's engineers tried valiantly to recapture the record, and to the world's delight achieved a remarkable round-trip average of 27.09 knots from the old lady's veteran turbines in August. Weather and sea conditions were not in the Cunard ship's favour, though on her homeward journey *Mauretania* for a short time surpassed *Bremen*'s average, at an incredible 29.76 knots steaming between Plymouth and Cherbourg. From *Bremen*'s streamlined bridge Captain Ziegenbaum returned the courtesy of McNeil's visit to him in New York with a cordial personal message of good wishes and encouragement. In his autobiography, Captain McNeil recalls that *Mauretania*'s passengers, many of whom were devoted regular patrons, eagerly followed the ship's progress. Smoking-room conversation was of turbine revolutions, propeller slippage, quarter seas and headway. The cognoscenti would venture out on to the boat deck, look wisely down at the wake and then up to the funnels to ensure that smoke was issuing from them, turn and wave affably towards the bridge as though to say to *Mauretania* herself 'keep up the good work'. But, alas, some 22 years after *Mauretania*'s own Blue Riband victory over *Kaiser Wilhelm II*, the honours rightfully belonged to a new generation of geared turbine superliners. *Bremen* bettered her performance, while *Europa* set an eastbound record in March 1930, which stood until surpassed by *Bremen* in 1934.

The significance of *Bremen* and *Europa* was far greater even than their speed records. They represented a substantial break with tradition as the most radical development in passenger shipping since *Lusitania* and *Mauretania*. Moreover, their sophisticated hull forms, streamlined superstructures, functional internal layouts and modern passenger amenities were immediately seen by the general public as being up-to-date, in tune with the times and even futuristic. During the four days *Bremen* spent in New York on her maiden voyage, the ship was visited by some 70,000 people, keeping her crew busy the whole time. In those days, ship visits were encouraged as a means of promoting a new liner on the idea that a visitor today would be a passenger tomorrow. Open days would be arranged by the line and their agents to show off a new liner such as *Bremen*.

Both *Bremen* and *Europa* settled into regular service with a minimum of technical and operational start-up difficulties. The funnels proved to be too low, with large amounts of smoke and soot being blown down on to the decks. These were heightened by 16ft (5m) during 1930, much to the chagrin of Ernst Glässel, who particularly admired the original long-and-low profile of the ships. The major operational challenge of making the turnarounds in New York and Bremerhaven in a mere 30 hours, so that the two ships could maintain the weekly schedule, was met without undue difficulty. Later, *Europa* experienced some turbine difficulties for which she was returned to her builders in 1931 and again in 1935.

During their first year of operation the two liners secured an increase in Norddeutscher Lloyd's North Atlantic market share by 17.6 per cent. At the same time, however, the entire shipping industry was hard hit by the New York stockmarket crash of Black Thursday, 24 October 1929, and the ensuing world-wide economic depression. These figures were but fractions of a declining whole. The ships were built without state assistance to the account of their owners, against their calculated success in service. In 1925, the United States Government had, under the Young Plan for compensation of war reparations, agreed to indemnify German shipowners for the loss of their vessels seized in American ports during 1917.[4] Norddeutscher Lloyd's share of this was calculated to be $27.24 million (about 100 million Reichmarks), which was more than enough to guarantee the line's debt for their new ships. By the time the first installment on this was paid in 1930, HAPAG and Norddeutscher Lloyd had joined forces as the HAPAG Lloyd Union as a means of joint survival based on pooling routes and resources, and of equally sharing their profit and losses. Germany could then no longer meet its war reparations debt load, and the compensation plan was scrapped, with its value applied against the nation's debt. Only later would the Third Reich endeavour to revitalize and nationalize the nation's entire merchant marine with a view towards its own objectives of conquest.

IN THE WAKE OF THE TRENDSETTERS

Despite the Great Depression, those of vision and courage looked to the future and to further development of the new standards that had been set by *Bremen* and *Europa*. France, Great Britain, Italy and the United States were all eager to engage in head-to-head competition with the new German record breakers with advanced new tonnage of their own. The visionary American architect and designer, Norman Bel Geddes, himself a strong proponent of streamlining, was inspired by the example of *Bremen* to design a remarkable express liner he claimed to be capable of speeds as high as 50 knots. His ship would be of monocoque construction, combining the hull and superstructure within a single smooth-surfaced shell of both hydrodynamic and aerodynamic shape. Plans of the Bel Geddes ship published in 1932 showed within the futuristic interior an inspired adaptation of

Bremen's axial layout, with a similar plan of the promenade-deck public rooms and of the dining rooms on the decks beneath the cabins.

The concept was perhaps too avant garde for its time, when the world was in the depths of the Great Depression. Had it progressed to the stage of technical development where it could be built and engined, and if business backing could have been found, this might well have materialized as something of a streamlined latter-day *Great Eastern*. Existing propulsion technologies at the time would have been unlikely to have economically produced the performance to justify the great expense of building so large a vessel of such unconventional structural design. Once again, shipowners would look to a more evolutionary approach to creating their own mark in surpassing the performance of the new German superliners. Only a few of the largest and fastest ships built in the following years were to adopt streamlining.

Of the two Italian Blue Riband contenders, only *Conte di Savoia* featured a streamlined superstructure, while *Rex* followed a more traditional rectilinear form. The two ships were originally ordered by separate companies to be operated jointly on the more southerly Atlantic route between the Mediterranean and New York. The venture was backed by the Italian Government which established the Instituto Credito de Italiano to secure financing for major shipbuilding projects such as these. Clearly *Bremen* was the reference ship for these, as they were planned more or less as direct competitors in her own class at around 50,000 tons each. *Rex* was ordered by the Genoa-based Navagazione General Italiana (NGI) from the yards of G. Ansalso, Sestri, Ponente, while Lloyd

Left: *The Princess Gallery interior of the Italian Line's* Conti di Savoia *of 1932 , linking the principal First-Class public rooms as a single wide mirrored thoroughfare along the ship's port side.*
(Author's collection)

Conti di Savoia
Above, left: *enclosed promenade interior with its modern full-height windows and shades that could be lowered against the hot Mediterranean sun.*

Above, right: *Colonna Hall interior, a classic Italianate gem in the midst of the ship's other modern interiors.* (Author's collection)

Sabaudo of Turin booked the *Conte di Savoia* with Cantieri Riuniti dell' Adriatico in Trieste.

While these ships were being built, world economic and shipping conditions worsened, with the annual North Atlantic passenger traffic figures dropping from 1,069,000 in 1929 to as low as 689,000 for the year 1931. Against the possibility of construction of both ships being halted with the loss of national prestige and valuable overseas trade, the Italian Government took action to amalgamate NGI and Lloyd Sabaudo, along with the Cosulich Line, into a single financial and management entity with the Italian state as its majority shareholder. Initially called Italia Flotte Riuniti Cosulich-Lloyd Sabaudo-NGI this was later to be organized as part of the state-owned Italia Società Anonima de Navagazione, more widely known as Italian Line or merely Italia.

Rex was completed and entered service in September 1932, followed by *Conte di Savoia* two

months later. Both ships experienced engine trouble on their maiden voyages, and it was only in August 1933 that *Rex* took her lead over *Bremen*'s westbound record. The new Italian ship's westbound crossing was recorded at an average speed of 28.92 knots between Gibraltar's Tarifa Point and the Ambrose Channel Light Vessel at New York. Unfortunately, *Rex* never recorded an eastbound record, nor despite her streamlined superstructure did the slightly smaller *Conte di Savoia* ever make a record crossing. Her best performance was a 27.5-knot average reached in 1933. Nonetheless, both were otherwise commercially successful and very popular. The streamlined *Conte di Savoia*, with the added modernistic touch of her sides being absolutely flush all the way up to her boat deck without the usual outward projection of the promenade deck, was widely regarded as the loveliest Italian liner of all time.

Both ships were generally of a classic liner layout

with centreline uptake casings and a fairly conventional three-class division among their accommodation and public amenities. They were, however, designed to also make the best possible use of their open decks for the enjoyment of their passengers on the more temperate southerly Atlantic routes to and from the Mediterranean. This was especially well articulated in *Conte di Savoia*, which effectively set the standards for post-World War II developments in dual-purpose and cruise tonnage. The ship featured a large outdoor pool, located high atop the superstructure between the funnels, where the lifeboats provided protection from the lateral forces of the winds, and there was an opening through the deck above to the sky and sunlight. The whole area was given a greater sense of social focus with the inclusion of a lido café aft of the pool and overlooking the long sweep of open decks with their own sports and recreational facilities extending astern down to the aft end of the lounge deck. Here the indoor pool was lifted from its traditional lower-deck location since the days of White Star's *Olympic*, and effectively rendered as an indoor/outdoor space with direct access to the open decks at either side and astern. The feeling of openness and of being in harmony with the world beyond the ship's sides was also enhanced by the use of full-height windows along the length of the enclosed promenade surrounding the First-Class lounges. *Conte di Savoia* was one of the first major liners to use floor-to-ceiling glazing in this way, with the deck rail becoming a part of the window units as a handrail inside each of the nearly-full-height framed glass panels.

The axial layouts of *Bremen* and *Europa* were, however, to be of perhaps the greatest influence in a number of other significant liners built during the 1930s. Among the first of these was CGT subsidiary Compagnie de Navigation Sudatlantique's *l'Atlantique*, whose keel was laid at Chantiers et

Ateliers de Saint-Nazaire Penhoët on 28 November 1928, even before *Bremen* was commissioned. At 40,945 tons, she would be the world's largest and most prestigious passenger vessel in South Atlantic service, built in response to the challenge of Hamburg-Süd's 27,561-ton *Cap Arcona*, delivered by Blohm & Voss as one of the first large German ships to be built after World War I.

On first impression, *l'Atlantique* presented a rather traditional appearance externally, with three classic stovepipe steamship funnels, her lifeboats carried close to the deck under old-fashioned luffing davits and with traditional square-fronted superstructure lines. Yet on seeing her for the first time, many people must have taken a hard second look, wondering what it was that was so different about this massively handsome ship. Another glance at the hull lines, and the narrow white riband painted beneath the D-deck portholes, wold reveal that *l'Atlantique* was constructed somewhat like a building, with her decks running almost entirely flat from end to end, without the traditional lines of sheer curving upwards slightly towards the bow and stern. Although less apparent visually, the decks also lacked the usual side-to-side curvature of camber.

Sheer and camber were a part of traditional shipbuilding originating from the days of sail. Wooden ships were built with their decks curved upwards towards the stem and stern to increase the hull's effective depth towards its ends as an added safety measure against the pitching to which these smaller vessels were subjected. The decks were also cambered as a ready and effective means of perpetual drainage of the spray and seawater that inevitably washed over their gunwales. The aesthetic of sheer remained with the construction of larger steel steamships, long after there was any great practical need for it, while it became common practice for only the exposed upper decks to be cambered, while

Italian Line's **Rex** *of 1932*
Above, left: *dining room, reflecting a complementary style of architecture and similar indirect lighting scheme to the main lounge several decks above.*

Above, right: *ballroom interior, lavishly decorated and comfortably furnished for either daytime relaxation or evening concerts and dancing.* (Author's collection)

Opposite, bottom: Rex
Left: *Great Entrance Hall interior, with its rich dark wood panelling, comfortable furniture and large central reception desk.*
Right: *main hall interior on the promenade deck, providing a spacious hotel-like lobby area for passengers to meet and socialize informally on their way to other gatherings and functions in the nearby lounges.* (Author's collection)

Above: *Port bow view of Compagnie de Navigation Sud Atlantique's* l'Atlantique, *launched in 1931.* (Chantiers de l'Atlantique)

those enclosed within the hull beneath were built flat from side to side.

While the North Atlantic might have still called for a more pronounced expression of the traditional aesthetic as an outward expression of safety and stability, it was thought that the less formal nature of the River Plate service would be more receptive to something this radical. Thus, *l'Atlantique*'s builders decided to minimize the traditional lines of sheer with only a slight turn upwards towards the bow, and absolutely flat to the stern. In reality, one wonders how many of the ordinary people who travelled aboard *l'Atlantique* would have noticed that she was built almost entirely without sheer. Yet, surprisingly, people do seem to have an innate sense of what looks right, even if they have absolutely no idea as to why things are the way they appear.

On board, *l'Atlantique* presented her passengers with a spectacular and fascinating array of public spaces and luxurious sleeping accommodation. These were arranged on a sophisticated axial plan, with widely divided funnel and engine uptakes creating a central thoroughfare of some 16–20ft (5–6m) in width through each of the passenger decks.

Uppermost, on B deck, at the promenade level, the First-Class Grand Salon (main lounge) was located amidships, with the smaller radial plan Salon Ovale forward, with both of these spaces extending upwards through the two decks above. From a small vestibule created as part of the Grand Salon itself, a wide processional staircase descended into the Salle à Manger (dining room) farther aft on C deck, itself extending up through B and A decks above.

The combined effect of these three spaces, the principal First-Class public areas, with their orientation along the centre of the ship, was truly remarkable, providing a cohesiveness of function, yet also a marked separation of each room's own purpose. The Grand Salon and Salle à Manger were both rectangular volumes, extending sheer upwards through the decks above, without mezzanines or even so much as any interruption in the arrangement of their tall windows, whose outlook was divided between two decks outside them. Most remarkable of all was the forward Salon Ovale, with its atmosphere of richness and intrigue imbued through a colonnaded central dance floor, with vast art-deco chandelier above, ten surrounding rosewood-clad pilasters and large elliptical mural-painted extension up through A and boat decks. The intimate darker palette of this room was quite at contrast with the more open, and altogether lighter and brighter expression of the marble and glass milieu of the larger Grand Salon and Salle à Manger. The vestibule surrounding the stairway between the Grand Salon and Salle à Manger was also panelled in dark woods, providing a stronger visual separation of the two spaces.

Other First-Class amenities arranged farther aft on the upper decks included an elaborate complex of children's play rooms and dining room, a lido café and a large swimming pool, enclosed at its sides and open to the sky above. Deftly separated from the main public areas by the dining room and galleys aft-of-amidships, these areas were generally treated as informal daytime areas accessible either from the open promenade deck or by way of stairs from the cabin decks below.

Generally, the architecture of *l'Atlantique*'s public rooms was art deco, though rendered in a less flamboyant and garish style than aboard *Ile de France*. The palette was less vivid, and the greater use made of glass and marble in *l'Atlantique* generally created a quieter expression of understated luxury and elegance. This was achieved by the coordinating architect Albert Besnard, along with Pierre Patout et Messieurs Raguenet et Maillard, responsible for the First-Class interiors, without recourse to any nautical theme in itself, yet remarkably in harmony with the ship's own modernity and the essence and geometry of its structure.

Undoubtedly one of the greatest triumphs of *l'Atlantique*'s design was the straight-forward axial arrangement of her First-Class cabins along the for-

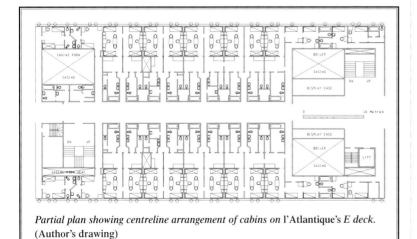

Partial plan showing centreline arrangement of cabins on l'Atlantique's *E deck.* (Author's drawing)

Left: l'Atlantique's *Grand Salon interior, looking forward along the ship's centreline to the Salon Ovale.*
(Archive Chantiers de l'Atlantique/Cliché Ecomusée de Saint-Nazaire)

Below: *The Hall d'Embarquement, looking aft along the centreline.*
(Archive Chantiers de l'Atlantique/Cliché Ecomusée de Saint-Nazaire)

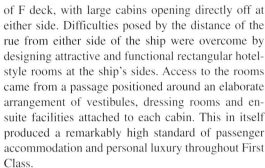

Above: *The chapel, located in one of the corners surrounding the Salon Ovale.* (Archive Chantiers de l'Atlantique/Cliché Ecomusée de Saint-Nazaire)

ward half of C deck and the greater part of D and E decks, where the single central passage was in effect given the status of a wide and attractive rue or street, complete with shops, vitrines and various services. Forward of amidships on E deck the rue widened to about nearly 27¾ft (8.5m), effectively creating a town square at the ship's entrance foyer, with florist and book shops, the purser's office, barber shop and beauty salon, bureau de change and various display cases, one of which was even large enough to display an automobile. At its centre, the town square was extended upwards through the two decks above, forming an atrium and giving these levels their own central visual focal point. The rue itself extended 430ft (130m) along the centres of E deck and below

of F deck, with large cabins opening directly off at either side. Difficulties posed by the distance of the rue from either side of the ship were overcome by designing attractive and functional rectangular hotel-style rooms at the ship's sides. Access to the rooms came from a passage positioned around an elaborate arrangement of vestibules, dressing rooms and en-suite facilities attached to each cabin. This in itself produced a remarkably high standard of passenger accommodation and personal luxury throughout First Class.

After being delivered to her owners in August 1931, *l'Atlantique* commenced her maiden voyage to Buenos Aires on 29 September. She was to share the French postal contract with her smaller 1920-built sister ship *Massilia* until the option for a second vessel of her own class was to be taken up. Owing no doubt to world economic conditions at the time, this was never realized, and nor was *l'Atlantique* herself immediately replaced after being gutted by fire while on her way to Le Havre for drydocking in January 1933. With little more than a year in service, this magnificent ship remained relatively obscure and little known in the experience of worldwide liner travel. Yet the individuality of her layout and magnificence of her architectural design were duly noted by her builders, as well as the parent company of her owners. *l'Atlantique* had set a standard by which both parties were soon to move forward to create one of the greatest and most legendary ocean liners ever built.

Axial planning of this type, with divided uptakes and vertical accesses, were prominent features of later ships such as Holland America's *Nieuw Amsterdam*, Swedish American Line's *Stockholm* and the HAPAG South Atlantic cargo-passenger liner

Left: *Swedish American Line poster from 1932, its style evocative of the modernity of the Line's white-hulled* Kungsholm, *serving both on the North Atlantic and worldwide winter cruising.* (Corbis)

Opposite left: *Salon Ovale, view into* l'Atlantique's *colonnaded central rotunda.*

Opposite right: *Salle à Manger on C Deck looking forward towards the grand processional staircase descending from a vestibule aft of the B Deck Grand Salon.* (Archive Chantiers de l'Atlantique/Cliché Ecomusée de Saint-Nazaire)

Patria. Also noteworthy in this regard were the three American-owned Panama Railway liners, *Panama*, *Ancon* and *Cristobal*, built at the end of the decade for service between New York and Cristobal. Yet the greatest and most sophisticated rendition of the idea was to materialize in France aboard *Normandie*.

THE INCOMPARABLE *NORMANDIE*

On the North Atlantic, France and Britain also lost little time in picking up the Blue Riband challenge of *Bremen* and *Europa*. CGT and Cunard each decided to respond decisively with substantially greater tonnage that would eclipse the new German liners the way they themselves had outclassed *Mauretania* and her contemporaries. Both lines had been considering their options for updating and expanding their fleets from as early as 1927. By the end of the decade, as the new German ships were settling in to their regular service routines, CGT and Cunard both made it known that they were intending to build significantly larger ships. Cunard signed a contract with John Brown & Co Ltd of Clydebank in May 1930 for the ship known then as yard number 534, whose keel was laid on 27 December the same year.

In France, CGT formalized their agreement with Chantiers et Ateliers de Saint-Nazaire Penhoët for their yard number T6, later to be launched as *Normandie*. Detailed studies and design work had been going on since the beginning of 1929, while space was being prepared for construction for what was to become, for a time at least, the world's largest and fastest ship. The building contract was finalized on 29 October 1930, and the first steel sections of the keel laid the following January.

Despite the more buoyant world financial circumstances prevailing as the ship was first planned, and the predictions of her success once in service, the owners found that they too could no longer survive without government support. As the building of this ship was considered to be a matter of national prestige for France, the Chamber of Deputies in Paris agreed on 3 July 1931 to guarantee a loan of 120 million francs to Compagnie Générale Transatlantique, and to assist with further measures to secure the line's long-term future viability.[5] This resulted in two further pieces of legislation being enacted: one to set up the company as a national corporation of combined public and private ownership, and the other to establish a new convention for calculating the postal subsidy to be paid to CGT. Finally, a codicil was added by the National Parliament in 1933 to specifically account for the line's building costs, amortization, interest and taxes for T6. Thus, effectively, CGT became the national flag-carrier and *Normandie* the flagship of the French nation.

T6 was required to perform as a 'five-day ship', departing from Le Havre 2:00 pm on day one, calling at Southampton later in the afternoon, and reaching New York in the morning of day five. A speed of 30 knots would be required to cover the 3,200-mile Atlantic crossing between the two ports with sufficient margin for normal losses of headway due to fog and heavy seas. Once the naval architects and engineers had completed the necessary mathematics, a displacement of approximately 60,000 tons emerged as representing the smallest, slowest and ostensibly most economical size of ship for the job. As detailed planning continued, precise dimensions established and internal volumes calculated, this would eventually translate to a gross registered tonnage of 79,280, as measured on the completed ship. Those in Liverpool and Glasgow working on 534 found that their own arithmetic produced similar results and that they too would need financial assistance, establishing a rivalry between these great French and British projects.

Of these two great ships, *Normandie* was by far the more avant garde in just about every aspect of her design, construction and outfitting. The greatest triumph of *Normandie*'s design was her magnificent hull, the revolutionary form of which was mainly suggested by Vladimir Yourkevitch, a Russian engineer, who had settled in France after leaving his homeland in 1917. Yourkevitch's approach dealt extensively with reducing the surface flank resistance created along the hull's sides at the waterline as the ship is propelled forward. He worked closely with the CGT technical team headed by Paul Romano, and with the Penhoët yard's design department under Fernand Coqueret, to develop a fully integrated solution, covering the complete underwater hydrostatics of the hull and its appendages, as well as the 'wave repellant' forms of the bow decks and bridge fronts and the aerodynamics of the superstructure and funnels.

At the waterline, *Normandie*'s hull was given a

Below: A fine aerial view of French Line's Normandie *at sea.* (Publicity photo, Chantiers de l'Atlantique)

curvilinear shape that would in effect follow as closely as possible the natural surface flow lines of the bow wave as the ship moved forward at speed. This was similar to the aerofoil principle where the lines of air flow over the top of an aircraft wing are kept as close to its surface as possible to create the minimum resistance. Yourkevitch's approach used a fine bow form, with a very small entry angle above the underwater bulbous forefoot to create the narrowest possible wave. This was kept close-in to the side of the hull, with a slightly concave shape aft of the bow, and ahead of the inflection point where the lines widened to the midbody, so the bow wave would splay out away from the ship's flank. There could be no flattening of the waterline form amidships, as a single uninterrupted sweep of line was required to limit the surface turbulence as much as possible so that the runnels of water between the bow wave and side of the ship would be prevented from breaking up and causing further flank resistance. The aft lines could be neither too long nor too short to their close at the stern, where the surface disturbances would wash away aft as wake.

Below the surface, the bulbous forefoot helped to diminish the effects of drag and stabilize the underwater lines of flow, reducing as well the bow wave's height above the surface. The forefoot also compensated for the slender waterline shape by providing an added reserve of buoyancy. Amidships there was a turning inwards, or tumblehome, of the hull's sides, converging very slightly inwards from below the waterline, also adding a compensating margin of buoyancy and vertical stability. Above the waterline, the forebody of *Normandie*'s hull was flared outwards to provide the internal volume required for the accommodation and working spaces, as well as to disperse large waves while navigating in heavy seas. This was given almost a clipper ship form, arched forward and with a distinctly curved bow line. Above, the foredeck was covered by a reinforced steel 'whale-back' shell and breakwater designed to protect the forward mooring machinery and to prevent high waves from breaking over the forward hatches, superstructure and bridge fronts.

Normandie followed the example of *l'Atlantique* in featuring an unusually large and dominant superstructure by the standards of the time. In *Normandie*'s case this extended along 71.5 per cent of the ship's overall length. Its front wall at promenade deck was semi-circular, mainly as a means of throwing off to either side whatever wash might breach the whale-back and breakwater. Above, the boat-deck deckhouse and wheelhouse fronts were similarly radiused, and the bridge wings swept back, presenting a pleasing modern and aerodynamic appearance. These same clean lines of form were repeated astern, where the fully-glassed-in aft ends of the boat, promenade and upper decks formed a graceful series of long terraces descending down to the ship's spoon-shaped, yacht-style stern. While much of this was a matter of carefully thought out modern styling, the funnels were considered to be aerodynamically sensitive. These were given a gentle ten-degree rake and a teardrop shape so as to minimize wind resistance.

Propelling a ship of such unprecedented size at a never-before-sustained maximum speed of 30 knots presented challenges of its own. While geared turbines appeared to be the most logical choice, there was concern as to whether the gearing could be machined in the sizes required without introducing levels of noise and vibration unacceptably high for use in a passenger liner. While direct-drive machinery, as had been used in ships such as *Mauretania* and *Ile de France*, would be quiet enough in operation, the turbine diameters needed for *Normandie*'s performance would be too large and cumbersome even for a vessel of her great size, and diesel was still unproven for such high-performance marine installations. The most satisfactory compromise was ultimately found to be turbo-electric propulsion, as had been used by P&O and was being introduced in Norddeutscher Lloyd's Far Eastern-service ships *Scharnhorst* and *Gneisenau*.

Although the machinery would itself be heavier and bulkier than a comparable geared-turbine installation, the transfer of power between the steam turbine plant and the propellers, being electrical rather than mechanical, allowed a greater degree of flexibility in the machinery layout within the working compartments below *Normandie*'s refined waterline. The four main steam-turbine sets, each directly driving its own electrical generator, could be arranged so as to keep the steam supply lines from the boiler plant as short as possible, with the four propulsion motors each being independently lined up with the propeller shafts, without the need for longer shaft runs. Turbo-electric propulsion also had the advantage of requiring no reverse turbines, as the motors themselves could be electrically switched to run in either direction. The plant as a whole also offered greater operating flexibility for the ship to be run efficiently at lower speeds in winter Atlantic service or cruising.

The ship had a considerable power reserve, even above her 30-knot maximum service speed. The motors were apparently rated to be run in service at a maximum 75 per cent of their full power, calculated to be their point of optimum torque. The turbo-generator sets were also capable of being pushed to a similar maximum overload margin if ever required. Although this was never disclosed to the public, and the official policy was that this reserve of power was never to be used in the ship's first year of service, there is room for speculation that the Blue Riband was to be won at great cost if need be. One noteworthy statistic publicized at the time of *Normandie*'s maiden voyage in 1935 pointed out that the ship's more-than-150-megawatt total generating capacity, including auxil-

Normandie.
Above: *View along the centre axis of the promenade deck, from the upper Hall d'Embarquement through the lounge vestibule to the main lounge beyond the glass doors (the sliding wall between the lounge and smoking room is closed, obstructing the view farther aft to the processional staircase and Café Grill).*

Right: *The Grand Salon, with tables set for afternoon tea, looking forward towards the lounge vestibule and upper Hall d'Embarquement. The Theatre entrance is visible in the far background.*

Above: *Axial view through the Fumoir towards the grand staircase leading up to the Café Grill on the boat deck aft.*

Left: *The Fumoir, prepared for tea time – note the preference for leather upholstery instead of fabric to avoid retaining tobacco odours in the smoking room.*

(All photos: Archive Chantiers de l'Atlantique/Cliché Ecomusée de Saint-Nazaire)

iary and emergency generators, was greater than the 130 megawatts then needed to run the entire Paris Metro system with its 150km of double track.

The all-important aspect of *Normandie*'s passenger accommodation and facilities can be seen as a significant further development of *l'Atlantique*'s planning. A cadre of prominent contemporary French architectural firms was engaged, including MM, Bouwens de Boijen, Expert, Patout and Pacon, among which Patout in particular had worked extensively on *l'Atlantique*'s interiors. *Normandie*'s overall design themes were again a more classic interpretation of art deco, and were more lavishly embellished with specially commissioned works of art. The general artistic theme was created around a historical treatment of the Normandy region of France itself, from the age of the Norsemen to modern times. Extensive use was made of bas reliefs in various metals and other materials, as well as decorative glass work, paintings, sculptures and other pieces in plaster of Paris and marble. Many of the glass items, including the large light standards in several of the public areas, were created by Lalique. At the time this was the greatest artistic programme for a ship's decoration that had ever been mounted.

The new CGT ship also featured an axial plan with divided uptakes and vertical cores, and likewise stressed a spectacular suite of First-Class public rooms of double-height throughout the uppermost decks. The superstructure was specially designed to create a clear 23¾ft (7.2m) height inboard of the enclosed promenades and extending up through the boat deck level, and spanning a clear width of 85ft (26m) without need of internal columns. This extensive openness of plan was kept as far forward as possible so that aft of the engine casings a more traditional structure could be retained as a means of suppressing possible propeller vibration.

One of the key differences from *l'Atlantique*'s plan, however, was that, in lieu of the earlier ship's upper decks dining room location, *Normandie* featured a spectacular triple-height Grande Salle à Manger extending through the centre of the ship four decks lower down. The processional stairway that had been a central focus of *l'Atlantique*'s public rooms was expanded into an even greater terraced feature leading up from the Fumoir (smoking room) on promenade deck up to the Café-Grill restaurant aft on boat deck overlooking the stern of the ship. The ritual dinner-hour grand descent to C deck was given a whole new interpretation by way of the connected upper and lower reaches of the ship's great multi-level Hall d'Embarquement. This offered a choice of sweeping majestically down a series of grand wide stairways arranged on converging U-shaped courses or riding in the comfort of the four spacious lifts.

The main focus of First-Class public life was a magnificent suite of rooms on the promenade deck, arranged along a 30ft- (9m-) wide thoroughfare

extending some 400ft (122m) along the centre axis of the ship. These included the Théâtre, one of the first of its kind at sea, and the domed upper gallery of the Hall d'Embarquement forward, the Grand Salon and Fumoir amidships, and astern of this the grand stairway to the Café-Grill, bringing the sequence up to the boat deck. From the stage of the Théâtre there was a direct line of sight through the entire suite of rooms and out to the open deck beyond the Café-Grill windows. Taking in the additional length of the Café-Grill itself, this was about the same distance as the visual panorama through *Bremen*'s public rooms. The remainder of *Normandie*'s considerably longer promenade deck was taken up with the Jardin d'Hiver (winter garden), library and writing rooms forward and by a block of deluxe veranda cabins aft beneath the Café-Grill, along with the Tourist-Class smoking room and enclosed promenade still farther astern.

As aboard *l'Atlantique*, the principal spaces comprising the Grand Salon and Fumoir, were rectangular, extended up through the decks above and arranged with double-height windows along their sides. Remarkably, The Grand Salon and Fumoir were designed as connected spaces, with a sliding wall between the two rooms allowing them to be joined together for larger social gatherings such as concerts or shows. The moveable wall was also fitted with a pair of double-wicket doors for through access while closed. The traditional function of both rooms was somewhat de-formalized by their location at the centre of the ship's grand axial plan, giving them instead the flexibility to serve as the forum of shipboard social activity, between the more fixed function Café-Grill aft and Théâtre forward, and amidst the daytime street life of the enclosed promenades to either side.

Together the two rooms could be used for special features, such as the ballet performance and fashion show staged during the inaugural festivities and maiden voyage, for ping-pong tournaments and other presentations, shipboard horse racing or dancing. The Grand Salon was provided with a small raised bandstand to the starboard side of the central thoroughfare. These rooms could also be more or less returned to a semblance of their original functions, although with the Fumoir having lost its usual place as an end-room, it could hardly retain its former sanctity as an exclusively male preserve.

Normandie's elegant 380-seat Théâtre offered the first permanent full-production entertainment facilities to be built aboard ship. With its acoustically engineered auditorium and production facilities occupying the full height of the promenade and boat decks, this was equipped with theatrical stage facilities as well as a rear-projection system for showing first-run sound motion pictures. This ocean-going arena would have been the rival, indeed the envy, of many smaller Paris, London or New York theatres or cinemas. In keeping with the informal open planning, the auditorium was separated from the upper Hall d'Embarquement only

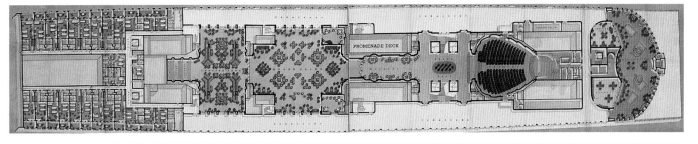

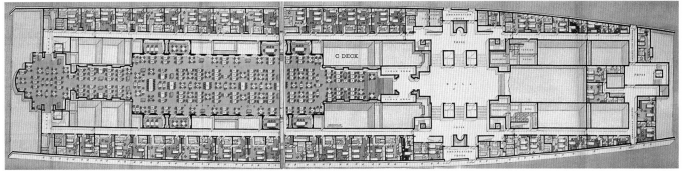

by a gated waist-high railing and full-height blackout curtains that could be used during film shows or to close off the Théàtre during rehearsals. The Hall d'Embarquement and the Grand Salon gallery farther aft served as the theatre lobby and no doubt the lounges themselves as the crush bar. A number of plays and other stage productions were mounted during the ship's career, as well as countless films being shown, establishing *Normandie*'s Théàtre as a valuable reference and prototype for other ships to follow.

The Jardin d'Hiver, library and writing room belonged to a separate outer circuit of daytime-focused spaces. These added to the then still flourishing social milieu of the enclosed promenade, the essence of the city park, with its exotic plants and caged birds, as well as the quiet retreats of places to read, update the diary or catch up with one's writing. Unconventional though it might have been for the library and writing room to be made part of the promenade's outer world, it was in reality an appropriate choice that located the predominantly daytime usage of these rooms away from the activity of the Théàtre, Grand Salon, Fumoir and Café-Grill along the ship's central axis.

Despite the lack of the nightclub life, casino gaming activity and the fitness and wellness facilities of today's cruise ships, social life in First Class aboard *Normandie* was remarkably full and sophisticated, even by present-day standards. It was also eminently more glamorous, with gentlemen requiring a dinner jacket or tuxedo for evening wear at dinner and in the public rooms, and ladies usually presenting themselves in long evening dresses or gowns. Knee-length cocktail frocks, showing silk stockings and high-heeled pumps, were only considered to be appropriate attire if elegant enough without appearing overly risqué. If nothing else, the First-Class dress code was an effective deterrent to

would-be interlopers from the lower decks.

Normandie's magnificent Grande Salle à Manger below on C deck called for, and indeed demanded, this sort of elegance. The vast room itself extended 305ft (93.3m) through the centre of A, B, and C decks at a width of 46ft (14m) and full height of 28ft (8.55m). This was like no other shipboard space ever before created, and few that have been realized since. As an entirely inboard space never reached by daylight, the room's deeply coffered plaster of Paris ceiling and moulded glass-tile walls shimmered eternally in the warm glow of 38 illuminated vertical wall fixtures, 12 tall decorative internally-lit Lalique glass standards and two vast overhead chandeliers. This great hall, along with its adjoining banqueting space and eight private dining rooms could elegantly serve all of *Normandie*'s more than 800 First-Class passengers at a single sitting, and in an atmosphere of luxury more suggestive of being akin to a contemporary ocean-going interpretation of Versailles than of anything appearing even remotely institutional.

Passengers entered the Grande Salle à Manger from the Hall d'Embarquement foyer half way between decks B and C where, upon passing through the great gilded bronze doors of this room's high entrance portal, they descended a wide stairway inside the room itself to be seated. For the ladies in particular, this was an opportunity to indulge in the grand gesture of making a theatrical entrance, to take in the scene from on high and to be seen by others – all part of the ritual of shipboard life. Service in the dining room was from a vast galley below on D deck by way of four double stairways discreetly concealed within the double walls at either side of the room.

Normandie's unique Hall d'Embarquement was a remarkable piece of vertical shipboard architecture for its time. Although hardly an atrium by today's standards, it nonetheless very effectively achieved

Above: *Part of an orthogonal plan showing (top) the* Normandie's *promenade deck, First-Class public rooms and upper Hall d'Embarquement, and (bottom) the First-Class Grande Salle à Manger, and lower Hall d'Embarquement on C deck. Note that the Café Grill was at the head of the ceremonial smoking room stairway (mid left) on the deck above the veranda cabins, and that the two Halls d'Embarquement were also connected by a series of wide stairways in addition to the four large lifts, thus making an elegant alternative processional descent to the dining room.* (©Association French Lines / French Lines Diffusion, Paris).

Normandie.

Above: *View along the centre axis of C deck from the lower Hall d'Embarquement, through the Grande Salle à Manger.*

Right: *Interior of the triple-height Grande Salle à Manger looking forward towards the room's main entrance from the lower Hall d'Embarquement, where the final stage of the descent from the public rooms four decks above was made by way of the steps inside the room.*

(Archive Chantiers de l'Atlantique/Cliché Ecomusée de Saint-Nazaire)

the same focus, access and sense of orientation about the ship, both horizontally and vertically. As already mentioned, the ship's main entrance hall was at a point half way between B and C decks, a half level above the Grande Salle à Manger and the embarkation hatches on C deck, from where it extended up two-and-a-half levels to the ceiling of A deck. This space was visually defined by four large lift towers rising as veritable columns opposite one another, two either side of the foyer floor. At the outer side of these, the foyer was open to all three decks, providing a distinct visual indication of its whereabouts in the long accommodation corridors at these levels. Above, on the upper deck there was a single-height space, serving as the vestibule for the purser's office, and shops, hairdressing and beauty salons were located there. Again, above this was the double-height domed Hall Supérieur on promenade deck with its access to the public rooms, enclosed promenades and other communal First-Class areas.

The four double-sided lifts were arranged with their outward sides opening to the accommodation passages on A, B and C decks, and their inward sides to promenade and upper decks, and the entrance hall for access to the public areas and various other services. This generally created a pattern of people moving through the lift cabins from one side to the other while going between the principal accommodation decks and other parts of the ship.

Additionally the Hall d'Embarquement also featured a series of wide stairways connecting its various levels on a grand processional route from top to bottom. These started at the promenade deck, extending forward along the outer sides of the lift towers, down to upper deck, forward again to A deck, where they turned at right angles, inwards towards the chapel vestibule on B deck, before descending a half level aft to the entrance hall. This created the grand illusion of some great contemporary château or palace where the passenger was guest, rather than the commercial Hyatt Hotel-style animation of today's cruise ship atria. Additional secondary stairways provided convenient connections between A and B decks, as well as to D deck, where the indoor swimming pool was located.

All together the Grande Salle à Manger and Hall d'Embarquement, and chapel and swimming pool, forward on A/B and C/D decks respectively, created an incredible series of totally inboard public spaces extending more than 500ft (150m) through the centre of Normandie's hull. As an offshoot of this plan, the First-Class standard cabins could be arranged along either side of the ship on a hotel plan of predominantly outside rooms with direct corridor access. The large Caen and Rouen suites and other deluxe accommodation were above the Salle à Manger on upper deck, which had a more conventional layout with the greater depth these rooms required. The vast 665sq.ft (200sq.m) Deauville and Trouville suites were above

the Café-Grill, where each had its own open deck space overlooking the stern.

The 24 veranda staterooms aft on promenade deck, each with its own private section of enclosed deck, were especially noteworthy as being a viable prototype for the veranda accommodation to be found aboard many of today's cruise ships. Eighteen of these were designed to accommodate three passengers each in modern American hotel-standard luxury, using two side-by side beds and a convertible sofa-bed as required for a third occupant. The arrangement was that of a comfortable bed-and-sitting room, now widely promoted throughout the cruise industry as an 'open-plan suite'.

All in all, Normandie was a ship of sophisticated and complex layout, of a style never again repeated. Yet little has been written of her Second- and Tourist-Class facilities. Although these were attractive enough in their own right, they were in reality dull and mundane compared with their First-Class counterparts. Normandie's designers were, for one reason or another, unable to achieve the continuity of shipboard experience among passenger classes achieved in Norddeutscher Lloyd's designs for Bremen and Europa.

At 6:40 pm, on Thursday 29 May 1935, following a week of celebrations aboard the ship, Normandie left the port's brand new Gare Maritime on her maiden voyage. She anchored off Southampton at 11:15 pm that evening to embark passengers from Great Britain, before starting her record-breaking Atlantic crossing at 3:07 am the following morning. After passing the Bishop's Rock lighthouse a few hours later at 11:48 am, Normandie reached New York in four days, three hours and 14 minutes, at an average speed of 29.94 knots, passing the Ambrose Channel Light Vessel at 11:02 am on Monday, 3 June. During the voyage, Normandie attained a top speed of 31.37 knots. Following five more days of celebration in New York, Normandie made her homeward voyage, departing at 12:30 pm, Friday 7 June and reaching Le Havre at 7:00 pm, Wednesday 12 June, after making a short call at Plymouth. The ship clinched her Blue Riband standing with an eastbound record at an average of 30.35 knots.

Among those first passengers to experience Normandie were Leonard and Doris Thompson, husband and wife proprietors of the Blackpool Pleasure Beach on Lancashire's Irish Sea coast north of Liverpool. Sixty-seven years after the experience, on the eve of her 100th birthday, the now late Mrs Thompson could still vividly recall the voyage and her impressions of the great French flagship.

Normandie was a magnificent sight, and the experience of approaching her on the water and boarding from the small ferry that had taken us out to meet her was quite remarkable. It was a very glamorous entry into the ship, despite having to ascend the steep gangways hung from *Normandie*'s sides. Once we were inside, we were greeted by the ship's boys lining the grand stairways going up to the lounge. There, the orchestra was playing the Lambeth Walk, which was the latest dance in England. Many on board were unfamiliar with the dance steps, so my husband and I took to the dance floor – we gave them a performance – it was all part of the great excitement of getting aboard *Normandie*. Onboard, the ship was spectacular – everything was very colourful and bright. *Normandie* didn't have the Cunard restraint. As we got out to sea in those lush interiors, though, I couldn't help but think, if I get seasick, looking at these things really won't help.[6]

The Thompsons were seasoned travellers, with Doris's own experience of liners going back to her early childhood, when her father, Blackpool Pleasure Beach founder William Beam, travelled frequently to America from Liverpool on the Cunard and White Star steamers. On the way to Liverpool, Doris and her brothers would make up little rhymes and limericks in their excitement of the occasion, beginning with something like: 'Seeing father safely on a ship, At the start of his trip...'.

As sad as the farewells might have been for little Doris, these occasions also offered the great opportunity to visit and explore the ships her father sailed aboard, including *Mauretania*, *Aquitania* and even one visit to the ill-fated *Lusitania*. Doris developed a keen interest in these great liners, and an avid appreciation for all of their interiors, furnishings and fittings. She would examine each and compare it with the others. Later, Doris travelled often with her parents, and after taking over the operation of the Pleasure Beach following her father's death in 1929, continued sailing with her husband and business partner Leonard Thompson. The experience of *Normandie* was no doubt of great interest to the Thompsons, who at the time were working on a large expansion and modernization of the Pleasure Beach, and were soon to engage the English architect Joseph Emberton to design a number of significant new art deco buildings at Blackpool.

Doris recalled *Normandie* as 'so different and so exciting'. The openness and uncomplicated layout of the ship's vast interiors created an altogether new sensation of the shipboard experience. Yet, despite her grandeur and greatness of scale, *Normandie* was in reality quite informal, with everything arranged along a wide boulevard running through the centre. The atmosphere seemed more alive and animated, as the ship's contemporary openness and abundance of colour and light brought an onboard social ambience of modern urban café life. The French themselves even referred to their *Normandie* as a 'ship of light'. One could more readily see what was going on and either participate or observe. It is these qualities, which are perhaps as much a part of *Normandie*'s

times and social life during the 1930s as they are of the ship herself, that made her the enduring legend she is.

'*Normandy* was spectacular' recalled Mrs Thompson, 'while British ships were neat, tidy and well groomed. They always had a very special warmth and coziness about them, and all of their fittings were so comfortable to use'. The Cunard *Queens*, and *Queen Mary* in particular, were her perennial favourites. Yet her one voyage aboard *Normandie* has always been an especially cherished memory. Seated in the beautifully restored art-deco Chairman's flat at the Pleasure Beach's Emberton-designed circular Casino building, Mrs Thompson succinctly concluded, after the lasting impression *Normandie* made on her, that 'deco is easy to live with'.

Despite *Normandie*'s otherwise stellar performance and claims of her exemplary fuel economy as being equal to that of the smaller and slower *Ile de France*, vibration presented a serious problem throughout her first season. During the winter months of 1935–6 she was returned to Penhoët for remedial work. The original three-bladed propellers were replaced with new four-bladed screws calculated to exert less pressure against the underside of the hull. Various other alterations were made to stiffen the ship's structures, with supporting columns being added in a number of the public rooms. The opportunity was also taken to make a substantial addition to the superstructure aft at the boat deck level. Here a large new Tourist-Class lounge was built aft of the First-Class Café-Grill, atop what had originally been a large expanse of open deck. Apart from adding structural reinforcement, this replaced the original, altogether unsatisfactory arrangement of the tourist lounge being completely enclosed by the First-Class accommodation aft on upper deck. Coincidentally, this addition also increased *Normandie*'s register to 82,799 tons, ensuring that France would still, against the by-then-known tonnage of Cunard's new *Queen Mary*, have the world's largest ship, even if her speed record was to be eclipsed by the British.

As new sea trials were run in early 1936, *Normandie* performed well, without the troublesome vibration. Just before making her first commercial voyage, it was found that she had mysteriously slipped one of her new propellers. In a delicate overnight drydocking operation, two of her original three-bladed propellers were attached to the inside shafts. Unfortunately the vibration returned with them, and *Normandie*'s passengers would have to wait until the following year before these could be replaced and the problem solved once and for all. What was learned from this, however, was that the propellers were the issue rather than Yourkevitch's hull design or the structural advances of *Normandie*'s vast open-plan interiors. If nothing else, she was still bigger than *Queen Mary*.

THE ST. LAWRENCE ROUTE *to* EUROPE

CANADIAN PACIFIC

THE ENDURING QUEEN MARY

While *Normandie*'s launch had been postponed twice, and her completion delayed by more than two years, construction of Cunard's 534 was halted altogether on 11 December 1931. Despite their market leadership position and cautious approach to doing business, even Cunard was unable to escape the economic troubles of the early 1930s. For the next 27 months, the owners, builders and the British Government all tried to find solutions to the eventual fate of 534, tackling various labour disputes with shipyard workers and others, and the national economy. Meanwhile, a herd of dairy cows sleepily grazed in a pasture by the Clyde, against a backdrop of the unfinished hull sitting high-and-dry on the stocks. It was an often photographed scene that aptly depicted the mood of the nation and the state of its affairs in those days.

After spending £1.5 million to build 534, Cunard had found that they no longer had the resources to complete the ship on their own. The Government was at first unwilling to lend assistance to what it viewed as private commercial enterprise. As work progressed across the Channel on *Normandie*, however, completion of the Cunard ship became a matter of national prestige. As lengthy negotiations continued between Cunard and the Treasury, a special committee of inquiry was set up to examine the viability of building new tonnage against falling passenger volumes. It also considered the alternatives of completing the 80,000-ton 534 against building two smaller ships of around 30,000 tons each. By the end of 1933 the committee were in favour of the larger ship, but also, surprisingly, requested a merger of the Cunard and White Star Lines into a new company, effectively creating the Cunard-White Star Line, which came into being on 1 January 1934. The Treasury would loan the new company £3 million for 534's completion and an additional £1.5 million in working capital, with provision for a further £5 million to be made available later if a second ship of 534's class was to be built. On 3 April 1934, those Clydeside cows were awakened to the clamour of shipyard activity as 4,000 men resumed work on the new Cunarder. On a rainy 26 September the ship was launched as *Queen Mary*.

Rather than following the examples of their European rivals, with turbo-electric propulsion, Yourkevitch hull forms or divided funnel uptakes with centre-axis layouts, Cunard chose instead to build on their own proven experience. They sought perfection rather than innovation, emphasizing the finest materials, engineering, structural fabrication and craftsmanship in the finishing trades. They decided not to opt for the additional vistas of open space that could be realized by placing the funnel and engine uptakes either side of their traditional places along the centreline, or the added margin of perform-

Above: Queen Mary's First-Class enclosed promenade, showing the curvature of the ship's sides and the longitudinal lines of sheer. (Gordon Turner collection)
Below: *The Cabin Class swimming pool, located down on D deck.* (CPL)
Opposite: *The* Queen Mary's *incomplete hull on the stocks at John Brown & Co. Ltd., Clydebank.* (CPL)

ance that a new hull form might realize. Instead they chose the 'wow factor' of creating a vast liner in the classic line and form. To quote an overworked advertising cliché, 'the surprise is, there is no surprise'. This would reduce the possibilities of vibration from newfangled hulls or machinery, soot being scattered over the decks from low 'designer' funnels or other difficulties resulting from anything new or less than totally proven. The new ship was thus designed as a significantly larger, faster and substantially modernized rendition of the line's own highly successful and much-loved *Aquitania*.

Cunard realized that they already had what is known in today's cruise industry as a valuable brand identity. This had grown as part of the line's corporate culture and out of Samuel Cunard's own original credo of 'safe, secure and comfortable passage'. The comfort, service and security offered by generations of well-tempered Cunarders, with their 'neat, tidy and well groomed' accommodation, were what brought thousands of loyal regular passengers such as Doris Thompson back to the Cunard and White Star liners again and again. These were British institutions, the daughters of the Clyde, Tyneside and Belfast-Queen's Island where they were built, and of their Empire home ports in Liverpool, London-Tilbury and Southampton. The neo-classic limestone Cunard Building, opened in 1916, still stands above Liverpool's Pier Head promenade, although no longer occupied by the line. It is flanked by the Royal Liver Building and Mersey Docks and Harbour Board, which collectively comprise one of the city's greatest architectural treasures, The Three Graces. Regrettably, the handsome Ocean Terminal built at Southampton to handle *Queen Mary* and *Normandie* (the first 'thousand-footers') was demolished in the early 1980s.

Cunard's cautious and traditional approach to *Queen Mary*'s design and construction certainly had its critics among those who felt that so great a ship needed to make a statement about the industrial and commercial progress of its home nation. Having praised Mewés and Davis's work aboard *Aquitania* in 1914, the architectural press was particularly vehement in its criticism of *Queen Mary*'s planning. They expressed the opinion that Cunard's plans of adopting their own British design leitmotif lacked a perspective of the nation's more contemporary hotel, domestic and commercial architecture. The purists, it seems, were worried that there might be a replication of the ersatz Tudor decoration tried in a recent refit of *Berengaria*'s Tourist-Class public areas. The line was, in effect, accused of pandering to the American fantasy of The Old Curiosity Shop and Ye Olde England. As Cunard was responsible to the Government only for the repayment of its loans, they felt no compelling obligation to patronize British industry nor to promote the latest trends of the architectural profession in any way beyond a fitness of

Above: Queen Mary's *First-Class main lounge interior.* (Gordon Turner collection)
Below: *The Cabin-Class children's play room, including a slide, miniature theatre and aquarium (behind the curved glass window).* (CPL)
Opposite: Queen Mary *on the building slip at John Brown & Co. Ltd., Clydebank.* (CPL)

purpose for the successful commercial operation of their ships.

Queen Mary's interior architecture was coordinated by Arthur Davis, whose office also designed the majority of First-Class interiors. The style was a sort of Cunard contemporary that was itself no more purely rationalist or modern than had Davis's work aboard *Aquitania* been period revivalist. It acknowledged the trends of the time without necessarily following them. The expression was neither art deco in the style of *Ile de France* or *Kungsholm*, nor moderne as *Normandie*, nor even set in the more functional rationale of P&O's *Orion*, completed a year earlier in 1935. The theme endeavoured instead to create the sort of comfortable and luxurious generic hotel ambience that pleases everyone, offends nobody and never tries to be beyond the understanding of its occupants in the same way that made Davis's earlier work for Cunard as successful as it was.

The layout of *Queen Mary*'s passenger accommo-dation, along with the shapes and orientations of the public rooms about the ship were all reassuringly familiar. The plan was in reality quite similar to *Aquitania*, with everything proportionally rendered in the larger scale of the new ship. The dome above the First-Class dining room was larger, extending up into the centre space between the accommodation passages on A and B decks above, and the prome-nade-deck public rooms were extended up through the boat deck as those aboard *Aquitania* had been. There was also a Long Gallery and the usual Cunard pattern of smoking room aft, main lounge amidships and some of the smaller rooms forward. The suite of public rooms aboard *Queen Mary* extended the length of the promenade deck, with the library, writing room, shops and other services surrounding the forward stairway vestibule, and for the first time aboard a Cunard Atlantic liner, a bar and observation lounge forward and overlooking the bow through the enclosed promenade. There was also a grill room aft

on the boat deck, which seems to have been added at a later stage of the ship's planning.

Belonging to no other existing design idiom, *Queen Mary*'s architecture avoided the sort of stylishness that can soon become outdated. In much the same way, *Normandie*'s classic richness of art and decoration would have given her modernity a more enduring quality had the ship herself not been destroyed after scarcely four years in service.

During *Queen Mary*'s construction, Cunard announced that she was to be a Cabin-Class ship, thereby absolving the line from having to apply the First-Class fares prescribed by the North Atlantic Passenger Conference. The Conference was established in the 1880s to set up standard transatlantic routes, as well as to maintain standards of practice. The aim was to thwart the destructive effects of cutthroat competition among its members, in much the same way that the International Air Transport Association (IATA) served the airline industry before

it was deregulated in the 1990s. While First-Class fares were fixed by the Conference, member lines were free to set their own rates for all other classes. Thus Cabin Class became the alternative of choice to First, where competitive pricing could be offered for essentially the same levels of service. The situation had become unworkable for all member companies, and by threatening to resign from the Conference if their classification of *Queen Mary* as a Cabin ship were to be disallowed, Cunard forced the policy of regulating First-Class fares to be dropped altogether.

Cunard chairman Sir Percy Bates had taken a great personal interest in every aspect of *Queen Mary*'s planning and building and gone to great lengths to ensure that every detail would be in order. The author Rudyard Kipling had provided great encouragement and moral support to his great friend Sir Percy throughout the build, and to recognize this, Sir Percy asked Kipling to coin a Latin motto which would be engraved on a medallion being struck for the ship's inauguration. Kipling, who had earlier deferred to John Masefield to write a poem for the ship, submitted his motto, which Bates in his usual cautious fashion passed on to be checked by the Royal Mint's Latin scholars. Sir Percy wrote to Kipling later, telling him that the Mint's learned people had simplified his phrase to 'Maria Regina mari me commisit' (Queen Mary committed me to the sea). In his reply Kipling wrote, 'Do you suppose I was ass enough to try to compose a Latin motto of my own? Tell your Whitehall pundits they'll find it in Horace's Odes.'[7]

A week before the ship sailed on her maiden voyage, London's well-known Trocadero Restaurant was elaborately made-over for five gala dinners to honour the new Cunard flagship. There was a five-deck scale wooden replica of the great new liner's bridge and forward superstructure. There were lifeboats from

Above: Queen Mary's *First-Class Drawing Room interior, essentially a ladies' lounge. The mural panels in the end wall conceal a consecrated sanctuary and altar, converting the room into a Roman Catholic church when needed for Holy Mass.* (Gordon Turner collection)

Left: *Dramatic bow view of the* Queen Mary *in dry dock, taken in 1951.* (CPL)

Left: A view of Queen Mary's *First-Class cocktail bar interior, with its semi-circular forward wall and panoramic windows facing ahead over the bow through the enclosed promenade.* (Gordon Turner collection)

Below: *An idea of the size of the* Queen Mary *can be gauged from the lone figure standing atop the bridge in this photograph of her as she completes fitting out.* (CPL)

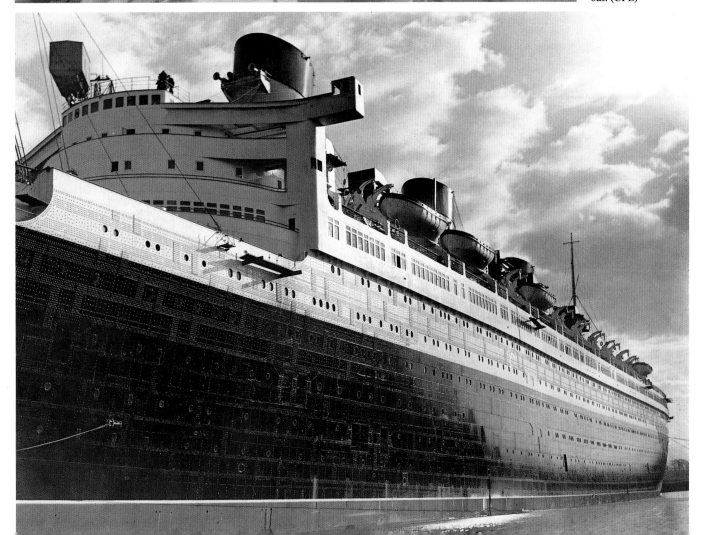

Right: *A humorous setpiece of two* Queen Marys, *the liner dwarfing the 23ft-long sailing boat of Halifax in which Captain Crowell and his dog Togo completed a circumnavigation.* (CPL)

Below: *Port bow quarter view with a Moran tug in the foreground, probably on her final call at New York, dressed all over and flying her paying off pennant.* (Gordon Turner collection)

which the orchestra played and deck chairs provided for the patrons. A hatch was cut in the wall of the building so that guests could 'board' by way of a gangway. Seated at a captain's table in the centre of the restaurant, *Queen Mary*'s master, Commodore Sir Edgar Britten, hosted each of these occasions and personally autographed the souvenir menus for his guests.

Cunard then brought about its next public-relations victories with *Queen Mary*'s Blue Riband record. Commodore Britten was instructed to 'run the engines in' on the maiden voyage and gradually work the new liner up to her maximum performance. On the first crossing to New York from Wednesday 25 May to Monday 1 June, *Queen Mary*'s triple-expansion geared turbine plant yielded an average speed of 29.13 knots without being pushed too hard. The crossing time between Bishop's Rock and the Ambrose light ship was only two hours 32 minutes longer than *Normandie*'s record time. Public interest was sustained as the great ship's performance gradually worked up to record crossings in August of 30.14

Left: Queen Mary's
First-Class dining
room interior,
dominated by an
Atlantic mural map.
(Gordon Turner
collection)

Below: Close-up of
the Atlantic mural
map, with its clock
and the routes on
which the ship's
position at sea was
indicated by a tiny
model. (CPL)

knots westbound and 30.63 knots eastbound. These were the first records above 30 knots, and the eastbound passage was the first to be completed in under four days, at three days, 23 hours and 27 minutes.

On her maiden arrival in New York, *Queen Mary* was enthusiastically greeted by what *The Times* called, 'a herbaceous border of humanity',[8] lining both sides of the Hudson all the way up to the Cunard pier. For five days of her turnaround time in New York the ship was fêted with dinners and banquets both aboard and ashore. At the same time she was practically picked clean of anything removable by the more than 14,000 people who toured her for a dollar a head.

The ship was hailed by a public who were yet to discover the great love affair they would have with her.

After the victory was theirs, Cunard made headlines again by refusing the Hales Trophy for *Queen Mary*'s record performance. This was an unofficial award struck by Harold Hales (1867–1942), the British Member of Parliament for Hanley in the 1930s, for the liner holding the transatlantic speed record. Himself formerly a marine engineer, Hales was keen to promote the cause of technological and commercial advancement in passenger shipping, acknowledging record speed on the North Atlantic as being the ultimate achievement. The trophy had been

Below: Queen Elizabeth *entering the King George V dry dock at Southampton in 1962. A rather posed photograph, it shows the 12-man team needed to handle the heavy ropes for tying up the liner.* (CPL)

America this year by R.M.S. "Queen Mary"

Cunard White Star

Previous page: *A 1930s Cunard White Star Line poster showing the new* Queen Mary *against a somewhat exaggerated impression of the Manhattan skyline.* (Corbis)

Left: *Cunard's* Queen Elizabeth, *steaming down Southampton Water on her way to Cherbourg and then New York, 1 December 1948.* (CPL)

Left: Queen Elizabeth *in
dry dock, Southampton,
January 1952.* (CPL)

Above: *View from the ship's deck showing one of the propellers, removed for annual inspection, May 1952.* (CPL)

Above: *View from beneath the stern, with the unshipped propeller in the foreground.* (CPL)

SHAW SAVILL LINES

DOMINION MONARCH

ENGLAND   SOUTH AFRICA
AUSTRALIA NEW ZEALAND

completed in 1935, acknowledging the Italia liner *Rex* as its first recipient, although it was actually first presented to CGT for *Normandie*'s record of that year. Cunard stated that they 'had taken no part in any competition', and politely refused the prize 'with thanks'.[9] It was part of the line's policy of never racing their ships, and of merely going about its business in the usual way. The prize was duly returned to Hales by CGT, and stored at Eric Pidduck's jewellery shop in Hanley until being enthusiastically accepted by United States Lines in 1952.

As Cunard-White Star Line and CGT had one award-winning liner each, they agreed to jointly maintain the weekly express service to New York with *Normandie* and *Queen Mary* sailing on alternate weeks in both directions. Cunard's *Mauretania* and *Berengaria*, along with the White Star Atlantic liners *Olympic*, *Homeric* and *Majestic* had all been withdrawn from service and scrapped, with the exception of *Majestic*, which served as the training ship HMS *Caledonia* until destroyed by fire in 1939. CGT's *France* of 1912 had been scrapped in 1934, and *Paris* was later to burn and capsize at her Le Havre pier in 1939.

In the longer term both lines were looking to the future, and to the eventual need for each to operate its own weekly transatlantic service. The keel of a second Cunard super-ship, John Brown & Co. Ltd. yard number 552, was laid in December 1936 and launched as *Queen Elizabeth* on 27 September the following year. In May 1939 it was announced by the French Ministry of the Merchant Marine that CGT had been authorized to order a second North Atlantic express liner similar to *Normandie*, for entry in to service in the spring of 1944. Both *Queen Elizabeth* and the new French ship, to be called *Bretagne*, were to be slightly larger consorts to their existing fleet mates, incorporating the latest developments in engineering and passenger service. *Bretagne* was expected to materialize at about 85,000 tons with a speed of around 32 knots, incorporating also a number of design refinements derived from *Normandie*'s service experience.

Other projects included two liners of about 60,000 tons planned for Italia, as well as the first of two 25-knot HAPAG ships for transatlantic service, the 41,000-ton *Vaterland*, whose keel was laid at Blohm & Voss in 1938. Yet this was but a prelude to the 36-to-38-knot *Amerika* being planned by Norddeutscher Lloyd in collaboration with Deschimag A.G. Weser, and with technical assistance from the nation's navy. This remarkably clean-lined modern ship with a single huge funnel was viewed with great interest by the Nazi government, which allowed its planning to proceed as *Viktoria* during World War II in the hope that

the great ship's completion would celebrate their ultimate victory.

Had the outbreak of World War II not intervened, the upward spiral of competition would probably have continued until most of its players had been bankrupted. *Normandie* was to all intents and purposes subsidized by the French government through their partial ownership of CGT and the mail contracts she held, and it is unlikely that as a publically held commercial venture she ever would have been profitable. Projects such as *Bretagne* and *Amerika*/*Viktoria* almost certainly would have been even less viable. Of the large express liners either planned or being built by the close of that most celebrated decade in passenger shipping history, only *Queen Elizabeth* was ultimately to materialize. And it was she that had the best pedigree for commercial success from the outset. ●

6

ALUMINIUM, TRANSITIONS AND THE JET AGE

At the end of World War II, the Cunard *Queens* had proven themselves to be a formidable force in the Allied victory. Winston Churchill estimated that these two great liners alone had probably shortened the war in Europe by at least a year, thanks to their tremendous ability to swiftly, safely and reliably mobilize vast numbers of troops from as far away as Australia, New Zealand, India, Malaya and Africa. Later huge numbers of troops were also mobilized from North America when the United States entered the conflict following the Japanese bombing of Pearl Harbor in December 1941. *Queen Mary* was laid up in New York from the beginning of the War in September 1939 until March 1940, when she was shipped to Sydney via Rio De Janeiro and Cape Town for conversion to a toopship for New Zealand armed forces. After being hurriedly completed for wartime service, *Queen Elizabeth* made a secret dash for New York in March 1940, two months ahead of her originally planned commercial maiden voyage. She remained in the American port until November that year, when she sailed to Singapore to be prepared for trooping before joining *Queen Mary* and *Aquitania*, along with other British and Allied ships, in trooping service.

While approaching her wartime base at Gourock on the Clyde on 2 October 1942, with a full contingent of troops onboard, *Queen Mary* accidentally struck and sank the anti-aircraft cruiser HMS *Curaçoa*, cutting the very-much-smaller naval vessel in half with the loss of 300 lives aboard the warship,

leaving only 72 survivors. The accident occurred as both ships were sailing on zig-zag courses to avoid enemy submarine attack, and HMS *Curaçoa* crossed too close under *Queen Mary*'s bows. Under strict standing orders never to stop his ship and put her valuable human cargo in peril of attack, the huge liner's master proceeded on at full speed as the cruiser's two halves slipped past her flanks, and other escort vessels proceeded to the rescue of her survivors. *Queen Mary* herself suffered only a fractured stem, which was temporarily bunged with concrete and later repaired in drydock at Boston Navy Yard. This was the most serious incident in the entire careers of both *Queens*.

Otherwise there had been only a few relatively minor incidents. There was a stubborn electrical fire in *Queen Mary*'s accommodations during her passage from Rio de Janeiro to Cape Town, and a few close calls, as when *Queen Elizabeth* was attacked by German submarines on 9 November 1942 while outbound to New York. Luckily, the two salvos fired missed their mark, sparing the ship and the lives of her company and the large contingent of civilian women and children on board being evacuated to North America. These and the greater majority of large liners that served along with them owed their survival to their speed.

The Cunard *Queens* alone carried 1.2 million troops and other wartime passengers, including prisoners of war transported to internment camps in Australia early in the war, over a total distance of

Opposite: *Launch of the Orient Line's* **Orcades** *at Vickers Armstrong Ltd's Barrow-in-Furness yard on 14 October 1947. She was first in a class of larger and slightly faster 22-knot postwar ships built for the co-operative services of Orient and P&O on their passenger and mail routes to Australia.* (CPL)

nearly a million nautical miles. From June 1943 until the German surrender in June 1945, the two great liners carried 320,500 of the 865,000 American GIs and other armed-forces personnel landed in Britain for combat duty. Each ship carried up to 15,000 people at a time, about seven times their normal peacetime passenger capacities. This was lowered to around 10,000 during winter North Atlantic crossings to reduce weight and maintain the added safety of increased vertical stability. While some 4,280 Allied merchant ships and another 490 vessels belonging to neutral nations are estimated to have been lost during World War II, the *Queens* carried on relentlessly with time out of service only for the most essential maintenance and overhaul.

The incredibly solid and robust construction of these ships, their machinery and auxiliary equipment allowed them to perform valiantly well beyond the circumstances of the peacetime commercial operations for which they were designed. As *Normandie* was about to be similarly re-fitted for trooping as USS *Lafayette*, concerns were voiced as to whether she had the structural stamina and stability to safely carry similar numbers of troops, likewise berthed en masse in her public rooms, and being exercised and battle-trained on her decks. The French liner had already shown herself prone to rolling stiffly in normal commercial service without additional personnel and equipment aboard. When fire broke out aboard the ship while being converted at New York's Pier 88 in February 1942, her stability was upset by the torrents of water used to extinguish the blaze. She heeled over on to her port side, where the prolonged process of her removal later became one of the epics of marine salvage. During the time Norddeutscher Lloyd's *Europa* was used by the United States as a troopship at the end of the war, it was found that she too was of a lighter construction and that there was some structural fracturing and various electrical problems with the original lead wiring used in her construction.

Of far greater long-term significance than the merchant marine's stellar wartime performance was the development of the polar Great Circle routes

Opposite: Queen **Mary** *in the King George V dry dock at Southampton, March 1947, undergoing repairs from war damage.* (CPL)

Below: *Three months later, workmen are pictured repainting the sides of the liner prior to her return to paying passenger service.* (CPL)

Above: *Cunard Line's 1939-built second* Mauretania *as a troopship, pictured in Australian waters in 1940 while carrying ANZAC troops to the Middle East.* (CPL)

Below: *Port stern quarter aerial view of Holland America Line's* Nieuw Amsterdam *inbound to New York.* (Author's collection)

across the Atlantic and Pacific Oceans, and networks of airports and radio-navigational aids set up in North America. These and the heavy four-engined bombers and transports were destined to form the backbone of post-war intercontinental civilian air services. The big Zeppelins had begun carrying small numbers of passengers above the seas in great luxury and comfort prior to the *Hindenburg* disaster at Lakehurst, New Jersey, on 6 May 1937, when 33 passengers and crew died as the huge hydrogen-filled dirigible exploded during landing. Pan American had introduced their first transatlantic Boeing 314 Flying Boat mail-and-passenger service between New York and Southampton in June 1939, only a matter of weeks before war was declared. While sea planes were to return after 1945, and vast new multiple-deck flying boats would be planned by Saunders Roe in the

1950s, the main thrust of post-war commercial aviation was to be land-based.

In the late 1940s a transatlantic flight from the tent city that was then London's new airport at Heath Row was likely to be a 15-hour odyssey of endurance in the cramped, cold and noisy cabin of a former Avro Lancaster bomber refitted and renamed for BOAC as a Lancastrian. The itinerary involved a dinner stop at Glasgow or Shannon, before the 10-hour overnight transatlantic leg, a refuelling stop and breakfast at Gander, Newfoundland, or Goose Bay, Labrador, before continuing on to New York or Montréal. Airfares were about double the Tourist-Class passage by sea. For many war-weary Britons and Europeans, the ocean voyage offered a welcome respite from the hardship of rationing and shortages of foodstuffs and other basic necessities. Most liners were provisioned at their New World terminals, allowing them to offer such welcome luxuries as steak, bacon, pastries and baked goods, butter, ice cream and chocolate. For the time being at least, steamship travel would regain its former prominence.

Released from national service in March 1946, and at long last fully fitted out for peace-time service, *Queen Elizabeth* started her belated commercial maiden voyage from Southampton to New York on Wednesday, 16 October 1946. Whatever performance might have been expected of *Queen Elizabeth* against competition from abroad when her keel was laid, the ship was never pushed to make a record crossing. Her machinery had already endured five years of heavy use, and her greatest Blue Riband rival, *Normandie*, was by then no more than a gutted hulk in a Brooklyn dock. Also, the pre-war Blue Riband ships *Bremen*, *Rex*, *Conte de Savoia*, along with Canadian Pacific's

Left: *The old Cosulich Liner* Vulcania, *which remarkably continued in service until 1965.* (CPL)

Overleaf: *The veteran* Aquitania *arriving at Gareloch on the Clyde to be scrapped, 22 February 1950. It was estimated that during her career she had steamed over three million miles and carried over a million people.* (CPL)

Below: *Workmen at Harland and Wolff's Belfast yard watch the launch of the new Union Castle liner* Pretoria Castle *on 19 August 1947.* (CPL)

Empress of Britain and P&O's *Viceroy of India*, were among the many well-known and much-loved ships the world over that had become casualties of war and were never to return.

Queen Mary remained in government service until September 1946, making a number of voyages to New York and Halifax under special arrangement with the United States government as a 'war-bride ship', carrying the wives and children of those servicemen who had married in Britain during the war to their new homes in North America. After also undergoing a thorough overhaul, *Queen Mary* returned to normal passenger service on Thursday, 31 July 1947. The restoration of both ships was highly publicized as a brave statement of winning the peace, lifting the burden of post-war gloom and austerity at home, and showing the rest of the world that Great Britain was recovering and returning to normality. Finally, Cunard had their two-ship express transatlantic service, almost 17 years after *Queen Mary*'s keel had been laid in December 1930.

Other familiar liners such as *Nieuw Amsterdam*, *Ile de France*, *Saturnia* and *Vulcania*, along with Cunard's *Aquitania* and second *Mauretania*, were likewise refitted, modernized and returned to regular commercial operations. Awarded to CGT in partial compensation for *Normandie*'s loss, Norddeutscher Lloyd's former *Europa* was extensively overhauled and strengthened at Chantiers et Ateliers de Saint-Nazaire Penhoët, emerging in 1950 as *Liberté* to run as consort to *Ile de France*. Royal Mail Line's clean-lined and modern *Andes* was one of several ships that were completed in the summer of 1939 and requisitioned immediately into government service upon her delivery. Her commercial debut came well after World War II in 1948. *America* was completed for United States Lines in June 1940 and used exclusively for cruising until being taken over for trooping a

year later as *West Point*, only making her North Atlantic debut in November 1946.

As Compagnie de Navigation Sudatlantique's long-awaited replacement for *l'Atlantique*, the distinctive *Pasteur* was scheduled to make her maiden voyage from Bordeaux to Buenos Aires in September 1939. After being used to take the French gold reserves to Halifax in August 1940, she was requisitioned by the British Ministry of War Transport for trooping service under Cunard-White Star Line management. In 1945 she was repatriated and subsequently used for government services under the French flag, including trooping to French Indochina, until being sold to Norddeutscher Lloyd in 1957, when she was extensively converted and remodelled as the line's fifth *Bremen*.

Above: *Passengers on board the* Andes *inspecting goods on sale in the shop, prior to her departure from Southampton on 22 January 1948. It was her first voyage as a passenger liner, having gone straight into service as a troopship upon completion in 1939.* (CPL)

Opposite: *Lit by pale winter sunshine,* Andes *pulls away from the Southampton dockside, which still shows evidence of wartime bomb damage.* (CPL)

Left: *French Line's* Liberté *of 1950 (ex-*Europa*) as she appeared shortly after being allocated to French Line.* (Chantiers de l'Atlantique)

Above: *A rare view of Compagnie de Navigation Sudatlantique's* Pasteur, *a ship little seen by the travelling public in her original form before going into wartime and later government service, before becoming Norddeutscher Lloyd's* Bremen *in 1959.* (CPL)

Opposite, top: *The* Bremen (ex-Pasteur) *under way.* (Author's collection)

Opposite, bottom: *Royal Rotterdam Lloyd's* Willem Ruys *of 1947, aerial port stern quarter view.* (Author's collection)

Below: *Aerial starboard side view of French Line's* Liberté, *under way.* (Author's collection)

Pasteur was a remarkable ship incorporating *Normandie*'s Yourkevitch-type hull form and adapting the essence of *l'Atlantique*'s distinctive internal layout to a more conventional plan with centreline funnel and engine casings. While *l'Atlantique*'s accommodation-decks' central 'rues' and the grand processional dining room staircase were lost to more rational planning, the spacious upper-deck Salle à Manger was repeated in a slightly more contemporary rendition and the earlier ship's Salon Ovale was adapted as the Grand Salon. One of the most distinctive features of *Pasteur* was her single enormous funnel located fairly far forward, and which can be seen perhaps as a reference for Norddeutscher Lloyd's vast unrealized *Viktoria*. It seems ironic that *Pasteur* should ultimately end up in their hands in 1959 as a latter-day namesake of *Bremen* of four decades earlier.

Royal Rotterdam Lloyd's *Willem Ruys* was also postponed by World War II after the keel was laid in January 1939. This was another ship of notable design, with nested lifeboats and powerful diesel machinery. The uncompleted ship remained at the

Royal de Schelde yard in Flushing, where her engines were run periodically to supply electrical power for the town when needed during the war. She was finally completed and entered service between Rotterdam and the Dutch East Indies in November 1947.

UNITED STATES

After realizing the tremendous benefit of large and fast ships as transports in times of war and other emergencies, the United States Government was anxious to possess such capabilities of their own. There was also a consensus among the American public that after its crucial and decisive role in the victory over Nazi Germany, the nation well deserved the prestige of having its own record-breaking liners on the North Atlantic. With commercial service on most sea routes curtailed during the war, there was insatiable and

seeming endless demand for passage to all parts of the world. At the same time the continuing war in Korea, the Berlin Blockade and other disquieting events showed that the world was still far from being at peace.

The Cold War had poised the United States and the Soviet Union on opposite sides of a political and ideological rift fed by propaganda, mistrust and hostility. Apart from a few traditionally neutral powers, most nations aligned themselves either with the US or USSR, and sought the protection of their chosen big brother in their own world affairs. There was good reason to assume that there would be the need for large troop movements. The heaviest military transport aircraft of the day could carry no more than about 200 combat-ready troops at a time against the capacity of huge ships such as the Cunard *Queens* to transport a whole infantry division. Aircraft needed airports with suitable runways and radio navigation

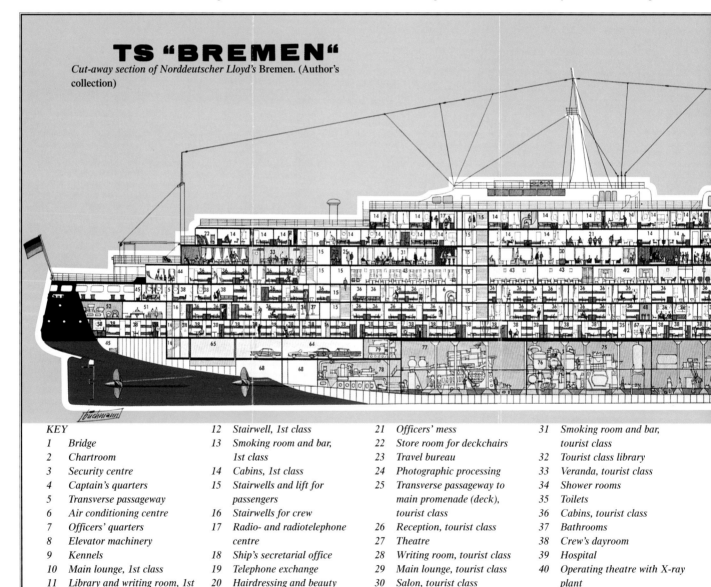

TS "BREMEN"
Cut-away section of Norddeutscher Lloyd's Bremen. *(Author's collection)*

KEY			
1 Bridge	*12* Stairwell, 1st class	*21* Officers' mess	*31* Smoking room and bar, tourist class
2 Chartroom	*13* Smoking room and bar, 1st class	*22* Store room for deckchairs	*32* Tourist class library
3 Security centre		*23* Travel bureau	*33* Veranda, tourist class
4 Captain's quarters	*14* Cabins, 1st class	*24* Photographic processing	*34* Shower rooms
5 Transverse passageway	*15* Stairwells and lift for passengers	*25* Transverse passageway to main promenade (deck), tourist class	*35* Toilets
6 Air conditioning centre	*16* Stairwells for crew		*36* Cabins, tourist class
7 Officers' quarters	*17* Radio- and radiotelephone centre		*37* Bathrooms
8 Elevator machinery		*26* Reception, tourist class	*38* Crew's dayroom
9 Kennels	*18* Ship's secretarial office	*27* Theatre	*39* Hospital
10 Main lounge, 1st class	*19* Telephone exchange	*28* Writing room, tourist class	*40* Operating theatre with X-ray plant
11 Library and writing room, 1st class	*20* Hairdressing and beauty salon	*29* Main lounge, tourist class	
		30 Salon, tourist class	*41* Dining room, 1st class

devices, while ships could go anywhere there was deep enough water and land their payload on a beachhead if necessary, as was later done during the Falkland Islands conflict in 1982.

While retaining a large express transport in readiness to move 15,000 troops was a contingency that might never have to be used, there was a compelling commercial rationale for repatriating America's fair share of the North Atlantic passenger trade. The United States had a minimal presence in the North Atlantic passenger business during the late 1940s, while Cunard's profitability was being largely supported by Americans travelling aboard their ships. By some accounts, Cunard's New York–Southampton trade was estimated to be worth $50 million a year. On the basis of meeting both these needs, arrangements were made for a ship to be jointly financed by United States Lines and the Pentagon, built to Navy specifications primarily for armed-forces service as

needed, but fitted out for her alternative role as an express North-Atlantic passenger liner.

The inverse concept of designing the ship first as a military transport and secondly as a liner was originally developed during the war by William Francis Gibbs (1886–1967), founder and senior partner of the well-established New York naval architectural consultancy, Gibbs and Cox. Gibbs himself had envisaged and planned great express ocean liners to sail under the Stars and Stripes since his early childhood. At the age of eight he and his younger brother Frederick had been on hand as First Lady Mrs Grover Cleveland launched the American Line Atlantic liner *St. Louis* at the William Kramp & Sons shipyard in Philadelphia, and young Gibbs decided to devote his life to ships. He avidly followed the development of White Star's *Oceanic*, Norddeutscher Lloyd's *Kaiser Willhelm II*, Cunard's *Lusitania* and *Mauretania* and White Star's *Britannic*, all the while devising his own

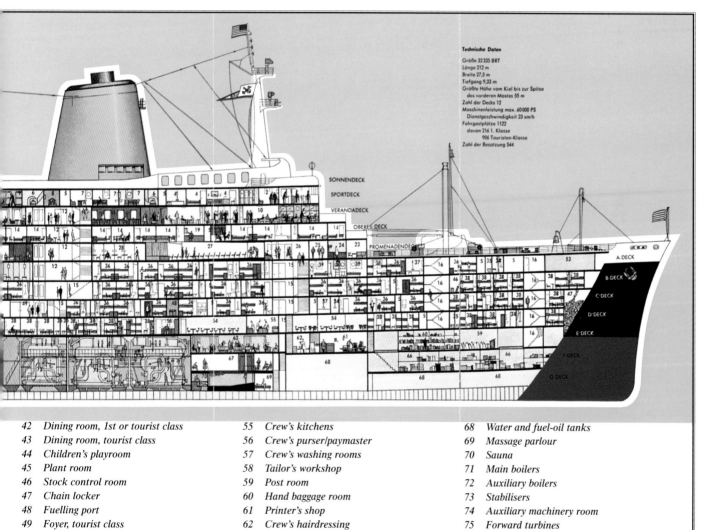

42 Dining room, 1st or tourist class	55 Crew's kitchens	68 Water and fuel-oil tanks
43 Dining room, tourist class	56 Crew's purser/paymaster	69 Massage parlour
44 Children's playroom	57 Crew's washing rooms	70 Sauna
45 Plant room	58 Tailor's workshop	71 Main boilers
46 Stock control room	59 Post room	72 Auxiliary boilers
47 Chain locker	60 Hand baggage room	73 Stabilisers
48 Fuelling port	61 Printer's shop	74 Auxiliary machinery room
49 Foyer, tourist class	62 Crew's hairdressing	75 Forward turbines
50 Purser	63 Pub	76 Seawater evaporation plant
51 Laundry	64 Automobile hold	77 After turbines
52 Rudder machine room	65 Car lift	78 Generator
53 Anchor capstan machinery room	66 Baggage rooms	79 Air-conditioner compressor
54 Crew's mess	67 Swimming pool	80 Double-bottom tanks

plans based on those features of their design he most admired. He produced detailed and feasible plans for thousand-foot express 30-knot liners as early as 1919, showing an inspired and remarkably sleek clean-lined combination of the hull lines from *Mauretania*, *Britannic*'s superstructure form and *Kaiser Wilhelm II*'s paired funnels. Without conventional steam machinery being available at the time to deliver the power needed for such high speeds, the Gibbs brothers had ascertained from their university connections that the General Electric Company was developing higher-powered electric drive for marine applications, also proposing its use for their then somewhat ethereal ships.

After working for a number of years under the name Gibbs Brothers, William Francis and Frederick were joined in 1929 by the noted American yacht designer Daniel H. Cox. The vast array of work handled by the company included ships, from passenger liners and freighters, to private yachts, tugs, coastal craft of various sorts and naval construction of fast destroyers and battle cruisers, as well as icebreakers and landing craft. The first passenger-ship designs supervised by Gibbs were for the Atlantic Transport Line's *Minnewaska* and *Minnetonka* of 1923–24, built by Harland & Wolff very much in the yard's own distinctive style. These were followed by his very advanced and individualistic design of the Matson Line Hawaiian-service liner *Malolo*, delivered by William Kramp & Sons in 1927. Meanwhile the company maintained a 10-year involvement in

the conversion, re-commissioning and operation of United States Line's *Leviathan*, leading eventually to design work on her American-built replacement, *America*.

Gibbs, who had avidly followed the progress of *Normandie*'s design and building, was later to make recommendations to the US Navy regarding her salvage and scrapping after the fire during her conversion as USS *Lafayette*. The firm was also involved in the conversions as troop carriers of the many ships taken over during World War II, including *George Washington*, *Ile de France* and *Pasteur*. Gibbs & Cox also converted the Norddeutscher Lloyd *Europa* for trooping as USS *Europa* at the end of the war in Europe. Although the conversion was itself successful, the ship was ultimately found to be deficient structurally and to lack the fuel and fresh-water capacities required for operations in the Pacific. She was thus returned to the United States Maritime Commission for disposal, ending up with a successful third career as *Liberté* after being extensively rebuilt in France.

Much of the early conceptual planning for what was at first generally known as 'the big ship' was done between 1943 and 1946 on Gibbs & Cox's own initiative for promotion to the Navy and United States Lines. From March 1946 onwards the company was engaged by United States Lines to work with the Navy and Newport News Shipbuilding. The formal business arrangement finally reached for the ship's construction was that United States Lines

Below: United States *arriving in New York harbour after trials, July 1952.* (CPL)

would pay $32 million of the $77 million building costs, with the remainder being borne by the Government. Finally realizing his childhood dream of building the world's greatest ship, William Francis's personal dedication and commitment to this project was so great that a substantial amount of his own money went in to the project. As plans progressed into reality, *United States* was chosen as the big ship's name.

The ship was designed to United States navy technical specifications with capacity for 14,000 troops and overall dimensions that would allow her to navigate the Panama Canal. As operation on the Pacific Ocean and in the Far East were also foreseen, accommodation was to be fully air-conditioned. The lack of airconditioning in the Cunard *Queens* and other ships used for trooping during World War II had caused great hardship in tropical waters, especially for those berthed on the lower decks.

Although her top speed remained classified for many years, it was long believed that she was capable of an absolute maximum in still water and air

Bellboys onboard the **United States.** (CPL)

conditions well in excess of 40 knots, fast enough to exceed the US highway speed limit of 55 miles per hour. She was powered by the same type of machinery installation as used in the Navy's *Midway*-class aircraft carriers. The propelling machinery comprised four compound triple-expansion turbine sets, with double-reduction gearing to the propeller shafts. It was later disclosed that the 53,209-ton ship's maximum output was 240,000 shaft horsepower, although at her regular North Atlantic service speed of 28 to 31 knots she developed around 158,000 horsepower.

Following naval practice of making the ship as resilient to attack or damage as possible, the machinery spaces were highly compartmentalized, with the turbine plant divided between two separate engine rooms and the steam plant likewise arranged in two boiler rooms, with separate compartments yet again for the auxiliary machinery. All of the necessary piping, electrical and control systems were provided so that any propulsion or auxiliary turbine set could be powered from either one of, or both, the boiler plants.

United States also had to meet naval standards for the watertight subdivision of the hull and fire proofing throughout all machinery spaces, working areas

and accommodation. The 14 bulkheads amidships extended up as far as A deck, with those forward and aft going up as far as the main deck above. The hull itself was built with an inner shell up to the height of B deck and with various other lengthwise watertight divisions below this level, effectively allowing the ship to remain stable and afloat with as many as four compartments flooded. This was well above the two-compartment standard usually followed for passenger ships, where the bulkhead height is usually one deck lower, and there is normally no inner shell above the double bottom. Gibbs had already adopted many of these same safety measures in his design of the Matson Liner *Malolo*, where he had also secured the remarkably high standard of quality control in her construction as would be called for in *United States*.

The ship's naval transport role called for unusually high fuel and fresh water capacities, as well as provision for the accommodation to be adapted quickly, and for a great deal of additional equipment and armament to be put in place as needed. To maintain stability against the additional weight of these items on the upper decks, the superstructure, funnels, lifeboats and their davits were constructed of aluminium. Light metal was also used extensively inside

Below: *United States Line's* United States *(above) and* America *(below) passing in the Hudson River off New York.* (Gordon Turner collection)

the ship for partitions and other internal structures that would otherwise have been made of wood. Altogether some 2,200 tons of riveted aluminium made *United States* one of the largest alloy structures of her time.

The need for safety above all else meant also that there could be none of *Normandie*'s structural openness on board, with triple-height public rooms and divided uptake casings. All deck openings had to be no larger than their function required of them, and these had to be as close to the centre of the ship as possible to maintain the greatest structural strength. The only double-height passenger space was the First-Class dining room on A deck where a central ceiling vault was allowed to break through the deck above. A similar space was also permitted above the theatre at the aft end of the promenade deck. All other public rooms were allowed only a single-storey height, with the ceilings on promenade deck being only slightly higher than the accommodation throughout the rest of the ship. The layout of First-Class public rooms was similar to *Queen Elizabeth*, with the sequence of ballroom, midships bar, smoking room and theatre interspersed forward-to-aft among the two funnel uptakes and engine casing. No

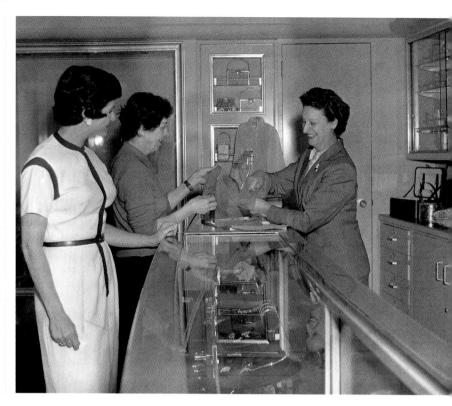

Above: *Lady passengers aboard* United States *shopping for nylon stockings, still fairly new at a time when the luxuriant femininity of Christian Dior's 'New Look' was setting trends in everyday fashion for women in all walks of life.* (CPL)

Left: *The time-honoured ministrations of a ship's bar steward in the modern surroundings of the ballroom aboard* United States. *The room's American-style sit-up bar is behind the illuminated decorative glass screens above the banquette, where the gentlemen passengers are seated.* (CPL)

Right: *Band musicians playing before a small audience of seemingly indifferent male passengers in the ballroom aboard* United States *– perhaps a cocktail hour interlude during the ship's record-breaking maiden voyage, when everyone was more concerned with the ship's own stellar performance.* (CPL)

Below: *Crowds of New Yorkers pack Pier 86 to wave off* United States *on 3 July 1952 as she embarks on her maiden voyage across the Atlantic.* (CPL)

panoramic windows or other large openings were allowed in the superstructure front, which was required to be a strength element as part of the ship's military role. The First-Class observation lounges were instead incorporated into the library and writing rooms, behind full-height windows located at the port and starboard sides of the ship forward of the enclosed promenades.

One of the most formidable challenges of *United States* as a passenger liner was to apply the navy's stringent fire-prevention standards without compromising the level of luxury and elegance expected by the travelling public. The ship's Method 1 Fire Prevention standard was based on the philosophy of avoiding as far as possible the mere possibility for fire to spread by allowing absolutely nothing that would burn to go into the ship's construction and outfitting. This extended to all furniture and interior fittings, draperies, carpeting and other soft furnishings. This was a cause that William Francis Gibbs himself, having personally surveyed badly fire-damaged ships such as *Morro Castle* and *Normandie*, enthusiastically championed almost to the point of fanaticism. All furniture, even for the most luxurious accommodation, had to be made of metal rather than wood. Wall- and floor-coverings, paints, upholstery and drapery fabrics all had to be entirely non-combustible. Teak was not even allowed for the deck coverings and handrails.

The only wood that passengers would ever come into contact with in the fittings aboard *United States* would be the specially fireproofed mahogany grand piano in the ballroom. This represented one of the very few major arguments the formidable naval architect ever lost during the building of his dream ship, as Theodore Steinway flatly refused to make an instrument out of aluminium. On the question of passenger classes, however, Gibbs emerged victorious from his confrontation over the number of passenger classes. United States Lines at first wanted the more modern approach of offering only two classes, as was being done with the American Export Lines *Independence* and *Constitution*, as well as aboard Norwegian America Line's new *Oslofjord*. William Francis, whose language could be most colourful and inappropriate in mixed company at such times, decreed categorically that there would be three classes, following the traditions of the Cunard *Queens* – and thus it was rendered without further discussion on the subject.

The architectural design of the interiors of *United States* was contracted to Eggers & Higgins, in collaboration with the interior design firm Smyth, Urquhart & Markwald, who had already worked with Gibbs & Cox on the Grace Line *Santa*-class liners and *America*. The *United States* commission was handled by partners Anne Urquhart and Dorothy Markwald. Gibbs particularly liked the subtly feminine touch that these women brought to their work,

as he believed that the choice of ship for an overseas voyage was most likely to be influenced by the lady of the household. The creativity of work done by both firms was no doubt circumscribed considerably by the need for all aspects of the ship's design to conform to the naval specifications and safety standards.

Some of the results achieved by the architects and interior designers were quite inventive. The Navajo Room, an intimate cocktail lounge on the promenade deck's starboard side, was decorated with wall panels bearing attractive geometrical Navajo tribal art rendered in coloured sands and bonded to metallic substrates. The windows in this room were large stylized portholes looking out to the enclosed promenade and fitted with metal frames and Venetian-style louvres. Creative use was made of cool, indirect fluorescent lighting as an architectural feature. The sense of a forum was created in the First-Class ballroom, largely by the use of circular lit ceiling vaults which defined the arrangement of glass screens separating the peripheral bar area aft of the central dance floor and bandstand. The central area of the main dining room three decks below could be seen as a stunningly contemporary rendition of *Europa*'s dining room from 22 years earlier. The cabins, where fireproofed soft furnishings would be a significant design feature, were bright and charming, with their tasteful use of colourful and patterned fabrics. It was no doubt here most of all that Gibbs foresaw Anne Urquhart and Dorothy Markwald's ability to appeal to the ladies who would choose this accommodation.

While the ship's interiors were ultimately considered by many to be bland and sterile in comparison with the warmth and richness of the Cunard *Queens*, their bright and functional modernity was very much in keeping with the times. It belonged to the international modernism of the post-war era, with the rebuilding of Coventry and Rotterdam as modern cities, the creation of Brazil's crisply modern capital, Brasilia, the growth of new towns in England such as Welwyn Garden City, Stevenage and Basildon and the urbanization of an affluent America during the baby-boom years. These developments ashore initiated many new ideas on urban construction and living, along with the widespread use of materials such as plate-glass, steel and reinforced concrete in domestic architecture. People wanted those same bright interiors and easily cared-for materials and finishes from the latest liners in their homes. Later, in controversy surrounding Cunard's planning for the replacement of their *Queens* during the 1960s, *United States* was cited as an example of the type of modernity most appropriate for the new British ship ultimately launched as *Queen Elizabeth 2*.

United States was built in a special drydock at the Newport News Shipbuilding and Drydock Corporation's yards in Virginia, where her keel was laid in February 1950. She was floated off her keel blocks with due ceremony on 23 June the following

year, and completed and delivered 12 months later. Yet as the Korean War broke out in July 1950, orders came from Washington that *United States* and three other large passenger liners under construction at American shipyards were to be completed for the Department of Defense as troop ships. The decision on the nearly-one-third-completed *United States* was reversed at the beginning of November, as the other three ships destined for American President Lines were to be completed for military service. While the future of *United States* was being decided in Washington her designers continued to work, based on William Francis's firm belief that, 'this will not happen', or perhaps his abject refusal to even think that it might.[1] Anne Urquhart was standing near Frederick Gibbs during the ship's christening ceremony, and she saw a single tear run down his cheek. She realized that, despite their professional stance of acknowledging a military call up as being a condition of the ship's building agreement, the near loss of their lifelong dream had indeed been a heavy blow to the two brothers.

On Thursday, 3 July 1952, at 12:07 pm *United States* began her record-breaking maiden voyage from New York's Pier 86, under the command of Commodore Harry Manning, with 1,600 passengers onboard. At 5:16 am London time, on Monday, 7 July, she passed Bishop's Rock, after a crossing of 3 days, 10 hours and 40 minutes from the Ambrose Channel Light Vessel (ACLV) at an average speed of 35.59 knots. At 3.9 knots greater than *Queen Mary*'s standing eastbound record, this was indeed a decisive victory for *United States*, America and especially for William Francis and Frederick H. Gibbs. The last American-built North Atlantic record-breakers were the Collins Line wooden paddle steamers *Atlantic*, *Arctic*, *Baltic* and *Pacific*, which had crossed the Atlantic in just under ten days at speeds of around 13 knots in the 1850s. Many of those aboard had partied all night in anticipation of the great event, with Champagne flowing and the ship's band playing a spirited rendition of *The Star Spangled Banner*. Later that same evening *United States* tied up for the first time in Europe at Le Havre's Gare Maritime, newly renovated after the war, from where *Normandie* had set out on her own conquest of the Blue Riband in 1935.

At Southampton on the afternoon of Tuesday 8 July, the American victors handled their great triumph with modesty and grace in response to the port and the city's warm welcome. William Francis Gibbs himself expressed it most eloquently, saying, 'We submit our effort with humility and friendliness for kind sympathy and consideration. We honour you for your achievements in ships. We have tried to emulate you.'[2] After leaving Southampton on 10 July, with a short afternoon call at Le Havre, *United States* made an almost anticlimactic homeward crossing in 3 days, 12 hours, 12 minutes at an average speed of 34.51

knots. After docking at her home pier in the evening of 14 July, the ship remained in New York for various celebrations, media and travel-industry events until 23 July, when she commenced her regular transatlantic sailing schedule with *America*. The Hales Trophy, which had been in storage ever since it was refused by Cunard, was brought to New York aboard *United States* and officially presented at a special dinner held aboard the ship in New York on 14 November.

During her first two years in service, *United States* spent 485 full days at sea, carrying 139,362 passengers back and forth across the Atlantic at an average speed of 30.73 knots. *United States* was a complex and highly sophisticated ship in operation. There were procedures for keeping her turbines idling at all times while in port away from home. Only during the ship's layovers in New York were these ever stopped. Oil samples were taken at the end of each voyage for chemical analysis to ensure that the powerful machinery was maintained in top condition. There were special electrical circuits for night lighting the public rooms and accommodation passages, which conserved power though retained a consistent lower

Opposite: The United States *approaches Southampton three and a half days later, gaining the Blue Riband on her maiden voyage.* (CPL)

Below: The view from the United States *as she prepares to dock at Southampton's Ocean Terminal.* (CPL)

Left: *Passengers and sightseers wave to one another as the* United States *docks at Ocean Terminal.* (CPL)

An original 1969 sailing schedule for United States. (CPL)

level of light throughout the ship. In service, the ship exhibited generally good sea-keeping characteristics and was remarkably free of vibration even at the never again repeated record-breaking speeds of her maiden voyage. In the public eye she embodied the energy, optimism and sleek modernity of her time, and the immense national pride of America and its peoples in their definitive ultimate conquest of the North Atlantic seaways.

Unfortunately, the three American President Lines Pacific-service liners *Presidents Jackson*, *Adams* and *Hayes*, completed for military service as the troop transports *Barrett*, *Geiger* and *Upshur*, were never to be boarded by the civilian public. Incorporating a number of progressive ideas from the noted American naval architect, George G. Sharp, these were designed with a two-thirds-aft machinery arrangement, beneath a pair of tall, slender side-by-side goalpost-style stacks. These were visually balanced against the absence of a traditional smokestack by expanding the navigating bridge, into a low, oval, funnel-like structure, containing also the officers' accommodation, ventilating equipment and emergency generator space. The superstructure front was semi-circular, enclosing large pie-slice-shaped cabins arranged on a radial plan around a circular central core. While these were retained through the conversion of the three ships, many of the other features of their proposed original passenger accommodation were never realized.

Sharp had been an avid proponent of what he called the Air Light accommodation plan, whereby inner and outer cabins would be arranged around enclosed courts or verandas at the ship's sides, with large windows admitting fresh air and daylight to the inner rooms. Arrangements of this type appeared in the four *Excalibur*-class cargo/passenger ships of American Export Line of 1931, as well as the Cosulich liner *Saturnia* completed a year later. No

doubt this would have been used extensively in the American President ships, had these been completed for commercial service. They would have also used various other features of Sharp's work, including lightweight furnishings and glass partitions between the main lounges and smaller fixed-function spaces such as the reading and card rooms, or between the ship's interior and open deck spaces, effectively bringing the inside and outside worlds together. Many of these ideas were, however, realized on the much smaller scale of the Mississippi Navigation Company's three *Del Norte*-class cargo-passenger ships.

Two other highly successful American ships of this period were the *Independence* and *Constitution*. These were remarkably modern fully air-conditioned ships with a high standard of accommodation throughout, built with the traditional touches of two tall steamship stacks and an old-fashioned counter stern. Aesthetically, these were at their best before their superstructures were extended forward in 1959 to add cabin accommodation. Their original interior layouts were very well articulated, with First-Class public rooms featuring a circular observation lounge surrounded by the enclosed promenade, main lounge amidships and a large club lounge with an adjoining enclosed terrace astern within the semi-circular aft

Above: *American Export Line's* Independence *of 1951; starboard view as built, before the superstructure was extended and the hull painted white.* (Author's collection)

Left: *main lounge interior.* (Author's collection)

Opposite: *The new Norwegian liner* Oslofjord *sailing up the Hudson River on 5 December 1949, at the conclusion of her first passage to New York.* (CPL)

end of the superstructure. The plan was simple and straightforward, with the main staircases and lifts divided at either side of the forward funnel casing. These, along with the dining rooms and a wide variety of cabins and suites, were designed in a luxurious contemporary style by Henry Dreyfuss, whose other work from this period included cabin interiors for the Lockheed Super Constellation and Electra airliners. Although the ships were built to Defense specifications for conversion as troop ships in times of war, they emerged with a slightly richer sense of style and elegance, perhaps by virtue of Dreyfuss's own approach or thanks to being less encumbered by Gibbs's personal obsession for safety and fire prevention.

THE MAGNIFICENT *FRANCE*

On Wednesday, 11 May 1960, the First Lady of France, Madame de Gaulle, launched *France* as a worthy successor to *Normandie*, whose great hull had also slipped into the waters of the Loire from that same building berth some 27 years earlier. Although the world's longest ocean liner, measuring 1,051⅔ft (315.5m) from stem to stern, the new 66,348-ton CGT flagship was to be a more agile vessel, created without aspirations of achieving world records. Within her slender hull was a quadruple set of geared steam turbines, built as an advanced and substantially automated rendition of the propulsion machinery

aboard Cunard's *Queens*. Following the example of *United States*, the machinery was arranged in two entirely separate engine rooms for the inner and outer pairs of propellers, and the boiler plant divided between two additional compartments located forward, ahead of two generator compartments and a block of fuel tanks amidships. The entire length of the eight machinery compartments was also enclosed within a double shell extending up to C deck, providing much of the same structural strength and security as the American ship.

France was created as a modern, comfortable and elegant liner for the 1960s, without the structural and decorative excesses of *Normandie*. Yet her design retained many distinctive features of the earlier ship. There was a whaleback over the bow and the paint scheme featured the same sheer line between the black hull and white upperworks, crossing the upper deck line of portholes in a gentle sweep up to the bow. Inside, the accommodation was designed around a conventional arrangement of the engine and funnel casings, stairways and other vertical accesses along the centreline, effectively eliminating any possibility of repeating the famed axial planning of *Normandie*'s First-Class interiors. *France* was also among several notable liners of her time, including P&O's *Oriana* and *Canberra*, to make extensive use of welded aluminium construction for her superstructure. About 800 tons of alloy was used in *France*'s topmost three decks and the

large funnels and fan housed above these.

France in essence repeated the sequence of *Normandie*'s public rooms, with the theatre forwardmost, followed by a sequence of lounges and other rooms extending aft to the open decks astern, and flanked on either side by the enclosed promenades. While the theatre occupied the full height of the promenade and veranda decks, with the stalls at its main level and a large dress circle balcony above, the sequences of rooms aft were in effect repeated on both decks, serving Tourist below and First Class above. A very similar approach was adopted in Holland America's new *Rotterdam*, completed in the Netherlands two years earlier. Both plans recognized an altogether more democratic approach to class segregation in the post-war era, as well as the more practical consideration of allowing all accommodation to be amalgamated for open-class cruising. The changeover could be made by simply changing deck accesses from the lifts and stairways. *France* used separate vertical cores for both classes, whose stairways and lifts would discreetly bypass the decks of the other class with the appropriate doors being closed during Atlantic voyages. The double interleaved 'trick staircase' aboard *Rotterdam* adopted the department store escalator principle to either combine or segregate the two classes, by way of opening or closing concealed partitions on each deck, with the lifts being electrically switchable for either style of service.

In essence these plans finally realized the approach proposed in the 1920s by Paul Biedermann for *Bremen* and *Europa*, and achieved a more satisfactory alternative to the type of integration schemes adopted by Swedish American Line and others in their dual-purpose tonnage of the 1930s. In both *Rotterdam* and *France* cabin accommodation for the two classes was also arranged horizontally, usually with First Class on the higher decks and Tourist Class along the ship's full length below. Thus each class could be given its own impression of having access to virtually all parts of the ship, without being exclusively confined forward, aft, below, or for that matter, above, as was First Class.

France reflected the architecture, art, society and lifestyle values of her own age, as *Normandie* and the earlier *France* had been in their own eras. The *France* of 1912 had belonged to the bon vivant of La Belle Époque, and *Normandie* to the ultimate grand luxe of the art deco era 20 years later. The new *France* was thus cast into the international modernity of the 1960s, with characteristically French flair and panache, yet rendered also with a sense of timeless classicism to avoid becoming quickly dated and retain her élan throughout a long service life. While the ship was built to the same Method 1 Fire Prevention standard as *United States*, with many of the same materials and finishes, her furnishings and decorations revealed a far warmer and richer palette.

Both suites of public rooms aboard *France* reflected a similar level of contemporary comfort and elegance. Apart from the addition of a few exclusive touches in the First-Class rooms themselves, the greatest difference was more a matter of ambience and service. The First-Class rooms on the veranda deck featured the Grand Salon amidships and a contemporary adaptation of the Fumoir as more of a versatile club room aft. On the deck below, the locations of these two rooms ware exchanged, with the tourist fumoir amidships, and Grand Salon aft where the greater length of the superstructure at this level provided better for the greater numbers of Tourist passengers. This room, which was also extended out to the deck's full width aft of the enclosed promenades, with its U-shaped American-style bar seating 27 people, claimed to be the world's largest shipboard

Below: A corner of France's Tourist-Class dining room, showing passengers seated in an atmosphere of contemporary French interior design, entirely appropriate to the shipboard milieu, yet without conveying any identifiably nautical leitmotif. (Chantiers de l'Atlantique)

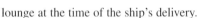

Above: *First class outer stateroom interior.* (Chantiers de l'Atlantique)

Left: *Passengers posing in the First-Class main lounge – the short cocktail dresses worn by the ladies indicative of more informal fashions in the 1960s.* (Chantiers de l'Atlantique)

Below: *The Tourist-Class smoking room bar area aboard the* France, *designed to meet the needs of an elegant yet more informal cross-section of an affluent and mobile 1960s international clientele.* (Archive Chantiers de l'Atlantique/Cliché Ecomusée de Saint-Nazaire)

lounge at the time of the ship's delivery.

Opposite the separate libraries and writing rooms of both classes, port side of the aft funnel casing and main stairways, the shop and a small cabaret bar were arranged one above the other for use by both classes. Each of these had its own stairway, providing First Class access to the shop on the promenade deck, and a discreet entrance for Tourist passengers to rub elbows with their First-Class shipmates in the veranda deck's bar. Remarkably, *France* featured no café-grill as there had been aboard *Normandie*. In fact, Tourist Class, or Rive Gauche (Left Bank) as it was called aboard *France*, had the benefit of a glass-domed indoor swimming pool and lido bar aft on the upper deck and a glass-roofed sports centre on the sun deck, while the albeit magnificently appointed

counterparts of these were located on the lower decks as entirely inside spaces.

Altogether, *France* had 17 First-Class public rooms, and 12 available to her Tourist passengers. These included a variety of speciality and fixed-function spaces such as the entirely separate infants' play-rooms, amusement arcade and soda bar for teenagers. The arrangement of *Normandie*'s music salon and ladies lounge as ante-rooms attached to the Grand Salon was retained. One had its own baby-grand piano for music recitals arranged adjacent to *France*'s First-Class Grand Salon, while the other, a similar music salon and card room, was likewise attached to the Tourist fumoir.

The quality of outfitting and finishing throughout the accommodation was of an unprecedented standard. *France* had the great luxury of being among the first liners to have carpeting fitted throughout her accommodation, including the stairways, deck lobbies and passageways. While this is taken for granted in today's cruise ships, it was then the height of ocean-going luxury. All cabins in both classes were, for the first time, provided with their own private en-suite toilet facilities, with those in First Class even having the added touch of de-misting vents to keep the vanity mirrors from fogging over while bathing or showering. Surprisingly for a French ship of such great luxury, the *Ile de France* and *Normandie* suites were the only accommodations fitted with bidets.

Electric lighting throughout the ship's interiors was carefully planned to achieve a balance between cool and energy-efficient fluorescent fixtures and incandescent elements. This was particularly important in achieving exactly the right nuance in the First-Class dining room dome, with its stunning combination of fluorescent halo surrounding star-like incandescent pot lights in the crown of the dome itself. Great care also had to be taken in balancing the light sources so as to avoid the wash-out effects prevalent with the type of fluorescent fixtures then in use.

France was one of several ships to introduce television in the public rooms and luxury First-Class suites. This was a closed-circuit black-and-white system, compatible with both the European and American formats, which was able to relay local broadcasting while the ship was in range of transmitters ashore. There was a small studio and an open-reel videotape machine, as well as camera connections in the main lounges, for live broadcasting of events aboard the ship. Very little use was actually made of these systems. P&O's Commodore John Wacher later said of *Canberra*'s television system, that far better use could have been made of it for entertaining the crew.[3]

With her wide variety of cabin accommodation and numerous public spaces, *France* offered something for every facet, mood and nuance of gracious modern living at sea. She was a product of the jet age, when already more people were flying than sailing. It was against this airborne competition that her owners recognized the need to offer something magnificent and extraordinary to entice passengers to choose a five-day ocean voyage over seven hours' flight across the Atlantic in an 'aluminium tube'. *France* was given a higher rating by the North Atlantic Passenger Conference than virtually any other ship in service at the time. Yet as the British shipbuilding trade journal *The Shipping World*'s correspondent wrote at the time of *France*'s maiden voyage, she was 'almost a never-never land, and perhaps sadly enough a never-again land, for it is most unlikely that such a magnificent ship will ever again be built.'[4]

THE NORTH ATLANTIC'S BIG FOURSOME

As *United States* was making her record-breaking maiden voyage, her master, Commodore Manning, received a message from *Queen Mary*'s Captain Harry Grattidge saying, 'Welcome to the family of big liners on the Atlantic'.[5] *United States* was the third ship to join *Queen Mary* after *Normandie*'s demise, followed in 1962 by CGT's *France*. *Ile de France* and *Liberté* were retired in 1958 and 1962 respectively, while *America* remained in service with *United States* until 1964, when she was sold to Chandris Lines, becoming *Australis*. Thus, by 1962, *Queen Mary*, *Queen Elizabeth*, *United States* and *France* were to be the world's only passenger liners in the over 50,000-ton class until the debut of *Queen Elizabeth 2* in 1969.

Of the four ships, the two *Queens* upheld Cunard's traditional standard of top-class service as they maintained their own weekly service between New York, Great Britain and Northern Europe. *United States* and *France* sailed on alternate weeks, offering much the same type of service, though in more modern and informal surroundings.

Cunard's *Queen Elizabeth* was a little larger than *Queen Mary*, and slightly more modern of the two. She had two freestanding funnels rather than the earlier ship's three, which were supported by guy wires and cables in the traditional manner, and no forward well deck, giving her a more rakish external appearance. Her interior architecture and decoration was modernized slightly towards the direction of Brian O'Rorke's interiors for Orient Line, to the point only of appearing perhaps a little austere compared with *Queen Mary*. One notable addition to the newer Queen's First-Class public facilities was the theatre, located aft on the promenade deck, although the indoor swimming pool was a disappointment following the magnificent art deco double-height swimming bath deep within the *Mary*'s lower decks.

Despite their slight differences in style and appearance, the Cunard *Queens* epitomised traditional first class grand luxe in the Post War liner era. Mr Keith Gledhill of Blackpool, who served in the purser's departments aboard both *Queens* between 1949 and 1954, and subsequently returned to *Queen Mary* with his wife as First-Class passengers in 1965, has experienced the ship from both the passenger and service viewpoints.[6] In the early 1950s he was one of 14 purser staff aboard *Queen Elizabeth*, when there would be a long retinue of film stars, celebrities and other notables from every walk of life aboard on every crossing. Until the rich and famous started jetting back and forth towards the end of the decade, the big liners were still regarded as the only way to cross, at least if you wanted to do it in real comfort and style. Cunard's *Queens* had the added advantage of tradition and service seniority over the more modern *United States* and *France*, according the Cunarders an added sense of luxury and prestige. Yet the polished linoleum flooring throughout even their most exclusive First-Class suites and public spaces, and the characteristically malodorous seawater flush toilets then in use, would hardly qualify as being luxurious by today's cruise ship standards.

Keith Gledhill recalls that life then aboard the *Queens* was quite formal and structured. The day started with breakfast being served in the dining rooms, although most First-Class passengers would have it brought to their cabins or suites. There were always those who preferred the splendour of the dining room and the attentive service to be found there at these early hours. The Turkish baths, swimming pool and squash courts would all open quite early in the nether regions of the ship's lower decks, drawing their bath-robed devotees discreetly by way of the accommodation passages. Others would start appearing on the promenade decks for their constitutional walks around the ship or to take up positions in their

reserved deck chairs. The first entertainment feature of the day would be a performance of classical music played on the organ in the main lounge at 10:45 am, while hot bouillon would be served on deck at 11:00 am. Elsewhere there might be an informal meeting of Lion's Club, Rotarians, Toastmasters or other service clubs likely to have members on board.

Lunch was served at 1:00 pm, with a programme of recorded classical music, perhaps a Furtwängler rendition of Beethoven's *Pastoral*, broadcast to the midships bar and also available over the cabin loud-speakers at 2:30 pm. There would be Bridge in the smoking room and perhaps a table-tennis tournament on the promenade deck. A trio from the ship's orchestra would play light music, perhaps a touch of Gilbert and Sullivan, in the main lounge at teatime. As passengers were preparing for dinner at 7:30 pm, newscasts from the BBC and Voice of America were broadcast to some of the public rooms and the cabins. The theatre would offer matineé and evening screen-ings of full-length films.

After-dinner entertainment usually featured bingo or shipboard horseracing in the main lounge, much as it would years earlier aboard Canadian Pacific liners. Dancing to the music of the ship's orchestra followed, as non-dancers among the gentlemen would retire to the smoking room for their Cognac and cigars, while waiting for the numbers for the Daily Tote to be brought down from the bridge. Betting on the Daily Tote would often be keen, with the winner, who chose the number closest to the ship's actual daily mileage, standing to win quite handsomely, often enough to cover their onboard expenses and gratuities, and occasionally even a good part of their passage money. As the rest of the ship fell quiet at midnight, the Veranda Grill would open, offering music, dancing, food and beverages for as long as there were takers.

Like so many, Mr Gledhill feels that these really were the glory years on the North Atlantic. Before there were cruise directors, casinos and extensive professional entertainment, there was instead a far greater emphasis on personal service and the social occasions of life at sea. With the exception of the first and last night out, evening attire was always formal, with gentlemen wearing tuxedos or dinner jackets and ladies in floor-length evening gowns. The per-sonal touch was everywhere, as the lifts were operat-ed by war veterans, sometimes amputees, who had served crown and country, and the dining room's glass doors were opened by ship's bellboys. There were magnificent displays of fruit and confectionary that were as much a treat for the eyes as they were for the palate. Freshly cut flowers brought an added touch of luxury and grace to the dining rooms, lounges and deluxe accommodation.

The segregation of passenger classes was strictly enforced, as Mr Gledhill recalls that the pursers and other ship's staff seemed to have a keen eye for spot-ting interlopers who strayed beyond their own domains. The errant passenger would be discreetly asked for his or her cabin number, and then escorted back to their own part of the ship.

During transatlantic voyages, virtually the only time the class barriers aboard the *Queens* were lowered was for religious services. A recording of church bells was broadcast over the Tannoy system on Sunday mornings as passengers of all three classes and off-duty crew would make their way to the First-Class main lounge, where 400 chairs had been set out for the interdenominational service, presided over by the captain, with the lesson being read by the staff captain. Passengers from the lower two classes and crew members would make their way to and from the lounge by way of the enclosed promenade deck. While the pealing of church bells was an unusual sound aboard ship, the assembly of these people from all walks of life and every strata of the ship's own social structure for church services was a familiar and comforting scene of the faithful gathering for worship as they do in communities on both sides of the Atlantic. Roman Catholic mass was held separately, while those of the Jewish faith were, for the first time in maritime history, provided with their own Scroll Room aboard *Queen Mary*.

Through the 1950s, passenger service in First-Class aboard the big liners was almost without peer anywhere else at sea or ashore. The Cunard *Queens*, for instance, were victualled with a huge variety of foodstuffs, catering to every taste and dietary need, including kosher and Japanese specialties. Passengers could even arrange for their meals to be cooked individually by a man-servant of their own, who would be given access to one of the ship's small service kitchens adjacent to the passenger's accommodation. At lunchtime, passengers in First Class at least could place individual dinner orders with the maitre d'hôtel. As many as a hundred of these private orders, requesting everything from caviar, *foie gras* and English or American sole, to charcoal-braised T-bone steaks, roast grouse and various dessert confections, would be typed during the afternoon and dispatched to the appropriate kitchen departments to be served that evening.

Service aboard *France* endeavoured to showcase legendary French gastronomy at its very best, while the individual attention given to passengers aboard *United States* stressed the modern hotelier luxury of round-the-clock service to the cabins. While much of the same attention could be had at the best hotels in London, Paris and New York, the cost of these would be charged to the guest's account whereas these extras tended to be included in steamship fares at the time. Apart from the cost of ingredients, the expense of serving light refreshments to a passenger cabin during the night could also run to paying overtime rates to the crew who could prepare and deliver it.

The luxury and service standards of *United States* and *France* reflected a sense of the altogether greater spirit of these ships' own modernity. They too developed their own loyal followings, among which United States Line was always especially proud to count the Duke and Duchess of Windsor. Edward's sensational abdication from the British throne in 1936 accorded him the freedom to marry American divorceé Wallis Simpson, who then became Duchess of Windsor. Perhaps this shift of the Windsors' loyalty from Cunard to United States was viewed as sweet revenge by the many Americans who would have so loved to see one of their own in Buckingham Palace.

Cunard's *Queens* had a rich and illustrious past that carried them forward, while *United States* and *France* were seen as belonging more to the future, and to identifying with the jet set and the space age. Passenger liners no longer inspired the awe and held the wonderment of their Victorian predecessors. The public gaze was cast ever more upwards to the world's conquest by commercial aviation and to the Sputnik, the 'Space Race' and President John F. Kennedy's promise to put a man on the moon before the end of the 1960s. At sea, the greatness of the express ocean liner was being challenged by supertankers, bulk carriers and container vessels. The year 1958 was the crossover point when the number of passengers crossing the Atlantic by sea began to decline. The figure dropped from its 1957 maximum of one million to 650,000 in 1965, while airline passenger volumes quadrupled from one to four million over the same time frame. Yet there remains to this day a devoted following of ocean travel by those who have the resources and the time to enjoy the luxuries of a shipboard passage, and who for one reason or another would rather sail than fly. Quite apart from 'old timers' who resist change or those who are afraid to fly, the sea has always continued to attract people of all ages and from every walk of life.

Claudia, an airline stewardess with a personal preference for sea travel, especially enjoyed the slick modernity of *United States* and *France*. Sailing in Tourist Class aboard both ships in the late 1960s, she felt that the contemporary style of their accommodation and service had a particular relevance to the jet age and to the way people wanted to live then.[7] Tourist sea passage was still an affordable alternative to intercontinental air travel at a time when there was limited availability of less-expensive excursion airfares, which were themselves restrictive and inflexible. Ships attracted a wide variety of younger and more active people, especially during the summer months, when many students, teachers and university professors had the time and resources to travel. There was always plenty going on, with the opportunity to circulate in stimulating company for a few days among people you had never met before nor were ever likely to see again.

As a woman travelling alone, Claudia preferred the greater sense of anonymity afforded by the larger ships such as *France*, where there could be more than

Opposite: Pictured here in 1966 in the partly-drained dry dock at Southampton, dock workers clear the Queen Mary's *hull of marine growth, which if allowed to remain would impede the ship's speed. (CPL)*

1,600 passengers in Tourist Class. There would be less chance of having to answer questions such as, 'Where were *you* during bingo yesterday evening?' Unattached women wanting a bit of shipboard romance were more apt to court the favour of officers or crew than their fellow passengers. Male passenger 'wolves' were in fact often the sort of people to be avoided. Claudia once resorted to putting on a false mid-European accent and wearing a brunette wig and dark glasses to avoid the advances of one fellow passenger, finding herself then being pursued by two different members of the ship's company, one each in her real and assumed personalities.

There was a far greater mystique in being invited behind doors marked 'Crew Only' or 'Equipage Seulement' to experience how the other half lives. As risqué as some encounters of this nature might appear, there seemed to be less risk in crew entertaining passengers in their own quarters, since they were still subject to the discipline of their employ-

ment and living arrangements on board. They were strictly forbidden to enter passengers' accommodation except in the line of duty, and were discouraged from bringing passengers into their own quarters, although privilege was a benefit of rank.

Whatever went on in an officer's cabin had to be handled quietly and discreetly, without giving the guest any cause for later complaint. Claudia recalls being aboard another ship where she was invited for cocktails by a junior officer who wanted to avoid being seen bringing anyone to his cabin. She was shown to the service deck behind the lifeboats and asked to enter by way of the window. This involved ascending the railing while holding on to one of the lifeboat davits, and then backing herself across the narrow deck space and in through the small window, stepping down onto a settee inside the room. Indeed no mean feat for a 5ft 10in (178 cm), 180lb (82-kilo) lady in a straight-line wool skirt and leather high-heeled shoes!

Below: *French Line's Flandre of 1952, seen here being manoeuvred by tugs at Manhattan's liner piers, was a rather austere intermediate-class passenger and cargo ship, one of two sisters, designed for the line's West Indies services, but instead put onto the North Atlantic run between Le Havre and New York.* (CPL)

OTHER SHIPS, SERVICES AND IDEAS

The post-World War II age was one of the most illustrious and diverse eras in the history of passenger shipping. From the immediate need to replace war losses came also the need to serve new emigrant trades and various new one-class services. Apart from the prestigious North Atlantic ships such as *United States* and *France*, there emerged other outstanding ships, such as *Leonardo da Vinci*, *Rotterdam*, *Windsor Castle* and *Oriana*. Taking a leaf from the progress in modern cargo shipping, a number of significant new liners such as *Southern Cross*, *Canberra,* and to a lesser degree *Rotterdam*, were built with their machinery and funnels aft so as to provide a fully uninterrupted volume of passenger accommodation amidships.

In the immediate aftermath of World War II, as thousands of military personnel were demobilized from the armed forces and left to seek accommodation and employment, many found that there was literally no place for them and their families in Europe's battle-ravaged cities and scarred countryside. Many people sought to emigrate and to find new lives in countries such as Canada, Australia and the nations of South America, which still maintained fairly liberal immigration policies. The government of the Netherlands went as far as to encourage those wanting a new start in life to leave the country, offering them free passage abroad and even a small amount of spending money.

These needs in turn fostered the creation of several new shipping lines, operating under various flags of convenience, using converted redundant tonnage of one sort or another. Home Lines, Arosa, Incras,

Sitmar Costa and Chandris were the best-known of these. Sitmar, Costa and Chandris were to fare best, going on to later become well-known brands in the cruise field, with Sitmar being absorbed into Princess Cruises, Costa now part of the Carnival group, and Chandris trading as Celebrity Cruises, now a part of the Royal Caribbean International group. Home Lines had become a pioneer in the luxury cruise field with their first new ship *Oceanic*, introduced in 1965, although unfortunately this very individualistic line was wound up a number of years ago.

In their early days, all these lines emphasized low-cost Tourist-Class service, much of it catering to the needs of those emigrating from Europe. Only a limited amount of First-Class accommodation was offered, mainly to satisfy the North Atlantic Passenger Conference requirements of having a prescribed level of premium-grade accommodation against which more competitive lower fares could be charged for Tourist-Class passage.

CGT and Holland America were among other lines to adopt a similar economy-oriented approach in the building of their first intermediate-class post-war liners in the 1950s. Although CGT's cargo/passenger liners *Flandre* and *Antilles* had a traditional predominance of First-Class accommodation, they were of a fairly austere standard. Their First-Class public rooms were aft on their boat decks with the Tourist communal facilities astern on the upper hull decks. While both ships were intended for the West Indies trade, *Flandre* made her debut in North Atlantic service to New York, where she served full time until 1958 and in high season up to 1962.

Developments in Japanese deep-sea passenger shipping during the post-war era was limited to but a

Below: *Port bow quarter view of Home Line's* Atlantic *of 1949 (ex-Malolo/Matsonia, 1927) under way.* (Author's collection)

few specialized vessels. Among these the handsome
10,000-ton *Brazil Maru* and *Argentina Maru* were
notable as versatile cargo-passenger liners designed
to carry a mix of Cabin and emigrant passengers
between Japan and South America. These crossed
from Kobe and Yokohama to Los Angeles, and then
proceeded via the Panama Canal to Rio de Janeiro
and the River Plate. They each featured cabins for 12
First-Class and around 70 Tourist passengers, each
with their own public rooms and Western as well as
Japanese baths, on the superstructure decks, and
basic dormitory accommodation for around 900
Third Class on the lower decks. Both ships were
modernized in 1965, with their Tourist- and Third-
Class accommodation amalgamated and upgraded
and the dormitories replaced by cabins. *Argentina
Maru* was later renamed *Nipon Maru* and put into

cruise service. *Shin Sakura Maru* was built in 1971
on a similar plan, with a large superstructure aft
housing accommodation for passengers, for use in
cargo service to Europe and to serve as a Japan
Industry Floating Fair exhibition ship. She was later
converted for cruising, with her accommodation
greatly expanded.

The *Ryndam* and *Maasdam*, completed for
Holland America Line in 1951 and 1952, each
accommodated only 39 First-Class passengers in luxury cabins on the boat deck, along with their own private dining room and club lounge. These privileged
few also had the full run of the ship's remaining public rooms, promenades and other deck spaces, with
the more than 800 in Tourist Class, who themselves
were barred from the premium-fare area above.
Swedish American Line's 1948-built cargo/passen-

ger liner *Stockholm* was an especially sad step-down from the magnificence of her immediate predecessor of the same name, which had been completed during the war, sold to Italian owners and subsequently sunk in July 1944 at Trieste. For a while ships of this type were seen by their owners as being the way of the future. Holland America claimed that their 'Economy Twins' were designed to 'do for the transatlantic traveller what Henry Ford did for the motorist'.[8] These lines very soon rediscovered the value of selling luxury and prestige, ultimately leaving it to the airlines to develop cheap transatlantic travel for the masses.

The five-ship *Ivan Franko*-class liners built during the mid-to-late 1960s at Mathias-Thesen-Werft in Wismar, East Germany, for the Soviet Union's state-run Morpasflot group, were a larger and more comfortable adaptation of the *Ryndam* and *Maasdam*.

Although these were operated as examples of class-less Soviet society, each was built with accommodation for 130 First-Class passengers on the promenade and boat decks, with their own lounge and bar above on the bridge deck. The dining room below was arranged so that First-Class passengers could be seated in its centre section where they had direct access from the forward staircase.

The remaining 620 passengers were accommodated in standard cabins, mostly arranged in interleaved two- and four-berth pairs so that each had its own portholes. The crew were likewise berthed in cabins of the same standard, port side on the second deck and part of the third deck Thus, these ships had the distinction of offering all outside accommodation for passengers and crew alike. Although by no means luxurious, the accommodation was generally bright,

Above: Swedish American Line's post-war intermediate cargo and passenger liner Stockholm, *shown on trials on 7 February 1948.* (CPL)

Below: Port stern quarter view of the **Alexandr Pushkin** *of the Baltic Steamship Company leaving Montréal, May 1975.* (Author's photo)

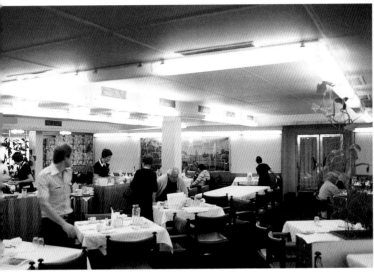

Above, left:
Restaurant at dinner time, aboard the Alexandr Pushkin, *September 1979.* (Author's photo)

Above, right:
Alexandr Pushkin's *music salon at teatime, September 1979.* (Author's photo)

airy and spacious, with a fairly wide variety of attractive and well-planned public rooms. These ships each featured an indoor/outdoor swimming pool with a sliding glass roof designed as a somewhat scaled-down rendition of *France*'s Tourist-Class pool and lido.

These ships were first used both for line service and cruising. In 1964 *Alexandr Pushkin* inaugurated a service between Leningrad and Montréal, with stops at Helsinki, Copenhagen, London-Tilbury and Québec City, and started making summer cruises from Montréal to St. Pierre et Miquelon, and as far afield as Bermuda and Cuba. *Mikhail Lermontov*, the last of the series to be completed in 1970, sailed to New York from Leningrad three years later. She was the first Soviet passenger ship in service to an American port since 1948, when several voyages were made on a trial basis using *Rossia*, the former HAPAG South Atlantic liner *Patria*. Soviet liners would occasionally turn up unexpectedly at various ports around the world on mysterious repatriation voyages, to bring Soviet diplomats and their families, returning defectors and Communist sympathizers back home to Russia.

Although *Alexandr Pushkin* carried only seven First-Class passengers and 29 in Tourist on her maiden voyage, the Soviet ships became very popular, particularly among younger people who were drawn to their lower fares and less formal lifestyle. The experience offered a rare opportunity to peek inside the mystery of life behind the Iron Curtain in those years of the Cold War. Apart from sampling the cuisines and cultures of the Soviet Union and its peoples, most passengers probably came back home with the realization that, as individuals, the Russian officers and crew were really little different from themselves. No doubt they were reined-in by their commissars and political officers, but the privilege of their service on those ships seemed to offer ample opportunities for the officers and crew to also indulge in the fashions, popular culture and rock 'n' roll of the West.

Some reactions were amusing, as in the case of Orville, who returned home from Europe aboard *Alexandr Pushkin* in the late 1970s, only because his Winnibego mobile home was too big to fit through *QE2*'s vehicle hatch. His red-neck diplomatic outlook was that anything beyond his immediate comprehension was simply a 'gawd-damned Commie plot'.[9] Orville was sure that his cabin was bugged, although it was unclear why he imagined anything he said would have interested the Kremlin in the least. Nonetheless, he was taking no chances, and decided to sleep in his big Winnibego, which was lashed to the ship's fantail and well stocked with canned pork and beans, Budweiser and freeze-dried Folgers. The crew took this all in their stride with benign amusement, making sure he was safe in his chosen accommodation and even hooking him up with power from the ship's electrical system. Yet, despite his foibles, Orville read widely from the library's large collection of translated contemporary and classic Russian works, and seemed generally to have enjoyed the crossing.

Remarkably, after *Ryndam* and *Maasdam* were withdrawn from the Holland America fleet, *Maasdam* was sold to Polish Ocean Lines, thoroughly refitted, and put into service between Gdynia and Montréal as *Stefan Batory*. She and *Alexandr Pushkin* continued to sail between Europe and Montréal until the early 1980s, usually calling at Le Havre, London-Tilbury and either Rotterdam or Bremerhaven. Sadly, *Alexandr Pushkin* departed from Montréal for the last time in the late summer of 1980, proudly bearing the insignia of that year's Moscow Olympiad, which had been boycotted by many Westerners in protest of the Soviet Union's involvement in Afghanistan. Affectionately known in Montréal as The Polish Love Boat, *Stefan Batory* remained in service as the last traditional transatlantic liner until 1986, when she was withdrawn.

As modern as things appeared to be, the majority of passenger ships built during the 1950s and 1960s were fairly traditional in concept with regard to the type of accommodation and service they offered, and to maintaining distinct classes of service. Of the great many very attractive Italian liners built during those years, most were solidly committed to a three-class service, and offered little contingency for their accommodation to be easily reconfigured for cruising or other services. Likewise, the style of accommodation and service aboard new passenger tonnage built in the late 1940s and early 1950s appeared to have changed little since the pre-war era, apart from the welcome addition of fin stabilizers and air-conditioning. Yet even Royal Mail Line's much admired *Andes* was still a product of 1930s social thinking, solidly committed to segregated passenger classes and only partially air-conditioned.

Shaw Savill Line's *Southern Cross* and *Northern Star*, along with Union Castle's *Transvaal Castle*, were among the very few liners to be built with but a single class of passenger accommodation. There had been numerous proposals for huge Atlantic liners to be built as cafeteria ships, based on a single class of service, with passengers paying separately for their meals, as was being done aboard ferries. The idea of this was to compete on the basis of the sort of highly standardized service that would ultimately develop with air travel. Vladimir Yourkevitch, who designed *Normandie*'s revolutionary hull form, proposed a very futuristic alternative to CGT's *Bretagne*, with luxury two-berth accommodation for 5,000 passengers priced at Tourist-Class levels, with passengers buying their own meals in a variety of restaurants offering different levels of service. These ideas were generally shunned by the established shipping lines as being outside their business profiles of operation in the luxury liner business.

When Shaw Savill Line began planning new ships for their service to Australia and New Zealand in 1952, the line's Chairman, Basil Sanderson, was keen to break with tradition on several issues. While it was customary for liners on these longer routes to also carry cargo, Sanderson wanted to exclude freight altogether from the new ships. Time would no longer have to be allowed for cargo handling, and the inevitable delays caused by pier availability and the persistent labour difficulties with stevedores and other unionized labour would be eliminated. The route to New Zealand would be extended right around the world, carrying on across the Pacific via Fiji and Tahiti, to the American West Coast, and then back to England via the Panama Canal and Atlantic ocean. Calculations based on the line's own experience with their earlier ship, *New Australia*, showed that a new 20,000-ton liner carrying 1,200 passengers on a strictly maintained schedule could profitably make four such voyages a year, of 76 days each at a service speed of 18.5 knots, with a 2-knot reserve for making up lost headway due to weather and other eventualities.

All passengers were to be carried in a single class of modern, fully air-conditioned accommodation, with a wide variety of public rooms and recreational facilities suitable for long voyages in tropical waters. Breaking with more than 100 years of steamship design tradition, and following the examples of the modern tanker and bulk cargo carrier, Sanderson succeeded in convincing his own technical advisers and the builders that his new liner should also be designed with her machinery aft. The idea was that if the engine room could be moved aft, three-quarters of the internal space amidships could be free of funnel uptakes, boiler casings and other obstructions. Apart from a few smaller ships built for North America's Great Lakes and the French coastal liner *El Djezair*, delivered in 1952, there was no precedent or prototype for deep-sea passenger liners with

Below: Soviet liner **Alexandr Pushkin** *and Polish Ocean Line's* **Stefan Batory** *(ex-Maasdam) together at the Port of Montréal in July 1980. These two ships were occasionally in Montréal together during the summer cruising season. Note the insignia for the Moscow Olympiad on* **Alexandr Pushkin***'s superstructure.* (Author's photo)

engines aft. One of the main design concerns was that, whereas the mass of the cargo itself would hold a tanker in proper trim, a liner of this type would need to be carefully ballasted forward against the weight of her machinery concentrated aft.

Harland & Wolff, who were contracted to build *Southern Cross*, as the new Shaw Savill ship was to be launched, produced an effective distilled-water ballasting arrangement. While this was achieved at the expense of increasing the ship's beam by 1ft (0.3m), there would be room for 20 extra cabins, and thus an additional 44 revenue-earning berths, more than would have otherwise been possible with a conventional plan. Her machinery was arranged tanker-style, with the boiler room aft of the turbine compartment and above the propeller shafts, rather than forward of the main machinery as is the normal arrangement for centre-engined ships. Thus the funnel is farthest astern, where its uptake least compromises the layout of the accommodation decks. The passengers were given virtually the full run of the ship from this point forward to the superstructure front, from the sun deck above all the way down to the bulkhead deck.

The lounge-deck suite of public rooms consisted of a large observation lounge forward, extending to the full width of the ship with windows overlooking the bow forward and the sea at either side. Midships, between the open promenades at either side, there was a smoking room and a double-height cinema lounge with a balcony above and a wide stage, while aft the tavern, another full-width space directly overlooking the sea, had access to the open decks either side of the funnel casing and astern. The two main staircases were divided either side of the centreline so that the cabin decks could each be oriented around a main central corridor, as had been done in earlier axial-plan ships such as *Bremen*, *l'Atlantique* and *Normandie*. There were, however, no central vistas through *Southern Cross*'s public rooms, as these were arranged to suit the cinema lounge's arrangement with auditorium-style seating and to provide central service pantries to this and the observation lounge forward. The saloon-deck layout was also arranged traditionally with the galley midships and the two dining rooms accessed directly from the forward and aft stairways.

Southern Cross became an immediate success from her first round-the-world voyage in 1955, sailing at more than 90 per cent capacity during her first two years in service. After the ship returned home from her first voyage, she was sent on three short cruises on the Atlantic and the Mediterranean to prove her suitability for this role, before the order was placed for a second ship. Built by Vickers Armstrong at Newcastle-upon-Tyne and named *Northern Star*, she was to operate westwards-about on the round-the-world service, sailing in the opposite direction to *Southern Cross*, with the two ships departing from Southampton at an interval of six weeks. Thus with concurrent circumnavigations of the globe in opposite directions, the line was able to offer a great variety of travel options. Sanderson and his colleagues firmly believed that sea travel offered a viable alternative to flying for those with the time to sail and who wanted the voyage itself to offer

Opposite: Southern Cross slides down the slipway as a Shaw Savill Line vessel after being launched by HM Queen Elizabeth at Harland and Wolff's Belfast yard on 17 August 1954. (CPL)

Below: Southern Cross; starboard aerial view under way. Note the unusual positioning of the funnel well aft. (Author's collection)

some relaxation and opportunity for visiting other places. In view of the competition from the airways, and the altogether more informal approach to living that came with the age's greater mobility, Shaw Savill also tried to create a more up-to-date approach to service on board. Following the example of their airborne competition, with its emphasis on female cabin service personnel, the line introduced the function of ship's hostess and to employ 'purserettes' in the purser's office and even a number of 'stewardettes' in the hotel department.

Union Castle Line's 32,697-ton *Transvaal Castle*, delivered by John Brown Shipbuilders in 1962, was outfitted on the idea of a modern hotel with no class barriers, to offer the same standard of service as the line's new two-class flagship, *Windsor Castle* completed two years earlier. During the interval between the commissioning of these two ships, BOAC and South African Airways had introduced a daily Boeing 707 jet service between London and Johannesburg in October 1960. Union Castle responded to the challenge by trying to update its style of service towards an ideal of the modern classless society, with all passengers having the full run of the ship's facilities and being able to enjoy the luxury cuisine and service.

The line's *Bloemfontein Castle* completed in 1950, as well as the smaller ships on their around-Africa services, was built for one-class service, generally with an attractive suite of public rooms and fairly basic grades of accommodation, mostly lacking private en-suite toilet facilities. *Transvaal Castle*, the only one-class ship built for Union Castle's flagship Southampton to Cape Town and Durban service, featured a single 499-seat restaurant and extensive promenade-deck suite of public rooms of a similar standard to those in First Class aboard *Windsor Castle*, with the variety of cabin accommodation effectively covering the range of First and Tourist Classes.

While the lowest cabin grades were scarcely any better than those aboard the line's earlier ships, *Windsor Castle*'s Tourist-Class public rooms were designed to a somewhat higher standard. These were arranged along the enclosed length of B deck beneath their First-Class counterparts. The Tourist main lounge was forward, with a large library and writing room and a smoking room, in reality a series of connected club rooms, arranged along the port side of the deck. The starboard side of this deck was occupied by the deluxe First-Class suites and cabins, effectively isolated from the Tourist public areas by the funnel casing and the separate stairways for the two classes amidships. The key difference between *Windsor Castle*'s First- and Tourist-Class public rooms was style rather than comfort and elegance. The First-Class rooms on both ships were designed by architect Miss Jean Munro, in a somewhat contemporary interpretation of traditional shipboard

architecture and furnishing, using modern wall coverings and fluorescent, indirect coffered ceiling lighting. *Windsor Castle*'s port-side Tourist-Class rooms were designed in an altogether more contemporary style by Michael Inchbald, using open planning and modern sectional furniture. Both architects were later to work together in the planning of *QE2*.

CANBERRA AND ORIANA

As the Dominions of India and Pakistan were created in 1947, and independence was granted to Ceylon and Burma the following year, P&O and Orient Lines were to lose a significant part of their traditional role of carrying government officials, troops and mails to and from the homeland. At about the same time, however, Australia was looking beyond its original colonial ties with Great Britain to developing new commercial enterprises of its own around the Pacific Rim, with Malaya, China, Japan, Canada and the United States. P&O and Orient Lines were both anxious to seize this opportunity to sustain and develop their own trading positions in the post-war era. The cultural diversity of the Pacific Rim and the attraction of tropical paradises such as Fiji and Hawaii were also seen to offer new opportunities for developing tourism and leisure travel to the more affluent and mobile populations of post-war Australia, New Zealand and North America.

An integrated network of services around the world was organized under the name Orient & Pacific Lines, extending and combining the traditional P&O and Orient Line routes with various other auxiliary and feeder services to such places as Manila, Hong Kong, Singapore and Yokohama. An alternative route to Australia and the Far East was also inaugurated by way of the Panama Canal and North American west coast ports. During the 1950s, Orient Line's *Orcades* began sailing westwards-about around the world via Panama to Australia and Suez in 1955, and P&O's *Chusan* was first to call at Vancouver, San Francisco and Los Angeles when she made her maiden trans-Pacific voyage from Sydney.

Competition on the Pacific was light, as Matson Line had ceased passenger services to Australia and the Far East to concentrate on their domestic services between the American west coast and Hawaii. After forfeiting their three *President Jackson*-class liners to completion as troop transports for the Korean War effort, American President Lines also was unsuccessful in obtaining Government assistance to build their planned express trans-Pacific liner *President Washington* of 43,000 tons with a 29-knot service speed. This ship, which was designed by Gibbs & Cox, would have somewhat resembled *United States* as a modern, fully air-conditioned liner with enclosed promenades. Although the Comet C4, Boeing 707 and Douglas DC-8 jets were already in transatlantic service, the 35-hour odyssey by air to

Opposite, above: Launch of Orcades *at Barrow in 1947. (CPL)*

Opposite, below: Orcades *arriving at Tilbury prior to her maiden voyage to Australia. This is November 1948, when she had just completed speed trials off the Isle of Arran. (CPL)*

Sydney with refuelling and crew-change stops en route was still too expensive and uncomfortable. Sea travel continued to be the favoured alternative for longer voyages, where people tended to be emigrating or making longer-term moves with the greater amounts of baggage and personal belongings that could be carried in a ship's hold.

The outlook for these services was so optimistic that both P&O and Orient Line decided to invest heavily in far larger and considerably faster ships, which would reduce the round-trip voyage times from Great Britain to Australia and New Zealand by a full two weeks. A service speed of 27.5 knots was determined to be optimum for the route with its many port calls, and a ship size of around 40,000 tons with a passenger capacity of 2,000 were found to offer the best economy of scale for commercial operation at the higher speed. Since the shorter voyage times would allow for more frequent sailings, the schedule could be maintained with fewer ships. P&O and Orient thus decided to build one fast superliner each for service on a pooled schedule.

Perhaps the greatest and most compelling rationale for building two such large ships was the Australian emigrant traffic, where the Australian authorities were given first priority on all Tourist-Class accommodation, virtually on a bulk charter basis. While the government-sponsored assisted passage cost each passenger a mere £10, the remainder of the actual £150 basic fare was fully compensated by the Australian government. At the time these ships were being planned, Australia's need for professionals and skilled tradespeople of all types as well as large numbers of ordinary workers and labourers seemed insatiable, with bright prospects of the nation's leading role in a 50-year cycle of Pacific Rim growth and development. Nobody then could have foreseen that by the end of the 1960s,

Australia's immigration needs would be restricted to those with specific skills, and that ultimately these people would travel exclusively by air.

Although both ships were to be of similar overall characteristics and performance, with nested lifeboats and remarkably large aluminium superstructures, each was designed and built independently of the other. Orient Line's *Oriana* was ordered from Vickers Armstrong and P&O's *Canberra* from Harland & Wolff. The more traditionally centre-engined *Oriana* was the ultimate career achievement of Orient Line's experienced naval architect, Charles F. Morris, as well as being the final expression of Brian O'Rorke's architectural work for the line since he began on *Orion* in the 1930s.

Canberra, with her machinery fully aft, was the product of a radical design approach on the part of P&O's progressive young naval architect, John West. Her interior architecture and elements of exterior styling were created by the noted contemporary British architect Sir Hugh Casson, working with his contemporaries, Barbara Oakley and John Wright. While both ships were regarded as being progressive and modern, *Canberra* was by far the more remarkable, as much for the clear, crisp modernity of her interior design as for her distinctive clean-lined exterior appearance, with her tall and slender oil-tanker-style funnels aft. In effect, *Oriana* carried the Orient Line fleet image in an apropos contemporary rendition, while *Canberra* conveyed the perhaps more youthful expression of an altogether new approach and expression brought about by the younger and more forward-focused minds that created her.

In her own right, *Oriana* was in many ways the more technically advanced of the two ships. Concerned about the sail-plane effects, Morris adopted a pyramid-like profile or elevation for the superstructure, rising from the bow and stern up to its

Below: *P&O's* Chusan *of 1950, one of several ships from both P&O and Orient Line that would be replaced by a new, fully integrated co-operative service between the two lines to be taken up in the early 1960s by* Oriana *and* Canberra, *reducing the voyage time between Southampton and Melbourne from 28 to 24 days.* (CPL)

highest point at the base of the funnel amidships. Having more than 85 per cent of the ship's whole side profile above the waterline would, he felt, significantly reduce the effects of wind resistance nearest the bow and stern, most critical while manoeuvring in port areas. To compensate for the loss of internal space at the opposite ends of the upper decks, *Oriana* was designed to use the spaces normally occupied by the engine room casing. These included baggage and store rooms at the lower levels, the two-deck-high cinema, the Tourist-Class midships bar and a small special-purpose reception room for First Class, all arranged with removable floor sections that could be opened up for access to the otherwise mechanically ventilated engine room as needed. (In point of fact it is very seldom, if ever, that this sort of service access is needed during a ship's service life.) This in turn left space available elsewhere for cabin accommodation and other facilities.

The stack, housing the air intakes for the engine-room ventilation system, was located immediately aft of the funnel amidships, though positioned lower down so as to avoid the possibility of drawing exhaust fumes back down into the machinery spaces. Although this was often mistaken for a second or dummy funnel, Morris himself had a particular aversion to dummy stacks, or indeed anything not entirely functional in the numerous liners he had a hand in designing for Orient Line since joining the company in 1944. He was fond of pointing out that when viewed against the sun, light passing through *Strathnaver* and *Strathaird*'s lounge beneath their aft-most funnels revealed unmistakably that these stacks were indeed dummies.

Concerned also that *Oriana* was to use a variety of smaller ports with lower pier heights, Morris took into consideration that the mooring decks needed to be lower than they might otherwise be for a ship of her size, in order to have the mechanical advantage of maximum purchase power on the lines. While it is customary for lower decks to be open at the stern of

a ship for such purposes, *Oriana*'s forward mooring gear was located on D deck, with openings in the forward hull shell plating for handling and securing the lines. This was two decks below the open fo'c'sle atop the hull where this gear would otherwise have been located.

Before they were awarded the building contract for *Oriana*, Vickers Armstrong (Shipbuilding) Ltd was hired by Orient Line in a consulting capacity to optimize the ship's hull form and to develop ways of achieving the maximum weight economy in her structural design. The welded aluminium superstructure was designed using techniques of modern aircraft construction to create a large and resilient structure that as a whole would form an integral strengthening element of the entire ship. As in aircraft construction, the inherent elasticity of the alloy would absorb the twisting and turning stresses of the ship's movement without loss of strength. These properties also allowed the superstructure to be constructed as a

Above: *P&O-Orient Line's* Oriana, *port side view showing the ship as built, with her hull in its original corn-colour and buff funnel.*
(Author's collection)

Below: *Starboard bow quarter view of* Oriana *off Auckland, still in line service, showing her later livery with white hull.*
(Author's collection)

Above, left & right: Oriana's Princess Lounge interior, August 1980. (Author's photographs)

Opposite, top: Canberra under construction at Harland and Wolff's yard, showing her aluminium superstructure. (CPL)

Opposite, bottom: Canberra sets off on her maiden voyage to Australia, 2 June 1961. (CPL)

Below, left: Starboard Gallery interior aboard Oriana. (Author's photo)

Below, right: Oriana's first class dining room interior, July 1979. (Author's photo)

stressed integral structure, without the need for expansion joints traditionally used in steel structures of this magnitude. *Oriana* also made wide use of the plane maker's technique of using profile cutouts in structural frames and beams as both a means of reducing deadweight and of providing a convenient routing for cables, plumbing and other services. All in all, the use of 1,100 tons of aluminium in *Oriana*'s construction was calculated to have achieved a weight economy of some 400 tons over conventional steel construction. In practical terms, this allowed the superstructure height to be increased to the height of one more deck than would have otherwise been possible.

Canberra's design was highly focused on the advantages of her fully aft machinery installation. While the examples of *El Djezair* and *Southern Cross* were valuable references, a great deal of design effort was required to develop a hull form that would support the concentration of powerful machinery aft against the fineness of waterline form forward needed to achieve the planned service speed of 27.5 knots. This had to be done in a way that would maintain low centres of buoyancy and gravity and a longitudinal centre of buoyancy as close to amidships as possible. Passenger comfort and safety could never be compromised in the interest of speed or the design ideal of having the engines all the way aft.

After a great deal of design work by John West and his colleagues at P&O, the technical department

of Harland & Wolff, and an extensive programme of model tank testing at the National Physical Laboratory, what finally emerged was, in effect, an adaptation of the *Normandie*-type Yourkevitch hull form. The added fullness of form aft required for *Canberra*'s machinery was compensated for by using a naval-style arrangement of exposed propeller shafts. This eliminated the added mass and drag of the steel bossings that usually enclose the shafts from the point where they pass through the shell back to the propeller brackets. Forward, the new P&O ship was given a fuller form below the waterline to help keep the longitudinal centre of buoyancy as near the midship point as possible. Above the water line the forward form was also flared out to a chine at D-deck level, increasing the accommodation space as far as possible and also, with the fullness of form below the waterline, providing vertical stability at speed.

Turbo-electric propulsion was chosen for *Canberra* as, despite its greater weight and cost, the drive motors could be positioned farther aft in the ship's confined stern compartments than could the larger steam turbines and reduction gearing of a conventional geared turbine installation. *Canberra*'s machinery was arranged with her three Foster Wheeler External Superheat D-type (ESD) boilers located farthest aft on a platform above the propeller shaft tunnels. The two doubled-up synchronous drive motors were in a compartment immediately forward

of this, where they were each aligned 2.35 degrees outwards to the line of the propeller shafts. The twin power-station-type, 6,000-volt, three-phase AC propulsion turbo alternator sets were in the main engine room immediately ahead of these. Above the boiler room, which itself extended up as far as D deck, there was a large conventional funnel casing, along with a smaller service and ventilation shaft extending up from E deck above the main engine room. All other auxiliary machinery spaces were below H deck, entirely beneath all accommodation and service areas for passengers and crew. The engine and boiler uptakes passed up through the accommodation decks immediately forward and astern of the aft main stairway, with only the Tourist-Class smoking room, pool and lido café being located aft of these on B and promenade decks.

The remainder of the four superstructure decks alongside and forward of the two casings, along with the corresponding midships spaces on C, D and E decks below, were the virtually exclusive domain of *Canberra*'s passengers. In his design of the First-Class public rooms, Sir Hugh Casson and his partners made extensive use of open planning, with the promenade-deck Meridian Room and its attached Century Bar, reading and writing rooms created as a flowing sequence of connected spaces entirely without inside corners. The dark and intimate Century

Above: Port bow quarter view of Canberra *under way towards New York, seen from the Verrazano-Narrows Bridge in 1978.* (Author's collection)

Bar was cosseted within an enclosed space at the main room's forward end, also housing a spectacular suspended spiral staircase ascending to the observation lounge three decks higher. At this uppermost level also was the First-Class ballroom, very ingeniously designed as an indoor/outdoor space with separate daytime and evening lives. A motorized sliding glass wall which descended into the deck allowed the teakwood dance floor to be joined with the lido sur-

rounding the immediately adjacent swimming pool. Thus the room served as a lido lounge during daylight hours, while after dinner dancing could be extended out to the pool on tropical evenings.

Although in themselves attractive and functional enough, the Tourist-Class rooms designed by John Wright never had quite the same design innovation and decorative richness of Sir Hugh Casson's First-Class spaces. Nonetheless, a number of these were very popular among *Canberra*'s passengers both in her original line services to Australia and the Pacific, and quite remarkably, later when both classes were amalgamated for cruising. The delightful cricket-themed Cricketers Tavern was an eternal favourite throughout *Canberra*'s 37-year career. The Island Room was also popular, as well as being a noteworthy modern, air-conditioned rendition of the 1935 *Orion*'s ballroom, with its glass side walls that could be opened to the outer deck and the tropical nights. The room was also fitted with a number of moveable interior glass partitions that could be arranged so that several activities could take place at the same time without interfering with one another.

By comparison, *Oriana*'s interiors reflected a more classic sense of Brian O'Rorke shipboard contemporary, as it had gradually modernized over the years since he had first worked on *Orion*'s design. There was a consistent sense of understated hotelier warmth and elegance throughout *Oriana* that was neither as crisply modern and high style as Sir Hugh's First-Class rooms aboard *Canberra* nor as stark as some of the P&O ship's tourist interiors were thought to be by some. The standard of *Oriana*'s Tourist public rooms in fact came closer to that of their First-Class counterparts than did those aboard *Canberra*.

Where the two ships did differ greatly was in their internal layouts. *Oriana* followed a traditional plan with public rooms on the uppermost decks, which placed these entirely above the nested lifeboats, recessed into the two uppermost cabin decks. In this respect, her plan was similar to the Royal Rotterdam Lloyd's *Willem Ruys* also built with nested lifeboats. *Canberra* was the first modern ship where the accommodation layout was planned to coincide with the lower location of the nested lifeboats. Thus the main suite of public rooms was located on the lowest superstructure deck, surrounded by the boat deck, where there was sufficient headroom beneath the boats themselves for this to serve as the principal promenade deck. This also allowed the public rooms to be used as muster stations in case of an emergency, where passengers could be assembled for quick and easy access to the lifeboats. The two decks both immediately above and below the main public rooms and promenade were occupied almost entirely by cabins. The dining rooms on the lowest passenger deck were beneath these, with a further suite of informal daytime public and recreation areas on the

uppermost decks above the cabins. *Canberra*'s plan has since become a reference for the design of large cruise ships, where a nested lifeboat arrangement is now mandatory in new safety regulations limiting the height of safety equipment above the waterline.

Both ships were laid out with First-Class accommodation forward and Tourist-Class aft. A court cabin arrangement of similar concept to George Sharp's Air Light accommodation plan was extensively used in both ships. These were a somewhat modernized rendition of the original idea, rendered on a remarkably compact plan using space-saving built-in fittings and features, such as convertible sofa-beds, to achieve the added sense of spaciousness and functionality needed on long voyages. In *Canberra*, these made up the majority of First-Class accommodation apart from the premium-grade suites and deluxe cabins and a small number of inboard single cabins on C and D decks.

Surprisingly for a ship with so much emphasis on an aft machinery location as *Canberra*, the opportunity was somehow missed to make full use of the court cabin arrangement to achieve an axial plan with single centre corridors on the accommodation decks as had been proposed in Sharp's original plans. Although centre passages were featured forward on *Canberra*'s B, C and D decks, the overall plan made less use of centre accesses than was done aboard *Southern Cross*. The most remarkable court arrangement was achieved on a radial plan inside the semi-circular superstructure front surrounding the spiral staircase. Thanks to the plan's greater radius at the distance of the courts from the main passage, the outer cabins could be virtually as large as the inner rooms despite the additional space needed for the courts themselves.

The court cabin arrangement was only adopted at a later stage of *Oriana*'s planning, with these being confined mainly to the midships and forward part of C deck for intermediate-grade First-Class, Tourist and interchangeable accommodation. Although both ships offered modern and luxurious First-Class accommodation, their enormous Tourist capacities were clearly aimed at the assisted passage Australian emigrant trade. Thus much of the Tourist cabin accommodation was decidedly sub-standard by North Atlantic convention. Although they were bright and modern, outfitted with attractive and serviceable fittings and finishes, many of the rooms were no more than minimalist four-berth emigrant cabins, with but a washbasin and otherwise served by communal bath and toilet facilities. Functionally, they

Opposite, bottom: **Canberra's Meridian Room interior with original furniture and ceiling fixture.** (Casson Conder Partnership Architects/Author's collection)

Below: *William Fawcett Room interior.* (Author's collection)

were little different from the Tourist-Third accommodation of the 1930s, while recent Atlantic liners such as *France* and Holland America's 1959-built *Rotterdam* were offering accommodation with en-suite toilet facilities as virtually standard throughout both classes.

As a concession to making at least some of this largely inside accommodation suitable for cruising and other services, both ships were fitted with blocks of cabins designed to readily convert as two-berth rooms with private showers and toilets. Using the type of ingenuity that usually goes into railway sleeping car design, these were built with one set of upper and lower bunks which folded away into a wall recess, revealing the concealed toilet and shower fittings. A fold-away partition with its own door completed the conversion, separating the compact en-suite from the rest of the room. The change-over could be made single-handed by a cabin steward in a matter of minutes.

Although of heavier and more conventional construction *Canberra* was without question the more attractive of the two ships. The structural and technical rationale of *Oriana*'s design and layout was lost to the casual comprehension of the average passenger or observer. *Canberra*'s clean-lined modern appearance, with her rounded superstructure front lines and the uncluttered appearance of her vast open upper decks and tall supertanker-style funnels, fulfilled a visual expectation in the public's eyes. Both inside and out she was very much of her time, an ocean-going symbol of the elegant 1960s, the jet age and even the space age. *Oriana* nonetheless developed

her own loyal following, on the basis of her stronger sense of Orient Line's particular onboard contemporary. While *Canberra* was crisply avant garde and rationalist, *Oriana*'s modernity tended more to be tempered with the various idiosyncrasies of plan and layout that have always made ships so interesting.

Oriana's upwards vista of the funnel, upper parts of the superstructure and bridge from the stadium deck well or from the sports deck aft, the stretches of traditional enclosed promenade deck alongside the First-Class lounge and galleries, were as much to be expected of the actual experience aboard ship as *Canberra*'s appearance presented the right impression externally. *Oriana* thus retained the special sensation of Orient's ships with their funnels and bridges amidships. Those little things one only discovers several days into the voyage, such as the grill room staircase behind the ballroom stage or those remarkable little spiral stairways joining the boat deck with the promenade, were part of an experience that has vanished with modern planning in which superstructure sizes are maximized and internal spaces optimized.

When *Oriana* and *Canberra* began sailing in 1960–61, they were a sensation worldwide. Following an enthusiastic media build-up to the event, *Oriana*'s maiden arrival in Sydney was announced in the Australian press with banner headlines proclaiming simply, 'She's Here!' When *Canberra* made a promotional voyage to North America's eastern seaboard in 1962, a broadcast of the popular morning television programme The Today Show from aboard the ship in New York was watched by an estimated 12 million viewers, believed

Below: *The Dutch liner* Willem Ruys *enters Grand Harbour, Valletta, on 8 January 1963, to take on some of the passengers of* Canberra (right), *which had been crippled by an onboard fire.* (CPL)

to have included President John F. Kennedy at the White House.

Then, before the advent of jet airline service to Australia from Britain, 26-day passage to Sydney could be booked for as little as £150 for a berth in a minimum-grade cabin without private toilet facilities, or £550 for a single cabin with its own bath, as opposed to £248 for the 35-hour flight from London to Sydney, with refuelling and crew-change stops en route.

A vast proportion of the passengers carried aboard both ships before they switched to full-time cruising in the 1970s paid only £10 for the one-way assisted passage as emigrants to Australia. This was in effect a bulk chartering arrangement giving Tourist-Class booking priority to the Australian government in what turned out to be the world's last great wave of emigration by sea. Yet despite the modernity of the ships and the services they offered, the quaint Victorian practice of segregating male and female passengers prevailed. Accommodation would usually be allocated within the groups of six-to-eight cabins surrounding each lateral passage leading from the main corridors, with men and boys sharing rooms one side, and ladies, girls and infants opposite. On at least one voyage, when the families in one of these enclaves found that there was a newly-wed couple in their midst, they took it upon themselves to exchange rooms in order to ensure that the honeymooners could enjoy the seclusion of one of the two-berth rooms alone.

One of *Canberra*'s masters later in her career, Captain Jock Lefevre, recalled that the ship's First-

Class trade 'engaged the last of the Raj'.[10] Among the last liners to ply the Commonwealth's traditional sea routes, she counted among her passengers the former Cabinet minister Lord George Brown, who later tried one of *Canberra*'s early Caribbean cruises, British newspaper magnate Lord Kemsley and famed Australian cricketer Sir Donald Bradman. The Australian and English cricket teams regularly travelled aboard the ship to and from their Test Matches, where they were popular with their fans onboard. The players would gather in the writing rooms during the morning hours on days at sea to autograph team photographs for passengers. *Canberra* was a favourite of the American film star Cary Grant, while part of the James Bond film *Diamonds are Forever* was filmed on board.

Canberra lived her early career as a liner in an age of modern informal elegance, once described as 'twin-set and tweedy days', when daytime wear in the fully air-conditioned public rooms and on deck tended to be then-fashionable twin-set sweater and cardigan ensembles for ladies, and gentlemen appeared in the dining room for dinner in their tweeds. Tea-time attire was usually jacket and tie for men and dress or skirt, seamed nylon stockings and high-heeled shoes for women. Full formal dress was generally only an option for First-Class gala occasions, with gentlemen's suits and ladies' cocktail dresses being equally acceptable.

Gin and tonic was the preferred pre-lunch drink, and scotch and soda the pre-dinner choice. Yet as the pop culture of the age was universally taking hold, and with many young people on their way to new lives in Australia, passengers in both classes were also dancing to the latest hits by Frank Sinatra, Petula

Above: Known as the 'Erections Bar' during the Falklands voyage, this is the Crow's Nest lounge as it appeared with the structural strengthening necessitated by the fitting of a helicopter deck above.
(Author's collection)

Above: *A rust-streaked* Canberra *on her triumphant return to Southampton on July 11, 1982, at the conclusion of her 'national service' in the South Atlantic.* (Author's collection)

Below: *The Meridian Room as it appeared later in the ship's career.*

Clark, the Beatles and Australia's own Bee Gees and Seekers. In those days, before the whirlwind of virtually round-the-clock activity expected aboard today's cruise ships, by midnight the band had put away their instruments, the bars were closed and the juke box in the Pop Inn fell silent. Apart from those on duty behind the scenes on the bridge, in the engine room and the galleys, and the crew who would clean the empty public rooms and swab down the open decks, *Canberra* slept until the first early risers appeared on deck at daybreak. A peculiarity of British domestic life from earlier times when sanitary facilities and hot water were in less abundant supply than they are today, both ashore and at sea, was that Saturday night was bath night in many households. In the early days of her career, *Canberra*'s engineers had to respond to a noticeable increase in demand for domestic hot water throughout the ship on Saturday evenings.

Of the two ships, ironically, the more lightly constructed *Oriana* was first to be withdrawn from service in 1986, becoming a tourist attraction in Beppu Bay in Japan the following year. Later moved to China where she still survives, albeit now in a static role, she ultimately outlived the more robust *Canberra*, which was decommissioned and scrapped in 1997 at the end of her illustrious service career of 36 years. ●

Left: *The Island Room, after its conversion as a night-club in the post-Falklands refit, showing an altogether plusher and more luxurious treatment of this formerly rather stark Tourist-Class space.*
(Author's collection)

Below: Canberra *in Southampton near the end of her career, with the new P&O cruise ship* Oriana, *delivered in 1995 and reflecting many of* Canberra's *distinctive design features, though very different in her absolutely flat rather than curvilinear sheered decks and inclusion of veranda cabins above the lifeboat recess.*
(Author's collection)

7

ENGAGING THE MODERN CRUISE ERA

The last traditional liners were completed and entered service in the mid 1960s, at a time when the airlines had already asserted their superiority over virtually all passenger liner services worldwide. Most of these ships were built for long-established lines that were in the passenger business since the early days of steam. While some were already diversifying into freight, containerized cargo, tankers and other services, for most, passenger liners were still a significant part of their corporate livelihood. Lines such as Cunard, CGT, Holland America, P&O and Union Castle all believed that, for the time being at least, they had an obligation to continue serving what remained of their loyal clienteles.

The great problem was to find alternative ways of making passenger shipping attractive and commercially viable against the new competition at a time when there were no business models, service precedents or reference ships for developing alternative or new types of service. Nobody then knew what the full impact of commercial aviation might be, nor whether there were enough people still preferring to sail rather than fly to make the continuation of service worthwhile, even with reduced schedules, smaller ships and less frequent sailings. The alternative of cruising was also an unknown factor at the time, when there was no certainty that the demand would expand widely to the more affluent younger generations of the 1950s and 1960s who now had the opportunity of jetting off to other parts of the world for coach tours or resort holidays.

Swedish American and Norwegian America lines had already captured a significant share of the elite luxury cruise trade, with its needs being specifically provided for in their North Atlantic ships. Since Swedish America's *Kungsholm* of 1928 and Norwegian America's first *Oslofjord* was delivered in 1938, both lines had put ever greater emphasis on the alternative cruising role of their fleets, stressing an ideal of the 1927-built Swedish cruise yacht *Stella Polaris* as a reference for design and service. The standard of accommodation adopted by the Swedish and Norwegian lines was based on a two-class Atlantic service for about 600 passengers in accommodation that was adaptable to single-class cruising for around 450 persons, using only the lower-berth capacities of the combined First and Tourist cabins.

During the 1950s and 1960s the building programmes of both lines emphasized greater comfort and luxury, with full air-conditioning and en-suite toilet facilities in every cabin, along with a wider range of cruise amenities such as outdoor swimming pools, lidos and deck cafés. The Swedish American ships were also designed with the additional luxury of exclusively outer cabins, each with its own portholes or windows.

Norwegian America Line's 1965-delivered *Sagafjord* and Swedish American Line's third *Kungsholm*, completed early the following year, were both deigned firstly for cruising and only secondly as Atlantic liners. As such, they were both essentially one-class ships, although a vestigial designation of

Opposite, top: *A photograph of the Queen's Room aboard the Cunard liner* Queen Elizabeth 2, *designed by Michael Inchald, showing the original furnishings and fittings with the trumpet-shaped columns being reflected in the shape of the chair bases. The room remained in this form until QE2's re-engining refit of 1986–87.* (Author's photo)

Opposite, bottom: *Italian Line's* Leonardo da Vinci *of 1960; the long sequence of afterdecks terraced from the First-Class pool on Lido deck down to Cabin-Class on Boat Deck, and Tourist farthest aft on Promenade deck.* (Author's photo)

Above: *Port-side near-profile view of the Swedish American Line's* Gripsholm *at sea, showing her classic liner appearance in a modern rendition with a 'cruising' white hull.* (Gordon Turner collection)

Above: *Swedish American Line's* Kungsholm *at the Port of Montréal in 1977 while cruising under charter to Flagship Cruises, showing the progression to a greater emphasis on cruising with an open pool area amidships on the boat deck, and lido protruding into the lifeboat line above.* (Author's photo)

Above: *Starboard bow view of Norwegian America Line's* Sagafjord, *departing from Montréal on a cruise in 1981. The luxury cabins above the bridge were added as a consideration of extended cruise service.* (Author's photo)

First Class was retained merely to satisfy the North Atlantic Passenger Conference's rating and membership requirements. *Sagafjord* was thus listed as having transatlantic accommodation for 85 First-Class and 704 Tourist Class passengers, while *Kungsholm's* figures were 108 First and 605 Tourist. For cruising the two ships were shown to each offer all-lower-berth accommodation for 450 passengers.

The two-class Atlantic line service appears to have been more ethereal than real, as there was virtually no discernible indication of which among the standardized luxury cabins and suites aboard either ship were designated as First Class. Aboard *Sagafjord* there was absolutely no provision for separation of public spaces to either class. *Kungsholm's* plan offered the possibility for some nominal division of public spaces, with the duplication of the cocktail lounges and libraries forward and aft of her amidships main lounge, as well as a forward observation lounge above on the boat deck, which could have been designated for exclusive use by premium-fare-paying passengers if required.

Sagafjord and *Kungsholm* introduced a number of features that have since been widely adopted in cruise ship design. These were among the first modern deep-sea passenger vessels to eliminate the traditional promenade decks surrounding the public rooms, either enclosed or open, in favour of extending the air-conditioned lounges and other social spaces fully out to the deck's full width with floor-to-ceiling windows along their outer walls. *Kungsholm*, the larger of the two ships, also featured a swimming pool, with adjoining lido decks and snack bar, located amidships between her two funnels. Glass windscreens protected the whole area along either side, and stairways ascended to the open sun terraces above. The concept of this, and indeed its physical relationship to the observation lounge and its enclosed verandas forward was fairly similar to *Canberra's* upper decks recreational facilities.

During their first years in service, the line operations of both ships and their respective fleet mates were drastically reduced in favour of cruising. Norwegian America Line's 15 transatlantic sailings in 1967 were reduced to only five the following year. Nine crossings were scheduled by Swedish American Line in 1966, dropping to three by 1970 and only annual positioning voyages being made between 1971 and 1975. The line suspended its passenger services altogether in 1975, selling *Kungsholm* and the 1957-built *Gripsholm*. *Gripsholm* was extensively rebuilt for Princess Cruises as *Sea Princess*, later becoming *Victoria* under the P&O houseflag, while *Gripsholm* went to the Greek Karageorgis family, cruising for many years as *Navarino*. Norwegian America's *Sagafjord* was followed in 1973 by a slightly larger ship of similar design, built exclusively for cruising, with both ships remaining in service until the line's later acquisition into the Norwegian

Left: *Starboard side view of Holland America Line's* Rotterdam *at sea late in her career, with a dark blue hull. The addition of wind-screening around her aft lido deck, and new excursion launches carried on the foredeck (replacing the aft-most lifeboats), were the only visible external modifications made for her full-time cruising role.* (Author's collection)

Kvaerner group and union with Cunard Line under the same parent corporation. *Sagafjord* continues to sail, as *Saga Rose* operated by UK-based Saga Holidays, while *Vistafjord* is now Cunard's *Caronia*. These ships had been unprofitable in cruise service for their original owners on account of the low passenger capacities they offered for their size. Operated on the basis of their transatlantic capacities or refitted to add extra accommodation, they have subsequently fared better, particularly in the larger fleets of P&O/Princess Cruises and Cunard.

Holland America Line's exquisite *Rotterdam* of 1959 was without doubt one of the ships to most successfully make the transition from line service to cruising. Like a number of her contemporaries including, nominally at least, *France*, Italia's *Leonardo da Vinci*, *Oriana* and *Canberra*, the new Holland America flagship was designed with an alternative cruising role in mind. This was an aspect of naval architecture generally viewed at the time as a matter of designing the passenger classes to be compatible and easily amalgamated, as well as offering the essential warm-weather amenities of open-air swimming pools, lidos and ample open deck spaces. *Rotterdam*'s original design, however, went further than most in asserting the right sort of onboard atmosphere and facilities for both types of service.

The afterdecks were laid out with a large swimming pool and vast surrounding lido with direct access from the Tourist Class veranda lounge and café on the promenade deck. The arrangement of the upper decks also provided excellent facilities for open-air activities, with two separate sports decks atop the superstructure, each with its own adjoining sun room inside a deckhouse also housing the lift machinery and air-conditioning plant. This was made possible largely thanks to *Rotterdam*'s three quarters-aft machinery arrangement, with two goalpost-style funnels aft, leaving space for the sports decks to be located amidships on the sun and boat decks. The

arrangement served both the purposes of class segregation in line service, and a greater diversity of places for different activities while cruising.

Rotterdam's entire layout was a masterpiece of planning, achieving far greater flexibility and adaptability in both her line service and cruising lives. At 38,650 tons and with a passenger capacity of 1,456, she had the economy of scale to be profitable in both types of service. Although rated below the elitist level of First-Class accommodation and service aboard *France*, *Rotterdam* offered a consistently higher level of luxury across all grades of accommodation in both classes than most ships of her time. There was clearly a lower proportion of inside cabins without portholes or windows than aboard *France*.

Apart from the deluxe suites and various other

Below: *The* Rotterdam *at her New York terminal on Easter Sunday, 17 April 1960, with a row of American cars in the foreground showing the automotive styling of the age, characterized by the gull-winged tail fin.* (Gordon Turner collection)

Above: *Rotterdam's original 'open promenade' after being adapted as a lido for full-time cruising, which entailed construction of a full-height glass windscreen at either side and an overhead brise soleil above the lido café, as seen in this 1986 view, looking forward.*
(Author's photo)

special rooms, *Rotterdam*'s cabins were of two fairly standardized plans. These included a larger First-Class layout designed for direct access from the main accommodation corridors, and a pair of smaller inner and outer rooms on a slightly wider fore-and-aft dimension occupying the same depth between the ship's side and passage, which could be booked at lower prices. To all intents and purposes, most of these were interchangeable between First and Tourist Class, as they were planned also to meet the requirements for luxury cruising. There was only a small block of minimum-fare Tourist cabins in B deck aft without en-suite showers and toilets, and no passenger rooms below the waterline. *Rotterdam* was, in fact, one of the few liners built to go cruising without any significant reduction of her full liner-service passenger capacity.

Throughout her accommodation, deck spaces and public rooms, *Rotterdam* had the same remarkable sense of comfortable human scale for which her older consort, *Nieuw Amsterdam* of 1938, was so popular. Neither ship was so big as to become impersonal, nor so highly populated as to ever seem crowded. Architecturally, *Rotterdam*'s modern interiors were an expression of classic elegance, expressed with a richness of finish and decoration reflecting but a slightly more contemporary rendition of the earlier *Nieuw Amsterdam*'s timeless ambience and elegance. This was especially apparent in the elegant double-height Ritz-Carlton Lounge, with its curving stairway and upper gallery, and the circular-plan Ambassador Room, with its dark and intimate corners and recesses.

The main defining difference between *Rotterdam*'s two suites of public interiors was that the layout and function of the First-Class rooms on the upper promenade deck were a little more formal than the promenade-deck Tourist-Class rooms. These

Tourist spaces included the large full-beam main lounge with its full-height panoramic windows and asymmetrical layout of the dance floor and bandstand, along with the veranda lounge and café aft, adjacent to the pool and lido. While each suite of rooms set the right tone for their own clientele in line service, their combination for cruising produced a wider variety of spaces to suite different functions and moods, in which no space seemed to be either too far above or below the ship's overall sense of luxury, elegance and good taste. Thanks to *Rotterdam*'s interleaved main 'trick staircase' the ship was able to achieve a virtually seamless cohesion of her accommodation, public rooms and deck spaces for cruising. There was absolutely no indication of duplicated functions, with the deck lobbies and other circulating areas fully opened up and concealing their remarkable ability to separate the two passenger classes when needed.

Although *Rotterdam* was operated mainly on line voyages between Rotterdam and New York during the early years of her career, cruising was introduced during her first year in service. In 1961 *Rotterdam* took over the line's annual round-the-world cruises, inaugurated in 1958 by *Statendam*. As the North Atlantic trade continued to decline, Holland America Line announced in 1968 their intention to concentrate their passenger services on cruising rather than crossings. *Nieuw Amsterdam* had already been modernized while *Rotterdam* was being built to bring her up to a similar standard of accommodation and service. *Statendam*'s public rooms were substantially remodelled. *Rotterdam*'s original Tourist-Class veranda lounge and café were entirely rebuilt into a large lido café and her accommodation upgraded to replace those cabins without en-suite facilities. Holland America's regular transatlantic services were closed by *Nieuw Amsterdam* in September 1971, with the much-loved older ship joining the newer *Statendam* and *Rotterdam* in full-time cruising for an additional two years before being finally withdrawn from service and sold for scrap at the end of 1973.

Among those of her contemporaries designed and built for dual-purpose operation, *Rotterdam* made the transition more readily and gracefully than most. While *France* had a similar arrangement of First- and Tourist-Class facilities, she lacked the open-air swimming pools, lidos, deck cafés and sports facilities required for cruising. Although both the the Tourist pool and sports centre had a glass roof, neither of these could be opened. While $4 million was spent on improvements to *Nieuw Amsterdam*, *Statendam* and *Rotterdam* for cruising in 1968, *France*'s conversion as *Norway* during the winter of 1979–80 cost $40 million, to enable her to do essentially the same type of year-round tropical island-hopping the Holland America ship had been doing since her inaugural year in service. The requirements for this were quite different from the few round-the-world voyages and other longer deep-sea cruises *France* had made during her 12-year service career, with the need for additional work being done to downgrade her powerful quadruple-screw machinery for economic service at lower speeds.

While other tropical liners such as *Transvaal Castle* already had the open-air pools and ample deck space for cruising, many were built with large amounts of general and refrigerated cargo space, making them uneconomical in any service without this capacity being used. When, as *S.A. Vaal*, this ship was bought by Carnival Cruise Lines in 1978, her extensive conversion as *Festivale* at the Kawasaki Heavy Industries shipyard in Kobe, Japan, involved converting her hold spaces to passenger accommodation and services, with the superstructure also being extended forward and aft above these.

Many considered the emigrant-class cabins lacking en-suite facilities that were prevalent aboard *Oriana* and the aft-engined *Southern Cross* and *Canberra* as substandard for cruising by the time these ships were seeking alternative deployment during the 1970s. *Southern Cross* was sold to Cia. de Vap. Cerulea S.A. in 1973, for cruising as *Calypso* and during her conversion the accommodation was extensively rebuilt and upgraded, unfortunately with the loss of her original axial layout.

Following an unsuccessful attempt to introduce *Canberra* into American-based cruising in 1973, P&O ultimately found that she and *Oriana* were more ideally suited to their British and Australian cruise markets, where there were more passengers willing to accept their many lower-grade cabins as an inexpensive alternative to the more luxurious accommodation. Both ships were perennial favourites, with *Oriana* continuing to make positioning voyages between her British and Australian cruise programmes until 1980, and *Canberra* making her annual round-the-world winter cruises until 1997, the year she was withdrawn from service.

No doubt the greatest disappointment was the limited success of the beautiful Italian Line ships of this era in making the transition to full-time cruising. These each featured several open-air swimming pools, ample deck space, magnificent suites of modern and functional public rooms and high standards of cabin accommodation and passenger service. But, alas, their owners continued to uphold a rigid adherence to their traditional standards of multiple passenger classes, with little concession being made to the full amalgamation of these for cruising. A modern standard of design was established in 1953–54 with *Cristoforo Colombo* and *Andrea Doria*, with the promenade deck divided between First-Class public rooms forward and those of Cabin Class aft, and with the accommodation for these classes on the decks immediately above and below. While these, along with the various swimming pools, cafés and deck

spaces, could be combined easily enough for cruising, the Tourist-Class public areas aft and the great numbers of smaller cabins on the lower decks were far less suitable.

Leonardo da Vinci, delivered in 1959 to replace *Andrea Doria* which had sunk after colliding with Swedish American's *Stockholm* in 1956, was a larger ship of similar overall layout and character. Largely as a result of *Andrea Doria*'s loss, a number of significant safety features were introduced into the design of *Leonardo da Vinci*. There was extensive watertight subdivision of the hull, with most of the watertight bulkheads being extended two decks higher than normal to the upper deck. The ship was fitted with bulkhead-mounted luffing davits capable of launching her motorized lifeboats against a list of up to 25 degrees.

The machinery was arranged with two entirely

Above: The First-Class ballroom of the Italian Line's Giulio Cesare, *showing an early post-war example of architect Gustavo Poulitzer's distinctive shipboard work.* (Gordon Turner collection)

Below: In comparison, Cristoforo Colombo's *First-Class ballroom, a slightly later and more 'international modern' Poulitzer design.* (Gordon Turner collection)

separate boiler and turbine plants in separate water-tight compartments, located forward and aft of the distillation plant located amidships. The forward installation drove the starboard propeller shaft and the aft plant the port-side shaft. Each of the two engine rooms was arranged asymmetrically, with two boilers arranged on the opposite side of the centreline to the turbine sets and double-reduction gearing. Nominal provision was made for the ship to later be converted to nuclear power, in the event that the American nuclear ship *Savannah*, being planned at the same time, was to gain public favour.

To make provision for a reactor to be installed amidships, *Leonardo da Vinci*'s dining rooms and galley were located on the foyer deck immediately beneath the promenade deck public rooms, and above the various ship's services and main fore-and-aft working passage along the starboard side of the deck directly below. From A deck down the accommodation was completely segregated by a block of working spaces amidships, directly forward of the funnel casing, arranged to accommodate a nuclear reactor if need be, with the most unfortunate conse-quence of the ship's lower-decks plan being severely fragmented. The lowest passenger-accessible corridor running the full length of the accommodation was located on the upper deck inboard of the working passage, with no fewer than 14 jogs and turns along its length, routed around the funnel casing, various stairways and other vertical cores and other obstructions. The change to atomic power was, of course, never made.

The 46,000-ton *Michelangelo* and *Raffaello* went into service as Italia's final two liners only 74 days apart in May and July 1965 respectively. The commissioning of two such large and prestigious liners as these in 1965 was indeed a tremendous gesture of confidence in the future of sea travel on the part of their owners. Sailing schedules were carefully arranged for the two new ships to be together at Pier 90 in the Port of New York on 3 August 1965 as a show of the new era in Italian passenger-liner service. Unfortunately, only 10 years later, both ships sailed from New York for the last time, first being laid up at Spezia, and then sold the following year for use as officer accommodation ships by the Iranian Navy.

The rationale for building these had originated in the late 1950s, effectively as replacements for the ageing *Saturnia* and *Vulcania*. With *Leonardo da Vinci*'s building taking precedence as an immediate replacement for *Andrea Doria*, orders for these ships were only placed in 1960, with their keels scheduled to be laid at about the time of *Leonardo da Vinci*'s completion. Originally they were to have been a slightly larger variant of the 33,340-ton, 23-knot *Leonardo da Vinci*, at 36,000 tons and a service speed of 26 knots. Later detailed planning revealed that a greater size of around 43,000 tons and speed of 26.5 knots would yield optimum performance at the power required to achieve the higher service speed, and would reduce the Atlantic crossing time by a full day. The order was revised accordingly, and the delivery date changed from 1963 to 1965.

The design of these ships was of considerable technical significance, as a two-thirds-aft adaptation of *Leonardo da Vinci*'s fore-and-aft segregation of her propulsion machinery and asymmetrical machinery arrangements. The two 43,500 shp propulsion aggregates were modelled after those of the United States Navy's *Independence*-class aircraft carriers. *Michelangelo* and *Raffaello* also featured extensive watertight subdivision of their hulls, and were outfitted to Method 1 Fire Prevention Standards, as had been *United States* and *France*. The nearly total absence of portholes and other shell openings below main deck was an added safety measure, albeit gained at the expense of all accommodation on A, B and C decks being rendered as inside spaces without the benefit of natural light or outside views. Provision was also made for later conversion to nuclear power, again with the unfortunate complete division of accommodation on these lower decks forward and aft.

The passenger accommodation layout and architectural design of *Michelangelo* and *Raffaello* were in essence an expanded rendition of that on *Leonardo da Vinci*. With the promenade and main suites of public rooms located on the first superstructure deck, and with the earlier ship's additional height repeated, virtually all First-Class cabins and suites, with the

exception of a small block of rooms port side on the main deck, were located on the two decks above promenade level. The farther-aft machinery location allowed for an upper-deck arrangement of the First-Class swimming pool, glass-enclosed lido and veranda café atop the superstructure, forward of each ship's pair of distinctive latticed funnels. The pools and other open-air amenities for Cabin and Tourist classes were arranged traditionally on the afterdecks, whose layout and extent were surprisingly unaffected by the location of a triple-height theatre on the upper decks aft of the funnels.

As aboard *Cristoforo Colombo*, *Andrea Doria* and *Leonardo da Vinci*, the main suites of First- and Cabin-Class public rooms aboard *Michelangelo* and *Raffaello* were arranged along the promenade deck, where they could easily be combined for cruising. One outstanding feature was the First-Class ballroom, extended out to the full-height windows at either side and featuring a central rectangular dome space through the deck above. The large cocktail bar, another exceptional feature, was designed as an intimate inboard space fully forward and flanked by the card room and library at either side overlooking the enclosed promenade. Apart from the belvedere deck above the bridge and the forward end of the boat

Below, left: Cocktail bar interior aboard the Leonardo da Vinci, *designed by Monaco and Luccichenti.* (Author's photo)

Below, right: View through the Promenade Deck *public spaces, where the lounges for all three classes could be combined for cruising by opening the interconnecting doors, as seen in this view looking aft from the* Leonardo da Vinci's *First-Class vestibule.* (Author's photo)

1   First Class Belvedere
2   Wireless and Radio Telephone Station
3   First Class Gymnasium
4   First Class Pool Verandah
5   First Class Swimming Pool and Lido
6   First Class Promenade
7   First Class Staterooms
8   Auditorium – Cinema – Theatre
9   Cabin Class Gymnasium
10   Cabin Class Promenade
11   Teenage Club
12   Cabin Class Verandah
14   Cabin Class Swimming Pool and Lido
15   Tourist Class Promenade
16   First Class Cocktail Lounge

18   First Class Lounge
19   First Class Ballroom
20   First Class Children's Room
21   Cabin Class Children's Room
22   Cabin Class Card Room
23   Cabin Class Lounge and Bar

Above: Cut-away longitudinal section of Italian Line's **Michelangelo** *of 1965. Note the cars stowed in the garage spaces amidships which would have become the reactor compartment if the ship were converted to nuclear power. The reactor would probably have been serviced from above by way of removable floor sections in the dining rooms, ballroom and swimming pool tank directly over this space.* (Author's collection)

deck, there was no view forward from any of the public spaces.

Although their layouts were virtually identical, the architectural design of the two ships was as radically different as it had been in the earlier *Cristoforo Colombo* and *Andrea Doria*. Each of the new ships was the work of a separate team of leading Italian architects, designers and artists. *Michelangelo*, which was among the last ship to bear Gustavo Pulitzer's creative signature, generally displayed a more typically Genoese style of sophisticated modernity. *Raffaello* was a little more progressive, adopting a lighter and brighter palette along with various decorative touches, such as the beautiful fluted ceiling panels of the dining rooms and the lighting schemes in a number of the other First-Class public rooms, that were in themselves individually distinctive. Of the two ships, *Raffaello* won the greatest public favour, being generally seen as more stylishly European in character. There was, however, a consensus of opinion among many that these ships never quite measured up to *Leonardo da Vinci*'s finesse of design and decoration.

Apart from the veranda café, children's room and library, located aft of these, the remaining Tourist-Class public spaces and accommodation were relegated to the lower decks. Most disappointing among these were the Tourist dining rooms in both ships, which were entirely inside spaces accessed from a long, featureless corridor running the length of main deck, parallel to the ship's working passage. Apart from the public rooms aft on the promenade deck, the

Tourist-Class facilities of the ships were generally considered to be less suitable for cruising, despite en-suite facilities being placed in all cabins. In cruise service the two new ships, as well as *Leonardo da Vinci* and *Cristoforo Colombo*, were operated with the majority of their Tourist public rooms unused, and with the better cabins in this class being sold at minimum fare and their occupants using the combined First and Cabin public facilities. The ships were therefore expensive to operate on cruises, with large amounts of unused space and an over-abundance of lounges and other rooms with little provision for professional entertainment or other specialized functions.

Initial public interest in *Michelangelo* and *Raffaello* was encouraging, as these ships were well booked during their first summer Atlantic seasons. The high point for Italian Line came in 1968 when they carried the most transatlantic passengers, a total of 81,069, against Cunard's second-place standing of 40,950. This was, however, a somewhat shallow victory, as Cunard's *Queen Mary* had been withdrawn from service in 1967 and sold to the City of Long Beach, California. This left only *Queen Elizabeth* on the Southampton–New York run during this, her last year before the new *Queen Elizabeth 2* was to make her debut in 1969. Nonetheless the Italia liners retained a loyal following among those still preferring to travel by sea, and whose homes or destinations were in Continental Europe where the train trip to Genoa was as convenient as that to Bremerhaven or Le Havre. The line's cruises from New York and

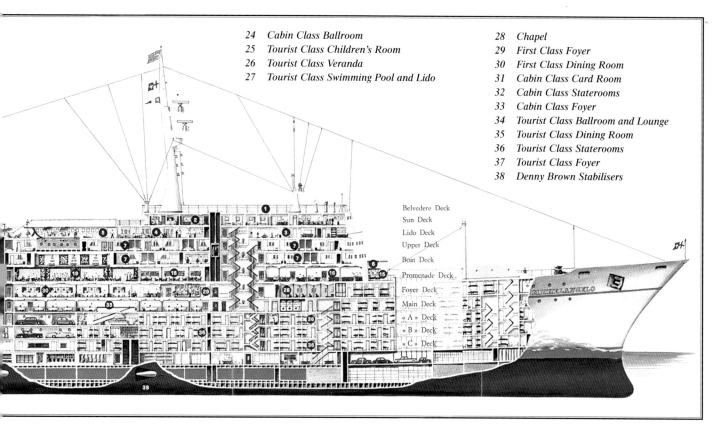

24 Cabin Class Ballroom
25 Tourist Class Children's Room
26 Tourist Class Veranda
27 Tourist Class Swimming Pool and Lido

28 Chapel
29 First Class Foyer
30 First Class Dining Room
31 Cabin Class Card Room
32 Cabin Class Staterooms
33 Cabin Class Foyer
34 Tourist Class Ballroom and Lounge
35 Tourist Class Dining Room
36 Tourist Class Staterooms
37 Tourist Class Foyer
38 Denny Brown Stabilisers

Belvedere Deck
Sun Deck
Lido Deck
Upper Deck
Boat Deck
Promenade Deck
Foyer Deck
Main Deck
« A » Deck
« B » Deck
« C » Deck

Fort Lauderdale were also popular, drawing mainly from the United States eastern seaboard in those days before airline connections to the port of departure were sold as part of the cruise.

The large liners *Oceanic* and *Eugenio C*, completed at about the same time as *Michelangelo* and *Raffaello* for other European owners, were more adaptable for alternative services such as cruising. Both were designed as two-class ships, with good provision for these to be combined as needed. Ordered for the Home Lines Cuxhaven–Southampton–Le Havre–Montréal line service, *Oceanic* was designed as a luxury adaptation of the *Ryndam* plan, having accommodation for about 172

first-class passengers on the boat deck, with their own exclusive lounge and forward-facing restaurant on the deck above. The ship went immediately into full-time cruise service from New York when she was delivered in 1965 with a single-class capacity of 1,200 passengers. *Eugenio C* featured a flexible *Canberra*-style fore-and-aft division between her First- and Tourist-Class public facilities, with First-Class cabins and suites above the promenade deck and Tourist accommodation below.

The public rooms and deck spaces aboard these ships were far better designed to take advantage of their structural layout with machinery two-thirds aft. One of the most outstanding features of *Oceanic* was

Below: Michelangelo, while running her speed trials off Genoa in March 1965, and showing the somewhat 'technical' rationale of her exterior form as a liner with machinery two-thirds aft, with latticed funnels. (CPL)

Above: *Costa Line's*
Eugenio C of 1966.
Virtually unchanged
externally since her
delivery, the ship is
seen in Montréal 20
years later on a North
American cruise, and
renamed Eugenio
Costa. *(Author's*
photo)

the enormous midships lido atop the superstructure, with two swimming pools and the world's first retractable Magradome glass roof. The essence of this spectacular rectangular space was reflected two decks lower down by the main lounge and a further two decks beneath this by the domed main dining room, both constructed entirely without internal supporting columns. As *Eugenio C* was designed for tropical service between southern Europe and South America, her midships lido was constructed without the Magradome, but with full-height glass windscreens at both lido deck and sun deck, above. The most spectacular feature of this ship was her layout of the promenade deck public rooms along a centreline axis through the ballroom, cocktail bar, forward deck lobby with its stairways and lifts divided to port and starboard, to the observation lounge with its large windows in the superstructure front. Among the notable aft-engined ships of this era, including *Rotterdam, Canberra, Oceanic, Michelangelo* and *Raffaello,* this modern adaptation of the 1930s centreline plans of *Bremen, Europa, Normandie* and the little-known *Stockholm* was only achieved aboard *Eugenio C.*

During their final years in the line services for which they were built, many of these ships were placed on alternative routes, as older tonnage was disposed of and the remaining vessels employed as effectively as possible. *Oranje* and *Willem Ruys* were switched from their original service between Amsterdam and South East Asia, with *Oranje* going into a round-the-world service via Australia and Singapore in 1950, and *Willem Ruys* making two North Atlantic crossings to Montréal for Europa-Canada Line before also going into round-the-world

service in 1958. After these two ships were sold to Flotta Lauro for conversion to cruising in 1964 and 1965 respectively, they were replaced on the round-the-world trade by *Ryndam* and *Maasdam,* with *Ryndam* then going on to serve for a while as replacement for *Seven Seas. Maasdam* continued to make periodic transatlantic voyages to Montréal until she was sold in 1968 to Polish Ocean Lines, becoming *Stefan Batory,* while *Ryndam* eventually ended up under the Greek flag as *Atlas* of Epirotiki Lines.

In the early 1970s Italia's *Raffaello* and *Leonardo da Vinci* were to have been transferred to the line's South American service as replacements for *Augustus* and *Giulio Cesare,* leaving *Michelangelo* and *Cristoforo Colombo* on the New York run. When *Giulio Cesare* was scrapped after developing rudder trouble in 1973, *Cristoforo Colombo* was transferred to the South Atlantic, where she served with *Augustus.* The sands of time were running out for Italia, as legislation was introduced in the Italian Parliament to begin a five-year phasing out of government subsidies for passenger services on long-distance ocean routes. As the remaining liners in the Italia fleet were disposed of, the line consolidated its activities in the cargo business.

What some of these changes and other contemplated moves showed was that the modern air-conditioned liners of the 1950s and 1960s were far more adaptable between various routes than were their predecessors, with their modern comfortable climate-controlled accommodation being suited to service conditions in virtually any part of the world. While some liners have been less easily adaptable for cruise service due to difficulties in amalgamating their multiple-class passenger accommodation or of effectively converting large amounts of cargo space, the accommodation and service standards of such outstanding liners as *Rotterdam*, *Oceanic*, *Sagafjord* and *Kungsholm* were ultimately to help set the pace of modern-day worldwide cruising.

Yet ships themselves seem to possess a remarkable quality of adapting themselves to what is expected of them. After spending many years in virtually continuous Caribbean cruise service, life aboard *Norway* took on the character of the ship's former career as *France* during the transatlantic positioning voyage she made in 1996. During the first two days of the voyage from Fort Lauderdale and New York, passengers started walking and gathering in the Champs Elysées and Fifth Avenue gallerias, as the original veranda deck promenades had by then become. The Club Internationale and North Cape Lounge began to take on the ambience of their original roles as the First-Class Fumoir and Tourist main lounge, as passengers, many of whom were not old enough to have experienced liner travel, began to unwind and adjust themselves to the pace of traditional shipboard life. There was less demand for the entertainment and other activities of modern-day cruising. By the third day, hot bouillon was being served on deck in the morning and afternoon tea was available in the lounges.

While *QE2*'s line service and cruising aspects have been developed into a sophisticated lifestyle product over the years, this marked change in routine aboard *Norway* for this one voyage showed, for those observant enough to notice it, a psychological difference between the experience of a line voyage with a purpose, and thus a destination as its ultimate fulfilment, and a cruise as a round-trip excursion which must itself offer complete fulfilment by modern-day standards.

Q3…Q4…QUEEN ELIZABETH 2

At about the time Italian Line were in the early stages of planning *Michelangelo* and *Raffaello*, Cunard had already been considering their options for replacing *Queen Mary* and *Queen Elizabeth* since as early as 1951. The venerable *Queens* were considered to be traditionalist compared with *Normandie* and *Nieuw Amsterdam* from the time of their building, becoming more so against newer competitors such as *United States*, *Rotterdam* and *France* as these came into service over the following 10 years. The *Queens* had been worked hard during their wartime service, and with *Queen Mary* reaching the age of 30 in 1965 at least one new ship would be needed as a replacement by then.

By 1960 Cunard had drawn up plans for a new transatlantic liner, codenamed *Q3*, of around 75,000 tons, of slightly smaller overall dimensions than the 80,773-ton *Queen Mary*, and with accommodation for 2,270 passengers against the earlier ship's origi-

nal capacity of 2,082. Rather than being booked at Clydebank, the great new liner was to have been built on the Tyne by a consortium of Swan Hunter and Vickers Armstrong. The British Government had agreed to lend Cunard £18 million towards the building cost, on the proviso that the ship was built to provide a three-class express North Atlantic service only. In late 1961, before the building contracts could be signed, Cunard's directors yielded to the concerns of those factions within the line's management in favour of a luxury express ship of about 58,000 tons that could also be used for cruising in the winter season. Vickers Armstrong were contacted again in May 1963 as technical consultants to Cunard on the design of *Q4*, as the more agile and versatile new ship was called.

The entire *Q3* approach was flawed in its premise that the North Atlantic express trade still demanded higher standards of luxury and a greater proportion of First-Class accommodation than were required for other line services and for cruising. This traditionalist approach also missed the point that modern air-conditioned and thus fully enclosed ships were by then quite adaptable to either tropical or North Atlantic trades, provided that sufficient stability and reserves of power were provided where regular Atlantic crossings were foreseen. If *Q3* had been built, she would probably have made her debut at about the same time as *Michelangelo* and *Raffaello* as a considerably larger rendition of these liners, without their swimming pools and lidos, and with an internal layout featuring upper and lower promenades similar to *Rotterdam* and *France*. Yet at a greater size than either of these, without even the minimal concessions to cruising made aboard *United States* and *France*, she would undoubtedly have been one of the least commercially viable ships of her time.

The *Q3* design was nonetheless quite advanced for a ship which was otherwise considered to be old-fashioned in overall concept. Vickers had already brought to the *Q3* much of the lightweight structural design and construction they had already developed for P&O's *Oriana*. As aboard the latest European examples of *Rotterdam* and *France*, the public rooms for each class were given the full run of a separate deck within the superstructure. This was probably the only instance in which this idea was carried to three classes. It was also taken a step further than the Dutch and French examples by also locating the dining rooms on these higher decks. This had been done primarily to allow greater flexibility in the exclusive use of the decks below for cabins. This in itself made a high degree of interchangeability among the three classes possible.

By the time the salvageable ideas from *Q3* had gone into the mix for *Q4*'s planning, the new ship's size had already crept up to over 60,000 tons. Cunard's management continued to insist that three,

Right: *An early model of the* Queen Elizabeth 2, *showing the original superstructure front with the Look-Out lounge's large forward-facing windows at the forward end of Upper Deck.*
(Author's collection)

Below: *One of Q4's four 19ft-diameter, 32-ton propellers being prepared for display at the International Engineering Exhibition at Earls Court, London, in April 1967.* (CPL)

rather than two, passenger classes was the only proper formula for their Atlantic service, despite the strong case to the contrary put forward by their own design department headed by the line's chief naval architect, Dan Wallace. While the class structure would for the time being remain sacrosanct, virtually every other design aspect of *Q4* was questioned and evaluated. Would dog kennels be needed? Should there be a cold room for storing passengers' furs as there had been on the old *Queens*? And, how many

pairs of shoes would a lady passenger on a world cruise want to put in her cabin wardrobe?[1] Among other things, it was decided that there should be a side-hatch-accessible garage for carrying passengers' cars as there were on the latest Italian liners, and that there would be stores and provisions capacities for a full cruise season of up to three months. On the basis of these overall criteria a building contract was finally signed on 20 December 1964 with John Brown (Clydebank) Limited at a price of £25,427,000, with the ship to be delivered in May 1968.

For all that was to be contained within the cocoon of her slender hull and dominant superstructure, the new ship had to be designed almost with an aircraft builder's approach to compactness and weight saving. A compact machinery installation of PAME-TRADA (Parsons Marine Experimental Turbine Research and Development Association) design was developed that would occupy only three of the ship's 15 watertight compartments, taking up less than half the space needed for the earlier *Queen Elizabeth*'s engine plant with its four turbine sets and twelve boilers. At 5,600 tons, the weight of this, the most powerful twin-screw steam-turbine installation then to be fitted in a merchant ship, was only about one third the mass of *Queen Mary*'s installation. In *Q4* the boiler room was located between the main turbine and auxiliary spaces as a means of minimizing the length of steam and water-piping runs and concentrating the funnel uptakes from all three compartments as closely as possible. The routing of all pipes,

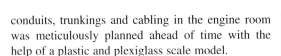
conduits, trunkings and cabling in the engine room was meticulously planned ahead of time with the help of a plastic and plexiglass scale model.

Other important space-saving measures involved the organization of all passenger dining rooms and crew messes around a single galley and service complex. The nine air-conditioning plants were arranged, as is now common practice in cruise ship design, along a central core between the two parallel accommodation passages on Three deck, rather than taking up valuable upper-deck space. With the emphasis on cabins at the ship's sides in preference over inside rooms, this space was ideally suited for such purposes, with its intake and return-air trunkings also being concentrated amidships around the boiler and engine room uptakes.

Structurally, Q4's welded steel hull and aluminium superstructure were fused together as a single load- and stress-bearing entity. Thus the superstructure as a whole could be designed to take the load normally borne by a single strength deck atop the hull, as was done in Oriana. The thickness of the uppermost rows of steel hull shell plating was reduced slightly, allowing some of the bending and twisting stresses of the ship's motion underway to be taken up by the superstructure. The thickness of plating and scantlings used in the superstructure was carefully controlled, with the materials being quite highly stressed to absorb the large movements inevitable so high up in the ship.

The arrangement of passenger spaces was in effect centred around and above a central core of propelling machinery amidships, the long expanse of air-conditioning plants following the centreline and a tight concentration of catering services, stores and crew facilities forward. The cabins were thus pushed outwards to the sides of the hull and upwards well into the superstructure. High up, atop these and all of the ship's inner workings, apart from the funnel and air-conditioning casings, three uninterrupted strata of public spaces were spread out to the ship's full beam. The required open deck spaces were laid out above these and in a series of long terraces stepping down four decks to the upper layer of cabins.

By the time Q4 was launched as Queen Elizabeth 2 on September 20 1967, her design had in fact just progressed to the last of three main stages in its evolution. The abandoned Q3 was the first stage, initially defining her as a large solely North Atlantic transport of fairly progressive technical design, followed by Q4 which rethought the concept as a fully versatile dual purpose ship. The third and final step was a complete rationalization of the accommodation design, which finally brought her fully up to date with the sophisticated lifestyles of the modern world into which she would emerge upon completion as Queen Elizabeth 2. This final stage would also at last settle the whirlwind of controversy that had surrounded not only the new ship's architecture since

the days of Q3, but also Cunard's whole design approach from the time of Queen Mary's planning.

It was through an unexpected turn of events that Cunard were given the time they needed to plan for such change. In late 1966 John Brown informed the line that the delivery of the ship had to be postponed from May 1968 to early 1969, ostensibly owing to a shortage of skilled steel workers. While Cunard would sacrifice the lucrative 1968 summer season at an estimated cost of £200,000 per week in lost revenue, the improvements to the ship which the extra time allowed would pay off in the long run. Although the hull had at this stage reached a fairly advanced stage of construction, with some items of machinery already in place and work on the lower strata of cabins begun, there was still time for change. The areas affected were primarily the public spaces which the overall design scheme had already relegated to the uppermost strata of the ship's integral hive of passenger spaces.

At the root of the rationalization was the fundamental change from Cunard's venerable three-class formula to a more loosely-defined two-class structure for Atlantic crossings only, with the ship otherwise open to a single-class service for cruising. This was a particularly hard-won victory over the strong traditionalist lobby within Cunard's management.

The rationalization of Queen Elizabeth 2's passenger facilities brought about a shift from the notion of an express vessel with hotel facilities added, to that of a modern ocean-going urban resort with mobility

Below: *The* Queen Elizabeth 2 *seen running her sea trials off the Isle of Arran.* (Architectural Press, University of Liverpool Archives)

Above, left:
View of the Queen
Elizabeth 2's *Quarter*
Deck promenade,
which also served as
the primary
circulation route
between the various
public rooms.
(Author's photo)

Above, right:
Passengers assembling
in the port-side
Quarter Deck
promenade for lifeboat
drill at the start of a
crossing to New York
in 1979.
(Author's photo)

and, when needed, North Atlantic express speed added. As such, she would provide equally for world-wide cruise passengers as for those whose travels would include an Atlantic crossing as part of a holiday or business trip. With the technical advances of her structural design and powerful twin-screw propulsion plant already rendered into reality, the remaining business of completing the ship would be highly concentrated on appealing to a then elusive new ocean-passenger market which *Queen Elizabeth 2* herself would ultimately help to define and develop.

This involved a near-total redesign of the public rooms on the uppermost three decks. Named Quarter, Upper and Boat decks, these were originally to have been allocated one to each class, giving First Class the full and exclusive run of Quarter deck, with Cabin and Tourist above on Upper and Boat decks respectively. Cabin and Tourist Classes were to share the Upper-deck dining room as a consequence of the amalgamation of catering services in a single galley complex. All passengers were also to have the use of the same theatre, following the example of *Rotterdam*, *France* and Italia's new *Michelangelo* and *Raffaello*. However, despite these concessions to the changing times, the smaller specialized spaces such as libraries and teenagers' rooms were still to have been rigidly segregated. The revised plan essentially combined the facilities of Cabin and Tourist classes on Upper and Boat decks into a suite of rooms complementing its First-Class counterpart below on Quarter Deck.

The large Tourist-Class lounge was created by breaking through the Boat deck and joining the original aft-located Cabin and Tourist main lounges. Aptly named the Double Room, this multi-function area with its spacious mezzanine was to serve as the focal point of shipboard entertainment. Its First-Class counterpart on the deck below would serve as a ballroom or take second place as the alternate showplace when needed as such. The remaining Tourist-Class rooms on Boat deck were eliminated, with their space being taken over by a shopping arcade amidships and the universally accessible nightclub, coffee shop, gallery and teenagers' room forward at the theatre's balcony level. The overall plan, which at various stages of its evolution included traditional open and closed promenades, was further reworked into a fully enclosed and climate-controlled circulating space around the perimeter of each deck, providing side access to the public rooms, stairways and other central services, as aboard the latest Scandinavian liners *Sagafjord* and *Kungsholm*.

At the same time these spaces were being rationalized and re-allocated by the technical departments of Cunard and John Brown Shipbuilding, changes were also being made in the selection of the design team that would eventually finish and decorate them. Cunard's original naming of designers for *Q4* in

1965 had done little to calm the grave concern being voiced in professional circles as to the new flagship's architectural and industrial design. Architects, designers and others in related fields were questioning the likelihood of the new ship demonstrating to the world at large a true and just impression of the very best that modern British design could offer. Undoubtedly the structural, engineering, navigational and other purely technical aspects of the ship would be near-perfect; but alas, Cunard's constant reputation for a characteristically traditionalist approach to the finishing and decoration of their fleet's interiors seemed unlikely to assure the same sort of advancement in the parts of the ship seen by her passengers.

The whirlwind of public controversy stirred up by the whole question went as far as being raised in the House of Commons as an attempt at bringing government pressure to bear on the owners' direction and choice of designers. Since the government's involvement with the ship was purely financial as lenders of capital, rather than the source of a grant, they had no direct authority to appoint any particular architects or designers. Meanwhile, Sir Basil Smallpiece, who had then recently taken over as Cunard Chairman, consulted privately with Sir Duncan Oppenheimer, chairman of the Council of Industrial Design, to work out the formation of a revised design team.

James Gardner, who was first engaged in 1961 to do the exterior styling of Q3, was retained and paired up with Dennis Lennon as joint design coordinators of the ship, working closely with the technical design team under Dan Wallace. Gardner would continue to be responsible primarily for the ship's exterior appearance while Lennon would head a team of professionals approved by Sir Duncan to handle the great number of interior spaces in his domain. While the design team had not been assembled early enough to exercise an enormous influence over the structural arrangements of their domains, the rationalization itself and postponed delivery certainly afforded them more flexibility than might otherwise have been possible.

Among those named to work on the interiors with Dennis Lennon and his own partnership were Jon Bannenberg, Stefan Buzas, Theo Crosby, Michael Inchbald, Jo Patrick (Mrs) and Gaby Schreiber. From among the Oriana and Canberra designers, Professor Misha Black was brought in to apply his special knowledge of the Jewish faith to design the synagogue, while Sir Hugh Casson supervised the work of two of his students from the Royal College of Art who designed the teenagers' and children's recreation areas. Each was given a fairly free hand in the design of the areas assigned to them, with a sense of harmony or unity being achieved through standardization of the linking passages, lobbies, stairways and perimeter promenades. These essentially important elements, along with the captain's quarters and by far the great-

est number of public rooms and other spaces, were designed by Dennis Lennon and Partners.

As demanded by her dual-purpose function, the standard of Queen Elizabeth 2's accommodation was as a whole substantially higher than that of any British ship then in service, including the old Queens. The average cabin area was 22⅓ft (6.7m) square, compared with only 14⅓ft (4.4m) square in the 1940-built Queen Elizabeth. Every one of the new ship's cabins had its own en-suite toilet with shower or bathtub. All cabin washbasins were relegated to the en suites, rather than being part of the room's furnishings in typical British boarding-house style. The cabins were carpeted throughout, and all passengers were berthed in hotel-style beds, usually arranged side-by-side or in convertible sofa-beds. Fold-away Pullman-type upper berths were only fitted in a number of the lower cabin grades, for use of families or groups of students travelling together at minimum fare.

Sophisticated architectural lighting was especially important in many of Queen Elizabeth 2's wide low-ceilinged spaces such as the larger lounges and dining rooms. Even during the sunny daylight hours spent in tropical cruising, electric lighting was required to maintain a uniform level of general visibility. In the dining rooms, automatic dimming devices were installed so that the level of electric light would actually increase with the brightness of the daylight and sun outside to avoid areas of comparative dullness within their interiors. For evening use the lighting of these rooms could be adjusted to create the right mood for various occasions of dinner service.

The overall lighting scheme consisted mostly of recessed flush or indirect fixtures. Spotlighting was also widely used to accent numerous decorative features including artwork and the plant boxes of the Queens Room and other such details. In the cabins special attention was given to the direct area lighting

Above: Fashionably 'mod' when the QE2 entered service, for many years the Theatre Bar on Upper Deck retained the essence of its original design by Dennis Lennon and Partners. (Author's photo)

Opposite: Part of the Double Down Room on Boat Deck, showing Jon Bannenberg's curved steel-and-glass staircase leading to the Double Up room on Boat Deck. By the time this photograph was taken in August 1979, the Double Up room had already been appropriated as a shopping centre. (Author's photo)

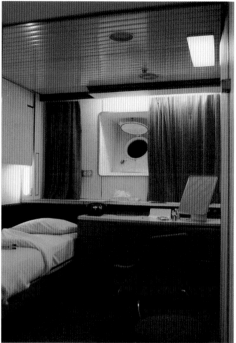

Above, left: Cabin 3076, port side amidships on Three Deck, was designed by Jon Bannenberg as one of the more ubiquitous types of First-Class accommodation throughout the ship. The bathroom seen in the background is beyond an entrance vestibule, with the cabin entrance to the left and walk-in closet to the right.
(Author's photo)

Above, right: Cabin 2008, port side forward on Two Deck, is a typical 1+1 Tourist-Class room, with single lower berth and fold-away upper Pullman that can be used for single or double occupancy. Note the traditionally nautical treatment of the porthole.
(Author's photo)

required for personal grooming, reading and writing. Being one of the first modern ships to be specially equipped for professional entertainment, a number of *Queen Elizabeth 2*'s public rooms were also equipped with additional theatrical lighting. The *Q4* Room and Club 736, which were the two original night spots along with the more general-purpose Double Room, were fitted with adjustable coloured spot lights and separate control panels for their use as needed by the performers.

One especially noteworthy example was the cinema/theatre, a double-height entertainment space of more-or-less fixed purpose. Along with the Grill Room Bar and Synagogue, this was one of the very few entirely inside public spaces, beyond the reach of natural light. Gaby Schreiber, who designed the theatre, adopted the powers of an architectural lighting scheme to set the mood of this otherwise plain fibre-glass-clad room to suit its various uses as a cinema, church, lecture hall and theatre. Two entirely separate lighting schemes were installed for cinema use and for the auditorium's alternative uses.

The cinema/theatre was fitted only with concealed indirect fluorescent fixtures for general ambient illumination of the auditorium itself. To this basic scheme were added production-quality pan-and-tilt theatre spotlights with automatic colour change. Full control of the whole lighting system was provided within the projection and control room, along with the latest Philips film projectors installed for showing wide-screen 70mm films, as well as separate units for 25mm and 16mm productions. In view of the ship's modern sense of worldliness the cinema/theatre was also equipped with simultaneous language translation facilities.

When the ship was finally completed,

Shipbuilding and Shipping Record subtitled their technical description of her: 'A ship with a past...and a future.'[2] In the *Architects' Journal*, Kenneth Anew wrote: 'Technically she is unusual in that innumerable small advances add up to something significantly new.'[3] Indeed, both sentiments endeavour to express the unique quality of universal timelessness which belonged to *Queen Elizabeth 2* alone. She embodied the more traditional elements of *Q3*'s big-liner influences, with its vide variety of custom-built accommodation and other North Atlantic features. The inspired lightweight centre-engined structural design of the Vickers Armstrong's *Q3* proposal and their work during the formative *Q4* gestation stage, backed by the eminent success of *Oriana*, helped to round out the new Cunarder's link, not only with the past, but also with some of the most sound shipbuilding practices of all time. The modern design of *Queen Elizabeth 2*'s accommodation, services and other creature comforts, along with numerous technical innovations in her engineering and various other supporting automation, gave her a running head start on the whole future of passenger shipping.

One of those many design advances which added up to making *Queen Elizabeth 2* into something significantly new was her distinctive and unmistakable exterior appearance. The importance of this image was considered to be vital to her ultimate success and of Cunard's promotion of her to the public. The rather esoteric appearance of ships like *Oriana* or *Willem Ruys* were accepted by their owners without deference to public appeal, while others succeeded with mundane and nondescript outer appearances. Cunard had too tough a marketing job ahead of them to take such chances. On the one hand there was the living image of the great bygone *Queens* to be upheld

Previous page:
Farewell to Queen
Mary *as she sets off
from Southampton on
her final voyage to
New York, 16
September 1967.*
(CPL)

in a traditional sense, and on the other, an entirely new conception of a modern dual-purpose ship to promote. Whether seen in a photograph, magazine advertisement, cruise brochure or in reality at the quayside or from the deck of a passing ship, an all-important strong first impression had to make the initial pitch for the ship. If that failed, then it would be more difficult to get a second chance.

What James Gardner succeeded so well in doing for *Queen Elizabeth 2*'s overall shape and appearance was to soften its lines of form and reduce the more severe expression of the traditional North Atlantic packet. At the same time he skilfully retained some elements of traditional appearance, even going as far as to deceive the eye in concealing the less attractive concessions the builders were compelled to make by way of technical expediency.

Slightly aft of amidships atop the superstructure, the funnel stood as James Gardner's greatest triumph. An ingeniously inspired combination of both very old and new thinking came together in its creation. The old idea was that of a tall and slender stovepipe steamer stack, painted black to keep it from looking soiled, and high enough to carry the exhaust gases well clear of the decks below. A lower, wider and more modern-looking white cowling was wrapped around the aft half of the stovepipe to push up return air from the ship's ventilation system and air-conditioning, driving the smoke and soot up higher and farther away from the decks. A broad and shallow wind scoop at the funnel's base was there to shovel clean air up from the slipstream to fill the low-pressure void behind the cowling. Perhaps most dramatic was the paint scheme, which made the only exception ever to the traditional Cunard black-and-red livery.

Instead of traditional black *Queen Elizabeth 2*'s hull was painted a dark charcoal grey, as in reality was the funnel's smokepipe. This change was made in consideration of the less dominating appearance of the ship's upperworks compared with the old *Queens*, or for that matter the relatively new *France*. Without the two or three huge funnels to offset its visual mass, James Gardner thought that a black hull would look too overpowering. The colour chosen was dark enough to give the right appearance for a large liner, yet just that much lighter to soften the effect sufficiently.

Queen Elizabeth 2's maiden voyage was postponed a second time when the turbines failed during the ship's sea trials, with an entire row of rotor blades sheering at their roots and being shredded into the following rows of blading, seriously damaging the inner workings of the machines. There were also problems with vibration and a considerable amount of finishing work needing to be completed in the accommodation. The maiden voyage to New York via Le Havre, Las Palmas, Barbados and Kingston, Jamaica, which was scheduled to leave Southampton on Friday, 17 January 1969, was cancelled outright.

The ship limped back to Southampton, where her troubled turbines were removed and flown to Clydebank for analysis and repair. After successfully running a second set of trials in April, where she achieved a top speed of 32.66 knots for a sustained period of six hours, a shakedown cruise was scheduled for 22 April and the long-awaited maiden voyage to New York finally got under way on Friday 2 May.

Keith Gledhill and his wife were among *QE2*'s passengers, both for the shake down cruise and her maiden voyage to New York. Mr Gledhill's first impressions fell short of what he had hoped for on the basis of his great appreciation for the old *Queens* and the traditional values of North Atlantic life and society they embodied.[4] Too many of the surfaces and finishes in the new ship, such as the inverted white trumped-shaped columns and matching white laminate furniture in the Queens Room had, to his experienced eye, the look of plastic, and he wondered how long these would stand up in service. He noted the absence of the raisable table edges and other refinements for service in rough weather, and was dismayed that there seemed to be scarcely a comfortable seat to be found anywhere on the ship.

The circular entrance foyer in deep purples and greens and with a fibreglass serrated ceiling, the Double Room with its sophisticated lighting and the deep red of the Princess Grill were all striking, different though these were from the Cunard he had worked and travelled with in the past. As the voyage progressed and Keith Gledhill chatted at length socially in the Midships Bar and the Queen's Room with the ship's naval architect, Dan Wallace, and with others among his fellow passengers, his impressions of the new ship warmed and mellowed. He began to appreciate *QE2* as being, 'with it, but also with a sense of tradition of her own'. The Gledhills have remained loyal repeat passengers, travelling often aboard the ship both on cruises and liner voyages, sometimes just for the enjoyment of a round-trip Atlantic crossing to New York, with lunch at the Plaza Hotel before starting the voyage home.

By the time *Queen Elizabeth 2* started her maiden voyage, *Queen Mary* had already been withdrawn from service at the end of her 1967 summer season, followed by *Queen Elizabeth* a year later. By the end of *QE2*'s inaugural summer season, *United States* was also gone, her sailing schedule suddenly cancelled in November 1969 in the face of rising operating costs and continuing labour difficulties with the ship's crew. *QE2* and *France* would remain as the only elite-class express liners on the North Atlantic until 1974, when the French liner's government subsidy would be curtailed and the ship withdrawn.

In January 1970, the 360-seat Boeing 747 wide-bodied airliner made its inaugural flight for Pan American World Airways between New York's John F. Kennedy Airport (formerly Idlewild) and London-

Heathrow Airport. BOAC, Lufthansa, Air France, KLM, Air Canada and others introduced their own translatlantic 747 services during the following months. BOAC's radio advertisement for their new 747 services introduced the airliner as 'The plane that's a ship – the ship that's a plane.'

The once-elitist jet age began to achieve the sort of universality that was once the exclusive preserve of the multi-class ocean liner. The original exclusivity of air travel was soon to yield ever more to inexpensive mass travel. The dreams visualized by Vladimir Yourkevitch and others for ferrying the masses back and forth across the Atlantic at minimum cost in vast liners had taken flight, and were finally being realized by the jumbo airliner. Ultimately the economy of scale offered by these new high-capacity aircraft would make long-distance travel available to greater numbers of people at far lower prices than the shipping lines could ever match. What then remained to be discovered was the future role of aviation in providing feeder services to the world's emerging full-time cruise industry.

Two months prior to *Queen Elizabeth 2*'s debut, the Anglo-French-developed Concorde supersonic airliner made its first test flights high above the pastures and vineyards of Gascony near Toulouse, where the plane was built at Aérospatiale's plant (today part of Airbus Industrie). Air France and British Airways both inaugurated supersonic service in January 1976, with services to Rio de Janeiro and Bahrain respectively. While flights to Washington DC were started in at the end of May, New York became a supersonic destination for flights to and from London and Paris in November 1977. Finally, the sleek delta-winged speed queen of the airways had taken her place among the North Atlantic's fastest and most prestigious leviathans, sharing the limelight with the new Cunard flagship alone, as *France* was by then already laid up at Le Havre. For the 100 passengers who travelled in the lap of luxury aboard Concorde, the three-hour-20-minute crossing between London–Heathrow and New York–JFK was to all intents and purposes the airborne equivalent of First Class aboard *QE2*.

The British Airways fleet of seven Concordes in fact became something of a consort to *QE2* through special arrangement with Cunard, whereby passengers could cross the Atlantic one way by sea and return via Concorde. The Gledhills, who make the crossing at least once a year and generally prefer to avoid flying, often used this arrangement before Concorde was withdrawn from service in 2003, usually preferring to sail westbound and travel home on Concorde, avoiding the discomfort of the usual overnight flight from JFK to Heathrow. Sea and sky were now unequal partners in the perpetual crossing of the Atlantic. ●

Below: *Cunard's* Queen Elizabeth *bows out in late 1968 at the end of a long and successful career in both war and peacetime, seen here dressed overall and flying her paying off pennant.* (Gordon Turner collection)

8

METAMORPHOSIS AND RENAISSANCE

Ever since entering service in 1969, Cunard's *Queen Elizabeth 2* has sailed back and forth between Southampton and New York through the high season between April and November. Her crossings are interspersed with shorter cruises, of usually seven-to-ten days each on either side of the Atlantic. Some of these have been as short as three-day voyages to Bermuda or Halifax, offered as affordable opportunities for prospective passengers to sample the ship. There were times also when round-trip passages could be booked from Southampton to Bremen and Cherbourg as part of the ship's European turnaround, or the Channel Crossing between Southampton and Cherbourg was possible as an alternative to the regular ferry services. During the winter months, *QE2* normally makes longer cruises, usually a three-month round-the-world voyage from January to April, in time to start the North Atlantic season.

Throughout the three decades she has been in service, *QE2* has retained her leadership position as a trendsetter and as the veritable gold standard against which the industry measures the worth and performance of other ships. This is a phenomenon retained through periodic refitting and conversion of the ship to keep abreast of latest trends in sea travel and cruising and the various stimuli from the luxury hotel, resort and service industries on land. *QE2* is undoubtedly the most extensively refitted and modified ship in history, with some of the changes arguably being less satisfactory than others.

In 1972 the original penthouse veranda suites were added, as a two-deck prefabricated unit built by Vosper Thornycroft ahead of time and hoisted into position as two sections. The restaurants were reorganized so that 1,700 cruise passengers could be served in a single sitting, with the result that the Tourist-Class Britannia restaurant was enlarged, and its escalator service from the central galley on the deck below replaced with its own kitchens, taking over the space occupied by the Look Out Lounge, which had been the ship's only public area with a view forward. Other changes included the addition of a casino in place of the original Tourist-Class library and writing room. An art gallery on the boat deck was eliminated and the shops relocated to the upper level of the mezzanine-plan Double Room, with deluxe cabins being added in the spaces formerly occupied by these facilities. More deluxe veranda suites were added in 1977.

After *QE2*'s services during the Falkland Islands conflict in 1982, she underwent restoration before returning to commercial service. At this time a health spa was added and the Quarter Deck public rooms were extended aft to include a glass-domed enclosure over the existing swimming pool. New indoor–outdoor lido areas were also created from the original lido lounge and nightclub.

Over the winter of 1986–87, *QE2* was completely re-engined at Lloyd Werft in Bremerhaven, with her too-often troublesome original boilers and turbines being replaced by a nine-engine diesel-electric installation. The opportunity was taken to make further

Opposite: *The* **Queen Mary 2's** *Britannia Restaurant, looking aft through the room's full-height central nave towards Barbara Broekman's tapestry depicting a mythical Cunard liner.*

(Author's photo)

Above: Queen Elizabeth 2 *seen here as she appeared during the mid-1980s, with the original Look-Out lounge windows plated over and penthouse suites added in the 1970s; the funnel changed from James Gardner's black-and-white paint scheme to the traditional Cunard colours; and the modifications having been made to the aft superstructure in the early 1980s.* (MAN B&W)

Right: Queen Elizabeth 2's *original Double Room has undergone numerous changes during the ship's life in an attempt to keep up with the latest standards of shipboard entertainment, eventually becoming the Grand Lounge, seen here while looking aft.* (Cunard/Author's collection)

modifications to the passenger facilities, with the addition of a further eight veranda penthouses, extension of the boat deck restaurant to accommodate the added capacity of the new suites, and reorganization of the previously installed computer learning centre into a business complex. The original Double Room was extensively modified to improve its suitability for staging live entertainment, becoming the Grand Lounge.

By the mid-1990s *QE2*'s whole plan had become rather fragmented through the many changes made over the years, losing much of its original character and identity. Most of the work had been done piecemeal, with little consistency of approach and no apparent longterm strategy. Thus Project Lifestyle was devised as a master-plan to bring the ship up to the latest cruise standards and restore the essence of her original rationale and clarity. The longterm programme would be carried out largely as part of her regular upkeep and maintenance. The first phase of Project Lifestyle was accomplished as a substantial refit by the Bremer Vulkan yard in Germany at the end of 1994.

The glass-domed lido area aft on Quarter Deck was completely reworked into a sophisticated lido restaurant, complete with its own galley and service facilities, bringing the area up to the latest cruise-ship standards as a full-service alternative restaurant and café. The pool and dome were completely removed, with the former Tourist-Class pool farther astern and one deck lower being upgraded and brought more closely together with the lido restaurant by way of new inside and outside stairways and its own service pavilion. The Grand Lounge was extensively rebuilt, adding fully terraced seating and, at long last, a large proscenium stage with full production facilities for live theatrical entertainment. This brought the room as close as the ship's existing structural limitations would permit to the standard of the multi-function American-style cabaret lounges of the newest Holland America and P&O/Princess cruise ships.

The overall plan was revitalized. The aft-most stairways were extended up to the boat deck and the circulating function of the original interior promenades were improved with a new aperitif bar adjacent to the restaurant on Upper Deck. Stairways to the Quarter Deck below joined the port and starboard promenades for the first time at their forward ends, providing direct access to all the ship's restaurants. The Yacht Club bar and lounge on Upper Deck were enlarged and arranged to close the circulation loop aft in the same manner as the lido restaurant on Quarter Deck below. These changes introduced an element of overall functional planning, stressing a gradual movement of shipboard activity farther aft from the restaurants during the evening hours, ending up with late-night and early-morning activities being concentrated farthest away from the bulk of *QE2*'s cabin accommodation. The original loosely defined segregation of First and Tourist Classes on Atlantic service has, over the years, generally diluted into little more than the designation of restaurant assignments according to cabin grade, with passengers otherwise being free to enjoy all services of the ship.

In addition to various upgrades of behind-the-scenes services and technical facilities, Project Lifestyle addressed the matter of upgrading the ship's sanitary facilities. The original en-suite toilet facilities

in all cabins were upgraded in stages, with new units featuring up-to-date fresh-water vacuum toilets and new water-efficient washbasins, bathtubs and shower fittings. The new units were designed especially for *QE2* as knock-down assemblies that could be easily brought aboard the ship by way of the accommodation passages and assembled inside the cabins and suites with minimum extra structural work required.

Thus *Queen Elizabeth 2* has continued to maintain her leadership position among the latest and most luxurious new cruise ships, while continuing to uphold the unique individuality of original design and construction.

DIVERSION TO MODERN CRUISING

In the years immediately following *QE2*'s 1969 delivery, *Hamburg*, completed a few months later for Deutsche Atlantik Line, and Norwegian America Line's *Vistafjord* of 1973 were the only two passenger liners built with provision for North Atlantic line service. Both of these vessels were of modest size and speed, nominally provided with the structural stamina and baggage-handling facilities for line serv-

Below, main picture: *With a new, larger funnel, carrying the uptakes from nine diesel engines,* **Queen Elizabeth 2** *sails past the Statue of Liberty, inbound to New York for the first time with her new diesel-electric power plant fitted in Germany over the winter of 1986–87.* **Below, inset:** *The Princess Grill, reinstated and restored to its original elegance as part of the 1994-95 Project Lifestyle, after having been modified in various forms and even disused during the ship's service career.* (Cunard Line publicity photos)

Above: *The circular entrance foyer of the QE2, redecorated (and perhaps somewhat downgraded from its original modernistic panache) as the central focus of a Cunard Line Heritage Trail integrated into the ship's refurbished interior design. (Courtesy of Met Studio, London)*

Above: *Although its scale is limited by existing structures, the Grand Lounge is finally fitted with a proscenium stage for cabaret-style entertainment as part of the Project Lifestyle refit. (Cunard Line publicity photo)*

Left: *The original First-Class Midships Bar on Quarter Deck, now upgraded and revitalized as the Chart Room bar, with a deeper sense of contemporary luxury and warmth as appropriate for today's sophisticated cruise clientele. (Courtesy of Met Studio, London)*

Below: Queen Elizabeth 2, *following the introduction of Project Lifestyle as a master plan for her continuing upkeep, as she appears at the time of writing. (Cunard Line publicity photo)*

ice, but otherwise outfitted to a luxury standard for worldwide cruise service. While *Vistafjord* was essentially a larger rendition of the line's 1966-built *Sagafjord*, with an additional superstructure deck and some refinements of her internal layout, *Hamburg* was a unique ship of remarkably progressive internal layout and design.

Hamburg's hull and superstructure were of fairly conventional design and robust steel construction and, adopting *QE2*'s structural approach of entirely flat decks amidships, sloped upwards in a straight plane towards the bow in place of the traditional curved sheer lines. Accommodation was arranged to create a sense of maximum space for 790 passengers in transatlantic service, reduced to 652 for cruising. The effect was accomplished largely through the space economy gained by extensive work- and service-flow planning of the closely integrated galley, restaurant and crew messing complex forward on the lower decks. This was linked by direct vertical cores to the lounges and deck service areas, likewise concentrated forward on the upper decks. The overall plan featured an axial layout with divided uptake casings and large standardized inner and outer cabins arranged either side of wide central passages through her three accommodation decks. The main public areas were concentrated forward, where the largest

lounges occupied the full width of the superstructure decks ahead of the two-thirds-aft engine uptakes. The theatre was the only major public area to be located aft of the funnel. As a key feature of her cruising role, the ship also featured a *Kungsholm*-style upper decks swimming pool surrounded by a glass-screened lido projecting into the lifeboat line forward of the funnel.

One wonders what *QE2* might have been like if a similarly progressive approach had also been adopted in her planning. Perhaps at least some of the Cunard flagship's extensive in-service refitting over the years might have been avoided. After serving with her original owners for only a few years, *Hamburg* was finally sold in 1974 to the Black Sea Shipping Company of the Soviet Union, becoming a very successful cruise ship in her own right as *Maksim Gorkij*.

Apart from these, passenger-ship building since 1969 has been almost exclusively for cruising and ferry services. Among the first of these were the modest 14,000-ton Netherlands-built *Cunard Adventurer* and *Cunard Ambassador*, originally ordered by Overseas National Airways and taken over for Cunard service during their construction. Modern first-generation tonnage was also delivered to new cruise operators such Norwegian Caribbean Line, Royal Caribbean Cruise Lines and Norwegian

Below: *Deutsche Atlantik Line's* **Hamburg** *of 1969, a steam-powered ship designed for Atlantic line service and extensive cruising, brought a number of technical innovations into liner service.* (Author's collection)

Above: *An artist's impression of Oy Wärtsilä AB's Superliner design from the 1980s, which examined concepts for a fast passenger ship with roll-on/roll-off vehicle and cargo capabilities, for use in high-speed line service derived from the FINNJET experience, most likely with North Atlantic service for Cunard Line in mind.* (Author's collection)

Cruiseships A/S of Oslo, whose *Sea Venture* and *Island Venture* later became the backbone of P&O's Princess Cruises fleet as *Pacific Princess* and *Island Princess*. The majority of these vessels were built for short cruises in tropical waters, with service speeds of between 18 and 20 knots. The gas-turbine-powered Baltic ferry *Finnjet* was delivered from the Helsinki yard of Oy Wärtsilä AB in 1977, then the only high-speed ship to be built since *QE2*. She was designed with a 30.5-knot service speed to enable her to cover the route between Helsinki and the German port of Travemünde in 22 hours, effectively replacing three smaller ferries on a three-times-a-week summer schedule.

At the end of 1981, as the cruise industry inevitably progressed to larger ships, HAPAG-Lloyd's 33,819-ton fifth *Europa* was delivered. Built essentially as a liner, she had the range and structural stamina for worldwide cruising and the capability to make long ocean crossings and other deep-sea passages in considerable comfort. New superships in the over-70,000-ton class, such as Royal Caribbean's *Sovereign of the Seas*, were built for cruising during the 1980s to rival and inevitably surpass the sizes of *United States*, *France* (by then converted for cruising as *Norway*) and *QE2*.

Cruise-ship accommodation and amenities became more oriented towards the concept of ocean-going resorts, with an emphasis on high superstructure blocks providing a predominance of veranda accommodation, extensive open-air recreation facilities above and main public rooms relegated to the upper hull decks. Some vessels also reintroduced aspects of traditional liner design. As cruise lines sought to broaden the range of their seven-day cruises or to offer longer worldwide itineraries, a number of large new ships were introduced. In the 1990s liners appeared with more slender and sea-kindly hull lines and with machinery capable of more efficient performance and higher service speeds.

Holland America's 20.3-knot *Statendam* was delivered in 1993 as the first of a series of 55,000-ton

cruise ships for worldwide itineraries with longer deep-sea passages in mind. Two years later the centre-engined *Legend of the Seas* made her debut in the Royal Caribbean fleet as the first of the line's 70,000-ton Vision Class vessels, with a 24-knot maximum service speed greatly increasing their effective range for seven-day tropical cruising. Four later ships in this series were built for a higher passenger capacity at a slightly reduced speed of 22 knots. P&O's new *Oriana* of 1995 and *Aurora*, delivered five years later, were designed both for the longer itineraries of the line's British market and to retain their trademark liner image of *Canberra* and the old *Oriana*.

Yet, despite their higher performance and more traditional expression of greater seaworthiness, ships of this class still lacked the structural strength and freeboard height for continuous deep-sea liner service, particularly on the North Atlantic. These also had none of the baggage rooms, kennels and other special facilities needed for line service, while those designed for more destination-oriented cruising would be unable to offer the diversity of onboard entertainment and activity that today's passengers would demand during uninterrupted sea passages of five or more days.

Meanwhile, a number of promotional designs for large and fast passenger ships intended for line service were created by the leading shipbuilders. The technical department of Oy Wärtsilä AB and their successor, Kværner Masa-Yards, produced plans in the mid-1980s for a North Atlantic liner capable of making a five-and-a-half day crossing between New York and Europe. Appearing as a further development of their earlier *Finnjet* concept, the ship also featured ferry-style car decks as well as a system for handling containerized cargo in watertight compartments below these and forward of the machinery spaces. This was later further developed into a unique monocoque passenger liner of lightweight construction and very refined hull form theoretically capable of economically achieving speeds of 35–40 knots using gas-turboelectric propulsion. Built to Panamax size, with spacious and luxurious accommodation for 2,000 passengers, the builders claimed that a ship of this type would be capable of making a round-trip cruise from Southern Florida to Rio de Janeiro in seven days, or a North Atlantic crossing in four days at competitive fares.

Q5...G32...QUEEN MARY 2

Cunard had been studying their longterm options beyond *QE2*'s foreseeable life expectancy ever since the early 1980s. A decade later, the line's technical department began planning a new dual-purpose transatlantic liner and cruise ship in collaboration with the Finnish consulting naval architectural firm Deltamarin. Code-named *Q5*, this ship was to have been of ultimate Panamax size at around 90,000 tons, with a maximum speed of 40 knots yielded by a highly efficient 240 megaWatt propulsion plant driving three screws. With its refined hull form and propellers designed for low pulse-induced pressure propellers, this remarkable liner was described as realising 'the impossible into a possible configuration'. With a somewhat traditionally balanced two-funnelled profile, featuring a *Canberra*-style nested lifeboat arrangement, Q5 would have offered accommodation for 2,500 passengers in 1,250 cabins and suites. Planning had reached a fairly advanced stage under a veil of great secrecy before this project was eventually cancelled as the line and its owners were ultimately unprepared to make the huge financial commitment to augmenting or replacing their flagship.

Only after Cunard was absorbed into Carnival Corporation in 1999 could specific planning begin for a new liner as part of the aggressive corporate fleet development programmes of Carnival and its subsidiaries. As the *Statendam*-class cruise ships had been designed and built under Carnival patronage following Holland America's acquisition earlier, so too Cunard's first new superliner since *QE2* would be planned with the benefit of the new corporate parent's amassed operational and technical experience in cruise shipping. Yet, as in the instances of Holland America and Costa, also part of the Carnival conglomerate, care would be taken to retain the line's individual identity and culture.

In Cunard's case this would, for the first time since *QE2*'s construction, involve planning a ship primarily for liner service and only secondarily for cruising. Cruise-ship design tends to give greater precedence to passenger amenities, such as veranda cabins, spectacular atria and extensive entertainment and recreational facilities, within the criteria for seaworthiness in temperate and tropical navigating conditions. In contrast, the new Cunarder's planning would have to revert to the more traditional approach of first addressing the requirements of structural strength and propulsion power for line service on the North Atlantic including winter sailings and other deep-sea crossings as part of world cruises and longer voyages. Where most large cruise ships are fundamentally capable of making occasional transatlantic positioning voyages, frequent or continuous deep-sea service of this kind demands greater structural stamina, higher levels of continuous power and various additional onboard services.

The hull and superstructure specifications are first determined for safely and comfortably withstanding long and frequent storms, packing gale-force winds that create 40ft- (12m-)high waves measuring 500ft (150m – about half the ship's waterline length) from crest to crest. The propulsion system must be capable of maintaining headway under such conditions at full speed against the force of more than 15,000 tonnes of turbulent seawater at relative head-on speeds of as

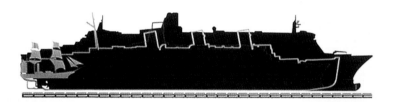

much as 45 knots. Only after this has been contended with can the cruise-ship features expected by today's travelling public be considered. The experience of liners such as *QE2*, *France* or *United States* could provide appropriate modern references for the naval architectural aspects of strength, stability and power calculations. Radically different thinking was required to design passenger facilities with a predominance of veranda accommodation while taking into consideration the additional freeboard height required for Atlantic service and providing for a somewhat different approach to onboard passenger lifestyle since the time of *QE2*.

After tenders were invited for the ship's construction, the final competition for the order was between a consortium led by Britain's Harland & Wolff and the Alston Chantiers de l'Atlantique yard of Saint-Nazaire in France. A letter of intent was signed with the French yard on 10 March 2000, with the contract for building hull number G32 being finalized on 6 November the same year. The new ship was to be Cunard's first North Atlantic liner to be built in France at the birth place of one-time rival Compagnie Générale Transatlantique's *Ile de France*, *Normandie* and *QE2*'s former opponent, *France*. This time there was no suspense or intrigue about naming, as *Queen Mary 2* had already been adopted as the logical name of choice.

Indeed this came as a very sad and bitter blow to the British shipbuilding industry, and particularly to the people of Belfast and to Harland & Wolff. While there had always been longstanding relationships with shipyards and suppliers in the times of the old Cunard *Queens*, with business arrangements being made on a handshake and a gentleman's agreement, the stark reality of business today is that, like most industries, shipping has become a globalized affair. Cunard itself is no longer a British institution, but

Above, top: An early rendering of Project Queen Mary, with the public rooms located two decks beneath the superstructure and with no turbine room atop the superstructure. (Cunard Line publicity photo)

Above, bottom: A comparison of the sizes of Britannia *from 1840,* Queen Mary *from 1936 and the* Queen Mary 2. *(Cunard Line publicity photo)*

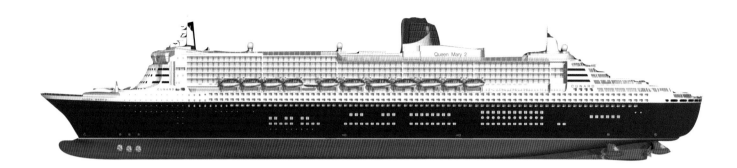

Above: *Port profile rendering of* Queen Mary 2, *clearly showing the irregular arrangement of windows in the hull, brought about by a highly innovative approach to the layout of public spaces within. In fact this is less apparent in the reality of the completed ship, as in daylight the windows usually appear dark against the similarly dark shell plating.* (Chantiers de l'Atlantique)

part of an international corporation headquartered in Miami with its technical department located in London, while Britain is now an integral part of the European Union, with an umbilical link to the Continent by way of the Channel Tunnel.

Concept plans for a 150,000-ton liner with a service speed of 30 knots and double-occupancy accommodation for 2,620 passengers were produced in a collaboration between Cunard's own newbuilding team, headed by Gerry Ellis and Carnival Corporation's Technical Services department in London, with Stephen Payne as project manager and senior naval architect. Once the contract was awarded, Chantiers de l'Atlantique's own design department also became involved in the detailed specification and planning of the ship under the direction of Alain Crouzols.

For Stephen Payne in particular, this project is the realization of a childhood dream. As part of a holiday bus excursion made at the age of nine with his parents and younger brothers in 1969, he had the rare opportunity of touring *QE2* in Southampton, and of seeing from the new Cunarder's decks *United States* making one of her last departures from the English port. That day set his career direction and life's objectives, with his mind made up to be involved in passenger shipping and ultimately to design great ships like these himself. Stephen soon started writing letters to seek out future employment opportunities and share his own thoughts with shipping lines such as Cunard, P&O, French Line and Holland America.

After BBC Television's Blue Peter programme for young people had shown footage of the old *Queen Elizabeth*'s tragic fatal burning in Hong Kong in January 1972 at the completion of her conversion as a floating university for the C. Y. Tung Group, and run an article in their Christmas annual magazine that year expressing the view the likes of such ships would never be seen again, Stephen wrote a letter expressing his hopes and views to the contrary. A kindly reply from the publishers praised young Stephen's enthusiasm, yet cautioned him against being too optimistic. When he was offered an interview by P&O at their Leadenhall Street head office a short while later, he had to ask if he could bring his mother along as she

was unwilling to let her 11-year-old son make the train journey to London alone. Although somewhat surprised to learn of his young age, the P&O people nonetheless obliged, and encouraged Stephen to continue his academic studies and to come back to them after finishing his schooling.

Stephen ultimately enrolled in the Ship Sciences and Naval Architectural Programme at Southampton University, where he chose for his study project to design a passenger ship based on a hypothetical specification obtained through his on-going correspondence with P&O. His professors thought that so sophisticated a ship might be too ambitious a project and encouraged Stephen to do something less complex, but he was adamant that it was passenger-ship design he wanted to learn. After graduating with honours, he served with the Royal Navy as a midshipman aboard HMS *Woodlark*. It was here that he acquired his great affinity for HMY *Britannia* from his commanding officer who had served aboard the royal yacht.

After working briefly for Marconi Marine, Stephen was contacted in 1984 by the London-based firm Technical Marine Planning with an offer to work in passenger-ship design for Carnival Cruises in response to an earlier application he had made. He later transferred to Carnival Corporation when they created their own Technical Services department in London. Here he designed large and sophisticated ships for Carnival Cruises, Costa and Holland America, as well as handling various conversions and modernizations of the Costa and Holland America fleets, including replacement of the much-loved 1959-built *Rotterdam*. As Senior Naval Architect and project manager for *Queen Mary 2*, Stephen has attained the most enviable, prestigious and responsible position in his field. He has also worked diligently on HMY *Britannia*'s preservation at Leith after her retirement from active service, and is still involved in plans to create a second life in a static role for *Rotterdam* in Amsterdam after she reaches the end of her service life as *Rembrandt*. Stephen's work is very much his life's passion, and in his own quiet way, brings to all his endeavours a sense of dedication and total commitment worthy of men such as William

Francis Gibbs, George G. Sharp and Isambard Kingdom Brunel.

In their approach to designing the new Cunard liner, Stephen and his colleagues began with *Queen Elizabeth 2*'s overall hull dimensions, passenger capacities, speed and service performance. Plans of *QE2* were spread out on a drawing board as the passenger and service areas were studied and either marked as needing to be substantially redesigned for the new ship or crossed off as being altogether inappropriate. While the essence of signature spaces such as the Queens Room and the full-width restaurants overlooking the sea would be retained, upgraded and brought up to current cruise-ship standards, the complex cabin layouts of Four and Five Decks, with their myriad secondary alleyways and large numbers of small inside rooms, definitely would have to go.

As *QE2*'s original Double Room has been adapted as best as possible to meet the requirements of professional cabaret entertainment through a number of successive refits and renovations, ending up as the Grand Lounge, the new ship would need a modern show lounge with a proper proscenium stage, full-production sound and lighting facilities and backstage amenities. Additional specialized modern facilities, including choices of alternative dining options and a health and beauty spa, would also need to be more fully introduced into the Cunard liner experience.

Other changes would involve adopting Carnival's highly rationalized approach to behind-the-scenes services and supporting facilities, established early in their own building experience and adopted aboard ships also built for their Holland America and Costa subsidiaries. Among other things this stresses the use of large marshalling areas on the lower decks, directly accessible through hatches in the hull's sides at pier level, from where the distribution of passenger baggage and ship's stores onboard are handled by the crew while underway, saving time and work while in port. Where *QE2*'s food and beverage service was originally planned around a single galley complex serving all passenger and crew dining areas, the demands for greater flexibility and diversity of service aboard today's ships calls for a more distributed approach, with a number of specialized galleys adjacent to the areas they individually serve, having direct access to stores and primary food-preparation areas, including the butcher's workshop and bakery.

Apart from the Captain and a handful of other senior officers given suites or cabins near the bridge, accommodation for all other officers and engineering staff would, as aboard virtually all cruise ships today, be located on the lower forward decks, rather than occupying prime revenue-earning space on the upper decks. Where *QE2*'s officers' dining room and lounge had pride of place across the boat deck's full width with windows overlooking the bow, the new Cunarder's corresponding spaces would offer premium passenger spaces.

With cruise amenities, such as a predominance of veranda cabins, higher emphasis on alternative dining facilities and wider range of entertainment venues and public spaces being taken into account and applied, the ship's size began to increase significantly in three dimensions. Where *QE2* was designed to fit through the Panama Canal as a consideration of her secondary cruise role, it quickly became apparent that the new liner would surpass the Panama Maximum's (Panamax) mark as the old *Queens* had done, thanks to the cruise influence on her primary line-service function.

Space for *QE2*'s original 1969 capacity of 2,000 passengers in accommodation, public amenities and service at the required luxury standard, along with adequate provision for 900 crew and stores, the ship's various working and stores areas, including holds, were all accommodated within an efficient envelope of hull and superstructure measuring 65,862 tons. At the time this was considered to be about the largest ship that could possibly navigate the Panama Canal, with her overall dimensions just fitting snugly into its famous 1,000ft (300m) locks, thanks to the lightweight aluminium construction of her upper superstructure and other economies of mass in her construction. While *QE2* had retained her unique market position and high standards of passenger accommodation through three decades of North Atlantic and cruise service, her alloy construction had been showing signs of fatigue for some time. Part of the work done during the ship's 1986–87 diesel conversion in Germany involved repairs to cracks and fractures of the superstructure plating.

With the new *Queen Mary 2* being planned for a 40-year service life, the decision was made to construct her entirely of steel. Although current design techniques allow Panamax cruise ships of up to around 90,000 tons to be dimensioned within the Canal lock size, the added requirements of length and beam for stability in Atlantic service and on other long ocean passages precluded limiting the new liner's size even to Panamax standards. To build a Panamax ship with the required liner characteristics of higher stability and greater seaworthiness, with longer fore- and after-decks entirely of steel, would have resulted in creating an overall package smaller than *QE2*. A review of *QE2*'s voyage schedules showed that the one passage of the Panama Canal per year made during her annual world cruise was scarcely worth the limitations of size the Canal restrictions would impose. With the Panama Canal restrictions removed, the practical concerns circumscribing the new liner's overall dimensions would revert to the turning space available at Southampton's Eastern Dock and the 1,000ft (300m) piers of New York's Consolidated Passenger Terminal, where a moderate extension into the Hudson's waters beyond the pierhead would be acceptable. A maximum draft of 33ft (10m) would allow for navigation without

Above, left: *An early architectural representation of Robert Tillberg's concept for a central walkway through the ship's public spaces.* (Author's collection)

Above, right: *The Deck 2 Grand Promenade looking aft from behind the Grand Lobby towards the Britannia Restaurant's entrance atop the stairs in the far background.* (Author's photo)

being dependant on the tides as were the old Cunard *Queens*, although an altogether new limiting factor since their time would be the maximum 206½ft (62m) clearance beneath the Verazzano Narrows Bridge at the entrance to New York's harbour.

In fact, the planned length and beam of 1,150ft (345m) and 136ft (41m) respectively would come closer to the 1,115⅔ft (334.7m) overall hull length and 135½ft (40.85m) beam of a United States Navy *Nimitz*-class nuclear aircraft carrier. Of course, these similarities are merely coincidental. Apart from the obvious differences in the two ships' functions, the strong visual impression of size, mass and might are created horizontally by the overhang of the aircraft carrier's flight deck rather than by its comparatively small superstructure to the starboard side, while it is the vertical dimension of the superstructure and funnels that inspire awe in the liner.

The new Cunarder's design emerged with the refined hullform needed to maintain a 30-knot speed in line service on the North Atlantic and through other deep-sea passages. The slender form of the hull's forebody, which is similar to *QE2*'s lines, was designed to optimize the ship's performance at speed while maintaining optimum stability over her waterline length of around 1,033ft (310m). The afterbody's shape was optimized with the fuller form needed for azimuthing-pod propulsion units and to also provide the additional buoyancy required to balance the bow's fineness of line and keep the longitudinal centre of buoyancy (LCB) as close to amidships as possible. The stern is in fact a combination transom and cruiser form, similar to that of Costa Line's *Eugenio C.*

Queen Mary 2's 86,000 kiloWatt power plant consists of a CODAG (combined diesel and gas turbine) arrangement of four 16-cylinder Wärtsilä 46C diesel engines and two General Electric aviation-style LM2500 marine gas generator sets. The diesels are of the latest Enviro type, using common-rail fuel injection for maximum efficiency and minimized smoke emission. A combination of two azimuthing and two

fixed pods is the first of its kind to be used in a passenger ship, with *QM2* being the only quadruple-screw liner to be built since *France* was delivered from Chantiers de l'Atlantique in 1961. The azimuthing units are farthest aft, with the fixed pods forward providing the additional power for cruising at full speed. The four 20 megaWatt Rolls Royce MerMaid pods are the largest encapsulated marine propulsion units of their type yet to be built.

While *QM2*'s machinery installation is unconventional in traditional liner terms, many of its components are already proven in service with other recently built cruise ships. Carnival Corporation has been a pioneering proponent of podded propulsion, first adopting the system for their cruise ships *Elation* and *Paradise* delivered in the late 1990s, as well as a partnering with Wärtsilä Diesel on adopting smokeless engine technology for passenger ships, as introduced in the year 2000 aboard *Carnival Spirit*. The Panamax cruise ship *Coral Princess*, completed by Chantiers de l'Atlantique for Princess Cruises scarcely a year ahead of *QM2*, served as a close half-scale prototype for the Cunard liner's diesel and gas-turbine generator installation.

Queen Mary 2's unique design also brings about the need for special new safety of life at sea (SOLAS) rules covering modern vessels of her class. For instance, in consideration of the freeboard height required for winter North Atlantic service, *QM2*'s lifeboats are nested 86½ft (27m) above the waterline, where the maximum height for cruise ships is only 50ft (15m). While located near the 150,000-GT *QM2*'s vertical midpoint, this is approximately the same distance to the water as from *QE2*'s upper decks lifeboat location.

Other liner considerations include the longer fore-deck, featuring a streamlined *Normandie*-style whale-back, and aerodynamically-shaped superstructure front. In the interest of structural strength there is no forward-facing open veranda accommodation. It is also noteworthy that, despite the need to access shallower ports in cruise service, *QM2* has a North

Atlantic draft of 32ft 10in (9.95m). This compares with a depth of only 28ft (8.6m) for Royal Caribbean's 137,278-GT *Voyager of the Seas*, currently one of the world's largest cruise ships.

During the ship's early planning stages, consultations were held with the renowned Swedish marine architect Robert Tillberg, whose career in passenger-ship design had begun with Swedish American Line's last *Kungsholm*, delivered by John Brown Shipbuilding in 1966, where *QE2* was being built at the time. Over the following years Arkitektkontoret Robert Tillberg AB's modest ship-design practice flourished and grew into an international operation with offices also in London and Fort Lauderdale, Florida. The firm's variety of work includes many ferries and cruise ships, large and small alike, trading on various services around the world.

Robert, then semi-retired, and his colleagues from both sides of the Atlantic worked out initial general layout and architectural design concepts for the ship's passenger spaces with Cunard's newbuilding team and Carnival's technical department. Their greatest challenge was to adapt the much admired liner-era features of ships such as *Normandie* and the old Cunard *Queens*, as well as more recent innovations from Holland America Line's fifth *Rotterdam* of 1959, and of course Cunard's own *QE2*.

Although Stephen Payne's responsibilities lay primarily with the more technical realm of naval architecture, and its considerations of hull forms and hydrostatics, structural strength and seaworthiness, power and propulsion, and development of the ship's overall plan, he also took great interest in her architectural and aesthetic design. Along with a few carefully chosen liners and cruise ships whose design he particularly admired, including *Rotterdam* and *QE2*, Stephen was keen for the architects to see Eltham Palace, near his own home in south-east London. Originally dating to the time of King Henry VIII, from which but part of the Great Hall had survived, the property was reconstructed as a private home for the British textile mogul Stephen Courtauld and his family in 1936. Built with a traditional exterior appearance in respect of the reconstructed medieval Great Hall, the interiors of the new additions were, however, a showcase of art moderne elegance with a strong ocean-liner influence, reflecting also no doubt Stephen Courtauld's personal interest in yachting, and his own steam yacht *Virginia*.

Now preserved by English Heritage, along with its gardens, as a public historical attraction, this is one of Britain's premiere surviving modern architectural sites of the period. The stunning main entrance hall, which is of a triangular plan with bowed sides in dark Australian blackbeam veneer panelling decorated with marquetry depictions of scenes from Florence, Venice and Stockholm, domed ceiling, cream-coloured terrazzo floor and circular carpet by Marion Dorn, were seen by both Stephen Payne and Robert

Tillberg to possess the elegance of style they wanted for the new liner.

Remarkably, this and a number of the reception rooms in the Courtaulds' magnificent new house were rendered at approximately the scale of the 1930s liner interiors that Stephen Courtauld himself so admired. The entrance hall was originally seen as offering a suitable reference for the ship's main lobby as a worthy successor to Dennis Lennon's striking circular main lobby aboard *QE2*, with its single central column in white and umbrella fibreglass ceiling with its serrations eddying outwards to the room's perimeter wall. Ultimately, Cunard's perception of passenger expectation and preference prevailed in favour of creating an atrium. Despite this concession being made, the influence of Eltham Palace is nonetheless apparent in a number of features of *Queen Mary 2*'s design, particularly in the Duplex Suites, which are clearly inspired by the design of Virginia Courtauld's circular bedroom.

Above: *View of the entrance hall of Eltham Palace as it appears from the east stairway, seen by Tillberg and Payne as a space offering the appropriate scale and elegance of style they wanted for the new Cunard ship.* (Author's photo)

Below: *External view of Eltham Palace from the east gardens, with the medieval Great Hall visible behind the house's south wing, seen on the left.* (Author's photo)

Right: *Sketch of the Illuminations dome being assembled onboard the ship, as visualized by Bernard Champy, an engineer with the yard's outfitting department.* (By courtesy of HMS, France)

Far right: *The Grand Lobby atrium, as seen from Deck 2 at the foot of its starboard staircase, showing part of the oval colonnade and the atrium space through Decks 4 to 6.* (Author's photo)

Below: *The Illuminations auditorium, with its planetarium dome in the raised position, allowing the room to be used as an auditorium and cinema. Note the dark gold seats beneath the dome that recline for planetarium presentations.* (Author's photo)

Tillberg Design's Swedish office in Viken was commissioned to handle most of the ship's architectural design, working jointly with the firm's London partners, SMC Design in London, where this huge enterprise was headed up by Andy Collier as project manager. The London-based firm designteam, headed by Eric Mouzourides, who himself had formerly worked with Robert Tillberg, was commissioned to create some of *Queen Mary 2*'s more specialized interiors, including the Illuminations auditorium, which is fitted with a retractable dome as the world's first-ever shipboard planetarium. Designteam also designed retail areas, speciality restaurants and

ConneXions, a more diverse adaption of the original Cunard University at Sea, introduced aboard *QE2* and operated now as ConneXions through Oxford University's Discovery Programme. The architects' overall design brief called for the Cunard fleet and 'product' image to be retained and further developed, as now conveyed through the unique atmosphere and experience of *QE2*. Yet the new ship was essentially to create an ambience and atmosphere all of her own, rooted in a contemporary classic cruising ultra-luxe. The schemes permitted, as Andy Collier explained, 'a tip of the hat to history and tradition, yet without setting any retrospective mood in themselves.'[1]

Queen Mary 2 is otherwise designed and built entirely as a ship of the present era. While references are certainly made to Cunard's history and background, and even to elements of the radical axial planning of ships such as the 1929-built *Bremen* and *Normandie*, there could be no recourse back to the traditional character of these ships or of the old Cunard *Queens*. The public amenities, particularly of liners built before World War II, generally provided for the shipboard lifestyles of those times, when the art of conversation and literary pursuits of reading and diary- or letter-writing flourished, and passengers were generally content to entertain themselves for most of the time.

In the 70-or-so years since these were built, society has changed dramatically, becoming more democratized and generally far more widely travelled. Even as late as the 1950s First-Class sea travel was still a privilege of the wealthy and the famed, or at least of those who had these reputations to live up to by family lineage, social standing or corporate position. The standards were set as much by the high levels of individual service and attention offered to the passenger, whose name and preferences would be remembered by ships' personnel from a passenger's earlier voyages with the same ship or line, as they were by the luxury of the accommodation and public amenities. Some passengers then still travelled with their own butlers and maids, and could arrange to have meals cooked by their own staff. In 1962 *France* was the last ship to provide a separate servants' dining room for her First-Class passengers.

Today, First Class has in essence become the defacto standard of the cruise industry, with luxury and service as its key selling points. The interaction between passenger and staff is now more personable than personal. Accommodation standards, entertainment and recreational facilities, gastronomy and the range of worldwide itineraries and destinations available in many ways surpass anything offered during the ocean-liner era. What has changed most is that there is now far greater emphasis on the cruise *experience* itself than on the type of individual attention First-Class passengers were accustomed to and expected. Today's ship passengers want the experience to be enriching and rewarding, perhaps by way of the itineraries offered, special onboard features of the ship such as fitness and sport facilities, business and learning centres, or the altogether more elegantly informal resort-inspired club-ship approach introduced into the German cruise market by Deutsche Seereederei's *Aida* in 1996 and subsequently adopted by a number of other lines.

While top cruise ships rival the best urban hotels and resorts ashore, today's cruise passengers and hotel guests also want the flexibility and freedom to serve themselves from individual mini-bars and to have choices of audio and video entertainment, as well as interactive digital services, computer access and worldwide communications, from the privacy of their own accommodation. Some of the more exclusive ships now do offer concierge service to those in their premium suites as an added luxury touch, as is offered aboard *QM2*. The passengers booking the most expensive suites today are more likely to be recording and film stars, successful business entrepreneurs and wealthy younger retirees, with either a sense of adventure or the wish to take some time out for themselves for a while, than the titled aristocracy who once took their morning walks around the promenade decks of Cunard's venerable *Queens*.

There is now a far greater proportion of the population that is accustomed to these levels of service both ashore and at sea than ever there was during the liner era. The travelling public is more affluent and adventurous than it has ever been. Social class barriers that once stratified society ashore and, most definitely at sea, have largely dissolved, with a greater cross-section of peoples from all walks of life and diverse backgrounds being brought together aboard trains, aircraft and ships around the globe.

The business policies of many hotel companies and shipping lines are often to upgrade their clientele to the best accommodation available at the time of the hotel stay or voyage as a means of offering the maximum satisfaction and an incentive to make future bookings at the higher-grade. Special fares and rates are also offered to travel and business groups, students and others, adding to the mix of people and in effect diluting the traditional sense of elitism and exclusivity of top-grade accommodation either ashore or afloat.

The expression of luxury has also changed throughout the hospitality industry, both ashore and at sea. Ships and hotels have taken on a more universal international style, brought about largely through the rationale of modular building techniques, with standardized guest room plans in each price range and an altogether more conscious approach to the productive use of the public spaces. The 'neat, tidy and well groomed' sense of Cunard's essentially nautical and shipshape onboard ambience that Doris Thompson always so admired during her travels as a young lady in the 1920s and 1930s, migrated upscale with the coming of *Queen Elizabeth 2* in 1969 to the contemporary international hotelier leitmotif of today's best hotels, resorts and cruise ships. Gone is the individuality of the old Cunard *Queens*, with the carpenter eclectic of their shipwright-made veneered cabin interiors, where virtually no two rooms were ever identical. The atmosphere is now more sleek and contemporary, perhaps at the expense of a little esoteric individuality, but ultimately to the greater serviceability of the ship as a whole over the long term.

Cunard, a company which has always tended to trade on public perception of tradition, nonetheless wanted their new liner to feature a layout of grand gesture with the long interior vistas so admired in the 1930s aboard *Bremen*, *Europa* and *Normandie*, to satisfy a popular impression of the liner era in all its former glory. While *Normandie* with her axial centreline plan and legendary public spaces was perhaps the obvious starting point, other plans were also examined. Frederik Johansson, who led Tillberg's Project Queen Mary design team in Viken, discovered that the Compagnie de Navigation Sudatlantique liner *l'Atlantique*, completed at Saint-Nazaire in 1931, once again offered a valuable design reference as she had for *Normandie*. The earlier ship's modern and spacious Salon Ovale ballroom, Grand Salon main lounge and Grande Salle à Manger main dining room, arranged forward-to-amidships on a remarkably simple plan as a series of centreline-accessed spaces, were seen to offer a less extravagant example better suited to modern passenger-ship planning.

l'Atlantique's Salon Ovale was in essence repeated aboard *Normandie* as the Café-Grill, located fully aft on boat deck and connected with the promenade deck public rooms by a grander rendition of the earlier ship's processional dining room staircase. A more contemporary single-level adaptation of the *l'Atlantique* plan and sequence of public spaces emerged during the 1960s in the axial arrangement of *Eugenio C*'s First-Class ballroom, bar lounge and oval-shaped forward observation lounge.

Robert Tillberg's own viewpoint was to adopt an axial plan for the new Cunard ship as a practical means of arranging the public rooms around a single wide Central Walkway through the centre of the ship between divided stairways, engine casings and other vertical service cores. He saw this as an opportunity to create the perfect ship's layout for clarity of function and for the ease of orientation from the passengers' perspective. The underlying idea was to simplify the plan to the point of it being straightforward and intuitive enough that directional signage would be virtually unnecessary.

The idea for *QM2* then emerged, retaining the concept of *l'Atlantique*'s Salon Ovale, Grande Salon and Grande Salle à Manger as an axial sequence of living spaces along a Central Walkway extending along the new Cunard ship's centreline. The sequence of these was rearranged to place the Salon Ovale amidships as an entrance lobby between the two rectangular spaces. At the stage this concept was introduced, *QM2*'s layout was being planned with public rooms assembled together throughout the promenade deck and two uppermost levels within the hull. The Salon Ovale-styled lobby was to be amidships extending through the three decks, with the main restaurant directly ahead of it on the two hull

decks, with the planetarium farther forward and the main galley beneath it. The show lounge was to be aft of the main lobby on these same decks.

The promenade deck was to have been arranged with the Queen's Room aft of the lobby and with the premium Princess and Queen's Grill restaurants forward, along with other rooms such as the Chart Room bar and Golden Lion Pub. The restaurants on this deck would have been served from their own finishing galley and pantries, with direct service-lift access from the main kitchens and prep areas three decks lower down. Remarkably, this plan was to have featured a *l'Atlantique*- or *Normandie*-style grand processional stairway descending to the main restaurant's lower level in the centreline space between the lift shafts, with the lifts themselves opening to vestibules at their outward sides on these decks.

The layout and location of the pubic decks went through a number of changes as the ship's plan evolved and the importance of various influences were evaluated and reassessed. There was the question as to whether *QM2*'s gas generators should be located in an engine room below decks along with the diesel machinery or in a deckhouse atop the superstructure as was being planned for *Coral Princess*. Was there to be an atrium? Would a high proportion of veranda accommodation be appropriate for Atlantic service, and if so, how would these be arranged to meet the strength and safety considerations of building a real liner?

Ultimately it was decided that the turbines should be housed above, directly astern of the funnel, doing away with the need for a second set of uptake casings and thereby increasing the amount of space available for passenger facilities. Unfortunately, plans for a *Normandie*-style processional dining-room staircase positioned between a pair of divided casings were ultimately dropped as the second pair of uptakes also disappeared. Although Stephen Payne and his colleagues in France would have preferred to minimize the number of additional multiple-deck open interior spaces as a consideration of structural integrity, the marketing and sales people still insisted that an atrium would be expected. They also won their case for a maximum of veranda cabins, with the result that the main suite of public rooms were in effect moved down to Decks 2 and 3, beneath three additional strata of cabins on the upper hull decks with verandas located behind openings in the upper strakes of the structural shell plating.

With the need thus to concentrate the veranda accommodation as high up as possible, the main suite of public rooms is concentrated relatively far down within the hull, on the lowest passenger-accessible decks. The inspiration of *l'Atlantique*'s arrangement of upper-decks public spaces for tropical service was thus to be realized aboard *QM2* at a relative height more akin to North Atlantic rationale of *Normandie*'s lower-decks dining-room. Yet the choice of a lower-

Below: *The Salle à Manger, Premiere Classe, of French Line's* Paris *of 1921, showing an approach to the overall arrangement of the room's mezzanine plan and illuminated ceiling similar to those of more than three quarters of a century earlier.*
(Archive Chantiers de l'Atlantique/Cliché Ecomusée de Saint-Nazaire)

deck venue for other principal spaces seems somewhat unusual. Since the primary function of many larger public spaces aboard ship is for evening entertainment, this ends up being both logical by its effective use of space on the lower decks and functional in its adjacency of these facilities to the dining room. While relatively low within the scheme of *QM2*'s great size, the height of these decks above water compares with the public room locations of contemporary cruise ships such as P&O's *Oriana* and *Aurora*.

The Grand Promenades, as Robert Tillberg's Central Walkways became, extend as wide boulevards through the centres of Decks 2 and 3, each offering long vistas through the ship's centre axis from the Royal Court Theatre forward, all the way through the Salon Ovale-inspired Grand Lobby atrium amidships to the large Cunard Liner mural on the aft wall of the Britannia Restaurant astern, a distance of some 400ft (125m). The classic liner opulence of these *l'Atlantique*- and *Normandie*-inspired interiors is conveyed largely by the luxury of overhead spaciousness, thanks to the 15ft (4.5m) height of Decks 2 and 3.

Yet despite its links to 1930s grand gesture, the rationale for the divided uptakes and central promenade aboard *QM2* is entirely modern and appropriate to today's ocean-going living. The various public rooms on these decks are entered in a direction going from inboard to outboard, where the view of the sea beyond the ship's sides always lies ahead in the same way that one's attention is drawn towards the stage or screen when entering a theatre or cinema. This is

something of a reversal of the perimeter circulation approach extensively introduced in 1969 aboard *QE2*, where one circulated about the ship near its sides and then moved away from the sea on entering any of the public rooms with the focus being drawn inwards, away from the sea.

Owing to the lower-decks location of *QM2*'s public rooms and current safety restrictions against excessive open spaces in passenger ships, the overall arrangement conveys a perhaps less open feeling than did the processional promenade through the

Above: *The enclosed forward part of the main promenade on Deck 7 of the* Queen Mary 2, *where it passes inside the superstructure front in the traditional style of the* Rotterdam *and* Canberra. (Author's photo)

Left: *View aft beneath the room's central ceiling vault, above the square parquet dance floor, looking towards the Hollywood Bowl-styled stage.* (Author's photo)

Above: *The* Queen Mary 2*'s main promenade beneath the lifeboats, appearing much like the boat decks of the old* Queens, *the* United States *and the* France, *where sunlight reached the deck in the space between the boats and superstructure wall. Note also the traditional arrangement of deckchairs.* (Author's photo)

centres of *Normandie*'s principal public rooms. The function is more of a circulation artery external to the public spaces themselves rather than a promenade directly through them as in the earlier French prototypes. A greater sense of openness might have been possible if a space such as the Winter Garden could have been located amidships in place of the atrium and its required separate egress stairways. If Stephen Payne and Robert Tillberg's preference for a single-deck-height lobby based on the example of Eltham Palace's Entrance Hall had prevailed, this could have been located on either of the two decks, leaving space on the other for alternative uses. The layout of these decks and location of the ship's entrance lobby had to take in to account the location of gangway access hatches to coincide with existing passenger terminal facilities in Southampton and New York.

Instead of trying to repeat the Gallic marble-and-glass-moderne decorative splendours of the 'Ship of Light', as *Normandie* was known, *QM2*'s architects chose to base their work on an appropriate contemporary approach, drawn in part from the lustrous veneered interiors of the original Cunard *Queens*. This they felt would best satisfy the public perception of the characteristic Cunard tradition of luxury and elegance, while also achieving the creative latitude to offer the diversity and special features demanded by today's cruise and travel market.

The Grand Promenades, Grand Lobby atrium and their adjacent spaces in particular, are block-panelled in various fire-resistant veneers including rosewood, eucalyptus burr and macassar, with inlaid banding in the woodwork inspired by the original *Queen Mary*'s design. The etched-glass stairway and balcony balustrade panels bear art moderne motifs reminiscent of *Normandie*'s glass-tile artwork. The Grand Promenade is decorated in the style of *Normandie*'s *verre eglomise* (decorative mirrored glass), a tech-

nique developed in France during the 1920s and 1930s for large architectural murals. The bas relief panels aboard *QM2*, executed in bronze resin, depict the four Seasons, the four elements, and the northern and southern hemispheres of the globe.

Among the iconic images depicting the United States, including pioneer covered wagons, a Native American in full-feathered headdress, a baseball player, the Statue of Liberty and the space shuttle, the artists surreptitiously added a tiny image from the current popular animated television series *The Simpsons*, depicting Homer Simpson, remote control in hand, blissfully watching TV. Nothing was said to Cunard of this addition, and Homer was left to stow away aboard the new ship until being discovered by passengers on one of her early voyages. Thirty years ago the subject of this sort of artistic fun would no doubt have been Archie Bunker from television's *All in the Family*.

The main Britannia Restaurant and Queens Room reflect the greatest sense of Cunard tradition among the ship's main public rooms. The mezzanine-plan restaurant in particular, with its pearlescent double columns, cherry and walnut veneer panelling, etched glass balustrades and illuminated glass domed ceiling, is an epic ocean-liner interior with a style reminiscent of the 1920s art nouveau opulence of French Line's *Paris*. While the *Normandie*-style processional staircase was sacrificed during *QM2*'s structural planning, passengers can still make their grand arrival from the raised podium at the Deck 3 entrance or sweep down from Deck 3 by way of the twin curved staircases inside the Britannia Restaurant. On the rear wall opposite the room's principal entrances hangs a 20x30ft (6x9m) tapestry by artist Barbara Broekman of the Netherlands, depicting a mythical Cunard liner emerging through a cluster of industrial steelwork against a backdrop of New York skyscrapers. The piece's presence is appropriately evocative of the Arcadian landscape that adorned *Ile de France*'s Grande Salle à Manger and Canadian artist Helen Banynina's trio of tapestries that hang in the forward Quarter Deck lobby aboard *QE2*, depicting the ship's launching.

Rather than trying to adapt the original 1960s mod-chic of *QE2*'s Queens Room, the architects designed the ballroom for *QM2* as an altogether new space, reverting to a somewhat art-moderne ocean-liner leitmotif. This 133sq.ft (40sq.m) room, decorated in regal hues of red, blue and yellow, is far too large for any adaptation of the trumpet-shaped white columns and delicate illuminated latticed ceiling from *QE2*. With a height of about 16ft (5m), the new ship's Queens Room has a coffered ceiling with concealed indirect lighting, somewhat reminiscent of the public spaces aboard Italia's *Rex* of 1932. There is a single fore-and-aft central vault with a pair of moderne chandeliers above the 330sq.ft (100sq.m) parquet dance floor. Extending up into the space between Deck 4's cabin corridors above to a height of 25ft (7.5m), this follows the stage's Hollywood Bowl-styled proscenium arch.

A double colonnade towards either side of the room, at a location coinciding approximately with *QE2*'s width, visually delineates elevated seating areas to either side of the ship overlooking the sea through large windows. In what would traditionally be a promenade-deck space, these in effect offer the essence of there being inner and outer spaces within the room as a whole. They also diminish any inherent sense of prejudice against the Queens Room's location several decks beneath the open promenades, and whatever impression this may create of being inside the hermetically-sealed fuselage of some great aircraft.

With passengers spending six continuous days at sea in North Atlantic service, the Queens Room is one of several spaces designed to also serve the traditional function of a ship's day lounge in addition to its main role as a ballroom. Care was thus taken to make the room equally suited to its alternative uses for lectures, afternoon tea, tea dances, social gatherings such as the Captain's reception, and various other entertainment features including concerts or fashion shows.

The Royal Court Theatre and Illuminations Planetarium belong to the more modern realm of cruising, with the theatre in particular being very similar to those aboard many recent cruise ships, including Holland America's newest *Rotterdam*, delivered in 1996. This is also true of the G32 Nightclub fully aft of the Queens Room, created as a high-tech multi-functional entertainment venue. The manicured industrial motif of this space was inspired by the shipyard and building of the ship herself, with the room named for the builders' yard number, as was the original 736 club aboard *QE2*.

Although featuring a modern-art decorative theme, Illuminations is otherwise a sophisticated modern facility of considerable technological complexity, outfitted as the first planetarium ever to be built aboard a passenger ship. Cunard wanted a special feature that would be unique to *QM2*, offering a memorable experience for their passengers beyond the realm of normally expected shipboard diversions. Yet they also wanted something more apropos to the liner experience than the rock climbing walls, ice-skating rinks and other 'pursuit of wow factor' extras being added by the cruise lines. The inspiration for Illuminations came from the London Planetarium as being a distinctive and popular tourist attraction on a scale that could be fully adapted to a shipboard space. As celestial programmes are fairly specialized, the room also had to function equally as an auditorium, lecture theatre and cinema. Located far enough forward on Decks 2 and 3 to be where the hull lines begin to converge towards the bow, the space itself already offered the ideal pie-slice plan, widest across

the single plane of its steeply raked seating and narrowing towards the focal points of its stage and projection screens at its forward end.

The planetarium dome itself is fitted above the auditorium's centre, with its crown nested between the Deck 4 cabin corridors. The lower part of the dome telescopes up into the ceiling around its crown while Illuminations is being used in its other roles. For celestial shows, iMax or other virtual-reality-type presentations, the dome's moveable segment is lowered, with a series of flaps opening like aircraft ailerons to complete the perfectly hemispheric, seamless projection surface over the 170 reclining seats within its viewing area at the room's centre. Having a diameter of 42ft (13m) at its 'equator', the dome is only slightly smaller than that of the London Planetarium.

With its dome retracted, Illuminations serves as a 473-seat recital hall and lecture theatre, with an impressive range of sound, projection and other audio/visual facilities including three large-format digital LCD video walls. Outfitted also with twin 35mm motion-picture projectors, the auditorium serves as an excellent cinema, the likes of which were last included aboard liners such as *Rotterdam*, *France*, *Michelangelo*, *Raffaello* and *QE2*.

QM2's requirement for a large variety of public spaces to serve the needs of passengers during a six-day Atlantic crossing has given rise to a number of special design considerations that had to be addressed by the naval architects and architectural designers. Where cruise ships normally feature an arrangement of public rooms with a full-width theatre at one end of the deck and the restaurant or a second show lounge at the other, the new Cunard liner needed to have multiple full-beam spaces, both forward and aft, along with the means of providing simultaneous access to each of these without passengers needing to pass directly through any of the others. This was accomplished by the ingenious arrangement of 'hidden promenades' or galleries as they are

Below: *The Winter Garden, rendered as a flexible and modern adaptation of a venerable liner-era shipboard institution, in which the forebears of today's passengers would have whiled away the days at sea..* (Author's photo)

referred to on passenger maps, inconspicuously bypassing the theatre and restaurant along either side of the ship at a half-level between Decks 2 and 3, designated as Deck 3L.

From full-beam deck lobbies on Decks 2 and 3 at the aft end of the Grand Promenades, the Deck 3L galleries bypass the main Britannia Restaurant, itself about two-thirds aft, en route to the Queens Room and G32 Nightclub farther astern. By virtue of the Britannia Restaurant's height of nearly 30ft (9m) through Decks 2 and 3, with its central illuminated dome extending up into the centreline space of Deck 4, the galleries are concealed between the room's main and mezzanine levels. These are arranged vertically so that ceiling heights beneath the mezzanine progressively increase inboard from the ship's sides, and the floor level of the mezzanine itself rises in three stages towards the outer walls, in both instances increasing visibility to the room's centre. This also creates a 9⅓ft- (2.8m-) high space at the ship's sides between the Deck 2 ceiling and mezzanine floor for the Deck 3L galleries. Appearing as bright enclosed promenades overlooking the sea, these serve as the photographers' display space and as art exhibition spaces, without the neat trick of their ingenious location and routing through the ship's structural webs being at all apparent from within the restaurant. The Queens Room and G32 Nightclub are located at about the height of Deck 3L, where the ballroom in particular is a remarkably spacious high-ceilinged space with large windows overlooking the sea along its sides.

Forward, the Deck 3L galleries pass to either side of the Royal Court Theatre, behind the upper reaches of the raked Deck 2 orchestra- or main-level seating, and beneath the raised outer extremities of the audi-

torium's Deck 3 balcony, where this extends out to the ship's sides. Ahead of the theatre, these access the Illuminations planetarium auditorium diagonally from a pair of vestibules to either side of the ship. A second pair of galleries beneath these on Deck 2 serve the ConneXions college at sea and business centre, located beneath the upper reaches of the planetarium's steeply raked seating, projection booths and control rooms. Secondary stairways to port and starboard connect with the Illuminations vestibules above.

From the Illuminations Planetarium's vestibules forward, the Deck 3L galleries are continued upwards in a gradual slope surrounding the auditorium itself to the forward-most passenger stairway and lifts where they join, forming a loop enclosing the forward public spaces on Decks 2 and 3. The slope upwards to Deck 3 is quite steep, and almost reminiscent of the remarkably pronounced sheer of *Canberra*'s forward decks. With but a few portholes along its outer sides, these galleries represent the sort of structural shipboard spaces that cruise passengers seldom have the chance to experience aboard most modern cruise ships. Indeed the carefully thought-out plans of these decks, where no room serves as a thoroughfare to other parts of the ship, are among the most sophisticated ever to be devised, to some extent dissolving Robert Tillberg's original vision of his perfect and completely intuitive layout.

Another consideration in creating an ocean liner rather than a cruise ship is the capacities and scale of passenger spaces. Although somewhat styled on the great ocean liners, *QM2*'s public spaces differ in that for the most part they are expected to handle the ship's entire complement of more than 2,500 passengers, rather than the 500–700 in First Class as did the rooms used as references for their design. The Britannia Restaurant, for instance, must serve 1,347 persons each in two dinner sittings, compared with *Normandie*'s Grande Salle à Manger which accommodated all 800 or so First Class passengers for a single service. This is still reflected in *QE2*'s dining arrangements where the main Mauretania and Caronia restaurants seat only 464 and 580 respectively. The luxury of size allows for a spacious arrangement of furniture throughout *QM2*'s Britannia Restaurant, with the arrangement of the room's periphery areas and mezzanines offering a sense of intimacy for those dining beyond the grandeur of the room's central area. One unavoidable concession to scale was that the traditional French service, as offered in *QE2*'s main restaurants, had to be forgone in favour of plate service for the Britannia Restaurant.

These considerations of scale are less critical in other cruise-derived spaces such as the theatre, various entertainment venues and informal dining areas where there are no liner-era references. There is also the consideration that in fact food and beverages car-

Below: *The Golden Lion Pub, first introduced aboard* QE2 *as a Project Lifestyle reincarnation of the original Upper Deck Theatre Bar, seen here repeated as a rather spacious ocean-going interpretation of a contemporary British public house, with wainscotted walls, wooden tables, Windsor chairs and an upright piano.* (Publicity photo, Chantiers de l'Atlantique)

ried the standard of passenger service aboard *QE2*, which has long suffered from her lack of full-production entertainment facilities in comparison with other modern cruise ships. *QM2*'s far superior facilities thus provide for the entertainment, spa and other services to all function together to offer a more fully rounded product of exceptional standing.

Four decks higher up, where the divided uptakes converge into a single centreline casing, the open expanses of Deck 7 are about equivalent to the height of *QE2*'s open Boat Deck, at 77ft (24m) above the waterline. Serving also as the new ship's boat deck, the teak-planked promenade here forms a continuous 1,860ft (580m) loop at the base of the superstructure, enclosed at its forward end behind windows in the curved superstructure front, and with access to an open observation deck farther ahead, to the breakwater at the end of the whaleback. The inspiration for these features comes from the Upper Promenade Deck layout of Holland America's 1959-delivered *Rotterdam*, a ship greatly admired by Stephen Payne.

In many newer cruise ships, the lifeboats are fully recessed within the ship's sides, with the open deck space minimized and, in some instances, even restricted to use for emergency purposes alone. *QM2*'s Deck 7 promenade is especially remarkable for the great spaciousness afforded by the ship's overall size. The massive semi-gravity lifeboat davits straddle a space between the inner sides of the boats and the superstructure wall wide enough to offer a view upwards between these to the decks above. When the sun is either directly ahead or astern of the ship around the middle of the day there is a lighting effect on Deck 7 that is incredibly reminiscent of the Cunard *Queens*, *United States*, *France*, and one of most recent constructions with wide-enough boat decks, *Finnjet*.

Public space on Deck 7 includes the spa forward, the Winter Garden and Kings Court informal dining area amidships and the exclusive Queens and Princess Grills aft. This deck's central feature is the open-plan Kings Court, which is a marché-type eatery, open around the clock and offering different culinary themes each day. This always-open space also forms part of the wide port-side indoor promenade extending the length of Deck 7.

This layer of public spaces at *QM2*'s vertical midpoint somewhat replicates *Canberra*'s sandwich-like plan, with the cabin decks being divided above and below the boat deck. This was long attributed to the great success of the earlier P&O ship's popularity with passengers, providing the almost-magical sense of function and orientation she possessed. In *QM2* this arrangement again serves to divide the cabin decks, reducing the instances of passengers moving vertically through the entire height of the 'hotel block' as they go about the ship from one place or activity to another. The scheme is of course larger and more sophisticated, with the three public strata

each being of somewhat different function and character. The atrium extending the Grand Lobby rotunda up to the boat deck and the inclusion of panoramic glass lifts in the superstructure lend added dimensions of orientation and direction for passengers.

Above the boat deck, the centre-body width of *QM2*'s superstructure is reduced in the interest of weight economy and vertical stability to gain the advantage of adding an extra deck. This follows current design trends aimed at maximizing the frontage available for veranda accommodation. The three strata of cabins below the superstructure are arranged either side of a wider centre core, with their verandas behind openings in the upper hull shell plating in a manner somewhat similar to the eight deluxe suites aboard Swedish American's 1930s-designed *Stockholm*.

From the forward end of Deck 7 two panoramic glass lifts are discreetly tucked into the superstructure inset aft of the bridge front, providing access to

Above: *The Library, comprising an elegant nautical interior with its dark wood panelling, white cornice and ceiling, and the contemporary touch of its illuminated bookcases.* (Author's photo)

Below: *'G32' night-club, looking to starboard on the upper level.* (Chantiers de l'Atlantique)

a number of forward-facing public rooms on Decks 8 to 11, as well as the unique feature of private entry for two of the ship's exclusive Royal Suites. Among the forward-facing public spaces on the upper superstructure decks are the Library and *QM2* Bookshop on Deck 8 and the Commodore Club on Deck 9. These are modern rooms with distinctly liner-era nautical themes, conveyed by the understated elegance of their décor with flat white ceilings and dark wood panelling recalling the 1960s chic of *Canberra*'s Meridian Room, and their forward outlook from within the curved and raked superstructure front through large round-cornered vertical rectangular windows overlooking the bow. Apart from their intended functions, these are places for curling up in

a comfortable easy chair, gazing out over the bow in mid-ocean and reminiscing or daydreaming. Featuring a collection of over 8,500 books, along with periodicals, CDs, audio/visual and digital material, the likes of this professionally-staffed ocean-going bibliothèque have been unseen probably since the days of the old *Queens* and the original Quarter- and Upper-deck libraries aboard *QE2*.

Directly above on Deck 9, the Commodore Club presents itself as an entirely up-to-date adaptation of the *Queen Mary*'s famous Observation Lounge, with a wide sweep of full-height windows overlooking the bow. The full-beam Commodore Club, with the sweeping curved line of its large forward windows overlooking the bow, has its own access to the scenic lifts and extends aft of these to an executive reception room and cigar lounge to port and starboard. It has an American-style centrepiece sit-up bar, behind which there is a 11½ft- (3.5m-) long illuminated model of *Queen Mary 2*, made in the Netherlands by Henrik Brandwijk, effectively in place of A. R. Thomson's mural painting 'Royal Jubilee Week' above the bar in the room's venerable art-moderne forebear, now preserved aboard the Queen Mary Hotel in Long Beach, California.

About as high above the water as the tops of the *Queen Mary*'s funnels, the new Cunarder offers a number of sport and recreational facilities and vast areas of open deck space, despite the large area at her funnel's base occupied by the gas-turbine housing on Deck 12. Forward of this is the Pavilion pool and lido area, extending across the superstructure's full width, beneath a retractable glass roof. This cruise-ship-style indoor/outdoor area features a large swimming pool, whirlpool baths and golf simulators, along with its own bar, occasional seating and entertainment area with a small bandstand. Along either side, sliding glass doors open to an open deck cantilevered beyond the superstructure's sides, and extending aft to a large open deck astern of the turbine house and accessing the Deck 13 lido space and viewing gallery atop the bridge forward. Two additional outdoor pools are located astern at the aft ends of Decks 6 and 8, where these are terraced in much the same way as *QE2*'s afterdecks, even to the point of repeating her tapered windscreen. Another thoughtful touch in the planning of the ship's outer deck spaces is the inclusion of an open viewing gallery, reminiscent of the Cunard *Queens*, following the bowed lines of the superstructure front on Deck 11 forward beneath the bridge.

Queen Mary 2 offers a wide variety of passenger accommodation, ranging from some of the largest and most luxurious suites and double-level apartments currently afloat to standard-cruise-ship veranda cabins and cozy compact inside rooms. These are arranged throughout Decks 4 to 6 and Decks 8 to 12, with more than 80 per cent of them featuring individual private verandas. Most spectacular among

these are the five two-storey Duplex Suites arranged across the aft end of Decks 9 and 10, along with Royal Suites occupying the forward end of Deck 10.

The location of the Duplexes and their panoramic outlook over *QM2*'s terraced afterdecks suggests a modern rendition of *Normandie*'s ultra exclusive Sun Deck Trouville and Deauville suites. Although without need of the adjacent servants' accommodation of their counterparts from the earlier ship, *QM2*'s Balmoral, Windsor, Holyrood, Buckingham and Sandringham Duplexes each feature a spacious reception room on their entrance level, a double-height solarium space overlooking a private terrace and housing a curved staircase sweeping up to the circular-plan bedchamber above. Clearly showing the design influence of Virginia Courtauld's bedroom at Eltham, the upper level of each Duplex is arranged to offer an unobstructed view out to sea from the bed. Other amenities include separate 'his and hers' bathrooms, walk-in storage space, exercise area, along with a guest lavatory and butler's pantry downstairs, adjacent to the reception room with its own dining area. There are options for combining these suites, along with two adjacent Penthouse Suites on Deck 9 by way of double soundproof doors.

The four Royal Suites fully forward on Deck 10 occupy the corresponding location, two decks beneath the navigating bridge, that had housed the officers' accommodation and ward room aboard *QE2*. The larger Queen Mary and Queen Elizabeth Suites wrap around the ship's port and starboard sides, with outlooks forward, beam-wise and aft along the superstructure, where each also encompasses the first veranda space and has its own private access to one of the external panoramic lifts. The smaller Queen Anne and Queen Victoria Suites are in essence a single-level adaptation of *QM2*'s Duplexes. All four suites can be combined in pairs or into a single vast apartment occupying the entire forward end of Deck 10. When this is done, the sitting areas of the two middle suites are connected in such a way as to

form the unique feature of a private internal promenade across the front of the ship.

Most of the standard-grade accommodation is generally similar to those of other large recently-built luxury cruise ships. *QM2* does, however, offer a greater number of inside cabins than are usually available on cruise ships, with these and some rooms in other grades also fitted with upper Pullman-type berths that fold away flush into the ceiling.

The broad range of facilities offered by *QM2* endeavours to serve the needs of the diverse cross-section of society that today can be expected to want to make transatlantic crossings. Yet to all intents and purposes she remains a product of the luxury cruise industry, as the complete lack of single-berth cabins and of truly economy-grade amenities priced for family and group travel would have fallen short of the North Atlantic Passenger Conference's criteria in its day. As times have inevitably changed, *QM2* and other modern passenger ships now make provision for passengers with various mobility and cognitive difficulties, offer wheelchair accessibility to virtually all public and deck areas, with cabins outfitted for use by handicapped passengers in most grades. Perhaps most remarkable among these is the Queen Victoria Suite, where the needs of those with disabilities are incorporated into the architectural design in such a way as to avoid the often rather orthopaedic appearance that often comes with these provisions. Those who book the suite without need of its spacial services will scarcely be aware of their existence.

QUEEN MARY 2 MAKES HER DEBUT

As soon as the idea of a new liner was first mooted after Carnival Corporation's acquisition of Cunard in 1998, prospective passengers started mailing in US $1,000 deposit cheques to secure places on the maiden voyage, no matter when and where that was to take place. This real prospect of a new Atlantic liner created a buzz of excitement around the world, at a

Above, left: The Balmoral Duplex Suite, looking inwards from the rear solarium wall to its reception room and dining area on Deck 9, with the staircase visible to the left.
(Author's photo)

Above, right: The Balmoral Suite bedchamber, again looking inwards from the solarium, and showing the influence of Eltham Palace in the room's layout and illuminated circular ceiling vault.
(Author's photo)

time when the greater part of the population is too young to have experienced the first liner era, yet is familiar with its romance and mystique, and with the Cunard name. With the building contract at last secured, the great and venerable Cunard Line was seen to be making a strong comeback, entering a new era and breathing with a new life.

The books were opened for passenger reservations and brochures released in July 2002, with those who had previously made deposits given first choice at the beginning of July, followed by passengers who had travelled aboard *QE2* during 2001 and clients of Cunard's 100 top-performing travel agents. Reservations were opened to the general public on 1 August. Response was overwhelming, with the majority of those who had previously made deposits making their bookings firm, and Cunard's newly expanded website and extended telephone reservation systems both being brought down periodically by the sheer volume of traffic during the first days of August. A special collector's edition of the brochure was produced and circulated to the line's best customers, with the side effect that, within days of its release, one of these was sold at auction on the internet, fetching a price of US$359. By September, US$50 million-worth of reservations had already been taken for *Queen Mary 2*'s first season, with four sailings designated as maiden voyages, each introducing a different aspect of her line and cruise services to passengers.

Queen Mary 2 bade a bittersweet farewell to Saint-Nazaire as she was officially handed over to Cunard Line on Monday, 22 December 2003. In a lecture paper prepared at the time of *Canberra*'s delivery in 1961, Sir Hugh Casson wrote that the joy and excitement of completing a job well done is tempered by a sense of loss experienced by the design-

ers, and indeed all those involved, when the ship is no longer theirs as she passes from their domain into the hands of her owners and goes into commercial service.[2] *Queen Mary 2* had featured as a key ingredient in the economic lifeblood of the city and France's entire Pays de Loire region, bringing thousands of visitors to see the ship taking shape at the Chantiers de l'Atlantique yard.

Visitors to France during *QM2*'s building were treated to several special exhibitions. '*Queen Mary 2: Naissance d'un Légende*' was mounted at the Musée Nationale de la Marine in Paris on the initiative of Chantiers de l'Atlantique with Cunard's sanction and assistance, presenting the ship along with the backgrounds of her owners and builders. This unusual move on the part of a shipyard reflects the great pride in the project and support of it on the part of yard and its people, the population of the Saint-Nazaire region and indeed the whole of France. Chantiers de l'Atlantique also operated tours and established its own presentation at the yard in response to the great public demand from around the world of those wanting to see where the great new liner was being built. Saint-Nazaire's remarkable Vielle Port Esca-l'Atlantique, a remarkably evocative museum of passenger liner shipping built inside an old German submarine base and featuring many full-scale reconstructions of liner interiors, featured their own remarkable graphic preview of the new Cunarder, called 'à bord du *Queen Mary 2*', which ran from April 2003 until January 2004.

The mood prevailing over *QM2*'s farewell to her birthplace was subdued by the unfortunate loss of 15 lives five weeks earlier when a gangway had collapsed while shipyard workers and their families were being given an opportunity to visit the ship. As *QM2* turned her bows to the west and made her way

Below: Queen Mary 2, *in the Loire estuary, heading towards the open sea as she makes her final departure from Chantiers de l'Atlantique on 22 December 2003, after being officially handed over to her owners Note the sign reading 'Merci Saint-Nazaire' hung from her boat deck, acknowledging the good relationship between owners and builders.*
(Courtesy of Maurizio Eliseo)

out to sea for a few days of technical trials and crew familiarization, her starboard side revealed to the crowds of well-wishers gathered along the beaches of the Loire estuary a large banner bearing the words 'Merci Saint-Nazaire'.

After arriving in Southampton at 1:00 pm, on Saturday, 27 December, the ship made a number of short preview cruises for the press and travel industry over the New Year weekend before being officially named by HM Queen Elizabeth II on Thursday 8 January. Since the new trends in cruise-ship building have dispensed with the traditional launching ceremony, as hulls are now floated off blocks in drydock often in foreign and distant yards, a post-delivery naming event has now become the official christening rite. Wearing an elegant dress and coat in pink with a purple hat, Her Majesty spoke the words, 'I name this ship *Queen Mary 2*. May God bless her and all who sail in her,' before pressing a button to release a jeroboam of Veuve Clicquot champagne to shatter against the new hull plating as a cover was drawn away from over the ship's floodlit name on her bow. An announcement was also made that *Queen Mary 2* would carry an RMS (Royal Mail Ship) designation, linking her with the Cunard Line's traditional role of carrying overseas mails to and from ports in the United Kingdon and other ports in the British Commonwealth, and allowing her to officially fly the Royal Mail pennant from her mast.

Apart from the 2,000 invited guests who attended the naming, music and fireworks display at Southampton's Queen Elizabeth II terminal that rainy January evening, thousands more gathered in a nearby park to watch the programme on large video monitors. For the people of Southampton the event recalled the city and port's former glory days as a gateway to the whole world, when passengers, mails and cargoes passed through the harbour the way that they now do at London's Heathrow Airport.

For the Queen this was her second launching of a Cunard superliner, having presided in 1967, when *Queen Elizabeth 2*'s hull had slid down traditional inclined launching ways into the River Clyde, also at the touch of her finger. On 26 September 1934 her grandmother, Queen Mary, had launched Cunard's first *Queen Mary* during the last years of King George V's reign.

During the final weeks of *QM2*'s completion in Saint-Nazaire, BBC Television's Blue Peter programme went to France to learn firsthand of how Stephen Payne had realized the dreams and aspirations about the future of great ocean liners expressed in the letter he write some 32 years earlier as an optimistic and hopeful schoolboy. Stephen was interviewed both in London and at Chantiers de l'Atlantique. Later in Southampton, Stephen conducted a filmed tour of the completed ship for the Blue Peter crew, shown on British television, along with footage of *QM2*'s departure from the port on her

maiden voyage and the original clips of the old *Queens* and the magazine item that he had seen as a boy. Stephen was also presented with a gold Blue Peter badge.[3]

Meanwhile Robert Tillberg took a well-earned retirement from his professional life at the age of 84, with *Queen Mary 2* being the jewel in the crown of his long and distinguished career. The work of Tillberg Design is continued by Frederik Johansson, Andy Collier and their colleagues in Sweden, Britain and the United States, where Tillberg Design US is headed-up by Robert's eldest son, Tomas. Stephen was made a Fellow of the Royal Institution of Naval Architects through his long service to the Institution, and was recently promoted to the position of Vice President Chief Naval Architect at Carnival Corporation. He was also awarded an OBE (Order of the British Empire) for his services to the shipping industry. In his acceptance of this honour, Stephen characteristically made a point of acknowledging the support of others in *QM2*'s success:

> I believe that the success of *Queen Mary 2* was attributable to the tremendous team effort of everybody involved in the project, notably LRS, SMC-Tillberg, Project International, designteam, MCA, Chantiers de l'Atlantique, CCS London and Saint-Nazaire and our colleagues at Cunard Line...[4]

Queen Mary 2 sailed from Southampton on her maiden voyage on Monday 12 January 2004. This was an Atlantic crossing from Southampton to Fort Lauderdale, with calls in the Canary Islands and the Caribbean en route. The ship performed well in high winds and heavy Atlantic seas encountered during

Above: *The* Queen Mary 2 *making her maiden arrival at New York's West Side passenger terminal, where with the help of the port's Moran tugs she is being warped against the Hudson River currents and into her berth in traditional fashion.* (Thomas Kralovic)

the crossing and arrived at Fort Lauderdale with no more than the usual teething problems to be expected with a large new liner. Baggage handling had proven to be one of the greatest difficulties, largely as a result of the sheer number of items to be loaded and unloaded, resulting in a delayed sailing in Southampton and one passenger missing airline connections after a late disembarkation in Fort Lauderdale. A series of winter and early spring cruises from Fort Lauderdale followed, reaching as far south as Rio de Janeiro for Brazil's Carnival celebrations, in essence repeating *Normandie*'s Carnival cruises in 1938, with passengers once again using the ship as their luxury hotel during the festivities.

After returning from Fort Lauderdale to Southampton by way of Dakar, the Atlantic Islands and Lisbon, *Queen Mary 2* made her inaugural express transatlantic crossing from Southampton on 16 April, arriving in New York on 22 April. For many, this was rightfully regarded as the new Cunarder's real maiden voyage, made in line service on the tra-

ditional transatlantic route between Britain and America. *QM2*'s inaugural east-bound New York to Southampton crossing was made in tandem with *Queen Elizabeth 2*, before the older liner assumed her full-time cruising role. Remarkably, this was the first time that two Cunard *Queens* have ever made an Atlantic crossing together, although the old *Queens* often passed each other bound in opposite directions.

Coincidentally, *QE2* closes her transatlantic service career after 35 years at about the same age that the older *Queens* and P&O's *Canberra* were decommissioned. Yet, at the time of writing, the much-loved *Queen Elizabeth 2* still has a number of years in full-time cruising ahead of her. Although built for the rigours of the same express line crossings as the older *Queens* and their contemporaries, the newer *France* and *QE2* have led less strenuous lives. With the airlines able to offer a fast alternative means of travel, liners such as these no longer needed to maintain year-round North Atlantic schedules and could be sent cruising during the winter months at lower and more economical speeds in friendlier tropical climes. Nor did either of the ships have to withstand the years of continuous wartime service endured by the Cunard *Queens*, as they carried up to five times their regular passenger complements in trooping operations around the world.

Although *Canberra* and *QE2* were requisitioned by the Admiralty and used in military service during the Falkland Islands conflict in 1982, their tenures in National Service were comparatively short. While these liners have lived somewhat charmed lives, *United States* has languished through one of the longest odysseys of inaction and lay-up since being withdrawn from service in 1969. Yet despite now being stripped of her furnishings and fittings and ravaged by years of neglect, she remains structurally sound, still with prospects of being revived for a second career as a cruise ship.

Among those who chose to acquaint themselves with the new Queen on the inaugural crossing to New York rather than the earlier voyage to Fort Lauderdale were Mr and Mrs Gledhill, who boarded earlier to include a four-days cruise to the Channel Islands and Cherbourg, extending their time on board to ten days. After a three-day stay in New York they returned home on *QE2*'s final line crossing of the Atlantic.

Keith Gledhill feels that *QM2* is 'quite spectacular' and that she will be enjoyed by everyone who sails in her, especially the younger people who will make the most of the ship's extensive array of facilities and services. He points out, however, that those accustomed to the Signal Deck suites and Queen's Grill Restaurant aboard *Queen Elizabeth 2* will notice some differences in the approach to services, bearing in mind the new ship's technological efficiency and greater size against the more traditional standards, higher level of individual attention and the

Below: Bow view of Queen Mary 2, *emphasising the breadth of her superstructure, alongside the pier in Fort Lauderdale at the end of her 12 January 2004 maiden voyage.* (Author's photo)

special relationships formed with numerous regular and repeat passengers such as the Gledhills. Doubtless *QM2* will develop her own loyal following in time, with individual relationships flourishing between repeat passengers and long-serving crew members.

Yet among the younger people for whom Keith Gledhill feels *Queen Mary 2* ultimately has the greatest appeal is Fiona Lang, special Projects coordinator of Toronto-based The Cruise People Limited, a leading travel agency specializing in cruises, passenger-ship and freighter travel. Herself too young to have experienced the old *Queens*, she has travelled several times aboard *QE2*, as well as a number of other liner-era ships remaining in cruise service. Fiona and her good friend Thomas went to New York for the *QM2* inaugural festivities, where they made a short familiarization cruise aboard the new liner.

Saying that she really can't understand how such things can be of so new and modern a vessel, Fiona feels that *Queen Mary 2* seems to have been already born with the sort of character or spirit that a popular ship may gain from the influences of her officers, crew and the passengers who sail aboard her over a number of years. 'I thought that was something that could only come with time once a ship is in service,' says Fiona, 'but *Queen Mary 2* already has an identity of her own while she has only been sailing a few months.'[5] Fiona feels that perhaps it comes from a 'pride of production' that has gone into the creation of this ship, from the determination of those at the top in the line and among the architects, designers and the builders, along with their subcontractors and suppliers and passed on through to virtually everyone, including the ordinary yard workers and other trades peoples whose manual labour brought the concepts into reality.

Fiona and Thomas were at the pier awaiting the ship's early morning arrival. They had somehow succeeded in manoeuvring themselves around the armed security personnel, crowd and riot-control squads, the bomb-detection technicians, their sniffer dogs and all else that has now become the mandatory paraphernalia of public safety. As the ship's whistle thundered into the chilly early morning air and her immense black bow appeared around the outward end of the pier, Fiona felt from the depths of her heart that this was 'a siren song from a great and glorious past, echoing into a new era'. Finally aboard the ship after a long process of security screening and embarkation, Fiona heard the distant sound of a piper, perhaps coming from the cabin loudspeaker. Venturing out on deck, she discovered to her delight that a man aboard one of the Moran tugs was playing his bagpipes to serenade the new Queen as she prepared to sail.

As one who yearns for the sensations of ships she grew up with as a child, Fiona was thrilled by her experience of this latest great ocean liner of the North

Atlantic. Yet, she poignantly makes the distinction that, as a new ship, *QM2* offers her own sensations and stimuli of being aboard, without some of the characteristic sounds and smells of her forebears. There is no creaking of wood panelling, and the conversation and other sounds from adjacent cabins is silenced by modern soundproofing and the barely perceivable, though soothingly analgesic, hiss of the air from the climate-control system. Gone also are the odours from the old plaster lagging used to insulate exposed pipes, the tinctures of steam and oil once drawn into the accommodation from the vent cowels, the smell of carbolic soap and, alas, the pungency of those old seawater lavatories.

One of the key things that *QM2* will be able to provide her transatlantic clientele of the 21st century, be they young working professionals or retired 'boomers', is time out of their busy lives to find enjoyment and personal fulfilment. An important part of Cunard's strategy is to promote the transatlantic crossing as something to be enjoyed as a periodic break from the pressures of life at home, rather than merely being thought of as an elitist once-in-a-lifetime experience.

In 1840, more than 160 years ago, the steamship company started by Samuel Cunard were pioneers in the development of modern steamship travel. Some 35 years ago in 1969, the new Cunard flagship *Queen Elizabeth 2* made her debut, as the last traditional liner to be built as well as being a trendsetting modern luxury cruise ship. Now, as this book goes to press, *Queen Mary 2* encapsulates the wealth of cruising experience gained during the first three-and-a-half decades of *QE2*'s service life distilled into the creation of an altogether new dual-function liner and cruise ship for a new generation. As *Queen Elizabeth 2* continues cruising and relinquishes her transatlantic role to *Queen Mary 2*, the continuum of liner travel by sea under the Cunard houseflag, albeit for some years now on the seasonal basis, is maintained and revitalized. ●

Above: Starboard bow view alongside the pier at Fort Lauderdale. (Author's photo)

·CHAPTER NOTES·

CHAPTER 1

1 Tom Hughes, *The Blue Riband of the Atlantic*, p. 27
2 F. Lawrence Babcock, *Spanning the Atlantic*, p. 60, quoted from Charles Dickens, *American Notes*, first published by Chapman & Hall, London, 1842
3 John Malcolm Brinnon, *The Sway of the Grand Saloon*, p. 15
4 Babcock, *op. cit.*, p. 59
5 C. R. Benstead, *Atlantic Ferry*, p. 40
6 Hughes, *op. cit.*, p. 41
7 David Howarth & Stephen Howarth, *The Story of P&O*, p. 48

CHAPTER 2

1 John Maxtone Graham, *Tribute to a Queen*, p. 24
2 R. R. Palmer & Joel Colton, *A History of the Modern World*, pp. 559–61
3 C. R. Benstead, *Atlantic Ferry*, p. 113
4 From author's discussions with Kai Liljestrand, Senior VP, Kvaerner-Masa Yards Inc., Helsinki, May 1997.
5 James Dugan, *The Great Iron Ship*, p. 44

CHAPTER 3

1 Frederick A. Talbot, *Steamship Conquest of the World*, p. 328
2 James Dugan, *The Great Iron Ship*, p. 23
3 Tom Hughes, *The Blue Riband of the Atlantic*, p. 124

CHAPTER 5

1 Paul Biedermann, H. Hein, *der Zeitschrift des Vereins Deutscher Ingenieure*, Nr. 21, 1930, p. 10. (Translated by author)
2 N.R.P. Bonsor, *North Atlantic Seaway* (1955 edition), p. 179
3 *Shipbuilding and Shipping Record*, August 23, 1928, p. 202
4 Arnold Kludas, *Record Breakers of the North Atlantic*, p. 112
5 François Robichon, *Normandie Queen of the Seas*, p. 15

6 In conversation with the author at Blackpool Pleasure Beach Casino, 31 October 2002.
7 Neil Potter & Jack Frost, *The Mary*, p. 126
8 Potter & Frost, *ibid*. p. 141
9 Kludas, *op. cit.* p. 128

CHAPTER 6

1 Frank O. Braynard, *The Big Ship*, p. 66
2 Braynard, *ibid.*, p. 123
3 Interview with author in Southampton, September 1982
4 *The Shipping World*, 7 February 1962, p. 171
5 Braynard, *op. cit.*, p. 116
6 Keith Gledhill was first contacted by the author in December 2002.
7 The author met Claudia aboard *QE2* in 1979.
8 Stephen Payne, *Grand Dame*, p. 23
9 The author met Orville aboard *Alexandr Pushkin* in 1979.
10 Philip Dawson, *Canberra*, p. 73

CHAPTER 7

1 Neil Potter & Jack Frost, *QE2*, p. 137
2 *Shipbuilding and Shipping Record*, January 31, 1969
3 Kenneth Anew, *The Architects' Journal*, 9 April 1969, p. 987
4 Through correspondence with the author from 2002.

CHAPTER 8

1 From discussions with the author, May 2001 in London, and November 2003 in Saint-Nazaire.
2 From material given to the author by the late Sir Hugh Casson in 1982.
3 From discussions with the author in early 2004.
4 News item by Keith Hamilton on internet site (www.nqsouthern.com).
5 From discussion with the author aboard *Spirit of Ontario*, 19 June 2004.

■ APPENDIX A ■

SHIPS' PROFILES

Following are the overall specifications and brief service details of the major ships discussed in this book. While the intention is to provide a similar presentation for each ship, some details of older ships, particularly those of the mid-nineteenth century, are unavailable. It should also be remembered that the rules for measuring tonnage have changed periodically, and that the figures given here generally reflect the measurements made at the time of construction and certification of each ship.

■ *Alexandr Pushkin* (1965): 19,860 GT; length overall, 577.6ft (176m); beam, 77.4ft (23.6m); draft, 27.25ft (8.3m); passengers, 130 First class, 620 Tourist Class (see text); crew, 220; speed, 20 knots; machinery, two Sulzer low-speed diesel engines direct-driving twin screws at 21,000 SHP. Built by Mathias-Thesen-Werft, Wismar, German Democratic Republic (DDR) for the USSR Baltic Steamship Company, Leningrad. Sailed from London-Tilbury to Montréal on 13 April 1966 and served on the route Leningrad, Helsinki, Copenhagen, Bremerhaven, London, Le Havre, Quebec City, Montréal until 1980, with the calls at Helsinki, Copenhagen and Quebec City being dropped. During the 1970s the Soviet ships became more actively engaged in cruising, with *Alexandr Pushkin* making high-season summer St Lawrence River cruises to St Pierre and Miquelon and winter cruises in the Caribbean. In 1975 she made her first cruise from Montréal to Havana and Bermuda. *Alexandr Pushkin* was sold to Orient Lines in 1993, and with her accommodation extensively upgraded was reintroduced as the cruise ship *Marco Polo*. As the second of the five-ship *Ivan Franko*-class, *Alexandr Pushkin* and the fifth ship *Mikhail Lermontov* were perhaps the best known, as both served on the North Atlantic for a number of years.

■ *Aquitania* (1914): 45,647 GT; length overall, 901.5ft (274.8m); beam, 97ft (29.6m); draft, 36ft (11m); passengers, 618 First Class, 614 Second Class, 1,998 Third Class; crew, 972; speed, 23.5 knots; machinery, four sets of triple-expansion steam turbines driving four propeller shafts, 60,000 IHP. Built by John Brown & Co, Ltd, Clydebank, for the Cunard Steam-Ship Company, Liverpool. As one of the longest serving ships in Cunard's history, *Aquitania* steamed some 3 million miles and carried 1.2 million passengers before being withdrawn from service in 1950. She served through both World Wars, was converted to oil firing in 1919, and her accommodation was modernized in 1922, 1933 and 1947. The ship was broken up at Gourock, with the work completed the following year. One of her bells was placed aboard *Queen Elizabeth 2* in 1969 and another is at All Saints Cathedral in Halifax, Nova Scotia.

Below: Aquitania *leaving Southampton in February 1950 on her final voyage, to be broken up on the Clyde.* (CPL)

■ *Bremen* (1929): 51,656 GT; length overall, 938.7ft (286.1m); beam, 101.7ft (31m); draft, 32ft (9.75m); passengers, 811 First Class, 500 second class, 300 Tourist Class, 617 Third Class; crew, 966; speed, 26.3 knots; machinery, four sets of triple-expansion steam turbines driving quadruple screws through single-reduction gearing at a ratio of ten-to-one to a shaft speed of 200 rpm, total 105,000 SHP. Built by Deschimag, AG Weser, Bremen, for Norddeutscher Lloyd, Bremen. *Bremen* held the North Atlantic speed from the time of her maiden voyage until surpassed eastbound by *Europa* from 1930 to 1934 and westbound by Italia's *Rex* in 1932, finally relinquishing the honours altogether to CGT's *Normandie* in 1935. *Bremen* made a number of long winter cruises circumnavigating South America in the late 1930s. In September 1939 she deadheaded from New York to Murmansk, then positioned to her home port of Bremerhaven in 1940, where she was used as a floating barracks until bombed and burned out in March 1941. She was scrapped in 1946. Sister ship *Europa* was of similar specifications, built by Blohm & Voss, Hamburg, entering service in March 1930 and holding the Blue Riband record as noted above. After being used by the Nazis as a troop transport during World War II, she was awarded to CGT in compensation for *Normandie*'s loss, being extensively refitted as *Liberté*, and serving until 1962, when she was decommissioned and scrapped at La Spezia.

■ *Britannia* (1840): 41,139 GT; length overall, 228ft (69.5m); beam, 34ft (10.4m); draft, 16.8ft (5.1m); passengers, 115 Cabin; crew, 89; speed 9 knots; machinery, 2 side-lever steam engines driving paddle wheels, 741 IHP; three-masted barque sailing rig; wooden hull. Built by Robert Duncan & Co., Port Glasgow, Scotland, for the British and North American Steam Packet Navigation Company (The Cunard), Liverpool. Sister ships *Acadia*, *Caledonia* and *Columbia* were delivered 1840–41 by the Clyde shipyards of John Wood, Robert Wood and Robert Steele. *Britannia* sold in 1848 and sunk as a target ship in 1880. *Acadia* sold in 1849 and scrapped in 1858. *Caledonia* sold in 1850 and wrecked in 1851. *Columbia* wrecked near Halifax on Devil's Limit Rock, 2 July 1843.

■ *Canberra* (1961): 44,807 GT; length overall, 820ft (249.93m); beam 102ft (31.08m); draft 32.5ft (9.9m); passengers, 548 First

Class, 1,650 Tourist Class; crew, 960; speed 27.5 knots; machinery, power-plant installation of 2 AEI turbo-alternator sets, comprising 17-stage, single-cylinder steam turbine driving a 600 volt 32,200 kVA alternators, two switchable double 42-pole synchronous motors, direct-driving a 4-bladed 6.24m diameter fixed-pitch propeller yielding 88,000 SHP. Steam raised by 4 Foster Wheeler type ESD boilers at 53kg/cm² at 515°C; aluminium superstructure. Built by Harland & Wolff Ltd at Musgrove Yard, Queen's Island, Belfast, for P&O-Orient Lines Limited, London. Completed 28 April 1961, the ship commenced her maiden voyage to Australia, New Zealand, Hawaii and the Pacific ports of Canada and the United States, on 2 June 1961. As the demand for line service decreased, *Canberra* was repositioned to New York for cruising in 1973, and as a result of being under-booked was laid up off South Carolina. She returned to the UK, where she was refitted for cruising in the British market. In April 1982 the ship was requisitioned by the Admiralty for service in the Falkland Islands conflict; refitted and returned to commercial service in September. Participated in the D-Day 50th anniversary celebrations in June 1994. *Canberra* arrived home to Southampton at the end of her last cruise on 30 September 1997, after which she was decommissioned and scrapped in Pakistan.

■ *City of Glasgow* (1850): 1,509 GT; beam, 34ft (10.4m); draft, 25ft (7.6m); passengers, 52 First Class, 85 Second, 400 Steerage; crew [unknown]; speed 8.5 knots; machinery, 2 geared beam engines of 350 HP driving a single 12ft- (3.7m-)diameter two-bladed screw propeller, three-masted barque sailing rig carrying a large amount of canvas; iron hull. Built by Tod & McGregor, Glasgow, Scotland, for Inman and International Steamship Company Ltd. Lost at sea without trace in 1854.

■ *Conte di Savoia* (1932) – see *Rex*

■ *Etruria* (1885) – see *Umbria*

■ *Europa* (1930) – see *Bremen*

■ *France* (1962): 66,348 GT; length overall, 1,035.2ft (315.5m); beam, 110.9ft (33.8m); draft, 34.3ft (10.4m); passengers, 407 First Class, 1,697 Tourist Class; crew [unknown]; service speed, 31 knots; machinery, four Parsons-type turbine sets manufactured by Chantiers de l'Atlantique, each with four ahead turbines driving four propellers through single-reduction gearing to the

Above: **Canberra** *in Sydney, having just completed her maiden voyage on 29 June 1961.* (CPL)

Above: *French Line's* **France** *of 1962, port stern quarter aerial view under way.* (Author's collection)

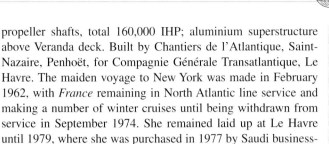

propeller shafts, total 160,000 IHP; aluminium superstructure above Veranda deck. Built by Chantiers de l'Atlantique, Saint-Nazaire, Penhoët, for Compagnie Générale Transatlantique, Le Havre. The maiden voyage to New York was made in February 1962, with *France* remaining in North Atlantic line service and making a number of winter cruises until being withdrawn from service in September 1974. She remained laid up at Le Havre until 1979, where she was purchased in 1977 by Saudi businessman Akkram who intended to use her as a floating hotel. The ship was purchased in 1979 for conversion to the Norwegian Caribbean Line cruise ship *Norway*, remaining in service as such since 1980.

■ *Great Britain* (1843): 3,270 GT; length overall, 324ft (98.8m); beam, 48ft (14.6m); draft [unknown]; passengers, 252; crew, 130; speed, 10 knots; machinery, chain-geared trunk engine of 1,500 IHP driving a single 15.5ft- (4.72-)m diameter wrought iron six-bladed propeller; six-masted sailing rig. Built by Patterson of Bristol for the Great Western Steamship Company. Originally entered transatlantic service, later trading to Australia by way of Cape Horn, and converted as a sailing ship while in this service. Beached at Port Stanley in the Falkland Islands in 1886, returned to Bristol 1970 and being restored as a museum ship.

■ *Great Eastern* (1858): 18,915 GT; length overall, 689ft (210m); beam, 82.8ft (25.3m); passengers, 596 Cabin, 2,000 Steerage; crew [unknown]; speed 13.5 knots; machinery, 2 oscillating steam engines, 3,400 IHP, for paddle wheels, one oscillating steam engine, 4,900 IHP, for propeller; sail area 54,900sq.ft (5,100sq.m); iron hull; built by J. Scott Russel & Co., Millwall, London, for Eastern Steam Navigation Company and finally delivered to the Great Ship Co., London. After limited service on the North Atlantic between 1860 and 1863, including a voyage to Québec City in 1861 under charter to the British Government. Following the Great Ship Co's liquidation *Great Eastern* was used for laying the North Atlantic and Aden–Bombay undersea telegraph cables. During this time she made one final voyage to New York, bringing passengers to Brest for the Paris Exhibition of 1867, before future crossings were cancelled owing to a lack of bookings. She ended her days in the Mersey as a floating bazaar and billboard for the David Lewis company in 1886, before finally being sold at auction and broken up at Birkenhead between 1889 and 1891.

■ *Great Liverpool* (1840) – see *Liverpool*

■ *Gripsholm* (1925) – see *Kungsholm* (1928)

■ *Hindostan* (1842): 2,018 GT; length overall, 240ft (73.1m); beam 35ft (10.6m); passengers, 150 Cabin; crew [unknown]; machinery, direct-acting steam engines driving paddle wheels, 520 HP; three masted sailing rig; wooden hull. Built along with sister ship *Bentinck* for Peninsular and Orient's service from Suez to India and the Far East, sold in 1856.

■ *Ile de France* (1927): 43,153 GT; length overall, 791ft (241m); beam, 92ft (28m); draft [unknown]; passengers, 670 First Class, 408 Second Class, 508 Third Class; crew, 800; speed, 23 knots;

machinery, quadruple turbine sets driving four propellers, total 64,000 SHP. Built by Société des Chantiers et Ateliers de Saint-Nazaire, Penhoët, for Compagnie Générale Transatlantique, Le Havre. Entered Le Havre–Plymouth–New York service on 22 June 1927, achieving great popularity for her modernity of style. After the outbreak of World War II, the ship was requisitioned in New York, and taken over at Singapore by British forces for use as an Allied troopship. She was thoroughly refitted, with the aftmost of her original three funnels removed, following the war, and returned to transatlantic service until 1958, sailing from Le Havre as *Furanzu Maru* in 1959 to Osaka where she was broken up. *Ile de France* is historically significant for her art deco interiors and the great popularity these accorded her throughout her long and distinguished career.

■ *Imperator* (1913): 52,117 GT; length overall, 919.3ft (280.2m); beam, 98ft (29.8m); draft, 35.5ft (10.8m); passengers, 706 First Class, 611 Second Class, 2.732 Third Class and Steerage; crew, 1,178; speed, 22.5 knots; machinery, Curtis-AEG-Vulkan steam turbines, arranged with one high-pressure turbine on each of the two inner shafts, feeding an intermediate-pressure turbine on the opposite inner shaft and then one of two low-pressure units on each of the two outer shafts, with reverse power being provided by two additional sets of high- and medium-pressure turbines, shaft speed 185rpm driving four-bladed propellers of 16.5ft (5m) diameter, 62,000 SHP. Built by Vulkan-Werke, Hamburg, for the Hamburg-Amerika Linie, Hamburg. Maiden voyage from Cuxhaven to New York on 10 June 1913; some difficulties were experienced with vertical stability resulting in measures being taken to reduce the weight of fittings on the upper decks. At the outbreak of World War I, the ship was laid up in Hamburg, where she remained until 1919. After first being handed over to the United States to be used as a troop transport, the ship was allocated to Britain in 1920 and chartered to Cunard. She was purchased by the line in 1929 and refitted and placed in North Atlantic service as *Berengaria*. After being seriously damaged by fire at her New York pier in 1938, the ship was eventually scrapped the following year.

■ *Kungsholm* (1928): 20.223 GT; length overall, 609ft (185.6m); beam, 78ft (23.8m); draft, 29ft (8.8m); passengers, 115 First Class, 490 Second Class, 970 Third Class; crew, 340; speed, 17 knots; machinery, two Burmeister & Wein 8-cylinder four-stroke air-injection diesel engines, directly driving twin propellers, total 17,000 BHP. Built by Blohm & Voss, Hamburg, for Brostroms group/Swedish American Line, Gothenburg. Atlantic service and luxury cruising from 1928 to the outbreak of World War II. Sold to the United States Maritime Commission in 1942 and converted for trooping as USS *John Ericsson*. After being seriously damaged by fire at New York in 1947, the ship was sold back to the Brostrom group, repaired and transferred to Home Lines as *Italia*, serving first in emigrant service to South America from Genoa, then transferring in 1952 to service from Hamburg, Southampton and Le Havre to New York, her North American destination being changed to Montréal in 1958. Converted for cruising at Genoa in 1960, and finally used as a floating hotel in the Bahamas before being broken up in 1965. *Kungsholm* and her earlier sister ship *Gripsholm*, built by Armstrong Whitworth & Co, Newcastle in 1925 were notable early North Atlantic motor ships, and significant for the adaptability of their passenger accommodation for cruising. *Kungsholm*'s interiors were of a notably modern Swedish design until rebuilt after the 1947 fire. *Gripsholm* was transferred to Norddeutscher Lloyd and renamed *Berlin* in 1954, became the first German-flag passenger ship to sail to New York after World War II. She finished her career as *Berlin* and was duly broken up in 1966.

■ *Kunsgholm* (1966): 26.678 GT; length overall, 653ft 3in (201.2m); beam, 84ft 11in (26.5m); draft, 26ft 3¼in (8.08m); passengers, 108 First Class, 605 Tourist Class; crew, 438; speed, 21 knots; machinery, 2 two-stroke, single-acting 9-cylinder, crosshead Gôtaverken VG-9U diesel engines, direct driving twin fixed-pitch propellers at a maximum of 124 rpm at 27,700 IHP.

Above: *Port side profile view of model of* Kungsholm *of 1966, superimposed on a seascape.* (Gordon Turner collection)

Built by John Brown and Company (Clydebank) Limited, Glasgow, for Brostroms group/Swedish American Line, Gothenburg. The ship sailed on her maiden voyage from Gothenburg to New York on 22 April 1966 and soon becoming primarily engaged in luxury cruising, making many round-the-world cruises and other longer voyages. In 1975 she was sold to Flagship Cruises and registered at Monrovia, changing hands again in 1978, when she was purchased by P&O's Passenger Division. After an extensive refit at Bremer Vulkan when her accommodation was extended and her forward funnel removed, the ship was delivered to her new owners as *Sea Princess*. She has served with P&O's Australian and British cruise operations and as part of the Princess Cruises fleet, later being renamed *Victoria*.

■ *l'Atlantique* (1931): 40,000 GT; length overall, 733ft (226.7m); beam, 92ft (28.1m); draft, 29.5ft (9m); passengers, 488 First Class, 88 Second Class, 662 Third Class; crew, 663; speed, 21 knots; machinery, four sets of triple-expansion steam turbines driving quadruple screws through single-reduction gearing, total 45,000 SHP. Built by Chantiers et Ateliers de Saint-Nazaire, Penhoët, for Compagnie de Navigation Sudatlantique, Le Havre. Maiden voyage Bordeaux–Buenos Aires–Bordeaux on 29 September–31 October 1931. The ship's funnels were lengthened by 16.5ft (5m) in 1932. On 3 January 1933, fire breaks out aboard *l'Atlantique* while she is deadheading to Le Havre for drydocking, and burns for two days before the ship is taken in tow to Cherbourg, remaining there as a constructive total loss until being towed to Port Glasgow in 1936 where she is scrapped.

■ *Liverpool* (1838): 1,150 GT; length overall, 235ft (71.6m); beam 35ft (10.6m); passengers 50 Cabin; crew [unknown]; speed

8 knots; machinery, side-lever steam engine driving paddle wheels, 646 HP; three-masted barque sailing rig; wooden hull. Built by Humble & Milcrest, Liverpool for shipowner Sir John Tobin; sold 1840 to P&O, enlarged to 1,600 GT with the addition of a second deck, and renamed *Great Liverpool*. Wrecked off Cape Finisterre, 24 February 1846.

■ *Lusitania* (1907): 30,822 GT; length overall, 787ft (239.9m); beam, 87ft (26.5m); draft, 37.5ft (11.4m); passengers, 560 First Class, 500 Second Class, 1,400 Third Class; crew, 800; speed, 24.5 knots; machinery, two high-pressure turbine sets driving the outer propeller shafts and two low-pressure turbines driving the inner shafts, shaft speed 200rpm, total 70,000 IHP. Built by John Brown & Co, Ltd, Clydebank, for the Cunard Steam-Ship Company, Liverpool. *Lusitania* held the North Atlantic speed record alternately with her sister ship *Mauretania* until May 1915 when she was torpedoed by the German submarine *U-20* off Old Head of Kinsale on the Irish coast and sank with the loss of 1,198 lives.

Above: Lusitania. (CPL)

■ *Mauretania* (1907): 31,988 GT; length overall, 787ft (239.9m); beam, 87ft (26.5m); draft, 37.5ft (11.4m); passengers, 560 First Class, 500 Second Class, 1,400 Third Class; crew, 800; speed, 24.5 knots; machinery, two high-pressure turbine sets driving the outer propeller shafts and two low-pressure turbines driving the inner shafts, shaft speed 200 rpm, total 70,000 IHP. Built by Swan Hunter & Wigham Richardson at Wallsend-on-Tyne for the Cunard Steam-Ship Company, Liverpool. *Mauretania* held the North Atlantic speed record alternately with her sister ship *Lusitania* until May 1915, and on her own until 1929. The ship was extensively used for cruising from 1933, with her hull painted white, and was withdrawn from service in 1935 and scrapped at Rosyth.

Above: Mauretania. (CPL)

Above: *Starboard-side aerial view of the Italian Line's* Michelangelo *of 1965 passing the Statue of Liberty inbound to New York.* (Author's collection)

■ *Michelangelo* (1965): 45,911 GT; length overall, 904.9ft (275.81m); beam, 101.7ft (31.0m); draft, 30.6ft (9.3m); passengers, 535 First Class, 550 Cabin Class, 690 Tourist Class; crew, 720; service speed, 26.5 knots; machinery, two Ansaldo double-reduction geared turbines, arranged in separate engine compartments, each with two Ansaldo-Foster Wheler ESD II watertube boilers, maximum power 104,000 SHP; aluminium superstructure above boat deck. Built by Ansaldo, Sestri Ponente, Genoa for Italia Societé per Azione de Navigazione, Genoa. *Michelangelo* began her maiden voyage to New York from Genoa on 12 May 1965, followed on 25 July by the near-identical *Raffaello* built by Cantieri Riuniti dell' Adriatico, Trieste. As the need for line services declined, both ships were used for cruising on both sides of the Atlantic. They returned from New York to Genoa in 1975, where they were laid up at Spezia and sold at the end of the following year to the Imperial Iranian Navy and moved to Bandar Abbas for use as accommodation ships, where they were eventually destroyed by neglect and act of war.

■ *Mikhail Lermontov* (1972): see *Alexandr Pushkin*

■ *Normandie* (1935): 79,280 GT; length overall, 1,029.3ft (313.75m); beam, 117.7ft (35.9m); draft, 36.6ft (11.2m); passengers, 848 First Class, 670 Tourist Class, 454 Third Class; crew,

1,345; speed, 30.0 knots; machinery, steam turbo-electric, using four main turbo-alternator sets with in-line multi-stage turbines and three-phase alternators producing 6,000 volts three-phase AC at a maximum 2,430 rpm, powering four synchronous motors, direct coupled to 16ft- (4.87m-) diameter propellers running at a service maximum of 225rpm, total 130,000 SHP. Built by Chantiers et Ateliers de Saint-Nazaire, Penhoët, for Compagnie Générale Transatlantique, Le Havre. *Normandie* made her record-breaking maiden voyage in May 1935, and after her first season was refitted with extensions to her superstructure and new propellers to correct vibration problems. She was laid up alongside Pier 88 in New York Harbour at the outbreak of World War II in September 1939, and acquired by the United States Maritime Commission in December 1941. On 9 February 1942, while undergoing conversion as the troop transport USS *Lafayette*, fire broke out, resulting in the ship keeling over onto her port side and sinking alongside Pier 88. After one of the most elaborate salvage operations in maritime history, the wreck was righted and towed to Port Newark in December 1946 and eventually scrapped there, with the work completed October 1947.

■ *Olympic* (1911): 45,000 GT; length overall, 882.75ft (269m); beam, 92.5ft (28.2m); draft, 34.5ft (10.5m); passengers, 735 First Class, 674 Second Class, 1,026 Third Class; crew, 860; speed, 21.5 knots; machinery, two sets of four cylinder triple-expansion reciprocating steam engines driving the port and starboard propeller shafts at 15,000 IHP each, and a low pressure steam turbine turning the centre shaft, at 1,600 IHP. Built by Harland & Wolff, Queen's Island, Belfast, for the White Star Line, London. Remained in service with White Star Line and from 1934 Cunard White Star Line Ltd, until withdrawn from service in 1935 and scrapped at Jarrow in 1936–37. Part of the original panelling from the ship's First-Class dining room was purchased from its owners and used in the Olympic Restaurant aboard the cruise ship *Millennium*, completed in the year 2000.

■ *Oriana* (1960): 41,923 GT; length overall, 796ft 2in (245.05m); beam, 98ft 7in (29.57m); draft, 32ft 1¼in (9.63m); passengers, 638 First Class, 1,496 Tourist Class; crew 899; speed, 27.5 knots; machinery, 2 sets of Vickers/PAMETRADA triple-expansion steam turbines driving twin 4-bladed fixed-pitch screws of 20ft 3½in (6.09m) diameter at 147rpm through double-reduction gearing, yielding 80,000 SHP. Steam raised by 4 Foster Wheeler type ESD boilers at 53 kg/cm² at 515°C; aluminium superstructure. Built by Vickers-Armstrong Ltd, Barrow in Furness, for P&O-Orient Lines Limited, London. The ship made her maiden voyage from Southampton to Australia, New Zealand, Hawaii and the Pacific ports of Canada and the United States on 13 November 1960. As the demand for assisted passages to Australia and other line services declined, the ship's role gradually switched to full-time cruising. *Oriana* made her first cruise to the St. Lawrence River and Montréal in July 1980, calling at Vancouver for the last time later the same year as she was switched to full-time cruise service based in Sydney, Australia. In 1986 *Oriana* was retired from P&O service and sold to Daiwa House Group in Japan for use in a static role as a congress centre, restaurant and museum at Beppu Bay on the Island of Kyushu.

■ *Orion* (1935): 23,371 GT; length overall, 665.17ft (202.74m); beam, 82ft (25m); draft, 30.17ft (9.2m) ; passengers, 486 First Class, 653 Tourist Class; crew, 466; speed, 19 knots; machinery, two S.R.G. turbine sets driving twin propellers, total 24,000 IHP. Built by Vickers Armstrong, Barrow-in-Furness, for Anderson Greene and Company, London, managers of Orient Line. Maiden voyage from London to Australia in September 1935, served as a troop ship during World War II and resumed regular passenger and cargo service in 1947. Withdrawn from service in 1963, sold and used as a hotel ship in Hamburg for three months before

Above: Orion *leaving Tilbury for Australia on 25 February 1947, her first passenger trip since the end of the war.* (CPL)

being broken up In Belgium. *Orion* is historically notable for her trendsetting modern interior architecture, as Orient Line's first ship with the corn-coloured hull paint scheme and first to have a single mast forward of the superstructure.

■ *Persia* (1856): 3,414 GT, length overall, 390ft (118.9m); beam 45ft (13.7m); passengers, 200 Cabin, 50 Second Class; crew [unknown]; speed 13.5 knots; machinery, 2 side-lever engines driving paddle wheels; iron hull; built by Robert Napier & Sons Ltd, Glasgow, for the British and North American Steam Packet Navigation Company (The Cunard), Liverpool. Held the North Atlantic speed record in 1856. Sold in 1868 for further trading and broken up at Thames Yard in 1872. Sister ship, *Scotia*, built in 1862, and sold to the Telegraph Construction Maintenance Company 1879 and converted to a twin-screw cable ship. Wrecked in Guam, Ladrone Islands 1904.

■ *Queen Elizabeth* (1940): 83,673 GT; length overall, 1,031ft (314.2m); beam, 118ft (35.9m); draft, 38.9ft (11.8m); passengers, 823 First (Cabin) Class, 662 Tourist Class, 798 Third Class; crew, 1,296; speed, 30.0 knots; machinery, four sets of single-reduction geared turbines, each consisting of one high-pressure, two intermediate-pressure and one low-pressure stages engaging the gearing through its own pinion, total 200,000 IHP. Built by John Brown & Co, Ltd, Clydebank, for the Cunard-White Star Line, Liverpool. After serving as a troopship during World War II, she was refitted for passenger service, making her commercial maiden voyage to New York in October 1946. She was modernized and outfitted for off-season tropical cruising in 1966. She was withdrawn from service in 1968 and sold for conversion to a hotel and conference centre at Port Everglades, Florida. In 1970 the ship was sold to C.Y. Tung and moved to Hong Kong, where she caught fire and was destroyed 9 January 1972 in Junk Bay after undergoing conversion as the ocean-going college *Seawise University*. She was scrapped where she lay two years later.

■ *Queen Elizabeth 2* (1969): 65,862 GT; length overall, 963.2ft (293.57m); beam, 105ft (32m); draft, 32.5ft (9.91m); passengers, 564 First Class, 1441 Tourist Class; crew, 906; service speed, 28.5 knots; machinery, two sets of John Brown/PAMETRADA double-expansion steam turbines, HP and LP turbines running at 5,207rpm. Driving twin controllable-pitch 6-bladed screws of 18½ft (5.79m) diameter at 174rpm through double-reduction gearing at a maximum of 110,000 SHP. Steam raised by 3 Foster Wheeler type ESD boilers at 60 KG/CM² at 510.2°C; aluminium superstructure. Built by John Brown and Company (Clydebank) Limited, Glasgow, for Cunard Line Limited, Liverpool. The ship sailed on her maiden voyage to New York on 2 May 1969, inaugurating a service pattern of Atlantic crossings interspersed with cruises based in both Europe and North America, and of world cruises and other longer voyages being undertaken during the winter months. During her career *Queen Elizabeth 2* has undergone a number of major refits and refurbishments, keeping her accommodation and passenger amenities up to the cruise industry's highest standards. On 26 October 1986 *QE2* underwent a 179-day re-engining at Lloyd Werft, where her original steam machinery was completely replaced with a modern diesel-electric power and propulsion plant. Apart from her North Atlantic voyages, *QE2* has cruised extensively around the globe, was requisitioned for trooping during the Falkland Islands conflict and participated with *Canberra* and the Royal Yacht *Britannia* in the 1994 Spithead Naval Review and festivities marking the 50th anniversary of D-Day. At times the object of IRA and PLO terrorist threats and on one or two occasioned suffering total loss of power while at sea due to failures of her original machinery, she has secured an enviable position as one of the world's best-known and most-loved passenger ships.

■ *Queen Mary* (1936): 80,773 GT; length overall, 1,019.5ft (310.7m); beam, 118ft (35.9m); draft, 38.8ft (11.8m); passengers, 776 First (Cabin) Class, 784 Tourist Class, 579 Third Class; crew, 1,101; speed, 30.0 knots; machinery, four sets of single-reduction geared turbines, each comprising one high-pressure, two intermediate-pressure and one low-pressure stages engaging the gearing through its own pinion, total 200,000 IHP. Built by John Brown & Co., Ltd., Clydebank, for the Cunard-White Star Line, Liverpool. After entering service in May 1936, the ship made record Atlantic crossings in August the same year, secur-

Above: *Cunard's* Queen Mary *with tugs and a motor launch in the foreground, probably in the Solent.*
(Gordon Turner collection)

ing the Blue Riband once again for Britain. *Queen Mary* served as a troop ship during World War II, and was restored to commercial service in August 1947. She was modernized, with two sets of fin stabilizers installed in 1958, and an extensive refit of her accommodation in 1966 aimed at attracting more cruise passengers. In 1967 *Queen Mary* was sold to the City of Long Beach, California, for use as a hotel and tourist attraction, where she remains active as such to the time of writing.

■ *Queen Mary 2* (2003): 151,400 GT; length overall, 1,131ft (345m); beam, 135ft (41m); draft, 32.67ft (10m); passengers, 2,600; crew, 1.253; speed, 30 knots; machinery, combined diesel-and-gas turbine arrangement using two GE LM2500+ aero-derivative gas generator sets and four 16-cylinder Wärtsilä 46C diesel engines feeding up to 118,000 mW of power to the main switchboards for distribution to propulsion and auxiliary systems as well as hotel and domestic services. The ship is propelled by four 20 mW Rolls Royce MerMaid pods, with two azimuthing units and two fixed pods forward. Built by Alstom Chantiers de l'Atlantique, Saint-Nazaire, for Cunard Line, London. *Queen Mary 2* began her maiden voyage on 12 January

2004, a 14-day voyage from Southampton to Fort Lauderdale via Madeira, Teneriffe, Las Palmas, Barbados and St Thomas. She begins her career as the world's largest-ever passenger ship, and as the only quadruple-screw liner to be built since *France* was delivered in 1962.

■ *Raffaello* (1965): see *Michelangelo*

■ *Rex* (1932): 51,062 GT; length overall, 879ft (267.9m); beam, 97ft (29.6m); draft, 31.1ft (9.5m); passengers, 604 First Class, 378 Second Class, 410 Tourist Class, 866 Third Class; crew, 756; speed, 27.5 knots; machinery, four sets of triple-expansion steam turbines driving quadruple screws through single-reduction gearing, total 100,000 SHP. Built by G. Ansalso, Sestri, Ponente, Genoa, for Navagazione General Italiana as booked and completed for 'Italia' Flotte Riuniti Cosulich-Lloyd Sabaudo-N.G.I. Made her maiden voyage – Genoa, Naples, Gibraltar, New York – in September 1932, securing a victory over *Bremen*'s westbound record in August 1933. *Rex* remained in transatlantic service until June 1940, when she was laid up, first at Pola and then at Capodistria, Trieste. She was sunk in shallow water by Royal Air Force rocket attacks in 1943, and broken up where she lay in 1947. *Conte di Savoia* was of similar specifications, built by Cantieri Riuniti dell' Adriatico, Trieste. After being withdrawn from commercial service in 1940, she was likewise sunk in 1943, refloated in 1945 for rebuilding, but ultimately scrapped in 1950.

■ *Rotterdam* (1959): 38,650 GT; length overall, 748.4ft (228.12m); beam, 94ft (28.65m); draft, 29.5ft (9m); passengers, 655 First Class, 801 Tourist Class; crew, 776; speed, 20.5 knots; machinery, 2 sets of De Schelde triple-expansion steam turbines driving twin 3-bladed fixed-pitch screws of 20⅛ft (6.1m) diameter at 135.5rpm maximum through double-reduction articulated gearing at a maximum of 38,000 SHP. Steam raised by 4 De Schelde V2M boilers at 50 kg/cm² at 460°C. Built by De Rotterdamshe Droogdok Mij N.V, Rotterdam, for Nederlandsche-Amerikaansche Stoomvaart Maatschappij, Rotterdam. The ship made her maiden voyage from Rotterdam to New York on 3 September 1959, calling at Le Havre and Southampton. During her first year in service, *Rotterdam* also made her first three cruises. In 1961 she took over the line's annual round-the-world cruises, inaugurated two years earlier with *Statendam*, going into full-time cruise service from 1970 onwards. *Rotterdam* remained in the Holland America fleet until 1997, being refurbished and mod-

Above: *Holland America Line's* Rotterdam, *1959, as built in the line's 1950s livery with a grey hull.* (Author's collection)

ernized several times, though always retaining her exterior profile and interior warmth and elegance. She was sold to Premier Cruises, becoming *Rembrandt*. Plans for the ship to return to the city of Rotterdam in a static role made when she was retired from Holland America Line service are still in place against her eventual retirement from active service.

■ *St. Laurent* (1866): 3,413 GT, waterline length, 355ft (108.2m); beam 43.75ft (13.3m); passengers, approx 128 First Class, 54 Second, 29 Third; crew [unknown]; speed 12 knots; machinery, inverted compound engine, driving a single screw, 3,300 IHP; three-masted auxiliary sailing rig; iron hull. Built by Chantiers de l'Atlantique, Penhoët, France, for Compagnie Générale Transatlantique. First transatlantic liner built in France. Served Le Havre–New York, later sailing to French Panama, re-engined 1875-76 with triple-expansion machinery, scrapped in Italy 1902.

■ *Titanic* (1912): 46,328 GT; length overall, 882.75ft (269m); beam, 92.5ft (28.2m); draft, 34.5ft (10.5m); passengers, 735 First Class, 674 Second Class, 1,026 Third Class; crew, 860; speed, 21.5 knots; machinery, two sets of four cylinder triple-expansion reciprocating steam engines driving the port and starboard propeller shafts at 15,000 IHP each, and a low-pressure steam turbine turning the centre shaft, at 1,600 IHP. Built by Harland & Wolff, Queen's Island, Belfast, for the White Star Line, London. The ship sank during her maiden voyage to New York with the loss of 1,635 lives after colliding with an iceberg off Cape Race, Newfoundland on 14 April 1912.

■ *Transvaal Castle* (1962): 32,697 GT; length overall, 760.2ft (231.7m); beam, 90ft (27.4m); draft, 32ft (9.8m); passengers, 728 in a single class; crew, 426; speed, 22.5 knots; machinery, two sets of single-reduction geared triple-expansion turbines, driving twin screws of 21.5ft (6.55m) diameter at 111rpm, total 40,000 SHP. Built by John Brown & Co, Ltd, Clydebank, for the Union Castle Mail Steamship Company Ltd, London. Entered service between Southampton, Cape Town and Durban, in January 1962, transferred to the South African Marine Corporation in 1966 and renamed *S. A. Vaal*. After being withdrawn from service in 1977, the ship was sold to Carnival Cruise Lines Inc and renamed *Festivale* under Panamanian registry. She was extensively rebuilt and converted for cruising by Kawasaki Heavy Industries at Kobe before commencing cruise service in 1978.

■ *Umbria* and *Etruria* (1884–85): 7,718 GT; length overall, 520ft (158.4m); beam, 57.25ft (17.4m); passengers, 550 First Class, 800 Steerage; crew [unknown]; speed, 19.5 knots; machinery, three 3-cylinder compound engines driving a single screw, 15,000 IHP; three-masted auxiliary sailing rig, steel hull. Built by John Elder & Co., Glasgow, for the Cunard Steam-Ship Company, Liverpool. *Umbria* and her near-identical sister ship *Etruria* held the North Atlantic speed record, alternately improving on each other's and their own records over five years. *Umbria* scrapped 1910, *Etruria* 1909.

■ *United States* (1952): 53,209 GT; length overall, 990ft (301.7m); beam, 101.4ft (30.9m); draft, 30.2ft (9.2m); passen-

Above: *United States Line's* United States *passing the Statue of Liberty outbound from New York.* (Gordon Turner collection)

gers, 871 First Class, 508 Cabin Class, 549 Tourist Class (alternatively adaptable to carry 15,000 troops); crew, 1,093; line service speed, 31.0 knots; machinery, four cross compound triple-expansion Westinghouse turbine sets, with double-reduction gearing to the propeller shafts. The four 18ft- (5.48m-) diameter propellers were arranged in pairs with four-bladed units driven at 139rpm on the outer shafts and five-bladed screws running at 141rpm on the inner shafts at normal service speed, total 240,000 IHP; aluminium superstructure. Built to US Navy specifications by Newport News Shipbuilding and Drydock Corp. Newport News, Virginia, for commercial service with United States Lines, New York. *United States* made her record-breaking maiden voyage in July 1952, surpassing *Queen Mary*'s mark by a decisive 3.9 knots. Full details of the ship's technical specifications and top performance remained classified during her service career, while she ran at service speeds of 28.5 to 31 knots, first with America, and later on a pooled schedule with *France*. *United States* was withdrawn from service on 8 November 1969 and laid up, first at Newport News and later at Hampton Roads. She was transferred to the United States Maritime Administration in 1973 and moved to Norfolk, Virginia. The ship was later sold to private enterprise, where numerous attempts to revitalize her as a cruise ship have failed. *United States* is still regarded as the world's fastest liner and the legitimate holder of the Hales Trophy, despite a number of faster one-off crossings having subsequently been made by lightweight aluminium catamarans. In April 2003 *United States* was purchased by Norwegian Cruise Line to be restored to service for cruising under the American flag.

■ *Victoria* (1931): 30,822 GT; length overall, 540ft (164.6m); beam, 68ft (21.3m); draft, 24ft (7.3m); passengers, 239 First Class, 145 Second Class, 100 Third Class, 80 Fourth Class; crew, 260; speed, 22 knots; machinery, four Italian-built Sulzer 8-cylinder two-stroke crosshead diesel engines, arranged in two separate engine rooms, and each directly driving one of four propellers at 132rpm, total 18,900 IHP. Built by Cantieri Riuniti dell' Adriatico, Trieste, for Lloyd Triestino, Trieste. Originally entered service on the route between Trieste, Venice, Brindisi and Alexandria, later extended to India and the Far East. Became a casualty of war on 23 January 1942. *Victoria* is historically notable as the fastest motor ship of her time, and for her outstanding modern interior design. ●

TIMELINE

1492: Christopher Columbus reaches the West Indies, effectively discovering The New World.

1497: The sea route to India around Africa and the Cape of Good Hope discovered by the Portuguese explorer Vasco da Gama.

1600: The English East India Company is founded as the official organ of trade and commerce between England and India. Similar Dutch and French companies were also established.

1620: The Pilgrim Fathers settle in New England.

1770: The first British penal colonies are founded in New South Wales (Australia) and Van Diemen's Land (Tasmania).

1784: The machine age begins in earnest, as James Watt patents the commercially viable double-acting low-pressure rotary steam engine.

1819: The American paddle steamer *Savannah* crosses the Atlantic from Savannah, Georgia, to Liverpool.

1829: The 24km Baltimore–Ellicots Mills line is opened in the United States as the first section of the Baltimore & Ohio Railroad.

1830: First passenger rail service opened in Britain, running between Liverpool and Manchester with the steam locomotive *Rocket* built by Robert Stephenson.

1832: Electric telegraph invented by Samuel Morse, inventor also of the dot-and-dash Morse code for its use.

1835: The Ludwigsbahn is opened as the first railway in Germany, with the Stephenson-built locomotive *Adler* running between Nuremberg and Fürst.

1837: Victoria ascends to the British throne.

1840: Transatlantic steamship service is inaugurated by Samuel Cunard's British and North American Royal Mail Steam Packet Navigation Company.

1842: The Compagnie des Chemains de Fer (forerunner of today's SNCF) founded to develop and operate rail services in France.

1847: HAPAG (Hamburg-Amerika Linie) is founded in Hamburg by a group of the city's prominent shipowners and merchants, with Adolf Godeffroy appointed as chairman.

1851: The Great Exhibition is held in London at the iron-and-glass Crystal Palace especially built for the event in Hyde Park.

1852: P&O inaugurates steamship service to Australia from Singapore, calling at King George's Sound, Adelaide, Melbourne and Sydney.

1856: Norddeutscher Lloyd is incorporated in the city of Bremen as the amalgamation of four smaller companies owned by the Meier family.

1857: The Indian Mutiny is put down, establishing British rule of India until 1947. The East India Company is wound up as commercial enterprise is brought under direct government control.

1858: The Egyptian Railway is completed linking the ports of Alexandria and Suez by way of Cairo.

1861: Compagnie Générale Maritime is reconstituted as Compagnie Générale Transatlantique and the Chantiers de l'Atlantique shipyard is commissioned at Penhoët in Saint-Nazaire in the estuary of the Loire River.

1864: Compagnie Générale Transatlantique (French Line) commences service between Le Havre and New York aboard their first ship *Washington*.

1864: First through train service introduced between Calcutta and Delhi, with rail coaches being carried by ferry across the river at Allahabad.

1865: George M. Pullman's *Pioneer* is built in America, as the prototype of modern railway sleeping car design, with fold-away lower and upper berths.

1866: The Atlantic cable laid by *Great Eastern* between Ireland and Newfoundland goes into service.

1866: Yamuna road and rail bridge completed, directly linking Delhi with Calcutta by rail.

1869: Suez Canal opened.

1869: The Aden–Bombay cable laid by *Great Eastern* completed.

1869: Transcontinental rail service opened in the United States, between New York and San Francisco.

1870: A rail connection is established between Bombay and Calcutta over the Thull Ghat at Jubbulpore (Jabalpur) from Itarsi.

1873: The Holland America Line is founded in Rotterdam as Nederlandsche Amerikaansche Stoomvaart Maatschappij (NASM).

1877: The Orient Line is founded to operate a passenger and emigrant service to Australia by way of the Cape of Good Hope and returning through the Suez Canal.

1884: The Greenwich Meridian is internationally recognized as the prime meridian by which the time of day and date are recognized around the world.

1886: Canadian Pacific Railway inaugurated transcontinental service connecting Québec City and Montréal with Vancouver.

1886: The automobile age begins as Gottlieb Daimler produces his first automobile in Germany.

1886: 28 October, the Statue of Liberty is dedicated in New York harbour as a gift of international friendship from the people of France to the people of the United States.

1892: Ellis Island is opened as an immigration processing centre for passengers entering the United States through New York Harbour.

1897: The Waldorf Astoria is opened in New York by John Jacob Astor IV as the world's largest hotel.

1898: The first Ritz hotel opens at the fashionable Place Vendôme in Paris.

1899: The White Star Liner *Oceanic* is completed as the world's first liner to exceed *Great Eastern*'s overall length.

1900: Following the destruction of its original wooden buildings by fire in 1897, the Ellis Island Immigration Center reopens in its present Beaux Arts-style buildings.

1900: 1 July, Count Ferdinand von Zeppelin's airship lifts above Lake Constance at Friderichshafen as the first flight of a powered dirigible.

1901: 22 January, Queen Victoria dies.

1901: *Kaiser Wilhelm der Grosse* and *Lucania* are the first liners to be fitted with Marconi wireless sets.

1901: 11 December, Guglielmo Marconi receives the first transatlantic Morse-code radio message, transmitted from Cornwall to Newfoundland, proving the viability of long range radio telegraphy.

1903: 17 December, the aviation age begins as the first controlled powered flights carrying a human are made by Wilbur and Orville Wright at Kitty Hawk, North Carolina.

1907: 7–13 September, Cunard's *Lusitania* makes her record-breaking maiden voyage from Liverpool to New York.

1907: 16–22 November, Cunard's *Mauretania* makes her maiden voyage from Liverpool to New York, but only secures her own Blue Riband record later.

1908: The Ford Model T automobile goes into production in the United States as one of the world's first mass-manufactured consumer products.

1912: On the night of 14–15 April, the White Star Line's *Titanic* sinks after colliding with an iceberg off Cape Race, Newfoundland, with the loss of 1,635 lives. The Morse code SOS signal is used for the first time.

1912: The Danish ship *Selandia* enters The East Asiatic Company's service between Copenhagen and Bangkok as the world's first successful deep-sea diesel motor vessel.

1913: 10 October, the Panama Canal is opened, connecting the Atlantic and Pacific oceans through the Isthmus of Panama.

1914: 29 May, the Canadian Pacific liner *Empress of Ireland* sinks in the St Lawrence River after colliding with the Norwegian freighter *Storstad* in fog, with the loss of 1,023 lives.

1914: 4 August, Great Britain declared war against Germany, commencing its involvement in The Great War, with the United States becoming an allied force in 1917.

1915: On the afternoon of 8 May, the Cunard liner *Lusitania* is torpedoed and sunk by a German submarine off Old Head of Kinsale on the Irish coast, with the loss of 1,198 lives.

1915: 11 December, Swedish American Line commences service as their first ship *Stockholm* sails from Gothenburg bor New York.

1917: 6 April, the United States of America declares war against Germany, joining Great Britain and its allies in Europe. German ships laid up in American ports are seized and their crews interned.

1918: 11 November, the armistice ending World War I is signed in a guarded railway carriage at Compiègne in Belgium at 11:00 am.

1920: 16 January, Prohibition begins as the 18th Amendment of the United States Constitution bans the production and sale of alcohol throughout America.

1927: 20–21 May, Charles F. Lindbergh makes his solo flight in *Spirit of St. Louis* from the site of New York's La Guardia Airport to Le Bourget Airport in Paris.

1928: 28 November, the keel is laid at Chantiers et Ateliers de Saint-Nazaire Penhoët for the Compagnie de Navigation Sudatlantique's express South Atlantic liner *l'Atlantique*.

1929: 16–21 July, the Norddeutscher Lloyd liner *Bremen* makes her record-breaking transatlantic voyage from Bremerhaven to New York.

1929: 7–29 August, the airship *Graf Zeppelin* completes a 19,500-mile circumnavigation of the globe from Lakehurst New Jersey with 36 crew and 16 passengers on board, stopping en route only at her German home base in Friedrickshafen, Tokyo and Los Angeles before returning to Lakehurst.

1929: 24 October, Black Thursday crash of the New York Stock Market, as 13 million shares are traded in a rush of panic selling, effectively beginning the Great Depression as one of the world's worst economic downturns.

1930: March, the Hapag-Lloyd Union is created by HAPAG and Norddeutscher Lloyd as a cooperative venture aimed at securing the survival of both lines through the world depression.

1930: May, Cunard announces plans to build a very large ship to compete with *Bremen* and *Europa*.

1930: 27 December, John Brown & Co., Clydebank, lays the keel for yard number 534, later to be launched as the Cunard North Atlantic liner *Queen Mary*.

1931: January, Chantiers et Ateliers de Saint-Nazaire, Penhoët lay the first sections of yard number T6, later to be launched as the CGT express North Atlantic liner *Normandie*.

1931, 1 May, the 102-storey Empire State Building is opened in New York as the world's tallest skyscraper.

1931: 3 July, the French parliament agrees to guarantee financial assistance to the Compagnie Générale Transatlantique for the construction of *Normandie* with a provision for the Company to be organised under combined public and private ownership.

1931: 29 September-12 October, *l'Atlantique* makes her maiden voyage from Bordeaux to Buenos Aires, calling 30 September at Vigo, 1 October at Lisbon, 9 October at Rio de Janeiro, 10 October at Santos, 12 October at Montevideo, and returning to France for 17 to 31 October.

1931: 11 December, work is suspended indefinitely on construction of John Brown & Co. yard number 534, the new liner for Cunard.

1932: 2 January, the Italian Line, 'Italia' Flotte Riuniti Cosulich-Lloyd Sabaudo-N.G.I. is created by merger of Navagazione General Italiana (N.G.I.), Lloyd Sabaudo and Cosulich Line.

1932: 27 September, Italia's *Rex* starts her maiden voyage from Genoa to New York, but only achieves a record passage in August the following year.

1932: 29 October, *Normandie* is launched by France's First Lady, Mme Lebrun, wife of the President of the Republic, at Chantiers et Ateliers de Saint-Nazaire, Penhoët.

1932: 30 November, Italia's *Conte di Savoia* starts her maiden voyage from Genoa to New York.

1933, 3 January, fire breaks out aboard the French liner *l'Atlantique* while deadheading without passengers to Le Havre for routine drydocking. The ship burns furiously in the English Channel for two days before being taken in tow to Cherbourg.

1933: 16 June, the New Deal begins in America as President Franklin D. Roosevelt signs the National Industry Recovery Act to stabilize and revitalize the nation's economy and end the depression.

1933: August, Italia's *Rex* makes a record crossing to New York, surpassing *Bremen*'s top westbound performance.

1933: 5 December, the 21st Amendment of the United States Constitution is passed ending 14 years of Prohibition in America.

1934: 1 January, the Cunard-White Star Line is formed by merger of the two companies, with loans made by the British Government for completion of yard number 534's construction and interim working capital.

1934: 3 April, work resumes on construction of John Brown & Co., Clydebank's yard number 534 for Cunard.

1934: 26 September, Cunard's *Queen Mary* is launched by Her Majesty Queen Mary at the John Brown & Co. Clydebank shipyard.

1935: 29 May–3 June, CGT's *Normandie* makes her record-breaking maiden transatlantic voyage from Le Havre and Southampton to New York.

1936: February, at Cherbourg the burned out *l'Atlantique* is consigned by her underwriters after a lengthy dispute with the owners to Smith & Houston Ltd. at Port Glasgow to be broken up, with the work finally being completed at the end of September the following year.

1936: 25 May–1 June, Cunard-White Star Line's *Queen Mary* makes her maiden voyage to New York.

1936: 20–24 August and 26–30 August, *Queen Mary* makes record Atlantic crossings westbound and eastbound.

1937: 6 May, after completing ten successful transatlantic voyages, the German Airship *Hindenburg* explodes in a huge fireball while landing at Lakehurst New Jersey, killing 37 passengers and crew.

1938: 3 July, a Gresley A4 Pacific-class streamlined Mallard steam locomotive makes railway history by setting a world speed record of 126 miles per hour on the London North Eastern Railway main line near Peterborough.

1937: December, the keel is laid at John Brown & Co., Clydebank, for yard number 552, later to be launched as Cunard's *Queen Elizabeth*.

1938: 27 September, Cunard's *Queen Elizabeth* is launched by HM The Queen Elizabeth at the John Brown & Co. Shipyard, Clydebank.

1939: 28 June, Pan American World Airways begins scheduled transatlantic Boeing 314 Flying Boat mail-and-passenger service between New York and Marseille via the Azores and Lisbon.

1939: 8 July, Pan American World Airways begins scheduled transatlantic Boeing 314 Flying Boat mail-and-passenger service between New York and Southampton.

1939: 3 September, Britain declares war on Germany and its allies. *Normandie* and *Queen Mary* are laid up in New York.

1940: 27 February, Cunard's newly completed *Queen Elizabeth* secretly sails from the Clyde directly to New York.

1940: July, United States Lines takes delivery of *America*, using the ship for cruising until she is requisitioned as a troop transport the following year.

1941: 7 December, the United States Pacific Fleet is attacked at its home base in Honolulu by 360 Japanese war planes launched in a surprise attack, bringing the United States into World War II. Britain declares war on Japan the following day.

1941: 12–16 December, *Normandie* and 13 other French ships laid up in American ports are seized by the United States Maritime Commission, and their French crews interned at Ellis Island.

1942: 2 October, the Royal Navy anti-aircraft cruiser HMS *Curaçoa* is sunk killing 300 of her company, after accidentally converging on the zig-zag course being sailed by *Queen Mary*, causing the naval vessel to be severed in two pieces by the liner.

1943: Ellis Island is used as a internment centre for aliens of enemy nationalities living in the United States.

1944: 31 May, the British Government discloses plans to develop a new London airport at Heath Row in Middlesex County, appropriating land under its powers of compulsory wartime purchase, and starting construction of runways in an RAF triangular plan.

1944: 6 June, the D-Day Allied invasion lands tens of thousands of combat troops by air and sea on the beaches of Normandy to begin the liberation of Europe and defeat of the Axis Powers.

1945: 7 May, World War II ends in Europe, as Germany's final surrender is accepted at a small red schoolhouse in Reims, France, near the headquarters of Allied Supreme Commander Dwight D. Eisenhower.

1945: 11 August, Japan's surrender is accepted, after the cities of Hiroshima and Nagasaki are each destroyed by a single nuclear bomb on 6 and 9 August respectively.

1946: 16–21 October, after six years of wartime service and an extensive overhaul, Cunard's *Queen Elizabeth* makes her maiden commercial voyage from Southampton to New York.

1948: New York Idlewild Airport opens, using temporary terminal buildings and control tower.

1949: 27 July, the de Havilland D.H.106 Comet jet airliner makes its first test flight at Hatfield, achieving a speed of 500 mph.

1950: February, construction begins on the new American superliner later to be launched as *United States*.

1950: 25 June, South Korea is invaded by troops from the Communist north of the divided nation, with United Nations forces of American, British and Australian troops coming to the defence of South Korea.

1951: 23 June, *United States* is launched as she is floated off her keel blocks in the drydock where she is being built.

1951: 28 November, an informal ceasefire ends fighting in Korea at the 38th parallel originally dividing North and South Korea.

1952, 15 April, the United States officially ends World War II in the Pacific with the signing of a peace treaty signed by President Harry Truman at the White House in Washington.

1952: 2 May, the jet age begins as BOAC inaugurates de Havilland Comet passenger service on their Empire Route between London and Johannesburg. With stops en route at Rome, Beirut, Khartoum, Entebbe and Livingstone, the one-way flight on the 36-seat jetliner takes only 21 hours.

1952: 3–7 July and 10–14 July, *United States* makes her record-breaking maiden transatlantic crossings eastbound and westbound .

1953: 14 January, Italian Line's first post-World War II North Atlantic liner, *Andrea Doria*, starts her maiden voyage from

Genoa to New York, followed 15 July 1954 by her sister ship *Cristoforo Colombo*.

1953, 3 April, BOAC inaugurates de Havilland Comet jet passenger service between London and Tokyo.

1954, April, the first permanent passenger terminals, control tower, service and office buildings of London's Heathrow Airport come into operation, and are officially opened by Her Majesty Queen Elizabeth II in December that year.

1954: The Ellis Island Immigration Center closes after processing more than 12 million immigrants since the first facilities were opened there in 1892.

1955: The first permanent buildings at New York Idlewild Airport go into operation, including the International Arrivals Building and control tower complex, along with the first separate terminals of each major airline serving the Manhattan area.

1956: 25 July, *Andrea Doria* collides with the Swedish American Line *Stockholm* off Nantucket, capsizing and sinking in 225 feet of water early the following morning.

1957: 4 October, the Space Age begins in earnest as Sputnik-1 is launched by the Soviet Union as the world's first un-manned satellite, then known also as an artificial moon, orbiting Earth in 95 minutes at an altitude of 500 miles.

1958: 4 October, BOAC inaugurates de Havilland Comet 4 jet passenger service between London-Heathrow and New York-Idlewild.

1958: 28 October, Pan American World Airways inaugurates Boeing 707 jet passenger service between New York-Idlewild and Paris-Orly.

1960: 11 May, CGT's *France* is launched by Madame de Gaulle at Chantiers de l'Atlantique in Saint-Nazaire.

1960: 17 June, Italian Line's *Leonardo da Vinci* starts her maiden voyage from Genoa to New York.

1961: 27–29 May, after being officially handed over to P&O at Greenock, *Canberra* makes her way to Southampton over the Whitsun holiday weekend, staying close to the shoreline around the Isle of Man, the Welsh and North Devon coasts, Land's End and along the southern shores of England to show her off to the press and the public.

1961: 2 June *Canberra* sails from Southampton on her maiden voyage to Sydney, Auckland, Honolulu, Vancouver and San Francisco.

1961:28 June, *Canberra* makes her maiden arrival in Sydney.

1962: 3–8 and 11–16 February *France* makes her maiden transatlantic crossings to and from New York

1965: 12 May, Italian Line's *Michelangelo* starts her maiden voyage from Genoa to New York, followed by *Raffaello*, departing from Genoa on 25 July.

1965: 2 July, the first keel plates are laid at John Brown & Co., Clydebank for yard number 736, later to be launched as Cunard's *Queen Elizabeth 2*.

1967, 20 September, Cunard's *Queen Elizabeth 2* is launched by Her Majesty Queen Elizabeth II at the John Brown & Co. Clydebank shipyard.

1967: 22 September, *Queen Mary* sails from New York for the last time before being withdrawn from service and sold to the City of Long Beach, California, as a hotel and tourist attraction.

1968: *Queen Elizabeth* is withdrawn from service at the end of her summer season and sold to American interests for use in a static role.

1969: 2 January, *Queen Elizabeth 2* returns to Southampton after cutting short her sea trials as a result of engine trouble, with her maiden voyage and a number of subsequent sailings being cancelled.

1969: 2 March, the Anglo-French-developed Concorde supersonic airliner makes its first flight at Toulouse, with the British Concorde flying for the first time at Filton, Bristol on 9 April.

1969: 2–7 May *Queen Elizabeth 2* makes her maiden transatlantic voyage from Southampton to New York.

1969: 21 July, television viewers around the world watch US Apollo 11 astronauts Neil Armstrong and Edwin 'Buzz' Aldrin as they become the first human beings to walk on the moon's surface, after blasting off from Cape Kennedy, Florida four days earlier.

1969: 9 November, *United States* is withdrawn from service and laid up indefinitely at Newport News, Virginia.

1969: Making only 13 Atlantic crossings that year, most of which were positioning voyages, Holland America officially renames its passenger operation as Holland America Cruises.

1970: 22–23 January, Pan American World Airways inaugurates Boeing 747 wide-body jumbo-jet transatlantic service between New York-JFK (formerly Idlewind) Airport and London-Heathrow.

1970: 12 September, four New York-bound airliners hijacked in Europe by Palestinian terrorists, who blew up three of the aircraft in the Jordanian desert, and a Boeing 747 at Cairo (the fifth target, an El Al 707, escaped the attempted takeover), precipitating the modern age of airline security.

1971: September, *Nieuw Amsterdam* makes her last Atlantic crossings, ending 98 years of transatlantic service for Holland America, as the line turns its passenger operations exclusively to cruising.

1972: 9 January, *Queen Elizabeth* is destroyed by fire in Hong Kong harbour, after being sold to Orient Overseas Line and converted to a floating university, renamed Seawise University.

1974: 11 September, *France* is taken over by her crew who force Captain Pettré to anchor at the entrance to Le Havre with 1,226 passengers aboard to protest the ship's pending withdrawal. Passengers are ferried ashore the next day.

1974: 9 October, the crew occupation of *France* ends after 28 days of negotiation of the terms of their redundancies as the ship finally docks at Le Havre.

1974: November, the new Consolidated Passenger Ship Terminal is opened in New York, replacing the 1930s-built 1,000ft piers 88, 90 and 92. By the time the new terminal opened only Cunard's *QE2*, Italia's *Leonardo da Vinci*, *Michelangelo*, and *Raffaello* and the Soviet Union's *Mikhail Lermontov* were making regular Atlantic crossings from New York.

1975: 21 April, *Raffaello* sails from New York for the last time, bound for Naples, Cannes and Genos, followed by *Michelangelo* on 26 June.

1976: 12 December, *Michelangelo* and *Raffaello* are sold to the Imperial Iranian Navy and moved the following year to Bandar Abbas for use as accommodation ships.

1979: 26 June, the laid-up liner *France* is purchased by Kloster Rederi, Oslo, for conversion as a cruise ship.

1979: 19 August, *France* is renamed *Norway* and towed to the Hapag-Lloyd shipyard in Bremerhaven for conversion.

1980: Norwegian America Line's passenger ships and cruise

operation are acquired by Norwegian shipowners Leif Høegh & Co. forming Norwegian America Cruises.

1980: September, the Soviet liner *Alexandr Pushkin* departs on her last transatlantic voyage from Montréal, following a lightly booked summer cruise season during the American-led boycott of the Moscow Summer Olympics.

1981: 27 September, TGV (Trains à Grande Vitesse) service is inaugurated by the French National Railways (SNCF) between Paris and Lyon, virtually halving the journey time to 2 hours, 40 minutes and inaugurating a new era of European express rail travel.

1982: April, following an invasion of the Falkland Islands by Argentinian forces, *Canberra* is the largest of several British merchant ships requisitioned for Admiralty service as part of a task force dispatched to the South Atlantic. After a quick conversion at Southampton, where helicopter decks and a field hospital facility are installed, *Canberra* sails on 9 April with more than 2,000 troops, naval and medical personnel aboard.

1982: 12 May, *Queen Elizabeth 2* is requisitioned for service in the Falklands conflict and, after a single voyage, is refitted and returned to commercial service on 14 August.

1982: 11 July, *Canberra* returns to a jubilant welcome at her home port of Southampton at the conclusion of her Falklands Islands engagement, having steamed 25,245 nautical miles during 94 continuous days at sea.

1982: 11 September, after being extensively refurbished at Southampton, *Canberra* returns to regular commercial service, resuming the remainder of her 1982 cruise schedule.

1982: 21–22 November, *Raffaello*, by then located at Bushire, is bombed and sunk in 40 metres of water by Iraqi aircraft. The hulks of *Michelangelo* and *Raffaello* are reported offered for sale as scrap in 1987.

1983: Leif Høegh & Co. sells Norwegian America Cruises to Trafalgar House, owners of Cunard Line, creating Cunard-Norwegian America Cruises with *Safafjord* and *Vistafjord* transferred to Bahamian registry.

1985: 7 October, the cruise ship *Achille Lauro* (former liner *Willem Ruys*), while on charter to Chandris Lines with 454 passengers aboard, is hijacked by PLO terrorists between Port Said and Alexandria, and released three days later. An elderly American male passenger is shot and thrown overboard, allegedly for antagonizing his captors. The hijackers were to have been flown to Palestine, but the plane carrying them was intercepted by US fighter jets and forced to land in Sicily.

1986: 15 February, *Mikhail Lermontov* sinks after striking underwater rocks near Port Gore on the South Island of New Zealand while on a cruise from Sydney, Australia, with one crewman reported missing.

1986: 4–6 July, the Statue of Liberty is rededicated amid three days of gala Independence Day celebrations after extensive multi-million-dollar restoration.

1987: 7–21 October, *Stefan Batory* sails from Montrèal to Gdynia for the last time, ending regularly scheduled transatlantic service between Canada and Europe.

1989: 17 January, purchase of Holland America Line by Carnival Corporation is finalized.

1990: 10 September, the Ellis Island Immigration Museum is opened in the restored Immigration Center buildings.

1991: 2 June, Developed by Deutsche Bahn (DB) as the Inter City Experimental train, ICE goes into service in Germany as Inter City Express at speeds of between 250 and 280km/h.

1994: 6 May, the Channel Tunnel (Eurotunnel) is opened by Queen Elizabeth II and French president François Mitterand, with HGV freight and Le Shuttle tourist car trains between Folkestone and Coquelles (near Calais) by the beginning of June, and direct Eurostar high-speed passenger rail between London, Paris and Brussels inaugurated 14 November.

1997: 30 September, *Canberra* returns to Southampton at the end of her last cruise and is decommissioned at the end of her 36-year service life. She later sails with a skeleton crew to Pakistan for scrapping.

1997: 30 September, Holland America's last purpose-built North Atlantic liner *Rotterdam* is withdrawn from the line's cruise fleet and sold to Premier Cruises, becoming *Rembrandt*.

1998: May, Cunard Line is acquired from its previous owners, Kvaerner Group by Carnival Corporation.

2000: 6 November, a contract is signed with Alston Chantiers de l'Atlantique of Saint-Nazaire for the construction of hull number G32 to be delivered at the end of 2003 to Cunard Line as *Queen Mary 2*.

2000: 19 December, in Toulouse, Airbus Industrie unveils plans for their 550-seat A380 double-deck airliner, with the first planes foreseen to be in service by 2006–07.

2002: 4 July, keel-laying ceremonies are held at Chantiers de l'Atlantique's Saint-Nazaire yard as the first hull section, engine-room block number 502, starboard side, was lowered in to position in the building basin.

2003: 14 April, Norwegian Cruise Line announced their purchase of the American liners *United States* and *Independence*, both to be converted for cruise service in American territorial waters.

2003: 25 May, the NCL cruise liner *Norway*, formerly *France*, suffers an engine room explosion and is subsequently towed to Bremerhaven for inspection where she is laid up and withdrawn from service indefinitely.

2003: 24 October, British Airways flight BA002 from New York-JFK to London-Heathrow closes the era of supersonic travel as the Concorde airliner's last commercial flight.

2003: 15 November, 15 people lose their lives and an additional 32 are injured when a gangway collapses during a visitors' day for shipyard workers and their families aboard the nearly completed *Queen Mary 2* at the Chantiers de l'Atlantique shipyard in Saint-Nazaire, France.

2003: 23 December, Cunard's *Queen Mary 2* is handed over to Cunard Line at the Chantiers de l'Atlantique yard in Saint-Nazaire, France, sailing late afternoon for final technical trials at sea over the Christmas holiday, before arriving in Southampton 27 December.

2004: 8 January, Her Majesty Queen Elizabeth II officially christens the new Cunard liner *Queen Mary 2* at an evening ceremony held in the ship's British home port of Southampton.

2004: 12–26 January, Cunard's *Queen Mary 2* sails on her first maiden voyage from Southampton to Fort Lauderdale by way of Madeira, Tenerife, Las Palmas, Barbados and St Thomas.

2004: 16–22 April, *Queen Mary 2* makes her maiden westbound transatlantic voyage from Southampton to New York.

2004: 25 April–1 May, *Queen Mary 2* makes her maiden eastbound transatlantic voyage from New York to Southampton in tandem with *Queen Elizabeth 2*. ●

▪ BIBLIOGRAPHY ▪

Articles

Anew, Kenneth, in *The Architects' Journal*, 9 April 1969

'Aspects of Large Passenger Liner Design', James L. Bates, Ivan J. Wanless, Transactions of the Society of Naval Architects and Marine Engineers, New York, 1946

'Bremen, ex Pasteur?' Stephen Tetlow, *Sea Breezes*, Liverpool, September 1957

'C.G.T. Liner Lafayette of 1929', J. H. Isherwood, *Sea Breezes*, Liverpool, August 1985

'Der Schnelldampfer Bremen', der Zeitschrift des Vereins Deutscher Ingenieure, Berlin, Nr. 21, 1930

'Der Vierschrauben-Turbinen-Schnelldampfer L'Atlantique', *Schiffbau, Schiffahrt und Hafenbau*, Hamburg, Vol. 33, 1932

'Die Einrichtung der neuen Bremen des Birddeutschen Lloyd', Dipl.-Ing. Eckart Hammerstroˆm, Hansa, Hamburg, Nos 33/34, 1959

'Dutch Shipping', *Shipping Wonders of the World*, Waverly, London, Vol. 3, 1935–6

'European Passenger Liner Construction', *Marine Engineering and Shipping Review*, New York, June 1940

'Exterior Design of Passenger Liners', E. Th. Christiansson, *Shipbuilding and Shipping Record*, London, November 5, 1953

'French Shipping', *Shipping Wonders of the World*, Waverly, London, Vol. 3, 1935–6

'German Shipping', *Shipping Wonders of the World*, Waverly, London, Vol. 3, 1935–6

'Hitler's Super Railway', Anton Joachimsthaler, *Trains*, USA, August 1984

'Holland-America Liner Nieuw Amsterdam of 1938', J. H. Isherwood, *Sea Breezes*, Liverpool, June 1982

'Informality in Ship Furnishing', *Shipbuilding and Shipping Record*, London, December 26, 1935

'Italian Shipping', *Shipping Wonders of the World*, Waverly, London, 1935–6, Volume 3

'Launch of the Bremen and Europa', *Shipbuilding and Shipping Record*, London, August 23, 1928

'La Décoration du Paquebot France', Françoise Siriex et Philippe Conquer, *303: Arts Recherches et Créations*, Nantes, France, 1992

'Le Paquebot France', Charles Offrey, *303: Arts Recherches et Créations*, Nantes, France, 1992

'Le Paquebot Pasteur', Raymond Lestonnat, *L'Illustration*, Paris, September 9, 1939

'Lloyd Triestino Liner Victoria of 1931', J. H. Isherwood, *Sea Breezes*, Liverpool, October 1978

'Messageries Maritimes Liner La Marseillaise', J. H. Isherwood, *Sea Breezes*, Liverpool, June 1978

'Quadruple-Screw Passenger Steamship L'Atlantique', *Shipbuilding and Shipping Record*, London, October 1, 1931

'ss Great Britain – Brunel's Masterpiece', Peter Rolt, *Maritime Life and Traditions*, Denville, NJ, USA, No 15, 2002

'Some thoughts about ss France', C. M. Squarey, *Shipbuilding & Shipping Record*, London, February 8, 1962

'Streamlining', Norman Bel Geddes, *The Atlantic Monthly*, New York, November 1934

'Sud Atlantique Liner L'Atlantique of 1931', J. H. Isherwood, *Sea Breezes*, Liverpool, December 1975

'Sud Atlantique Liner Pasteur of 1939', J. H. Isherwood, *Sea Breezes*, Liverpool, April 1984

'The Atlantic Liner Bremen', *The Shipbuilder*, London, October/November 1930

'The Bremen and the Europa', *Shipping Wonders of the World*, Waverly, London, Vol. 3, 1935–6

'The Bremen', *Shipbuilding and Shipping Record*, London, August 1, 1929

'The Diesel-Electric ship Patria', *The Shipbuilder and Marine Engine Builder*, London, February 1939

'The French Quadruple-Screw Steamship Pasteur', *The Shipbuilder and Marine Engine Builder*, London, May 1940 (continued June and July 1940)

'The Motorship Wilhelm Gustloff', *The Shipbuilder and Marine Engine Builder*, London, November 1938 (concluded December 1938)

'The New Italian Passenger Liner Conte Di Savoia', *Shipbuilding and Shipping Record*, London, December 1, 1932

'The Nieuw Amsterdam', *Shipbuilding and Shipping Record*, London, May 19, 1938

'The Nieuw Amsterdam, A Floating Palace of Art', The London Studio, London, July 1938

'The Norddeutscher Lloyd Liner Europa', *The Shipbuilder*, London, April 1930

'The Rex and the Conte Di Savoia', *Shipping Wonders of the World*, Waverly, London, Vol. 3, 1935–6

'The Swedish American Liner Stockholm', *The Shipbuilder and Marine Engine Builder*, London, May 1940

'The Traveller and His Stateroom', *Shipbuilding and Shipping Record*, London, December 26, 1935

'Trans-Atlantic Liner France: Luxury passenger liner for the French Line', *The Shipping World*, London, 7 February, 1962

'Victoria–The Fastest Motorship', *Shipbuilding and Shipping Record*, London, July 30, 1931

Books

Babcock, F. Lawrence, *Spanning the Atlantic*, Alfred Knopf (New York, 1931)

Benstead, C. R., *Atlantic Ferry*, Methuen & Co. Ltd (London, 1936)

Biedermann, P; H. Hein & W. Cogh, *Schnelldampfer Bremen*, VDI Verlag GmbH (Dusseldorf, 1987)

Bonsor, N. R. P., *North Atlantic Seaway*, T. Stephenson & Sons (Prescott, UK, 1979)

Bonsor, N. R. P., *South Atlantic Seaway*, Brookside Publications (Jersey, Channel Islands, 1983)

Bowen, Frank C., *A Century of Atlantic Travel*, Sampson Low, Marston & Co. Ltd (London, 1930)

Braynard, Frank O., *By Their Works Ye Shall Know Them: The Life and Ships of William Francis Gibbs, 1886–1967*, Gibbs & Cox Inc (New York, 1968)

Braynard, Frank O., *Lives of the Liners*, Cornell Maritime Press (New York, 1947)

Braynard, Frank O., *The Big Ship: The story of the SS United States*, The Mariners Museum, Newport News (Virginia, 1981)

Brinnon, John Malcolm, *The Sway of the Grand Saloon*, Delacorte Press (New York, 1971)

Bush, Donald J., *The Streamlined Decade*, George Braziller (New York, 1975)

Cable, Boyd, *A Hundred Year History of the P & O*, Ivor Nicholson and Watson Ltd (London, 1937)

Le Corbusier, *Towards a New Architecture* (translation), Dover Publications (New York, 1986)

Dawson, Philip S., *British Superliners of the Sixties*, Conway Maritime Press (London, 1990)

Dawson, Philip, *Canberra: In the Wake of a Legend*, Conway Maritime Press (London, 1997)

Dawson, Philip, *Cruise Ships: An Evolution in Design*, Conway Maritime Press (London, 2000)

Dugan, James, *The Great Iron Ship*, Harper & Brothers (New York, 1953)

Fletcher, R. A., *Steam-Ships and their Story*, Sidgwick & Jackson Ltd (London, 1910)

Frampton, Kenneth, *Modern Architecture, A Critical History*, Thames and Hudson Ltd (London, 1987)

Hardy, A. C., *History of Motorshipping*, Whitehall Technical Press (London, 1955)

Harris, C. J. and Ingpen, Brian D., *Mailships of the Union Castle Line*, Patrick Stephens Ltd (Bar Hill, Cambridge, 1994)

Heskett, John, *Industrial Design*, Thames and Hudson Ltd (London, 1987)

Howarth, David and Stephen, *The Story of P&O*, Weidenfeld & Nicolson (London, revised edition, 1994)

Hughes, Tom, *The Blue Riband of the Atlantic*, Patrick Stephens Ltd (Bar Hill, Cambridge, 1973)

Huldermann, Bernhard, translated by W. J. Eggers, *Albert Ballin*, Cassell & Co Ltd (London, 1922)

Kludas, Arnold, *Die Grossen Passagierschiffe der Welt*, Gerhard Stalling Verlag (Oldenburg/Hamburg, 1974)

Kludas, Arnold, *Die Schnelldampfer Bremen und Europa: Hôchpunkt und Auskland einer epoche*, Koehlers Verlagsgesellschaft (Herford, 1993)

Kludas, Arnold, *The Record Breakers of the North Atlantic: Blue Riband liners 1838–1952*, Chatham Publishing (London, 2000)

Kohler, Peter C., *The Lido Fleet*, Seadragon Press (Alexandria, VA, USA, 1998)

Koltveit, Bard, *Amerikabâtene*, Norsk Sj⁻fartsmuseum (Oslo, 1984)

Mattsson, Algot, *The White Viking Fleet*, Tre Böcker (Göteborg, 1983)

Mattsson, Algot, *Vägen mot Väster*, Askild & Kärnekull (Stockholm, 1982)

Maxtone-Graham, John, *Queen Mary 2: The Greatest Ocean Liner of Our Time*, Carpe Diem Books (Portland, Oregon, 2004)

Maxtone-Graham, John, *The Only Way to Cross*, Macmillan (New York, 1972)

McNeil, S.G.S., *In Great Waters*, Harcourt, Brace and Company (New York, 1932)

Miller, William H. & Hutchings, David F., *Transatlantic Liners at War: The story of the Queens*, David & Charles (Newton Abbot, Devon, 1985)

Miller Lane, Barbara, *Architecture and Politics in Germany 1918–1945*, Harvard University Press (Cambridge, Massachusetts, 1985)

Munro-Smith, R., *Merchant Ships and Shipping*, Hutchinson & Co. (London, 1966)

Musk, George, *Canadian Pacific*, Holt Rinehart and Winston (Toronto, 1981)

Palmer, Robert Roswell & Colton, Joel, *A History of the Modern World*, McGraw-Hill Publishing Company (New York, seventh edition, 1983)

Payne, Stephen M., *Grande Dame: Holland America Line and the s.s. Rotterdam*, RINA Ltd (London, 1990)

Potter, Neil & Jack Frost, *Queen Elizabeth 2: The authorised story*, George G. Harrap & Co. Ltd (London, 1969)

Potter, Neil & Jack Frost, *The Elizabeth*, George G. Harrap & Co. Ltd (London, 1965)

Potter, Neil & Jack Frost, *The Mary: the inevitable ship*, George G. Harrap & Co. Ltd (London, 1961)

Prager, Hans Georg, *Blohm+Voss; Ships and Machinery for the World*, Koehlers Verlagsgesellschaft mbH (Herford, 1977)

Robichon, François, (ed.) *Normandie: Queen of the Seas*, The Vendome Press (New York, Paris, Lausanne, 1985)

Smith, Eugene W., *Passenger Ships of the World Past and Present*, George H. Dean & Co. (Boston, Massachusetts, second edition, 1978)

Steele, James, *Queen Mary*, Phaidon Press Limited (London, 1995)

Talbot, Frederick A., *Steamship Conquest of the World*, William Heinemann (London, 1912)

Turner, Gordon, *Empress of Britain: Canadian Pacific's Greatest Ship*, Boston Mills Press/Stoddart Publishing Co. Limited (Toronto, 1992)

Tyler, David Budlong, *Steam Conquers the Atlantic*, D Appleton-Century Company Incorporated (New York, 1939)

Williams & de Kerbrech, *Damned by Destiny*, Teredo (Brighton, 1982)

Zimmermann, Eduard, *Flaggschiff Bremen*, Geschichte einer Schiffsfamilie, Norddeutscher Lloyd (Bremen, 1959)

·INDEX·

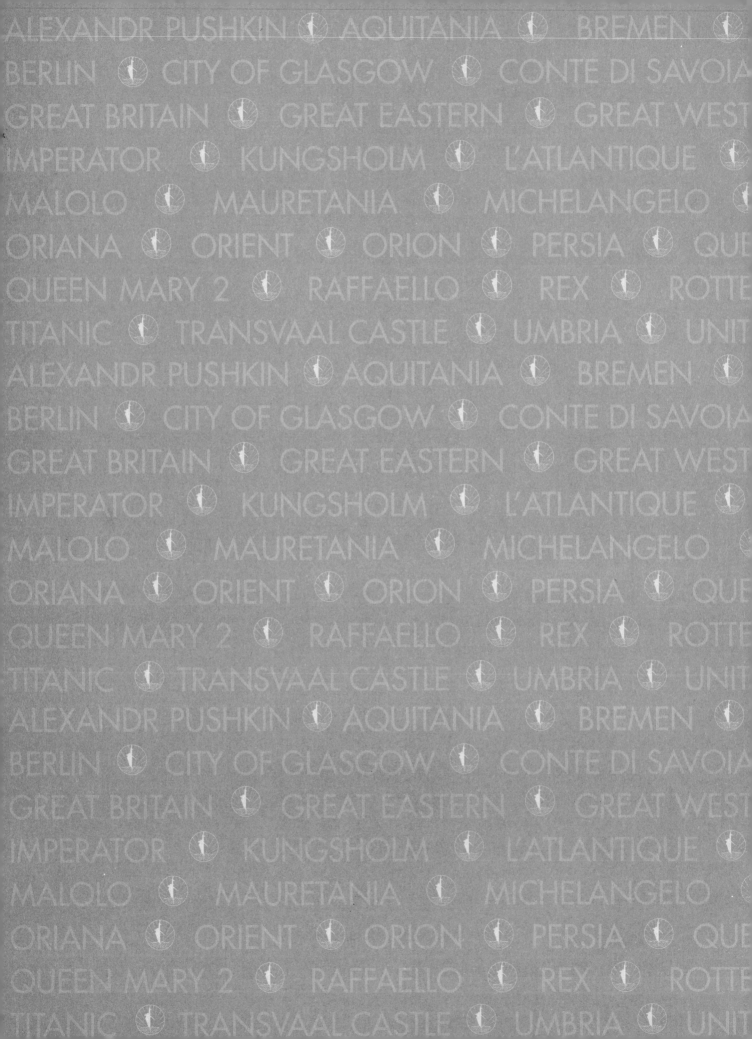